NEW PERSPECTIVES ON POTTERY MOUND PUEBLO

New Perspectives on Pottery Mound Pueblo

edited by Polly Schaafsma

UNIVERSITY OF NEW MEXICO PRESS ❖ ALBUQUERQUE

©2007 by the University of New Mexico Press
All rights reserved. Published 2007
Printed in China by Everbest Printing Company, Ltd.

12 11 10 09 08 07   1 2 3 4 5 6 7

LIBRARY OF CONGRESS
CATALOGING-IN-PUBLICATION DATA

New perspectives on Pottery Mound Pueblo /
[edited by] Polly Schaafsma.
     p. cm.
Includes bibliographical references and index.
ISBN 978-0-8263-3906-5 (CLOTH : ALK. PAPER)
1. Pottery Mound (N.M.)
2. Pueblo Indians—Antiquities.
3. Pueblo art—New Mexico.
4. Kivas—New Mexico.
5. New Mexico—Antiquities.
I. Schaafsma, Polly.
E99.P9N47 2007
978.9'92—dc22

                    2006039819

Images on page i–iv, 1, 15, 29, 55, 75, 85, 109,
137, 167, 207, and 229 from "Kiva Art of the
Anasazi," Hibben, 1975, K C Publications

Book and jacket design and
typography by Kathleen Sparkes

This book was typeset using
Adobe Minion Pro and
Berthold Akzidenz Grotesk

Text is Minion 10/13, 18P9/2 COL

Contents

List of Illustrations

FIGURES

TABLES

Preface

The important archaeological site of Pottery Mound, New Mexico, the subject of this volume, was occupied from the late fourteenth into the late fifteenth centuries. This was a time of significant reorganization and social change among Native peoples of the American Southwest, including the ancestors of today's Pueblo peoples of New Mexico and Arizona. Pottery Mound was excavated by the late, well-known archaeologist and University of New Mexico professor Frank C. Hibben, primarily in the late 1950s through the 1960s, when relatively little archaeological attention was focused on Ancestral Pueblo sites of the same age as Pottery Mound. Although Hibben published a few articles (Hibben 1955; 1960; 1966; 1967) and a book on the site's spectacular kiva murals (Hibben 1975), Pottery Mound remains poorly studied, underpublished, and largely neglected by today's southwestern archaeologists. Here, I briefly situate Pottery Mound in its time.

Pottery Mound was occupied for about a century, from ca. 1375 to 1475, within the Pueblo IV period of the Pecos classification used in the northern Southwest (Kidder 1927). Beginning 100 years earlier, in about 1275, vast areas of the Southwest that had long been densely inhabited were depopulated of full-time residents. For example, an estimated 6,000 to 10,000 people left the Mesa Verde region between 1275 and 1300 (Varien et al.

1996), and there appears to have been no year-round occupation in Chaco Canyon or much of the San Juan Basin after 1300 (Roney 1996). Outside of the Ancestral Pueblo area, the Hohokam cultural pattern in the uplands north of Phoenix and east and south of Tucson disappears after 1300 (Adams and Duff 2004). Portions of the Mogollon Highlands of central New Mexico and Arizona were also uninhabited after 1300.

Migrants from these areas sometimes joined settlements that were already occupied, or they formed new settlements, some of them very large and closely spaced so that a spatial cluster of settlements contained several thousand residents. In fact, very large settlements are a hallmark of the fourteenth- and fifteenth-century southwestern landscape (Adams and Duff, eds. 2004). Among the large and well-known postmigration settlements are those of the Galisteo Basin, Chama Valley, Zuni and Salinas districts of New Mexico, and the Middle Little Colorado, Anderson Mesa, and Hopi areas of Arizona (Adams and Duff 2004; Spielmann 2004). By far the largest, most elaborately constructed, most densely inhabited center (the term "city" is used) in the postmigration Southwest was Paquimé (Casas Grandes) in northern Chihuahua (Di Peso 1974). Paquimé is estimated to have housed about 2,240 people, with ceremonial architecture that included stone-faced platform mounds and T-shaped ballcourts. Originally thought to date to the 1000s by its excavator, Charles C. Di Peso, Paquimé is now securely dated by tree rings from 1253/1306 to 1359/1413, making it slightly earlier and roughly contemporary with Pottery Mound.

Today, southwestern archaeologists working on this time period are intensively investigating the nature of social interactions within and among postmigration settlements. Studies focus on comparing locations where settlements are composed of both migrants and local people with those where individual settlements in close proximity seem to be inhabited by one or the other (see papers in Adams and Duff, eds. 2004 and Spielmann, ed. 1998). Pottery Mound, on the Rio Puerco of the East, a Rio Grande tributary, manifests a diversity of Pueblo characteristics, some of Rio Grande Pueblos but some as well of the Western Pueblos of Acoma, Laguna, Zuni, and the Hopi villages.

Those leaving vast areas of the Southwest, at the end of the thirteenth century, were leaving their homes, shrines, burial grounds, fields, and traditional hunting and gathering territories, all those known places from which they and their ancestors had derived their livelihoods, and moving to places where they would surely have known people but where neither natural nor cultural landscapes could have been known in detail. In this kind of world, beset with novel fears as well as with new opportunities, institutions that could integrate people of heterogeneous backgrounds would be highly advantageous. Many of the very large southwestern archaeological sites of the fourteenth and fifteenth centuries do indicate the development of new religious beliefs and practices, forms of community organization, and regional interaction. These are reflected in distinctive regional and panregional art styles painted on ceramics, kiva murals, rock art, new networks of ceramic production and exchange, and in a change in architectural forms to fairly consistent use of settlements consisting of roomblocks massed around open-plaza spaces.

Some of the new painted imagery seems to have been used only within small localities. Other imagery is more widespread. Some of the imagery is repeated from earlier periods while some is new. Tantalizingly, some of the imagery is clearly recognizable today as part of the iconography of the katsina ritual system that is practiced in nearly all of the modern Pueblo villages. Some of the iconography is not katsina related. Recent archaeological attention focuses (sometimes refocuses) on the content and meaning of this iconography, the networks of communication reflected in various different media (for example, rock art versus kiva murals versus settlement layout), and on interactions maintained by exchange of pottery, especially Rio Grande glaze paint ware (Adams 1991; Adams and Duff 2004; Bernardini 2006; Crown 1994; Habicht-Mauche et al. 2006; Huntley and Kintigh 2004; Schaafsma 1994; Schaafsma and Schaafsma 1974; Shepard 1943; Spielmann, ed. 1998; Upham 1982).

Pottery Mound is crucial to all of these discussions. The site was first noted largely because its surface yielded abundant decorated pottery reflecting Rio Grande Pueblo, Acoma, Zuni, and Hopi cultural traditions of pottery (R. G. Vivian, this volume). Subsequently, the discovery of the many layers of murals in 11 of its kivas provided a uniquely magnificent archive of religious iconography of the period—again reflecting diverse traditions (Crotty 1995; Hibben 1975; papers in this volume). As R. G. Vivian (this volume) indicates, some of Hibben's (1966) interpretations of Pottery Mound, especially his discussion of a platform mound at the site, may reflect his knowledge of Paquimé, although at the time, Hibben and Di Peso thought Paquimé was at least 300 years older than Pottery Mound. Whether or not Pottery Mound was linked in some way with Paquimé, a reevaluation and investigation of Pottery Mound with knowledge of the potential role of Paquimé as a major southwestern center are warranted.

In the years when Frank Hibben brought the University of New Mexico (UNM) field schools to Pottery Mound, beginning in 1954 (R. G. Vivian, this volume), there was great professional and public awareness of the site. Unfortunately, though not uncommonly for field school sites of the day (see Spielmann 1998), Pottery Mound was never thoroughly studied. Publications were few and field records inaccessible. As Polly Schaafsma and Gwinn Vivian (this volume) note, Pottery Mound was marginalized in southwestern archaeology, and I believe largely forgotten by the public. In 1979 I directed a UNM field school that mapped and made systematic surface collections at Pottery Mound. Under the field supervision of Kathryn Sargeant, field school students also tested an area of the site that is expected to be lost as the bank of the Puerco comes to grade. Some of the information from that work is included in Vivian's contribution to this volume, in C. Schaafsma's (this volume) tabulations of ceramic types, and in unpublished papers (Cordell 1980; 2004; 2005).

Pottery Mound deserves to be acknowledged; it is a very important site. Yet, it is a difficult site to understand.

The pottery and kiva murals reflect more than one Pueblo tradition. Its architectural features are complicated and were not adequately exposed in excavations. It was excavated over many years by crews with varying levels of expertise, and written records of later work are few. Pottery Mound may at some time benefit from additional excavation, in the way that Steven A. LeBlanc (1983) "rescued" information from previously excavated and often heavily looted sites in the Mimbres Valley. Yet any such work would be premature without a thorough investigation of what we do know about Pottery Mound. The Hibben Center of the Maxwell Museum of Anthropology at the University of New Mexico, founded through a bequest

from Frank Hibben who passed away in 2002, now houses field notes and the archaeological collections from Pottery Mound (Ballagh and Phillips 2005).

In this volume, Polly Schaafsma has brought together scholars who had firsthand field experience at Pottery Mound along with others who later reviewed, studied, and analyzed the site's remarkable legacy. The papers in this volume provide many important insights and sensible direction for all those who will rediscover Pottery Mound for a better understanding of an especially dynamic period in Pueblo history.

Linda S. Cordell
Boulder, Colorado

REFERENCES CITED

Adams, E. Charles
 1991 *The Origin and Development of the Pueblo Katsina Cult.* University of Arizona Press, Tucson.

Adams, E. Charles, and Andrew I. Duff
 2004 Settlement Clusters and the Pueblo IV Period. In *The Protohistoric Pueblo World, A.D. 1275–1600,* edited by E. Charles Adams and Andrew I. Duff, pp. 3–16. University of Arizona Press, Tucson.

Adams, E. Charles, and Andrew I. Duff (editors)
 2004 *The Protohistoric Pueblo World, A.D. 1275–1600.* University of Arizona Press, Tucson.

Ballagh, Jean H., and David A. Phillips Jr.
 2005 Rediscovering Pottery Mound. Paper presented at "Pottery Mound and the Cultural Dynamics of Pueblo IV," 96th Annual Meeting of the Society for American Archaeology, Salt Lake City.

Bernardini, Wesley
 2006 *Hopi Oral Tradition and the Archaeology of Identity.* University of Arizona Press, Tucson.

Cordell, Linda S.
 1980 University of New Mexico Field School Excavations at Pottery Mound, New Mexico, 1979, Preliminary Report. Manuscript on file, Maxwell Museum of Anthropology, University of New Mexico, Albuquerque.

 2004 Advanced Seminar on Pottery Mound, School of American Research, May 11–12. Manuscript on file, School of American Research, Santa Fe, New Mexico.

 2005 The Pyramidal Mound at Pottery Mound. Paper presented at "Pottery Mound and the Cultural Dynamics of Pueblo IV," 96th Annual Meeting of the Society for American Archaeology, Salt Lake City.

Crotty, Helen K.
 1995 *Anasazi Mural Art of the Pueblo IV Period, A.D. 1300–1600: Influences, Selective Adaptation, and Cultural Diversity in the Prehistoric Southwest.* Ph.D. dissertation, University of California, Los Angeles. University Microfilms, Ann Arbor.

Crown, Patricia L.
 1994 *Ceramics and Ideology: Salado Polychrome Pottery.* University of New Mexico Press, Albuquerque.

Di Peso, Charles C.
 1974 *Casas Grandes: A Fallen Trading Center of the Gran Chichimeca,* Vols. 1–3, Series 9. Amerind Foundation, Dragoon, Arizona.

Habicht-Mauche, Judith, Suzanne L. Eckert, and Deborah L. Huntley (editors)
 2006 *The Social Life of Pots.* University of Arizona Press, Tucson.

Hibben, Frank C.

1955 Excavations at Pottery Mound, New Mexico. *American Antiquity* 21:179–180.

1960 Prehispanic Paintings at Pottery Mound. *Archaeology* 13:267–74.

1966 A Possible Pyramidal Structure and Other Mexican Influences at Pottery Mound, New Mexico. *American Antiquity* 31:522–29.

1967 Mexican Features of Mural Paintings at Pottery Mound. *Archaeology* 20(2):84–87.

1975 *Kiva Art of the Anasazi at Pottery Mound.* KC Publications, Las Vegas, Nevada.

Huntley, Deborah L., and K. W. Kintigh

2004 Archaeological Patterning and Organizational Scale of Late Prehistoric Settlement Clusters in the Zuni Region of New Mexico. In *The Protohistoric Pueblo World, A.D. 1275–1600*, edited by E. Charles Adams and Andrew I. Duff, pp. 62–74. University of Arizona Press, Tucson.

Kidder, Alfred V.

1927 Southwestern Archaeological Conference. *Science* 66(17):489–91.

LeBlanc, Steven A.

1983 *The Mimbres People: Ancient Pueblo Potters of the American Southwest.* Thames and Hudson, London.

Roney, John R.

1996 The Pueblo III Period in the Eastern San Juan Basin and Acoma-Laguna Areas. In *The Prehistoric Pueblo World, A.D. 1150–1350*, edited by Michael A. Adler, pp. 145–69. University of Arizona Press, Tucson.

Schaafsma, Polly

1994 The Prehistoric Kachina Cult and Its Origins as Suggested by Southwestern Rock Art. In *Kachinas in the Pueblo World*, edited by Polly Schaafsma, pp. 63–80. University of New Mexico Press, Albuquerque.

Schaafsma, Polly, and Curtis F. Schaafsma

1974 Evidence for the Origins of Pueblo Katchina Cult as Suggested by Southwestern Rock Art. *American Antiquity* 39:535–45.

Shepard, Anna O.

1943 *Rio Grande Glaze Paint Ware.* Contributions to American Anthropology and History No. 39. Carnegie Institution of Washington Publication No. 528. Carnegie Institution of Washington, Washington, D.C.

Spielmann, Katherine A.

1998 The Pueblo IV Period: History of Research. In *Migration and Reorganization: The Pueblo IV Period in the American Southwest*, edited by Katherine A. Spielmann, pp. 1–30. Arizona State University Anthropological Research Papers No. 51. Arizona State University, Tempe.

2004 Clusters Revisited. In *The Protohistoric Pueblo World, A.D. 1275–1600*, edited by E. Charles Adams and Andrew Duff, pp. 137–140. University of Arizona Press, Tucson.

Spielmann, Katherine A. (editor)

1998 *Migration and Reorganization: The Pueblo IV Period in the American Southwest.* Arizona State University Anthropological Research Papers No. 51. Arizona State University, Tempe.

Upham, Steadman

1982 *Polities and Power: An Economic and Political History of the Western Pueblo.* Academic Press, New York.

Varien, Mark D., William D. Lipe, Michael A. Adler, Ian M. Thompson, and Bruce A. Bradley

1996 Southwestern Colorado and Southeastern Utah Settlement Patterns, A.D. 1100–1300. In *The Prehistoric Pueblo World, A.D. 1150–1350*, edited by Michael A. Adler, pp. 86–113. University of Arizona Press, Tucson.

Acknowledgments

This book was initially inspired by a certain amount of badgering and a few informal conversations among "veteran students" of Pottery Mound from the late 1950s and early 1960s. Of these early students, I thank James Faris in particular for spurring me "to do something"—to take a new look at this important site from the perspective of 50 years or so later.

The dedicated efforts of many individuals and institutions have contributed to this volume. The project to examine Pottery Mound from diverse points of view formally began with a two-day seminar in May 2004, sponsored by the School of American Research in Santa Fe, New Mexico. This conference brought together scholars with various areas of expertise with which to address the archaeological issues and challenges presented by this site with its rich ceramic legacy and many painted kivas. Participants in the seminar were Michael Adler, Linda Cordell, Helen Crotty, Suzanne Eckert, Kelley Hays-Gilpin, Polly Schaafsma, Gwinn Vivian, Patricia Vivian, Laurie Webster, and David Wilcox. During the seminar, David A. Phillips of the Maxwell Museum of Anthropology, University of New Mexico, brought a preliminary compilation of the famous bulldozer trench profile of the site for the consideration of those of us presenting papers. We are all indebted to the School of American Research, with special thanks to Richard Leventhal, director; Nancy Owen-Lewis, director

of academic programs; Janet Stoker; and other SAR staff members for enabling this endeavor. Following the seminar, Tiffany Clark and Curtis Schaafsma were invited to contribute their areas of expertise to the book. Thanks also goes to Linda Cordell for her subsequent endorsement of this project. A grant from the Santa Fe Art Foundation for color reproduction of the incredible artistic legacy of Pottery Mound and contemporary ceramics is greatly appreciated. Thank you also to Lloyd Anderson and a number of anonymous donors for additional support.

I also express my gratitude to all of the authors for their enthusiasm, sustained cooperation, and patience during the preparation of the book manuscript. In fact, the seminar was continued via a constant dialogue and exchange of e-mails right up until the last days before the book manuscript was submitted to the press. Preparation of the volume has been greatly assisted by the committed support of the curators at the Maxwell Museum, University of New Mexico. I particularly want to thank David Phillips, curator of archaeology, and photo archivist Catherine Baudoin. Dave gave generously of his time and talents in providing documents, maps, and notebooks on request. His dedication to the construction of maps of the site on the basis of all known data at this time is an enormous and substantial contribution—a much needed foundation upon which future research on Pottery Mound can build. The maps are reproduced in Appendix A and a composite map illustrated in Chapter 1. In addition, on numerous occasions, Catherine made available to several of us the photographic documents, although they were still in a phase of organization.

Along the way, J. J. Brody and Charlie Voll provided critical information in regard to field school details that had otherwise escaped the recall of the rest of us who had worked at Pottery Mound in the mid-twentieth century. In addition, Carroll L. Riley kindly provided a photograph of the site. Appreciation also goes to Joan Mathien for her critical and supportive review of the book manuscript and valuable and helpful suggestions for final revisions.

I also express my thanks to Luther Wilson, director of the University of New Mexico Press; Lincoln Bramwell, editor; Maya Allen-Gallegos, managing editor; and Kathy Sparkes, senior book designer. The careful editorial reading of the final manuscript by Sarah E. Soliz is very much appreciated.

Finally, throughout the compilation of the volume, Curt Schaafsma's computer skills were of continuous value. At one point, he managed to save the manuscripts when the computer crashed as the volume was being assembled! Curt also worked out a myriad of technical details and computer-related organizational strategies that have been critical to getting the book on the road to publication.

CHAPTER ONE

Introduction
Revisiting Pottery Mound

Polly Schaafsma

Today, beside the Rio Puerco, about 70 mi north of the pueblo described by Gallegos, a low earthen mound thickly scattered with sherds marks the site of Pottery Mound (LA 416), a Pueblo IV village of coursed-adobe construction. Twelve miles to the east flows the Rio Grande (Figure 1.1). The Manzano Mountains rise in the distance beyond the river, and a few miles to the west of Pottery Mound, a forbidding dark volcanic hill called Hidden Mountain forms the edge of the nearby landscape (Figure 1.2). Beyond are high mesas of the Acoma country.

The immediate scene is bleak. The saltbush-dotted terrain surrounding Pottery Mound is flat and barren, having been overgrazed by cattle for decades. Dust storms, preludes to summer downpours, sometimes scream across the valley, and the Rio Puerco has cut a deeply entrenched, intermittent watercourse, whose flash floods have relentlessly gnawed at the adobe walls of the pueblo throughout the twentieth century. Little by little the northern portion of the site has been under-cut, collapsed, and washed away. Nevertheless, in better times, 600 years ago or so, Pottery Mound was the home to Pueblo people who built their houses near its banks and for over a century farmed the valley. That this was also a village of prodigious potters, mural painters, weavers, and participants in colorful religious rituals is all evidenced in the pottery sherds scattered across the site and in the 11 elaborately painted kivas buried beneath the

[We] . . . came to a pueblo of many houses three stories high. . . . In the houses we found many turkeys and much cotton and corn. . . . [We found] in the valley many cornfields like those of Mexico, and also fields of beans, calabashes, and cotton. . . . We found the houses very well planned and built in blocks, with mud walls, whitewashed inside and well decorated with monsters, other animals, and human figures. . . . The inhabitants have a great deal of crockery, such as pots (ollas), large earthen jars (tinajas), and flat pans (comales), all decorated and of better quality than the pottery of New Spain.

—Hernán Gallegos,
description of a Piro village, 1581[1]

1

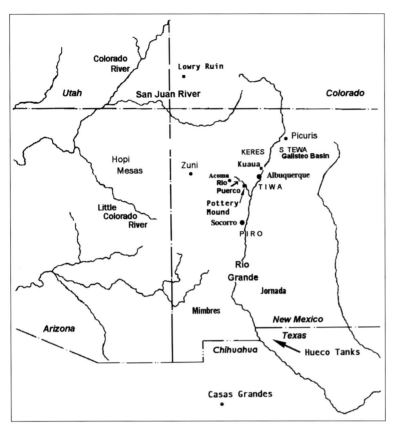

FIGURE 1.1

Map of the Pueblo IV world
and related regions.

silent clays of the valley floor (Figure 1.3) that belie this rich cultural heritage on the banks of the Rio Puerco.

It is generally conceded that Pottery Mound was occupied roughly between ca. A.D. 1370 and 1450–1475. Currently, the analysis of ceramics from controlled excavations (C. Schaafsma, Appendix D), supports this estimate. Some fluctuation at either end of this suggested time frame can be found among the various volume chapters. There are few absolute dates. One archaeomagnetic date of 1400 ± 33 is reported by Hibben (1987:4) from the Shaman's Room. In addition Eckert (2003:37) reports four noncutting tree-ring dates: 1381v, 1411v, 1418v, and 1427v, all of which were dated by Florence Ellis in the 1960s. These dates are, nevertheless, concordant with the ceramic evidence.

Contemporaneously, 12 mi to the east, neighboring villages existed closer to the Rio Grande itself (Figure 1.4). Mera (1940:20–21) recorded five sites in what he referred to as the Western Tiwa division in the vicinity of Los Lunas: LA 81, LA 951, LA 953, LA 954, and LA 957. These coursed-adobe pueblo sites have not been systematically excavated; some have sustained substantial damage from

historic developments in the valley, and nothing is known about their kivas (Franklin 1997:1; Schaafsma 1987:9). It is worthy of note that at Valencia Pueblo (LA 953) Franklin (1997:2) found some 70,000 potsherds in limited trenching. He states: "This alone attests to the incredible rate of pottery production during the early glazeware periods between about A.D. 1325 and 1490." A similar situation prevailed at Pottery Mound.

The murals from 11 kivas are, nevertheless, what contribute heavily to Pottery Mound's distinctiveness and, at the moment, seemingly unique place in Rio Grande prehistory. The paintings at Pottery Mound, along with the Jeddito murals on the easternmost Hopi mesa (Smith 1952), are unequivocally among the most elaborate and iconographically complex kiva paintings known. Among their content are narrative ritual scenes that picture ceremonial participants—some seemingly leaders and priests with ritual paraphernalia detailed to an unparalleled degree. Other paintings show supernatural entities, and transformational figures embodying human, animal, and/or avian characteristics are common. The potential that kiva mural paintings hold for understanding and therefore

FIGURE 1.2
View of Rio Puerco valley landscape from Pottery Mound (foreground) looking west.
Hidden Mountain is visible in the near distance. (Photograph courtesy of Carroll L. Riley.)

appreciating the metaphors of belief and cosmology of the recent Pueblo past is just beginning to be explored (Sekaquaptewa and Washburn 2004).

While it is not the purpose of this volume to pursue an extensive interpretation of the cosmology represented in the murals, the various chapters illuminate the context and significance of the murals in regard to culture history and social dynamics during early Pueblo IV. The contextual database of the murals in Rio Grande rock art, the heavy dominance of glaze wares, and adobe architecture preclude seeing Pottery Mound as a Western Pueblo intrusion into the Rio Grande—in other words, in most respects, it is a typical Rio Grande site. Nevertheless, seemingly Western characteristics at the site often dominate discussions about the ethnic composition of Pottery Mound. The small presence of Western ceramics (2 percent or less each from the Zuni-Acoma region and from Hopi; Appendix D), the Sikyatki mural style (Chapters 6 and 7), and kivas with benches and floors paved with sandstone (Chapter 6)

continue to raise questions concerning social diversity and how it may have been resolved. Several papers in this volume are concerned with those aspects of the archaeological record that reflect processes of social interaction and negotiation between Pottery Mound residents and the proposed Western Pueblo immigrants and with the Hopi in particular.

One would feel more confident assessing these issues if we had more concrete information about Southern Tiwa/Piro kivas with which to compare those of Pottery Mound. While data are scanty, historical references, in the form of late sixteenth-century Spanish eyewitness accounts, note the presence of wall paintings and include short descriptions of kivas in the Piro and Southern Tiwa districts about 100 years after Pottery Mound was abandoned. These references, brief as they are, do provide insight into a wider pattern of kiva features that need to be taken into consideration while evaluating Pottery Mound's place in Rio Grande prehistory. References to

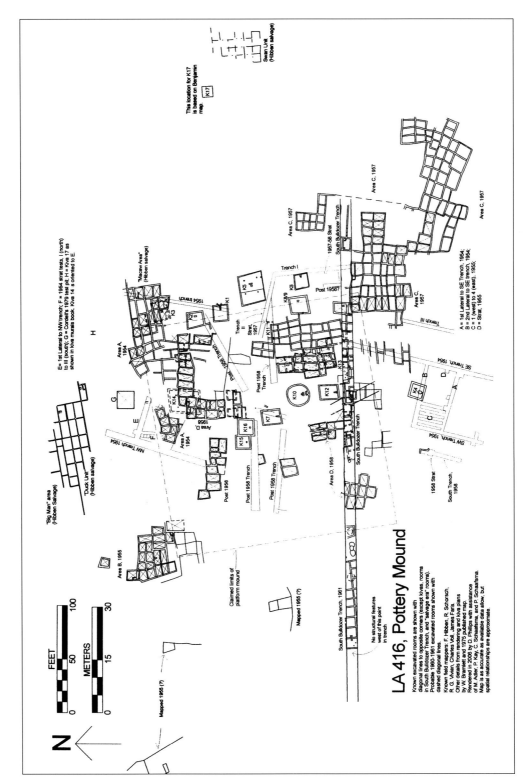

FIGURE 1.3

Map of Pottery Mound. (Photomerge of map tiles in Appendix A by David A. Phillips, Maxwell Museum of Anthropology, University of New Mexico.) See Appendix A for explanation of symbols and details, and Figure 3.3 for room numbers.

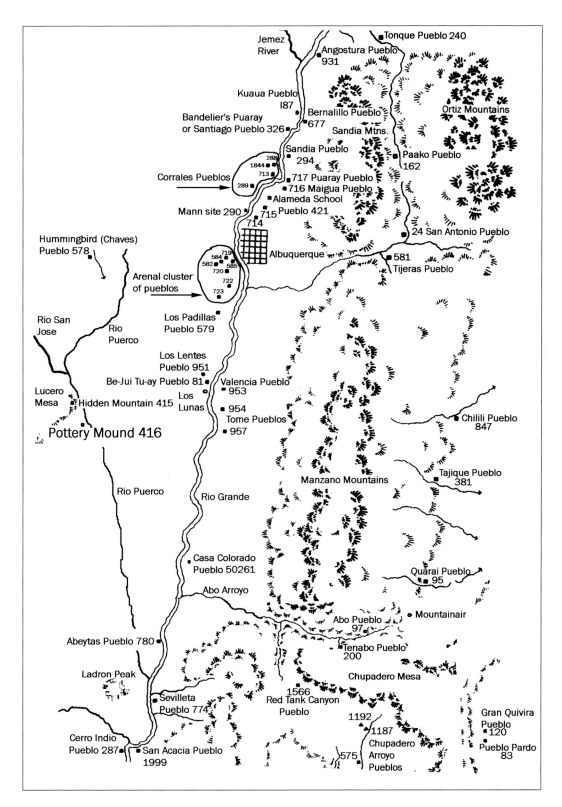

FIGURE 1.4

Detailed map of the central Pueblo Rio Grande showing topographic features and sites occupied contemporaneously with Pottery Mound. (Adapted from Mera [1940]. There is no scale in the original.)

the use of stone in Piro and Southern Tiwa kiva floor and bench construction would seem to preclude linking Pottery Mound to the Western Pueblos on the basis of architectural stone features (Dutton 1963:6; Hammond and Rey 1940:254–256; 1966:173; Winship 1896:520–522).

The Gallegos quote at the beginning of this chapter refers to wall paintings in a southern Piro village near Black Mesa, named San Miguel by the Spanish. Elsewhere other Piro walls "painted in many designs and colors" are described by Gallegos (Dutton 1963:8; Hammond and Rey 1966:83). Piro paintings were also alluded to by Gaspar Pérez de Villagrá, scribe of the Oñate expedition of 1598, who reported seeing paintings "of the demons they worship as gods" (Dutton 1963:12–13; Villagrá in Espinosa 1933:140). Finally from the Tiwa region are the famous so-called paintings of the martyred friars in Puaray (Villagrá in Espinosa 1933:132), although this interpretation of possibly some rather complex paintings is seriously called into question (Dutton 1963:13, Note 50). The probable nature of the sixteenth-century paintings observed by the Spanish is made evident by the Pottery Mound paintings, as well as by the murals at nearby Kuaua (Dutton 1963). If wall paintings were widespread as suggested by the Spanish documents, then perhaps the Pottery Mound murals were not unusual.

Yet there remain many unanswered questions, and on balance, we return to the archaeology. What will the archaeological record ultimately reveal about the numbers and nature of prehistoric Rio Grande painted kivas? How many Rio Grande villages with painted ceremonial rooms embraced the Sikyatki style—was it present at all in the murals beyond Pottery Mound itself? Certainly the small presence of Hopi Yellow Wares and Pottery Mound Polychrome with its Sikyatki designs, both rare occurrences in contemporaneous Rio Grande sites, indicate interaction with the Hopi region. This suggests that Sikyatki-style murals may have been limited to Pottery Mound in the Rio Grande. It is notable in this regard that Hopi Yellow Ware is almost completely absent in the surface collections from Rio Grande Glaze Ware–period pueblos recorded in the Rio Abajo survey (Marshall and Walt 1984:Appendix I, Table 7). Likewise, Franklin (1997) found no prehistoric Hopi Yellow Ware at Valencia Pueblo.

The life of this remarkable site on the Rio Puerco was relatively short. It is possible that the duration of Pottery Mound for approximately a mere 100 years or so may be explained on ecological grounds. The use of irrigation on the Rio Puerco floodplain to create extensive agricultural fields is well documented in a paper by Steven D. Emslie (1981), who reconstructs the immediate environment around the village on the basis of avifauna remains found at the site. It is well known that excessive salinity is a prime concern affecting all major streams in New Mexico (Clark 1987:410). Unless precautionary measures are taken, irrigation on flat, arid plains such as that in the vicinity of Pottery Mound will result in salinization of the soils within a hundred or so years. Although research in this regard has not been done for the Lower Rio Puerco, it is very likely that the muddy waters of the Rio Puerco, flowing through the Mancos shale sediments above Pottery Mound, would have produced adverse farming conditions in just about this amount of time. Thus the people at Pottery Mound would have had to move on. Such speculation rests on the premise that the Rio Puerco would not have been entrenched during the occupation of Pottery Mound. (For a good discussion of the geomorphology of the Lower Rio Puerco see Betancourt [1980].)

We are left with an intriguing bundle of archaeological data in regard to Pottery Mound. No other Rio Grande site has provided the wealth of information found in the visual texts of the murals. It is possible that the seemingly unusual large number of painted kivas denote a hierarchical ranking among sites in the Rio Grande theater. If so, then Pottery Mound may have had prestige status granted through its apparent control of ritual knowledge or "ritual completeness" as described by Elizabeth Brandt (1994). The questions raised by the Sikyatki presence in the murals and the answers proposed in Chapter 7 by Hays-Gilpin and LeBlanc may have some bearing on this issue.

At various times during the last half century, Pottery Mound has drawn the attention of archaeologists and art historians (see Chapters 2 and 5). In 1954 Frank C. Hibben, of the Department of Anthropology at the University of New Mexico, initiated field school excavations at the site (Figures 1.5 and 1.6). His proprietary interests in Pottery Mound over the span of several decades are described by Gwinn Vivian in the following chapter.

In addition to *Kiva Art of the Anasazi* (Hibben 1975), Hibben also authored several earlier articles (1955; 1960; 1966; 1967), some of which espouse controversial ideas. Other authors have published papers that discuss the murals and various other aspects of the site (see especially Crotty 1992; Emslie 1981; Garrett 1976; Vivian 1994). In addition, there are various unpublished reports, papers, theses, and dissertations that address Pottery Mound

FIGURE 1.5

The first week of the 1957 field school consisted of exploratory trenching in search of adobe walls. In the photo the first walls of Kiva 5 are about to be encountered. On the right, students Jerry Dobson, Mr. and Mrs. Hahn, and Sandra Strong are among the group around Frank C. Hibben (with camera). To the left are Robert K. Alexander, in trench, and Polly Dix (Schaafsma) above. The Rio Puerco is visible to the north in the background, beyond the school bus. (Photograph by R. G. Vivian, courtesy of the Maxwell Museum of Anthropology, University of New Mexico, catalog no. PM37.145.)

from the perspective of the murals, ceramics, and physical remains (Brody 1964; Clark and Eckert 2004; Cordell 1980; Crotty 1995; Eckert 2003; Emslie and Hargrave 1978; Mathien 1982; Ogilvie 1993; Schorsch 1962; Vivian 1961; Voll 1961; Walt 1981; among others). In spite of some continued research over the decades following the initial fieldwork in the later 1950s and early 1960s, the published information on the site is spotty, and Pottery Mound with its unusual wealth of archaeological potential has often been marginalized or overlooked altogether in regional syntheses of the Pueblo IV period (see Spielmann 1996: Figure 12.1).

Following the death of Frank Hibben in 2002, attempts are being made to correct this situation. The Hibben Center at the University of New Mexico, founded

with a bequest from Hibben, now houses the Pottery Mound collections. Material from Hibben's personal collections have been donated to the Hibben Center by his widow, Marilyn. Organization of these collections is in progress under the direction of David Phillips and Catherine Baudoin. Jean Ballagh, editor/archaeologist, has begun the task of writing up descriptive reports of the field schools based on student notebooks. These reports will be published in several volumes in the Maxwell Museum Anthropological Papers. Each volume will be dedicated to each year of fieldwork, beginning with 1954. A paper entitled "Rediscovering Pottery Mound" by Jean H. Ballagh and David A. Phillips Jr. (2005) was presented by Ballagh in the symposium Pottery Mound and the Cultural Dynamics of Pueblo IV at the 69th Annual Meeting of

FIGURE 1.6

The bulldozer cut in progress, 1961. As discussed elsewhere in this volume, this trench was dug under Hibben's direction in search of a hypothesized platform mound underlying the rooms. (Photograph courtesy of the Maxwell Museum of Anthropology, University of New Mexico, catalog no. PM37.227.)

the Society for American Archaeology in Salt Lake City. The paper describes the available documents and collections from Pottery Mound and the project to prepare the reports on the various field seasons.

The current book is the result of continuing research on the Pottery Mound collections at the Hibben Center, combined with the benefits that many decades of scholarly inquiry into Pueblo prehistory have contributed to reformulating hypotheses and research goals. The significance of Pottery Mound in identifying regional interaction, patterns of migration, cultural (including ritual) exchange, and shifting cultural identities and social processes in Pueblo IV cannot be overestimated. As we return to Pottery Mound today, we have acquired new information with which to evaluate the past, gained new perspectives, and thus generated new questions to be addressed,

while dealing with data gleaned decades ago, lying silent in collections, drawings, maps, photo archives, and student notebooks. The chapters that follow are largely the revised papers from the 2004 seminar on Pottery Mound at the School of American Research (see Acknowledgments).

Synthesizing and evaluating the available records has presented, however, a challenge. The intervening years and sometimes contradictory or incomplete records add a layer of uncertainty to interpretations, especially in regard to stratigraphy and architecture. The reader should not expect consensus, and she or he will note that Wilcox's commentary on some chapters is sometimes contentious. Points of disagreement and questioning, however, indicate future directions for research, which will lead to new views of Pottery Mound's past and place in Rio Grande prehistory.

The Many Dimensions of Pottery Mound

The chapters by R. Gwinn Vivian and Patricia Vivian review the history of the archaeological work at Pottery Mound. Their personal experiences in the field during the late 1950s and early 1960s provide useful insights into how work was conducted during that period. Gwinn Vivian's discussion focuses on the history of the projects directed by Hibben and includes a summary of the architecture of Pottery Mound. Importantly, Vivian's chapter also assesses Hibben's changing interpretations of the site between 1960 and 1966 and how these changes were influenced by other archaeological excavations in the Southwest and northern Mexico at the time. Chapter 5 by Patricia Vivian, in regard to work on the kivas, reviews student notes in connection with recording the murals. Especially valuable as a guide for all future studies of the murals is her description of her hands-on recording experiences during the summer of 1960 under a National Science Foundation–sponsored mural project.

The remaining chapters address the many archaeological dimensions of the site. Persistent themes throughout these discussions revolve around the dynamics of group interactions in the Pueblo IV past, including issues of migration (or immigrations), social integration, ritual specialization, and means of dealing with group identity in a diverse social milieu. In Chapter 3, Michael Adler reviews the Rio Puerco sites of Hummingbird (also known as Chaves Pueblo) and Pottery Mound through the lens of architecture, with special attention to techniques of construction. In the course of his discussion, Adler synthesizes for the first time what is known about the building of Pottery Mound and the social implications thereof, pointing out fruitful directions for research in the future. He cautiously concludes that "architectural data from Pottery Mound and Hummingbird Pueblo provide both strong and equivocal lines of evidence for monitoring the complex history of occupation, migration, and social organization at these settlements."

Suzanne Eckert (Chapter 4) details the social processes involved in Pueblo migration and reincorporation into host villages. She focuses on ceramics to address the social dynamics of immigration at Pottery Mound, examining temper types and the use of designs to see how Western Pueblo immigrants to Pottery Mound potentially negotiated their social space within a predominantly Eastern Pueblo society. In Chapter 6, Helen Crotty presents plan drawings of Pottery Mound kivas as she evaluates Eastern and Western Pueblo characteristics both in the kiva design and in the murals. Among the murals, the Sikyatki style and its distribution among the kivas, as well as non-Sikyatki stylistic conventions, form the substance of her discussion.[2] The pervasive presence of Sikyatki elements in the mural paintings has led Kelley Hays-Gilpin and Steven LeBlanc in Chapter 7 to script a view of this period of Pueblo history that is dynamic and provocative. They propose various social models to account for the discontinuous distribution of this style. These involve multi-ethnic communities that seem to have characterized many settlements during this period, as well as practice of craft and ritual specialization that was not limited to specific regions.

In Chapter 8, I compare mural iconography with that of the regional rock art, thus establishing a wide Rio Grande, or Eastern Pueblo, context for the murals' predominant visual text. This study also demonstrates that the closest iconographic and thus ritual relationships within the Rio Grande are with the Southern Tewa, Southern Tiwa, and Tompiro regions. Beyond the Rio Grande, questions are raised concerning the social dynamics between Pottery Mound and Antelope Mesa.

Hays-Gilpin and LeBlanc (Chapter 7) and Laurie Webster (Chapter 9) address an often overlooked component of prehistory that in this case is intricately pictured in the mural paintings—the rich archive of textiles, for the most part totally lost in the archaeological material record. The significance of textiles in transmitting ritual information and as items of trade and communication is explored in Chapter 7. In Chapter 9 Webster details the ritual costuming portrayed in Pueblo IV murals, with a focus on Pottery Mound. She compares the regional differences within the textile tradition of this period between Antelope Mesa and the Rio Grande valley as she describes garment styles as "components of coherent ritual assemblages." Her observation that "most styles of ritual clothing found in the Pueblo IV kiva murals appear to have entered the Southwest as part of an integrated costume repertoire influenced by distant ritual complexes in Mexico" is well supported by the commonalities in Pueblo ritual and cosmology with Mesoamerica as a whole as discussed elsewhere (Schaafsma 1999; 2001; Schaafsma and Taube 2006; Taube 1986; 2001).

In Chapter 10 Tiffany Clark reports the faunal remains from Linda Cordell's 1979 excavations, comparing these data from Pottery Mound with other sites in the region. The species identified reflect culinary patterns that were focused on the procurement of small game animals, while avian remains comprised a small percentage of the assemblage. Clark notes that these findings adhere to a generalized pattern characteristic of sites in the central Rio Grande.

In the final chapter, as outside discussant, David Wilcox brings to bear his own particular observations on each chapter and, importantly, his perceptions of Pottery Mound and its varied relationships within the larger context of the Southwest. His wide spectrum of interests and work on the Coalescent Communities Database (see Figures 11.2–11.5 and Table 11.1) place Wilcox in a particularly advantageous position for addressing the social relationships and cultural dynamics of the late fourteenth century to mid-fifteenth century in relation to Pottery Mound.

Wilcox brings into focus a need for a refined definition for the Sikyatki style and the implications in its spatial and temporal variations as they appear on various media. At Pottery Mound, because the Sikyatki style appears to be much more developed in the murals than on Pottery Mound Polychrome, questions are raised about its origin, an issue also addressed by Hays-Gilpin and LeBlanc (Chapter 7).

The problems encountered in trying to evaluate the information recorded in decades-old field journals and reports have become aggravatingly apparent through the production of this volume. Wilcox has raised a significant empirical question in regard to Cordell's 1979 test and the validity of the temporal divisions proposed in Chapters 4 and 10, through the use of arbitrary levels. The strata so divided are variously described as "sharply angled" (Sargeant in Cordell 2004:11) and elsewhere as manifesting "some down-sloping" (Cordell 1980:4). The implications of Wilcox's critique simply cannot be fully evaluated without further investigations at the site. (For additional comments see C. Schaafsma, Appendix D). The depth of the deposits in question (3.4 m, see Eckert, this volume) would seem to significantly reduce any problems in Clark's (Chapter 10) broadly conceived faunal analysis, inasmuch as she deals only with a two-part division (early and late).

The appendixes present data that supplement many of the discussions in the preceding chapters. The plan of Pottery Mound as can best be ascertained on the basis of the information currently available is pulled together in the maps in Appendix A, compiled by David A. Phillips at the Maxwell Museum. Additional critical architectural and stratigraphic data are presented in Appendixes B and C by Michael Adler. Appendix D by Curtis Schaafsma is

a compilation of ceramics excavated by and previously reported by Voll (1961), Cordell (1980), and Hibben (1987) but with limited distribution. These sources are the most reliable to date (see Field School Student Notes, R. G. Vivian, Chapter 2) and have never been integrated into a single study. The results of this synthetic analysis of over 44,000 sherds has important implications for the chronology of Pottery Mound overall (ca. 1370–1450). As this book goes to press, further studies are under way on Cordell's test by Hayward Franklin.

The Long View

This collection of papers puts Pottery Mound and the information it holds for understanding the central Rio Grande between ca. A.D. 1370 and 1450 on a new footing. Old data have been revived and new questions addressed within the framework of current archaeological paradigms. These discussions set a precedent for further addressing the social processes of the period via the variety of information—ceramic, architectural, the graphic and textile arts, and faunal remains—that Pottery Mound has to offer. I suggest that the rich cultural legacy of this site be examined in the future for its potential in investigations of past Pueblo leadership strategies as detailed in various chapters in Mills (2000). What contributions can be made via further studies of Pottery Mound murals and ceramics to understanding the use and distribution of ritual knowledge, power, and social ranking during the Pueblo IV period (see especially Graves and Spielmann 2000:45–59; Potter and Perry 2000:60–78; Van Keuren 2000:79–94)? Study of the wealth of information pictured in the murals has only begun, and the discussions herein relate more to understanding regional social relationships than power structures or even interpretive efforts. A focused and detailed iconographic analysis, as well, will at some point further enrich our perceptions of Pueblo religion and cosmology in the recent past. Just as the coherency of ritual attire pictured in the murals is noted by Webster in Chapter 9, a coherency of cosmological symbols and metaphors resides in these complex renditions of Pueblo ceremony, describing the Pueblo worldview when Pottery Mound was inhabited and the kivas active.

It needs to be emphasized again that to successfully review Pottery Mound in its regional perspective, we ultimately need more comparative data on central and southern Pueblo Rio Grande sites. As is always the case, interpretations offered at any given point in time are subject to change as more information becomes available. Nevertheless, we initiate here a long overdue dialogue on this important site and often overlooked region in the central Pueblo Rio Grande, with its implications for Pueblo prehistory overall.

Finally, as the papers in this volume, written with a focus on Pottery Mound, examine the many threads of social dynamics operative in the fifteenth century—trade, migration, craft and ritual specialists, the means of maintaining (or not) identity in a multiethnic community—a boldly textured picture of fifteenth-century Pueblo society emerges that points the way to research in the future.

NOTES

1. Epigraph drawn from Hammond and Rey (1966:82).

2. Discrepancies in the information presented by Crotty versus Hays-Gilpin and LeBlanc in their tabulations of Sikyatki painting in Pottery Mound kivas may relate to their each having access to different resources regarding the paintings. In a very few cases, differences appear to relate to differing views on what may be included in this style.

REFERENCES CITED

Ballagh, Jean H., and David A. Phillips Jr.

2005 Rediscovering Pottery Mound. Paper presented at the 69th Annual Meeting of the Society for American Archaeology, Salt Lake City.

Betancourt, Julio L.

1980 Historical Overview of the Lower Puerco–Rio Salado Drainages, N.M. In *Reconnaissance Study of the Archaeological and Related Resources of the Lower Puerco and Salado Drainages, Central New Mexico*, by Mark Wimberly and Peter Eidenbach, pp. 25–48. Human Systems Research, Inc., Tularosa, New Mexico.

Brandt, Elizabeth

1994 Egalitarianism, Hierarchy, and Centralization in the Pueblos. In *The Ancient Southwestern Community*, edited by W. H. Wills and R. D. Leonard, pp. 9–23. University of New Mexico Press, Albuquerque.

Brody, J. J.

1964 Design Analysis of the Rio Grande Glaze Pottery of Pottery Mound, New Mexico. Unpublished Master's thesis, Department of Art, University of New Mexico, Albuquerque.

Clark, Ira G.

1987 *Water in New Mexico: A History of Its Use and Management*. University of New Mexico Press, Albuquerque.

Clark, Tiffany, and Suzanne L. Eckert

2004 The Importance of Avifauna in Pueblo IV Ritual Systems: A Case Study from the Lower Rio Puerco, New Mexico. Poster presented at the 69th Annual Meeting of the Society for American Archaeology, Montreal.

Cordell, Linda S.

1979 Unpublished manuscript. Manuscript on file, Maxwell Museum of Anthropology, University of New Mexico, Albuquerque.

1980 University of New Mexico Field School Excavations at Pottery Mound, New Mexico, 1979, Preliminary Report. Manuscript on file, Maxwell Museum of Anthropology, University of New Mexico, Albuquerque.

2004 Advanced Seminar on Pottery Mound, School of American Research, May 11–12. Manuscript on file, School of American Research, Santa Fe, New Mexico.

Crotty, Helen K.

1992 Protohistoric Anasazi Kiva Murals: Variation in Imagery as a Reflection of Differing Social Contexts. In *Archaeology, Art, and Anthropology: Papers in Honor of J. J. Brody*, edited by Meliha S. Duran and David T. Kirkpatrick, pp. 51–61. Papers of the Archaeological Society of New Mexico Vol. 18. Archaeological Society of New Mexico, Albuquerque.

1995 *Anasazi Mural Art of the Pueblo IV Period, A.D. 1300–1600: Influences, Selective Adaptation, and Cultural Diversity in the Prehistoric Southwest.* Ph.D. dissertation, University of California, Los Angeles. University Microfilms International, Ann Arbor.

Dutton, Bertha P.

1963 *Sun Father's Way.* University of New Mexico Press, Albuquerque.

Eckert, Suzanne L.

2003 Social Boundaries, Immigration, and Ritual Systems: A Case Study from the American Southwest. Unpublished Ph.D. dissertation, Department of Anthropology, Arizona State University, Tempe.

Emslie, Steven D.

1981 Prehistoric Agricultural Ecosystems: Avifauna from Pottery Mound, New Mexico. *American Antiquity* 46(4):853–61.

Emslie, Steven D., and Lyndon L. Hargrave

1978 An Ethnobiological Study of the Avifauna from Pottery Mound, New Mexico. Paper presented at the 43rd Annual Meeting of the Society for American Archaeology, Tucson.

Espinosa, Gilberto

1933 *The History of New Mexico by Gaspar Pérez de Villagrá.* The Quivira Society Vol. IV. Los Angeles.

Franklin, Hayward H.

1997 Valencia Pueblo Ceramics. In *Excavations at Valencia Pueblo (LA 953) and a Nearby Hispanic Settlement (LA 67321), Valencia County, New Mexico,* edited by Kenneth L. Brown and Bradley J. Vierra, pp. 125–246. Office of Contract Archaeology, University of New Mexico, Albuquerque.

Garrett, Elizabeth M.

1976 A Petrographic Analysis of Thirty Pottery Mound Polychrome, San Clemente Polychrome, and Glaze C Sherds from Pottery Mound, New Mexico. *Pottery Southwest* 3(1):4–8.

Graves, William M., and Katherine A. Spielmann

2000 Leadership, Long-Distance Exchange, and Feasting in the Protohistoric Rio Grande. In *Alternative Leadership Strategies in the Prehispanic Southwest,* edited by Barbara J. Mills, pp. 45–59. University of Arizona Press, Tucson.

Hammond, George P., and Agapito Rey

1940 *Narratives of the Coronado Expedition, 1540–1542.* University of New Mexico Press, Albuquerque.

1966 *The Rediscovery of New Mexico, 1580–1594: Explorations of Chamuscado Espejo, Castaño de Sosa, Morlete, and Leyva de Bonilla and Humaña.* University of New Mexico Press, Albuquerque.

Hibben, Frank C.

1955 Excavations at Pottery Mound, New Mexico. *American Antiquity* 21(2):179–80.

1960 Prehispanic Paintings at Pottery Mound. *Archaeology* 13(4):267–74.

1966 A Possible Pyramidal Structure and Other Mexican Influences at Pottery Mound, New Mexico. *American Antiquity* 31(4):522–29.

1967 Mexican Features of Mural Paintings at Pottery Mound, New Mexico. *Archaeology* 20(2):84–87.

1975 *The Kiva Art of the Anasazi.* KC Publications, Las Vegas, Nevada.

1987 Report on the Salvage Operations at the Site of Pottery Mound, New Mexico, during the Excavating Seasons of 1977–1986. Manuscript on file, Laboratory of Anthropology No. P2662 and P2663, Santa Fe, New Mexico.

Marshall, Michael P., and Henry J. Walt

1984 *Rio Abajo: Prehistory and History of a Rio Grande Province.* New Mexico Historic Preservation Program, Santa Fe, New Mexico.

Mathien, Frances Joan

1982 Intermittent Excavations at Pottery Mound, June 7, 1980, through January 3, 1981. Manuscript on file, Maxwell Museum of Anthropology, University of New Mexico, Albuquerque.

Mera, H. P.

1940   *Population Changes in the Rio Grande Glaze-Paint Area.* Technical Series, Bulletin No. 9. Laboratory of Anthropology, Santa Fe, New Mexico.

Mills, Barbara J. (editor)

2000   *Alternative Leadership Strategies in the Prehispanic Southwest.* University of Arizona Press, Tucson.

Ogilvie, Marsha

1993   Sexual Division of Labor as Reflected in Skeletal Morphology at Pottery Mound, New Mexico. Manuscript on file, Cat. No. 93.28.10, Maxwell Museum of Anthropology, University of New Mexico, Albuquerque.

Potter, James M., and Elizabeth M. Perry

2000   Ritual as a Power Resource in the American Southwest. In *Alternative Leadership Strategies in the Prehispanic Southwest,* edited by Barbara J. Mills, pp. 60–78. University of Arizona Press, Tucson.

Schaafsma, Curtis F.

1987   The Tiguex Province Revisited: The Rio Medio Survey. In *Secrets of a City: Papers on Albuquerque Area Archaeology in Honor of Richard A. Bice,* edited by Anne V. Poore and John Montgomery, pp. 6–13. Archaeological Society of New Mexico Vol. 13. Ancient City Press, Santa Fe, New Mexico.

Schaafsma, Polly

1999   Tlalocs, Kachinas, and Sacred Bundles, and Related Symbolism in the Southwest and Mesoamerica. In *The Casas Grandes World,* edited by Curtis F. Schaafsma and Carroll L. Riley, pp. 164–92. University of Utah Press, Salt Lake City.

2001   Quetzalcoatl and the Horned and Feathered Serpent of the Southwest. In *The Road to Aztlan: Art from a Mythic Homeland,* edited by Virginia M. Fields and Victor Zamudio-Taylor, pp. 138–49. Los Angeles County Museum of Art, Los Angeles.

Schaafsma, Polly, and Karl A. Taube

2006   Bringing the Rain: An Ideology of Rain Making in the Pueblo Southwest and Mesoamerica. In *A Pre-Columbian World,* edited by Jeffrey Quilter and Mary E. Miller, pp. 231–86. Dumbarton Oaks Research Library and Collection, Washington, D.C.

Schorsch, Russell Lowell Gordon

1962   The Physical Anthropology of Pottery Mound: A Pueblo IV Site in West Central New Mexico. Unpublished Master's thesis, Department of Anthropology, University of New Mexico, Albuquerque.

Sekaquaptewa, Emory, and Dorothy Washburn

2004   They Go Along Singing. *American Antiquity* 69(3):457–86.

Smith, Watson

1952   *Kiva Mural Decorations at Awatovi and Kawaika-a.* Papers of the Peabody Museum of American Archaeology and Ethnology Vol. 37. Harvard University, Cambridge, Massachusetts.

Spielmann, Katherine A.

1996   Impressions of Pueblo III Settlement Trends among the Rio Abajo and Eastern Border Pueblos. In *The Prehistoric Pueblo World, A.D. 1150–1350,* edited by Michael A. Adler, pp. 177–87. University of Arizona Press, Tucson.

Stephen, Alexander M.

1936   *The Hopi Journal of Alexander M. Stephen,* edited by Elsie Clews Parsons. Columbia University Contributions to Anthropology Vol. 23. Columbia University Press, New York.

Taube, Karl

1986   The Teotihuacan Cave of Origin: The Iconography and Architecture of Emergence Mythology in Mesoamerica and the American Southwest. *Res: Anthropology and Aesthetics* 12:51–82.

2001   The Breath of Life: The Symbolism of Wind in Mesoamerica and the American Southwest. In *The Road to Aztlan: Art from a Mythic Homeland,* edited by Virginia M. Fields and Victor Zamudio-Taylor, pp. 102–23. Los Angeles County Museum of Art, Los Angeles.

Tichy, Marjorie Ferguson

1937 The Kivas of Paako and Kuaua. *New Mexico Anthropologist* 2(4–5):71–79.

Van Keuren, Scott

2000 Ceramic Decoration as Power: Late Prehistoric Design Change in East-Central Arizona. In *Alternative Leadership Strategies in the Prehispanic Southwest*, edited by Barbara J. Mills, pp. 79–94. University of Arizona Press, Tucson.

Vivian, Patricia Bryan

1961 Kachina: The Study of Pueblo Animism and Anthropomorphism with the Ceremonial Wall Paintings of Pottery Mound and the Jeddito. Unpublished Master of Fine Arts thesis, Department of Art, University of Iowa, Iowa City.

1994 Anthropomorphic Figures in the Pottery Mound Murals. In *Kachinas in the Pueblo World*, edited by Polly Schaafsma, pp. 81–92. University of New Mexico Press, Albuquerque. (Reprinted University of Utah Press, 2000).

Voll, Charles

1961 The Glaze Paint Ceramics from Pottery Mound. Unpublished Master's thesis, Department of Anthropology, University of New Mexico, Albuquerque.

Walt, Henry J.

1981 Kiva Murals. Manuscript on file, Acc. No. 81.32.68, Maxwell Museum of Anthropology, University of New Mexico, Albuquerque.

Winship, George Parker

1896 *The Coronado Expedition, 1540–1542.* Bureau of American Ethnology Fourteenth Annual Report. Smithsonian Institution, Washington, D.C.

CHAPTER TWO

Frank C. Hibben and Pottery Mound
Site Research and Interpretation

R. Gwinn Vivian

Introduction

Pottery Mound (LA 416 and LA 8683) is a large adobe Early Glaze period pueblo located approximately 25 mi southwest of Albuquerque, New Mexico. Site occupation is ceramically dated at approximately A.D. 1370 to 1450. The ruin mound has an estimated 500 rooms that may have surrounded several large plazas. Pottery Mound is best known for 17 excavated kivas, 11 of which contained multiple layers of murals on the walls. However, the presence of contemporary Zuni and Hopi pottery and a postulated two-tiered platform mound underlying a major portion of the site (Hibben 1966) also signal the site's archaeological importance.

The site was known archaeologically by at least 1926 (Warner 1928) and was recorded by the Laboratory of Anthropology in Santa Fe in 1930. However, subsequent work at Pottery Mound essentially became the exclusive domain of Frank C. Hibben, a professor of anthropology at the University of New Mexico (UNM) from 1935 to 1977. Hibben carried out work at the site in two phases. The first involved five field sessions of the UNM summer archaeological field school in 1954, 1955, 1957, 1958, and 1961. He also apparently did some work at the site in 1959, possibly with student volunteers, and in the summer of 1961 with the UNM Anthropology Club. The summer of 1960 was devoted to mural recording funded by the National Science Foundation (NSF) (see P. Vivian, this volume). In

addition, in 1975 under Hibben's supervision, Kiva 17, on the brink of the bank of the Rio Puerco, was excavated by Kathy Weidner (Mathien 1982). Hibben then returned for a second phase of work in 1977 to conduct salvage operations in a portion of the site that was collapsing into the eroding Rio Puerco. He sporadically continued these activities until 1986. During this second phase, Linda Cordell directed another UNM field school at the site in 1979. Cordell, field supervisor Kathryn (Kit) Sargeant, and students produced a topographic map of the site, made systematic surface collections, and excavated a 5 m by 5 m test unit in the northwestern portion of the site. After five 20 cm levels had been removed from the unit, Cordell divided the unit into quadrants and proceeded to excavate the southeast and northwest quadrants. The southeast quadrant was taken down 17 more levels to sterile, the northwest down 15 levels. In that same year, a survey for the Army Corps of Engineers, by Human Systems Research (Wimberly and Eidenbach 1980), in the Lower Puerco River valley included visiting Pottery Mound. The survey report contains several aerial photographs of the site.

In essence, other than Cordell, no other archaeologist collected data from Pottery Mound after 1954. Moreover, use of site data in four master's theses (Brody 1964; Schorsch 1962; Vivian 1961; Voll 1961) by students who had worked at the site in varying capacities was strongly controlled by Hibben. There were two notable effects of this exclusivity and control. First, a sherd-curtain of sorts was pulled down over the site, and archaeologists working in the Southwest and elsewhere increasingly forgot about Pottery Mound. Second, the occasional and often repetitive articles that Hibben published on Pottery Mound reflected an increasingly narrow focus on subjects that appealed to him. That trend culminated in his 1975 publication, *Kiva Art of the Anasazi at Pottery Mound*, in which he briefly summarized site archaeology but devoted most of the text to describing and interpreting the kiva murals. Although Hibben submitted a report on his 1977–1986 salvage excavations at Pottery Mound to the State Historic Preservation Office (SHPO) in 1987, he did not use these new data to revise his 1975 interpretation of site history.

During the 21 years between his first official work at Pottery Mound in 1954 and the publication of his major monograph in 1975, Hibben's writings reflect a notable shift in his identification of external cultural influences on the indigenous population. Initially, he interpreted the presence of early Zuni Glaze Wares and Hopi Yellow Wares as evidence for important trading ties with Western Pueblo

peoples. Moreover, the use of Sikyatki-style motifs in some murals suggested strong ritualistic links with Western Pueblos if not the actual presence of Hopi or other residential units at Pottery Mound. By 1966, however, his *American Antiquity* article, "A Possible Pyramidal Structure and Other Mexican Influences at Pottery Mound, New Mexico," marked his acceptance of Mesoamerican, or in his terminology "Mexican," elements at the site. This theme was more fully explored in his 1975 monograph. The evidence he used to support a southern source for cultural values and change at the site included mural subject matter, a few examples of material culture, and what he believed was a two-tiered platform mound or "pyramid" underlying a large portion of the site.

The case for a Mesoamerican source for personages and motifs displayed in some of the kiva murals is explored in other papers in this volume. A copper bell (Cordell 1980; Vargas 1995), five Ramos Polychrome sherds, and a clay bell "in obvious imitation of copper form" (Hibben 1966:525) constituted the relatively meager handful of Mesoamerican-derived or -copied items recovered from the site. The architectural evidence is equivocal. This is largely because of unrecorded or poorly recorded architectural data exposed at the site during field school excavations. This situation is a direct result of minimal field documentation (particularly at the supervisory level) and the lack of a consistent research plan. My intention is not to lay blame, but rather to clarify as much as possible the largely tenuous nature of Pottery Mound architectural information, including evidence for a pyramid or platform mound.

To provide context for evaluating the architectural data, I briefly describe site setting and condition, synopsize investigations at the site from 1926 to 1954, and then summarize methods and results of data collection during the UNM 1954–1961 field school sessions. Relevant data from Hibben's second phase of work at the site and Cordell's 1979 field season are referenced in this summary. I conclude with a short analysis of Hibben's changing views on sources of cultural influence at Pottery Mound and offer an explanation for his shift to a Mesoamerican interpretive theme.

Site Setting and Condition

Pottery Mound is located approximately 15 mi west and slightly south of Los Lunas, New Mexico (Valencia County), on the west bank of the Rio Puerco approximately

10 mi south of the junction of the Rio San Jose and the Rio Puerco on the eastern slopes of Mesa Lucero. The broad and relatively featureless Rio Puerco valley in this area is bordered on the west by Hidden Mountain and Mesa Carrizo, the northern slopes of the Sierra Ladrones to the south, and the western uplands of the Rio Grande valley on the east.

Elevation change within the valley is minimal, ranging between 4,800 and 5,000 ft; Pottery Mound is near the upper elevation, and the pueblo may have been constructed on a natural terrace above the valley flood-plain (see "Platform Mound" discussion below). Wimberly and Eidenbach (1980:61) describe the present habitat as "primarily desert grassland with some shrubs and sparse Juniper woodland on the valley slopes. The valley bottom is deeply eroded by the primary channel of the Rio Puerco and tributary arroyos on the east and west." They further note that "the major limiting factor on productivity in this habitat is water. Precipitation is generally in the range of 8 to 14 inches.... And there is not much variability in rainfall from one part of the area to another. Microhabitat differences do occur, however, and these are associated with such factors as the slope of the land, soil permeability and ability to hold water" (1980:61).

The northeastern margins of Pottery Mound have been eroding into the Rio Puerco since at least the 1920s (Warner 1928), and significant portions of the site, including Kiva 17, are known to have been lost in the past 35 years. In the 1950s the site covered at least 7 acres, but Warner (1928) estimated mound size at 15 acres in 1926, and rooms were already collapsing into the Rio Puerco at that time. The mound was always a noticeable cultural feature in the area as it rose as much as 20 ft above the surrounding plain; Warner's (1928) estimated mound height, often in feet, may be incorrect or reflect erosional changes at the site. Today, the mound is heavily pocked by years of legal and illegal digging and trenching, and the bulldozer trench cut in 1961 through the southern margins of the mound appears as a major scar on aerial photographs.

Site loss through long-term vandalism and encroachment of the Rio Puerco channel was curtailed to some degree in 1979 when the Huning Land Trust deeded the site zone to the regents of the University of New Mexico for continued "academic purposes." This transfer effectively placed the site under state archaeological protection. The following year the Huning Land Trust and the university fenced the site. At the same time the U.S. Army Corps of Engineers developed plans for improved

site protection from further Rio Puerco bank erosion. Hibben (1987:3) reported that "engineers of the New Mexico National Guard constructed a dam in part of the Puerco drainage around 1977," but this apparently did not totally prevent bank erosion. Cordell (2004) notes that a description of the corps project was filed with the Museum of New Mexico in March 1981. The Pueblo of Isleta now owns property around Pottery Mound and controls access to the site.

Archaeological Investigations at Pottery Mound: 1926 to 1954

Thor Warner (1928) wrote the first known description of Pottery Mound. Warner, a geologist, visited the site in 1926 when doing geological reconnaissance work in the Rio Puerco valley. He described both the mound and a nearby mesa-top site (LA 415) that he called "Fortification Mesa." His article contained two site location maps and a detailed plan of the mound showing the exposed adobe walls of a number of roomblocks. Warner named the site "Pottery Hill," but its designation on one map is "Ancient Pottery City" and on the second map is "Pottery Mound." Presumably Hibben was aware of this article, though he does not cite it in any of his publications. Considering his short time at the site, Warner provided a perceptively detailed architectural summary. He estimated that the mound covered about 15 acres, contained approximately 500 rooms of a fairly uniform size (6 x 10 ft), and rose some 10 ft above the valley floor. Noting that the base of an adobe wall exposed in the bank of the Puerco was 4 ft below the valley surface, he surmised that the pueblo might have been several stories high. The edge of the Rio Puerco at this time was "about 1000 feet from the center of the mound" (Warner 1928:90). Warner (1928:91) also dug several rooms to a maximum depth of 4 ft and recovered an "abundance of pottery fragments, a part of one human skeleton, corn-cobs, turquoise beads, ornaments carved in soft rock, and a number of crudely shaped stone implements."

The site was described briefly by Luhrs (1937:75–77) who refers to it as the "'Thor Warner' site or 'Pottery Mound.'" She notes that "'pothunting' has practically ruined this site as there are holes in every portion of the mound." More significantly, H. P. Mera visited the site on March 16 in 1930 and designated it as LA 416 in the Laboratory of Anthropology site recording system. According to Curtis Schaafsma, three additional dates on the current site card (3/26/30, 7/30/32, and 1/16/39) probably indicate subsequent visits to the site and possible updating of site information. The card includes a tally of collected ceramics, and Schaafsma (personal communication 2004) believes the reported ceramic types represent "the identifications done by Mera and/or Stan [Stanley Stubbs]." He also notes that "the text that appears prominently on the site card was added later, and my guess is all of that was added by Helene Warren who analyzed 'and culled' the survey collection in 1970."

A plan map of LA 416 is also filed at the Laboratory of Anthropology and is attributed to Mera. This plan shows two separate trapezium-like units oriented roughly north-south with a rectangular roomblock attached to the base of the southern unit. Polly Schaafsma (personal communication 2004) indicates that the map was made no later than 1939. David Wilcox (personal communication 2004) believes the map may show a much larger site akin to the 15-acre site reported by Warner (see Figure 11.1).

Mera referenced LA 416 again in 1940 in his discussion of sites in the West Tiwa Division of the Rio Grande Glaze paint area. His entry for LA 416 indicates, "Sherds of three distinct ceramic cultures are present in such quantities that it makes this village unique in the Rio Grande drainage. But as this paper deals principally with the duration of occupation it will suffice to say that this covered a span from A to E" (Mera 1940:18). Curtis Schaafsma (personal communication 2004) points out that Mera's identification of late glaze types at the site is contrary to all other reported ceramic identifications (Brody 1964; Cordell 1980; Hibben 1975; Luhrs 1937; Voll 1961). Laboratory of Anthropology site records also indicate that Pottery Mound was visited and a sherd collection made in 1953 by F. Fenenga and T. Cummings. This visit probably was in conjunction with archaeological pipeline surveys in the state.

The UNM Archaeological Field School at Pottery Mound: 1954 to 1961

Frank Hibben initiated research at Pottery Mound through the University of New Mexico summer archaeological field school in 1954. Although he reported excavations "during the years of 1954, 1955, 1958, 1959, 1960, 1961 and 1962" (Hibben 1966:523), there was a field school at the site in 1957, but not in 1959. However, inasmuch as the UNM Research Committee provided funding for work on kiva murals in 1959 (Hibben 1975:ix), Hibben may have

been at the site with students or volunteers that year. If so, this may explain the discrepancy between the number of mural layers reported in student notes for kivas opened between 1954 and 1961 and Hibben's (1975:Table 3) listing of "Layers with Murals" in these kivas. Similarly, though field schoolwork at Pottery Mound ended in 1961, Hibben apparently directed or was otherwise involved with Anthropology Club work at the site in 1962. There are no known records of this work, nor of any return visits he made to Pottery Mound until 1977, aside from the 1975 excavation of Kiva 17 mentioned earlier.

Hibben did not explain why he selected Pottery Mound for a field school in his first report on work there (Hibben 1955). He did note that the site had been "known for the last 2 decades to archaeologists and laymen alike as a place prolific in many kinds of pottery" (1955:179). He also was aware of the Hummingbird Ruin in the Puerco Valley upstream from Pottery Mound and may have been carrying out a simultaneous investigation of that site, although not with the field school. Field sessions ran for six weeks, beginning in mid-June and ending in late July or early August. Hibben's presence at the site varied each year; he was on-site once or twice a week in 1957. The field staff varied annually but always included Hibben as the general supervisor and a graduate student dig foreman. There was no supervisory apprenticing at Pottery Mound, though Russell Schorsch held the position of dig foreman in 1954, 1955, and 1961, and he directed the NSF-supported mural work in 1960 while Hibben was in Africa. Gwinn Vivian was dig foreman in 1957 and Charles Voll held the position in 1958. Staff members increased in 1961. Jim Harris did site mapping, Ronald Provencher was class supervisor, Jean and Jerome (Jerry) Brody were laboratory supervisors, and Ted Frisbie and Dennis Tedlock recorded murals with student help. Although kiva murals were discovered in 1954, there is no indication that a position to supervise mural exposure and recording was ever formally established. Natalie Vytlacil carried out this responsibility in 1954, 1955, and 1957. Jerry Brody, a student in 1954, devoted much of his time to recording murals in Kiva 1, and John Vaughn did similar work in 1955, possibly as a staff member. Brownie Hibben worked on murals every year as a volunteer , and she also made a documentary film on work at the site (DVD remaster of motion picture film on file at the Maxwell Museum of Anthropology, University of New Mexico).

The number of students enrolled for the field session at Pottery Mound essentially increased each field session. Student numbers are based on field session notebooks, but some notebooks are missing. I know of four students in 1957 for which there are no notebooks, and notebooks are missing for other students who are mentioned in curated student notebooks for other years. At least eight students were enrolled in 1954. In 1955 there were 13, but additional students may have been present. Twenty-nine students, including four with missing notebooks, were enrolled in 1957. Student numbers dropped to 19 or possibly 20 students in 1958. The numbers increased to at least 32 and possibly 35 in 1961.

The Hibben Center at the University of New Mexico curates documents from the field school period of research at Pottery Mound. These include student field/laboratory notebooks, site maps, a profile of the 1961 bulldozer trench through the southern edge of the mound, photographs, and field drawings—primarily of kiva murals. I made a preliminary review of site maps and student field notebooks in 2004 to better ascertain the quantity and quality of site data in these sources and briefly viewed the bulldozer trench profile. I did not examine site photographs and field drawings. Field notes or logs recorded by Hibben and student dig foremen (Schorsch, Vivian, and Voll) were not among the documents I examined at the Hibben Center. If Hibben made field notes they remain in his personal papers not yet curated by the Hibben Center. My personal recollection is that I did not keep notes or a log during the 1957 field session, and neither did Voll (personal communication 2004). Russell Schorsch (1961), the dig foreman in 1954, 1955, and 1961, did submit a paper for credit in 1961, but apparently he did not keep daily notes.

Although Hibben (1975:4) references site "excavation plans," I was not aware of those plans in 1957, and Voll (personal communication 2004) also did not recall any such plans for the 1958 field season. Though Hibben (1975:4–6) states that the excavation plans "for the whole structure included only limited testing in selected areas," we have no knowledge why particular rooms or groups of rooms were selected each year for excavation. I do remember that in 1957 my instructions were to select rooms that were sufficiently deep to ensure that each student would be in one room for the duration of the field season. Since Warner's time, the tops of adobe walls were visible on much of the mound surface, but kiva locations were unknown. Their excavation inevitably was the result of chance discovery, often through trenching in areas where room walls were not visible on the surface. Trenching may have been intended to locate kivas or plaza areas, but the rationale for their placement is unclear.

Site Architecture— Sources of Information

Hibben did not describe site architecture in detail in any of his publications. Instead, he wrote slight variations on a basic overview of primary structural features. The following is one of his most complete descriptions:

> Architecturally Pottery Mound consisted of adobe-walled rooms surrounding four large plazas in a plan usual at Pueblo IV sites. Including several additions, the structures covered approximately seven acres. During the 175-year period of active life of the site, three or four multi-roomed adobe pueblos were built. In several sections the buildings were three or four stories high. Some of the rooms within the pueblos were built on top of others in a seemingly haphazard fashion, the historical sequence of which has yet to be fully determined, i.e. room tiers had been burned or otherwise reduced to rubble and at later times other rooms were built on top of them [Hibben 1975:6–8].

However, according to Hibben the first structure at the site was not the earliest pueblo but rather a "pyramid" or two-tiered platform mound. He believed the structure was built sometime late in the Pueblo III period in this location because "in the whole Puerco region there is no place where a flat-topped structure of even modest dimensions would appear more imposing that at this spot"(Hibben 1975:11). The structure's use life may have been short, because "later Pueblo IV occupants built their pueblo immediately on top of the pyramid, covering it completely with structures extending down the sides of the pyramid and to a considerable distance around its base" (Hibben 1975:11). Hibben (1966:528) noted one additional structure at the site, "a sunken caliche-covered floor of unknown dimensions [that] may be a court, or an entrance to the structure, or possibly a ball court."

Hibben would have had to base his reconstruction of site architecture on data collected during the 1954–1961 field seasons. These would have included photographs, site maps, trench and "strat test" profiles, and field school student notes. Additional information on site architecture, not available to Hibben before 1975, now includes Cordell's (1980) report on the 1979 field school and Hibben's 1987 salvage excavation report. These documents contain varying degrees of data on rooms, kivas, plazas, and the postulated platform mound. I will briefly evaluate and summarize each source, other than photographs, relative to its potential value for contributing to an understanding of site architecture. Photographs were not examined in 2004 and are not considered here. Kiva architecture is not described. Hibben's 1975 monograph summarizes this information, Pat Vivian (this volume) provides additional details, and other papers in this volume reference this architectural form. Crotty's (1995: Figure 1 la–e) dissertation contains plans of several kivas drawn by Bill Bramlett (see Figure 6.1), Hibben's graduate assistant, in 1963. These plans are now curated at the Hibben Center.

Maps

The site map in this volume (see Figure 1.3 and Appendix A) is a compilation of several maps prepared during the 1954 to 1961 field school seasons and two maps accompanying Hibben's 1987 report. The first map was prepared in 1954 by Schorsch, and site mapping presumably was completed each field season, although a map of rooms excavated in 1955 was not found at the Hibben Center in 2004. Voll produced the most important map in 1958 when he plotted all rooms and kivas excavated to date at the site. There are two versions of this map at the Hibben Center, one without room numbers and another with room numbers. Importantly, this map assigns letters for each of the four years (1954 = A, 1955 = B, 1957 = C, and 1958 = D) of excavation at the mound. This composite map also shows rooms that were not excavated but that were visible on the surface—a feature first noted by Warner in 1926. These unexcavated rooms were not shown on Hibben's published 1975 site map. A separate map of rooms excavated in 1961 was not located at the Hibben Center. However, three roomblocks and six scattered rooms are shown on Hibben's published 1975 map that was prepared by Bill Bramlett. This map probably represents a 1961 update of Voll's 1958 composite map. This conclusion is supported by students referencing work in the southeast sector of the site where the largest of the three blocks (18 upper-level rooms) was located. Similarly, a plan of several rooms shown in John Speth's 1961 student notebook matches rooms in the northwest roomblock.

In the mid-1980s there were two updated maps. One was prepared by Ben C. Benjamin, a volunteer on Hibben's excavations between 1977 and 1986 (Hibben 1987:4), which has the date of "7/26/85." The other is a hand-drawn map that accompanied Hibben's 1987 report (Hibben 1987:Map I). This 1987 map is adapted from the 1975 published map (Hibben 1975:21). The 1987 map importantly shows the Duck Unit in the right place (see Figure 1.3 and Appendix A). However, from all indications it (and the published map) shows Kiva 17 in the wrong place (close to the Duck Unit). On the other hand, Benjamin's 1985 map evidently has Kiva 17 correctly located (see Figure 1.3 and Appendix A), but without any question it has the Duck Unit wrongly placed.

These, and many other inconsistencies, have been considered in preparing Appendix A and the composite map in Figure 1.3. A final note for future fieldwork is that Hibben's 1987 map is of interest because it includes "walls showing on surface" of at least six roomblocks and three apparent kivas on the west and northwest sides of the site. These additions are all plotted beyond the limits of Hibben's platform mound and almost double the site size.

Trench and Strat Test Profiles

Although a number of trenches and "strat tests" were placed in the mound each field season, culminating in the major bulldozer trench in 1961 (Figure 2.1), the only profile located at the Hibben Center in 2004 was of the bulldozer trench (see Adler, this volume). These profiles are important because Hibben both implies and states that a number of them were cut to reveal evidence for the platform mound. Thus, he stated that "when it became suspected that an artificial structure might be the basis for the entire sequence, some twenty tests of small areas were carried down through the several architectural levels to examine the structure beneath" (Hibben 1975:4–6). But, he also notes that "tests of small areas gave little information" (1975:6). However, these "tests" are almost certainly not the long trenches cut into the site from 1954 to 1961. Profiles of the long trenches, as noted, were not located at the Hibben Center. Three of these trenches—with laterals—were cut in 1954 on the north and south sides of the mound (Appendix A, Tiles N-Central [NC], S-Central [SC]). Two of these, the Northwest Trench and the Southeast Trench, could have cut through the platform mound, but student notes do not indicate their presence. On the other hand, the northern lateral of the Southeast Trench also bisected Kiva 4, but student notes make no reference to this kiva. Trenching in 1955 was limited to four short trenches cut between the 1954 Southeast and Southwest trenches on the southern edge of the mound (Appendix A, Tile SC). Again, no students reference this work. Trenching in 1957 was limited to two trenches (I and II) on the eastern side of the site (Appendix A, Tiles NC, NE). One of these, Trench II, extended into the

FIGURE 2.1

View of the completed bulldozer trench cut through Pottery Mound in 1961 (see Figure 1.3 for location of the trench within the site). (Photograph courtesy of the Maxwell Museum of Anthropology, University of New Mexico, catalog no. PM37.230.)

platform mound zone and according to Hibben exposed the east edge of the platform mound, which he shows as "e" on his 1975 published map. I was not aware of this exposure in 1957, nor of the potential presence of a platform mound. Neither was Voll (personal communication 2004) aware of the platform mound when he excavated the Central Trench and the South Trench in 1958. The central trench, located near the center of the mound, was almost precisely in the center of the zone identified as the platform mound. The South Trench is probably a cut shown on Hibben's 1975 map that crosses the southwest corner of Kiva 12 and was then bisected by the 1961 bulldozer trench. Five fairly short trenches placed in the mound in 1961 are briefly referenced in student notes.

The Hibben Center does curate a complete profile of the north face of the "South Bulldozer Trench" that was cut in 1961 (see Adler, this volume, and Appendix C). This trench was cut across the southern portion of the mound specifically to obtain evidence for the "pyramid" or platform mound. The bulldozer cut was approximately 10 ft wide and 260 ft long. Notably, Hibben (1966; 1975) provides no details on the excavation of this trench, and his published cross-section (Hibben 1966) is of a scale that has little value. The only student notes relating to this trench are Barnes's description of the architecture and several painted walls of Room F70 that was located near the southeast corner of the platform mound and was cut by the bulldozer.

Linda Cordell examined the profile at the Hibben Center and provided the following description of the profile that consisted of two sections.

> The longer of the two is composed of several sections taped together and is relatively clean. The shorter section appears tan and "old." . . . It is possible to link the profile with the profile published in the *American Antiquity* article (p. 251). The published map is not the full extent of the profile but ends at a trash pit mapped on the profile at 6' East. The full extent of the drawn profile is from 312' East to 240" West. The profile indicates the top of the mound above or on a red clay layer. In areas where there are adobe walls, there is sometimes a "greenish" clay layer and there are sand layers. The adobe walls mapped on the drawn profile average about 1.5' in thickness. The drawn profile clearly shows that walls under the surface are at different levels and do not align, and as Hibben noted in the 1966 article, walls are both on and set into the clay (mound) layer [Cordell 2004:9].

Field School Student Notes

As expected, notebook entries varied greatly by student, thereby leaving large information gaps in every field session. Generally, there was a tendency to record kiva and kiva mural data in greater detail than information on rooms. Most students provided a plan of the room they were excavating, but profiles of room fill and construction details were rare. Information on subfloor architecture, when exposed, also varied by student. Hibben's instructions to students in 1957 regarding note taking emphasized recording what they found in their rooms rather than describing room architecture. The content of student notes suggests that these were annual standard instructions. Thus, many of the student notebooks contain detailed notes and drawings on burials, and by 1961 at least 100 burials had been recovered from the site. Notebooks also contain the results of laboratory sherd and faunal analysis, but some comments in notebooks suggest that identifications may not be reliable.

C. Schaafsma (personal communication 2005) has noted that Bill Bramlett, Hibben's graduate assistant in 1963, used student notebook entries to write "an anonymous manuscript that describes the ceramics on the floors of various kivas." While this could provide evidence for a kiva chronology at Pottery Mound, the reliability of student ceramic identification remains a problem.

Architecture Summary

Rooms

At least 149 rooms were excavated at Pottery Mound in the 1954 to 1961 field seasons. Twenty-three rooms grouped in three clusters in the northeast quadrant of the mound were cleared in 1954 (Appendix A, Tile NC), a considerable number compared to other years, given the apparent limited number (eight) of students. The assignment of lowercase letters to the same room number in student notes probably reflects the discovery of subfloor or lower-level rooms because Hibben (1955:179) reports evidence for "three general Pueblo structures" in this area, the first of which was destroyed by burning. Shortly thereafter a second pueblo was constructed on the ruins of the first, but this building "was partially destroyed and partially abandoned" (Hibben 1955:179). "The third or last Pueblo was built directly over the preceding second. Many walls and floors of the uppermost structure incorporated portions of the earlier ones in their makeup" (1955:179). Hibben must have been recording notes during the excavation because the chronological sequence of buildings described above is not reflected in student notes.

Hibben's salvage excavations in the Duck Unit (Appendix A, Tile NC) sometime between 1977 and 1986 produced corroborating evidence for at least three architectural levels, which Hibben (1987:7) indicates was "a feature of the entire site." Twenty-four of the 29 rooms located in this unit were excavated and Hibben (1987:7) noted that "in most instances the underlying rooms show a plan different from the level or levels below and above." Hibben (1987:8) also reported that the Duck Unit was "marked on the northwest by an especially heavy (35 cm) adobe wall which was apparently the outside wall of the major pueblo in this area." The 1987 report also contains a fairly detailed description of Room 2 in the Duck Unit, a room Hibben (1987) called the "Shaman's Room" (Figure D.2).

The 1955 excavation opened 22 rooms in a single cluster on the northwest corner of the mound (Appendix A, Tiles NW, NC). The roomblock appears on Benjamin's 1985 site map. Subfloor rooms, if present, were not identified by different numbers or lowercase letters. The 29 rooms cleared in 1957 were primarily confined to the southeast quadrant of the site (Appendix A, Tiles SC, SE). Two additional rooms (28, 29) were excavated that year in the 1954 northeast quadrant roomblock to allow full exposure of Kiva 3 that was partially exposed in 1954 (Appendix A, Tile NC; see Figure 3.3). All of these rooms, with the exception of Room 27, are shown on Benjamin's 1985 site map. Again, good evidence for subfloor rooms was not collected.

Three clusters of D rooms (totaling 23 rooms) were cleared in 1958. The first cluster of eight rooms (1–6, 26, 27) were in the north-central portion of the mound and were bordered by (though not contiguous with) A rooms to the northwest and east that were excavated in 1954 (Appendix A, Tile NC; see Figure 3.3). A second cluster of eight rooms (7–10, 12–15) in the south-central portion of the mound (Appendix A, Tile SC) were not totally contiguous, and Rooms 9 and 10 were removed by the bulldozer trench in 1961. The final group of seven rooms (16, 18–20, 22, 24–25) was located in the southwest sector of the mound and within the southwest corner of the platform mound zone (Appendix A, Tile SC). Missing room numbers may have been assigned, but they are not shown on the 1958 map, nor were they referenced in student notebooks. They probably were assigned to rooms that were not excavated. Rooms 12 through 15 are not shown on Benjamin's 1985 map of the site. The partial wall of Room 22 is also missing on this map.

If post-1958 rooms and room clusters on Hibben's 1975 map are correctly assigned to the 1961 field season, 42 upper-level (F) rooms and at least 18 lower (SF) rooms were identified though not necessarily excavated in 1961. In addition, 20 new upper-level rooms and three lower-level rooms were identified or excavated in the bulldozer trench (Appendix A). Based on student notes, at least 52 of these 83 rooms were excavated in 1961. This was the first year that upper and lower levels were distinguished, though several lower-level rooms are shown on the 1975 map in the 1958 D cluster of rooms located west of Kiva 12. Presumably, F numbers correspond to previous annual letter assignments of rooms on the 1958 site map rather than designating upper (F = floor) and lower (SF = subfloor) levels.

There are no known E room numbers, but this letter may have been retained for rooms that might have been opened in 1960, though there is no record that any were excavated.

Student notebooks for 1961 indicate work in 31 upper-level (F) rooms and 21 lower-level (SF) rooms. The fact that there are only six corresponding F and SF room numbers

suggests that these six SF rooms lay directly below upper rooms, whereas other SF numbers probably represent partial or offset rooms below upper-level F rooms. Room plan maps in several student notebooks (e.g., Benham) and student notes (e.g., Briscoe) support this interpretation. Four of the upper-level rooms (70, 71, 75, 77) described in student notebooks were located in the sides of the bulldozer trench, but there are no notes for 16 additional upper-level rooms and three lower-level rooms shown on the bulldozer trench map. Walls of these rooms were exposed in the trench, but the rooms may not have been excavated.

Hibben's (1987:5) report indicates that two rooms of an estimated "dozen or more rooms" in the Swan Unit were excavated in 1981 (Appendix A, Tile NE). Both had subfloor rooms slightly offset from the upper room. Cordell's (1980) excavation units at the site in 1979 did not reveal any room architecture.

In sum, detailed analysis of student notes and comparison of room descriptions to site maps might give us a better understanding of site architecture. At present it is difficult, however, to confirm the presence of plazas at the site given our knowledge of room layout. It is also impossible to determine site growth from the available sources. Comparison of room size might provide a means for determining site growth, if it could be demonstrated that room size varied over time. Abandonment of rooms and subsequent construction of later roomblocks over early portions of the site are evident in a number of areas. Careful analysis of these data might also contribute to a better understanding of site chronology. Finally, there is virtually no evidence for multistory construction at the site, certainly not three- or four-story buildings.

Plazas

Hibben (1975:6) described Pottery Mound as "adobe-walled rooms surrounding four large plazas, in a plan usual at Pueblo IV sites," but no plaza was ever positively defined at the site. Adler (2004) tentatively concurs with Hibben, noting that plazas "emerge" on a "best guess" map when the open areas between architectural blocks are highlighted.

The relatively linear location of Kivas 14, 15, 16, 7, 10, 12, 13, and 4 in the middle of the mound and a similar arrangement of Kivas 3, 2, 1, 5, 8/9, and 6 on the east margin of the mound could reflect a more parallel street-type layout rather than enclosed plazas, a plan Cordell (2004:12) points out could reflect Western Pueblo influence. Polly Schaafsma (personal communication 2005) rightly questions prehistoric evidence for parallel street layout of pueblos, suggesting that this may occur largely in historic sites. Or, within-roomblock placement of some kivas may be a feasible alternative. Moreover, structural evidence for Kiva 6 suggested that it was at least partially constructed within a deep refuse deposit. Pole walls covered with adobe lined the pit that was excavated into the refuse.

Thus, the evidence for plazas at Pottery Mound remains clouded. Despite an initial belief that they were working in a plaza area on the northwestern edge of the site, Cordell's (1980) field school students ultimately determined that surfaces cleared did not represent a plaza. Cordell (2004:5) notes that Vargas (1995:96) incorrectly reports the provenience of the copper bell recovered in 1979 from this "plaza floor." Hibben (1987:5), on the other hand, assumed he was in a plaza when he trenched near the Swan Unit in 1981 and found no rooms.

Platform Mound

Evidence for the two-tiered platform mound seemingly is limited to features recorded on the north face profile of the South Bulldozer Trench cut in 1961 (see Figure 2.1, Appendix C, and Adler, this volume).

Hibben (1975:6) reports that "when it became suspected that an artificial structure might be the basis for the entire sequence, some twenty tests of small areas were carried down through the several architectural levels to examine the structure beneath." He does not indicate when he first suspected the presence of this structure or when the tests were made, but his 1960 article, "Prehispanic Paintings at Pottery Mound," makes no mention of clues for this building, As noted earlier, neither Voll nor I recall any discussion of this structure in 1957 or 1958. Thus, the decision to search for evidence of the platform mounds seems to have been made between 1960 and 1961.

Hibben (1966) then waited about five years to report the architectural details of this structure. Remarkably, the complete description of the "pyramid" is contained within two paragraphs (213 words). We learn that the structure had "sloping sides made of puddled adobe and trash fill with a smoothed caliche surface" (Hibben 1966:525), and that the lower level rose about 8 ft and was 220 ft east to west and 218 ft north to south at the base. Given a single trench, it is unclear how these precise dimensions were obtained. Remains of a narrow (25 in) set of stairs were located at the northwest corner of the lower level. An upper tier that was 207 ft on a side rose an additional 6 ft to a flat-topped surface. Again, it is unclear how these precise dimensions were obtained. Hibben (1966:525) noted that "if any features were originally on its summit, these have not yet been revealed or have been obliterated by later additions." However, on the 1975 site map legend Hibben (1975:21) noted that at "point d [the southeast corner of the platform] nine skeletons were found sprawled on the slope of the pyramid. These were not formal burials."

Although Hibben made it clear that he saw no architectural link between the platform mound and the subsequent Pueblo buildings—other than superposition of the latter on the platform mound—his interpretation of the composition and thereby the function of the early structure was wholly dependent on a single profile. The interpretive process he used in identifying this structure continued a pattern of drawing architectural conclusions from relatively poorly documented site field data. Hibben's evidence for the platform mound is extremely tenuous.

Given the current state of erosion at the site, obtaining additional data from the bulldozer trench is not feasible. Therefore, reexamination of the profile may be the only approach to resolving this issue. In this vein, Cordell (2004) has offered some provocative thoughts regarding clay deposits shown on the bulldozer trench profile and similar deposits located during her 1979 field session tests. Briefly, she points out that reddish and greenish clay bands on the bulldozer trench profile that presumably represent Hibben's caliche-covered mound surfaces may, in fact, be thick, natural, water-deposited lenses. Tom Lyons and Julio Betancourt, who visited Cordell's 1979 field school excavations, first noted this possibility. According to Kit Sargeant, Cordell's field supervisor, they suggested that "deposition on top of older prehistoric occupations would have occurred as a result of bajada erosion while the clay lenses in the formation may be the result of ponding following flooding or still water at the stream edge" (Cordell 2004:11). Sargeant had exposed a red clay layer in the Southeast Quad excavation unit and a "slightly greenish" (Cordell 2004:9) clay layer in the Northwest Quad. Cordell (2004:11) concluded that "Pottery Mound was probably on a natural terrace above the floodplain and that flooding may account for some of the clay lenses and remodeling of the site."

Architectural evidence at Pottery Mound for Mesoamerican influence ultimately can be based only on the postulated presence of a platform mound. All other architectural features are well within the Puebloan sphere. The failure to substantiate the presence of a platform mound considerably weakens Hibben's (1966:525) argument that "the flat-topped structure at Pottery Mound is, then, simply a northern extension of this type of ritual architecture." Personages and motifs in the kiva murals may then represent the best evidence for Mesoamerican ties at Pottery Mound.

Interpreting the Archaeology of Pottery Mound— Hibben's Changing Views

Although Hibben did not spend a great deal of time interpreting the prehistory of Pottery Mound, there is an interesting shift in his interpretive approach that I believe could be attributed to his close ties with the Amerind Foundation in southeastern Arizona. His first two articles on the site (Hibben 1955; 1960) reflect a broad interest in defining the cultural origins of Pottery Mound ceramics, architecture, and kiva mural art. This interest was primarily focused on ceramics and kiva murals and their stylistic similarity to the Western Pueblos and, more specifically, the Hopi. In his first brief report on work at Pottery Mound, he observed that the "considerable percentage" of "Jeddito Brown on Yellow and Sitkyatki [sic] Polychrome" presented "a strong possibility of an intrusion from the west of a large group of Hopi peoples" (Hibben 1955:179). This interpretation was soon bolstered by the presence of murals in Kiva 1 that were in some ways reminiscent of those reported by Smith (1952) from Awat'ovi and Kawaika'a.

By 1960, following four field seasons at Pottery Mound, Hibben (1960:267) acknowledged "architectural and ceramic connections with the Rio Grande pueblos." However, he continued to argue for strong ties with the Hopi and Zuni areas, noting that not only ceramics but "other material from the site strongly bears out these western connections" (1960:268). He did not identify the "other material." Observing that only two other sites in the Southwest (Kuaua and Awat'ovi) contained murals on a par with those from Pottery Mound, Hibben concluded that those from Pottery Mound were more sophisticated. Notably, he stated that while these murals showed "stronger affinities with the paintings at Awatovi," they exhibited "greater variation in style and color . . . [and] a much wider variety of subjects" (1960:272). At this time Hibben was already working with informants from Laguna and Acoma pueblos to identify personages depicted in the murals.

In 1966 Hibben signaled a major shift in his thinking about Pottery Mound in his *American Antiquity* article "A Possible Pyramidal Structure and Other Mexican Influences at Pottery Mound, New Mexico." Western Pueblo influences were now relegated to the notation that Zuni and Hopi ceramics were "fairly common" at the site (Hibben 1966:522), although he continued to acknowledge that Pottery Mound was closely connected with the Middle Rio Grande pueblos. However, he now argued that evidence from the site provided "evidence of more direct Mexican-Anasazi cultural contact" (1966:522). This evidence was expressed primarily in architecture and the kiva murals.

Although Hibben indicates that evidence for a pyramid beneath the roomblocks at Pottery Mound grew over the several years of field school excavations, this evidence was not cited in his earlier articles. Nonetheless, based on test pits and trench exposures, including the major bulldozer trench cut through the southern edge of the mound in 1961, Hibben (1966:Figure 1) defined a two-tiered platform mound as the initial structure at the site. Citing the presence of pyramidal buildings at Casas Grandes in Chihuahua and in the Hohokam area including the Gatlin Site, Hibben (1966:525) concluded that the Pottery Mound structure was "simply a northern extension of this type of ritual architecture." He also referenced the Hohokam and Casas Grandes association of ballcourts with platform mounds and suggested that a "sunken caliche-covered floor of unknown dimensions" south of the Pottery Mound building might have been a ballcourt (1966:528).

Hibben then noted that it was logical to assume the transmission of rituals associated with platform mounds and that "the major body of information as to Mexican ritualistic influence is contained in the Pottery Mound mural paintings" (1966:526). He identified four Mexican-inspired motifs in the murals. These included the frequent depiction of macaws or parrots, shield-bearer figures that resembled Mexican figures, an association of eagles and jaguars suggesting the eagle-jaguar cult, and horned and feathered serpents. Additional connections with more southern cultural systems included the presence of a number of sherds of Ramos Polychrome, a clay imitation of a copper bell, and shell jewelry.

A 1967 article in *Archaeology*, "Mexican Features of Mural Paintings at Pottery Mound," expanded only slightly on his conclusions in the *American Antiquity* paper and reinforced Hibben's interpretive shift from western to southern influences at the site. The same approach was taken in his 1975 book where he referenced the pyramidal structure and possible ballcourt and devoted a section of the text to "Mexican influences" in the murals. Apparently for the first time, Hibben (1975:21) also noted the presence of "nine skeletons . . . sprawled on the slope of the pyramid" and pointed out that they were not formal burials. Their location is identified on Hibben's 1975 map as in the bulldozer cut near the southeastern corner of the pyramid, so presumably notes and drawings on this portion of the trench contain additional information on the skeletons.

It is unclear if this shift in his interpretive scenario evolved from Hibben's analysis of the data or represented his buying into the then-current "Mesoamerican" sphere of influence explanatory model favored by a number of southwestern archaeologists, most notably Charles Di Peso. It may well be the latter, inasmuch as Hibben had a long association with the Amerind Foundation in Dragoon, Arizona. This began with his close relationship with William S. Fulton, the first director of the foundation, and his wife, Rose. The depth of that relationship is reflected in the dedication of his 1975 book not only to Hattie Cosgrove but to the Fultons, "the most beloved and respected figures in all of American archaeology" (Hibben 1975:v). This friendship continued after Charles Di Peso assumed the directorship of the Amerind Foundation, and Hibben (1987:3) reports that both Fulton and Di Peso carried out test excavations at Pottery Mound and the Hummingbird Ruin "in the 1970s." This could not have been inasmuch as Fulton had died in 1964.

Hibben was obviously aware of Di Peso's work at Casas Grandes, and the timing of the Casas field operations from late 1958 into 1961 coincided rather neatly with Hibben's shifting interpretation of outside influences at Pottery Mound. Although he did not publish his "pyramidal structure" paper until 1966, the trench that was bulldozed through the mound to help confirm the pyramid was cut in 1961. Di Peso's (1968) *pochteca* theory would only have reinforced Hibben's "Mexican" interpretation, as did the 1974 publication of Di Peso's eight volumes on the Casas project. Hibben may have believed that additional archaeological value would accrue to Pottery Mound if it could be shown that it represented a northern "pochteca" outpost in the Rio Grande valley. The presence of platform mounds and ballcourts similar to those at Casas Grandes would support such a premise. And the possibility that human sacrifice may have been practiced at Casas Grandes (Di Peso 1974:414–415) could have prompted the "discovery" of the nine skeletons "found sprawled on the slope of the pyramid" (Hibben 1975:21) at Pottery Mound. Hibben's 1987 report makes it clear that his conviction did not waver, even after Di Peso's dating of Paquimé and the presence of pochteca in the Southwest was seriously questioned by a sizeable segment of the southwestern archaeological community.

As is evident in the papers in this volume, the importance of Pottery Mound as an apparent nexus of multiple and diverse sources of cultural inspiration remains a viable and vital focus of research. Despite Hibben's controlling and sometimes controversial handling of the Pottery Mound data, we can acknowledge the role he played in provoking more detailed and comprehensive analyses of the site data. ▪▪

REFERENCES CITED

Adler, Michael

2004 Building Identities: Architecture and Cultural Affinities in Pueblo IV Settlements along the Rio Puerco. Draft of a paper prepared for the Pottery Mound Mini-Seminar held at the School of American Research, Santa Fe, New Mexico.

Brody, Jerome J.

1964 Design Analysis of the Rio Grande Glaze Pottery of Pottery Mound, New Mexico. Unpublished Master's thesis, Department of Art and Art History, University of New Mexico, Albuquerque.

Cordell, Linda S.

1980 University of New Mexico Field School Excavations at Pottery Mound, New Mexico, 1979, Preliminary Report. Manuscript on file, Maxwell Museum of Anthropology, University of New Mexico, Albuquerque.

2004 Advanced Seminar on Pottery Mound. Draft of a paper prepared for the Pottery Mound Mini-Seminar held at the School of American Research, Santa Fe, New Mexico.

Crotty, Helen

1995 *Anasazi Mural Art of the Pueblo IV Period, A.D. 1300–1600: Influences, Selective Adaptation, and Cultural Diversity in the Prehistoric Southwest.* University Microfilms, Ann Arbor.

Di Peso, Charles

1968 Casas Grandes and the Gran Chichimeca. *El Palacio* 75(4):45–61.

1974 *Casas Grandes: A Fallen Trading Center of the Gran Chichimeca.* 8 vols. Vols. 4–8 coauthored with John B. Rinaldo and Gloria J. Fenner. Amerind Foundation, Dragoon, and Northland Press, Flagstaff, Arizona.

Hibben, Frank C.

1955 Excavations at Pottery Mound, New Mexico. *American Antiquity* 21:179–180.

1960 Prehispanic Paintings at Pottery Mound. *Archaeology* 13:267–74.

1966 A Possible Pyramidal Structure and Other Mexican Influences at Pottery Mound, New Mexico. *American Antiquity* 31:522–29.

1967 Mexican Features of Mural Paintings at Pottery Mound. *Archaeology* 20(2):84–87.

1975 *Kiva Art of the Anasazi at Pottery Mound.* KC Publications, Las Vegas, Nevada.

1987 Report on the Salvage Operations at the Site of Pottery Mound, New Mexico during the Excavating Seasons of 1977–1986. Manuscript on file, Maxwell Museum of Anthropology, University of New Mexico, Albuquerque.

Luhrs, Dorothy Louise

1937 The Identification and Distribution of the Ceramic Types in the Rio Puerco Area, Central New Mexico. Unpublished Master's thesis, Department of Anthropology, University of New Mexico, Albuquerque.

Mathien, F. Joan

1982 Intermittent Excavations at Pottery Mound, June 7, 1980, through January 3, 1981. Manuscript on file, Maxwell Museum of Anthropology, University of New Mexico, Albuquerque.

Mera, H. P.

1940 *Population Changes in the Rio Grande Glaze-Paint Area.* Technical Series, Bulletin No. 9, Archeological Survey. Laboratory of Anthropology, Santa Fe, New Mexico.

Schorsch, Russell Lowell Gordon

1961 Field Techniques for the Pottery Mound Project, A Summary for Anthropology 199F. Student Paper, Maxwell Museum of Anthropology Catalog No. 2003.31.1, University of New Mexico, Albuquerque.

1962 The Physical Anthropology of Pottery Mound: A Pueblo IV Site in West Central New Mexico. Unpublished Master of Science thesis, Department of Anthropology, University of New Mexico, Albuquerque.

Smith, Watson

1952 *Kiva Mural Decorations at Awatovi and Kawaika-a. Reports of the Awatovi Expedition No. 5.* Papers of the Peabody Museum of American Archaeology and Ethnology Vol. 37. Harvard University, Cambridge, Massachusetts.

Vargas, Victoria D.

1995 *Copper Bell Trade Patterns in the Prehispanic U.S. Southwest and Northwest Mexico.* Arizona State Museum Archaeological Series No. 187. Arizona State Museum, University of Arizona, Tucson.

Vivian, Patricia Bryan

1961 Kachina, The Study of Pueblo Animism and Anthropomorphism within the Ceremonial Wall Paintings of Pottery Mound and the Jeddito. Unpublished Master of Fine Arts thesis, Department of Art, University of Iowa, Iowa City.

Voll, Charles

1961 The Glaze Paint Ceramics of Pottery Mound, New Mexico. Unpublished Master's thesis, Department of Anthropology, University of New Mexico, Albuquerque.

Warner, Thor

1928 Rio Puerco Ruins. *American Anthropologist* n.s. 30:85–93.

Wimberly, Mark, and Peter Eidenbach

1980 *Reconnaissance Study of the Archaeological and Related Resources of the Lower Puerco and Salado Drainages, Central New Mexico.* Human Systems Research, Inc., Tularosa, New Mexico.

CHAPTER THREE

The Architecture of Pottery Mound Pueblo

Michael A. Adler

Introduction

Archaeological syntheses of Ancestral Pueblo material remains along the Rio Puerco (of the East) have often typified this area as a poorly known frontier. In their seminal summary of the prehistory of the northern Rio Grande region, Wendorf and Reed (1955) use the drainage of the Rio Puerco as the far western border of the region. This "in between" area separates the Eastern Pueblo communities along the Rio Grande from those communities farther to the west, including near today's Acoma, Laguna, Zuni, and Hopi pueblos (Roney 1996). Surveys and excavations over the past century have documented a significant presence of sedentary villages in this frontier zone, including two large settlements, Pottery Mound (LA 416) and Hummingbird (Chaves) Pueblo (LA 578).[1] Our archaeological understanding of these settlements and the Rio Puerco as a whole has been influenced by the region's "frontier" status, making this a suitable topic for a study of architectural patterns at Pottery Mound. This chapter investigates the extent to which the architectural patterns at Pottery Mound and other Rio Puerco sites support the likelihood that population immigration and extralocal influences played important roles in the occupational history of this boundary area between the Eastern and Western Pueblos.

Frank Hibben is one of the few archaeologists to have worked at both Pottery Mound and Hummingbird Pueblo.[2] Hibben's work at Pottery Mound was heavily influenced by the role of extralocal influences on the occupants of the Rio Puerco region between about A.D. 1250 and 1450. Though Hibben's interpretations emphasized the role of long-distance influences from Mexico on the Pottery Mound community, others have implicated the spread of the katsina belief system (Crotty 1995; Eckert 2003; Chapters 4, 6, and 8, this volume) and the introduction of Puebloan migrant populations from the west (various chapters in this volume) as important factors in the archaeological patterning we see at Pottery Mound.

Both Pottery Mound and Hummingbird Pueblo provide research contexts that can enhance our understanding of local and regional population dynamics across the greater Southwest. This chapter focuses on a detailed analysis of architectural variability at Pottery Mound and Hummingbird Pueblo and considers evidence for population migration and social group differentiation at these settlements between the late thirteenth and fifteenth centuries. I review several lines of architectural patterning from each site, some of which I believe support the likelihood that population immigration was involved in the settlement histories of both settlements. At the same time, some of the architectural evidence remains equivocal with respect to the immigration question. Given that my interpretations address issues of cultural affiliation linking contemporary Pueblo communities to occupants of the ancestral Rio Puerco cultural landscape, I conclude my chapter with general comments on the contributions that archaeology can and should make in our understandings of cultural affiliation in the American Southwest.

Why Study the Architecture of Pottery Mound Pueblo?

Before we embark on a consideration of architectural patterns at Pottery Mound, it's important to reflect on the site's significant archaeological legacy of interpretation and contrasting explanations. Beginning with Hibben's early descriptions of Pottery Mound architecture (1955; 1966) and kiva murals (1960; 1967; 1975), and continuing up through the chapters in this volume, Pottery Mound's prominence rests in large part on it being a "destination point," a crossroads of migrants, exchange, and conceptual systems. This consistent theme of culture contact derives

in large part from two primary lines of material evidence. First, the site's rich ceramic assemblage (Brody 1964; Eckert 2003; Luhrs 1937; Voll 1961) not only provided the site with a fitting name but also contains a wide array of ceramic wares representing several different local and nonlocal ceramic traditions. Second, the famed kiva murals (Crotty 1995; Hibben 1966; 1975; Chapters 6, 7, and 8, this volume) uncovered at Pottery Mound depict a wide range of imagery and iconography. Depending on one's perspectives, these images may refer to ideological concepts and group histories emanating from local or nonlocal traditions, or an admixture of both.

The fact, then, that so much of Pottery Mound's material culture refers to "other places" has provided, and continues to provide, the inspiration for a wide range of interpretations regarding the settlement's history. Hibben's explanations emphasized Mexican influences in the mural depictions and the purported platform mound at Pottery Mound. Other scholars have placed more importance on influences emanating from much closer to home, including the adoption of religious ideologies, design motifs, and the possible immigration of Ancestral Pueblo peoples into Pottery Mound. One commonly cited source for these ideologies and immigrants are Puebloan communities located in the Zuni region to the west, as well as communities from the nearby Rio Grande valley (Baker and Durand 2003; Brody 1964; Dittert 1959; Eckert 2003; Ruppé 1990; Tainter and Tainter 1996; Voll 1961). In sum, Pottery Mound's past consistently raises questions of regional interaction ranging from the movement of ideas and hard goods to the migration and relocation of Ancestral Pueblo peoples.

Understanding Migration and Group Identity in the Puebloan Past

Before making my case for the amalgamation of socially and historically distinct populations at Pottery Mound and Hummingbird pueblos, it is important to contextualize these settlements as part of a dynamic regional landscape forming during the late prehistoric period in the Southwest. Though much of the significant archaeological research on Pueblo IV period settlements was done prior to 1950, Duff's (2002) recent reanalysis of regional Western Pueblo data points to the Pueblo IV period as a very likely time of regional population dispersal and ethnic group differentiation. In other words, local and regional conditions favored the widespread formation of regionally distinctive ethnic groups. Several lines of evidence support Duff's assertions.

First, the geographic spread of Puebloan settlements reduced by 30–50 percent during the period of A.D. 1250–1400 (Adler et al. 1996). This reduction in the spatial distribution of Pueblo settlement involved regional relocations of significant numbers of people, significantly altering the social landscape of the Southwest (Adams and Duff 2004; Adler 1996; Cameron 1995; Spielmann 1998). For example, archaeological research in and around the northern Rio Grande valley documents a substantial increase in both the number and size of settlements in the region during this period (Crown et al. 1996). The sharp increase in population is generally attributed to large-scale immigration from areas outside the Rio Grande valley. The integration of new, nonlocal populations would have provided fertile ground for the development of ethnic group identities.

Second, these changes in Pueblo IV period settlement strategies also precipitated changes in the scale of village communities and community clusters. Depending on the regional sample, settlement sizes increased two- to tenfold across the Ancestral Pueblo world (Duff 2002; Spielmann 1998). On a purely demographic level, this would have increased face-to-face interactions to levels rarely experienced in Ancestral Pueblo communities prior to this period. Pottery Mound was occupied during the span of this scalar change in community scale but does not appear to be part of a larger cluster of contemporaneous settlements, so it may provide useful insights into other Pueblo IV community dynamics.

Finally, as Olzak (1992) has pointed out, heightened levels of social conflict and aggression commonly provide contexts that engender social group differentiation. Recent research into the role of regional warfare documents a wide range of evidence that larger, more crowded Pueblo IV period communities were engaged in ongoing conflict (LeBlanc 1999; Wilcox and Haas 1994). So in addition to the "trading" emphasized in past work at Pottery Mound, we also need to consider the effects of "raiding" as well. There are trends toward increasingly defensive architectural layouts and clustering of potentially allied settlements for mutual defense during the Pueblo IV period, attributes of settlement strategies utilized by groups coping with widespread conflict and warfare during this period.

Given these conditions, we need to consider archaeological avenues that will enhance our understandings

of the disintegration and reintegration of social groups across the Pueblo IV landscape. Several material proxies for ethnic group diversity have been proposed (see Jones 1997 for a summary). There is insufficient space to review all of these approaches, so I focus on the use of architecture and built space at Pottery Mound Pueblo and the nearby Hummingbird Pueblo to assess local and extralocal influences on the occupational histories of Ancestral Pueblo communities.

Throughout the history of shelter and ritual, people have used architecture as a salient means for conjoining space, identity, and history. We cannot be certain that migrant groups self-identified as social groups, but given that ethnic and social difference often plays off of divergent origin locations, technological traditions, and other aspects of identity, built space often sets migrants apart in space and technology from their indigenous hosts. These dynamics have not been lost on archaeology where it has been common practice to try to "track" possible migrant populations through the material patterning of architectural features. This link between architectural variation and migrants is certainly not unique to the American Southwest. As one example, Aldenderfer and Stanish (1993) make a strong argument for the active role that domestic architecture, as a nonportable technology and medium of social expression, played in asserting ethnic identity in the southern Andes.

Recent research in the Southwest has expanded archaeology's methodological and theoretical insights into the linkages between architecture and social identity (Cameron 1998; 1999; Clark 2001; Mills 1999). Clark's (2001) Tonto Basin research indicates that a range of architectural evidence in domestic contexts can provide robust methods for differentiating between indigenous villagers and migrant populations moving into the region during the fourteenth century. Clark sets out several testable expectations regarding the expression of group differences in architectural features. Of particular interest to our research, Clark argues that we should pay attention to both highly visible and less visible characteristics in construction technology. Less visible characteristics of built space can be informative because technological traditions often tend to be relatively conservative and unique to localized populations sharing a common historical background. As an example, these less visible characteristics might include methods for preparing construction materials (adobe, masonry, mortar, etc.), particular ways of preparing footing trenches and foundation materials, and specific locations and configurations of storage, food processing, and hearth features within domestic contexts.

Variations in the scale and layout of pre- and post-contact Pueblo architecture may also provide evidence of social group differences. James (1994) and Baldwin (1987) both propose that regional ethnic traditions in the construction and use of built space are often manifested in room-size distributions. Mills (1999) has proposed that significant differences in floor area of Pueblo IV sites in the Silver Creek area may be due to the influx of migrants into an already occupied area. These studies do not fully explain the causal links between social organizational strategies, room size, and cultural identity, but these patterns may still provide useful starting points for research into group composition, immigration, and other aspects of Ancestral Pueblo group dynamics.

Along these lines, Cameron's (1999) recent assessment of Pueblo architectural variability provides one of the most comprehensive reviews of research linking room size to ethnicity, social organization, environmental constraints, and architectural techniques. She believes the most compelling explanations made to date are those linking architectural techniques to room size. Cameron emphasizes that the overall dimensions of roofed space in the Pueblo world were limited by the size of available roofing timbers, but in the final analysis she places more emphasis on the construction technique as a determinant of average room size, particularly during the precontact period in the Southwest.

In sum, there are many promising avenues for archaeological assessments of the relationships between social group identity and the material fallout that can result from cultural differences. The architectural data from Pottery Mound and Hummingbird Pueblo provide both strong and equivocal lines of evidence for monitoring the complex history of occupation, migration, and social organization at these settlements.

Goals and Limitations of Architectural Analysis

To date, little of the research at these sites has focused on the largest class of material culture, namely site architecture, to address the issue of local and extralocal influence in the Rio Puerco region. Pottery Mound is presently undergoing a second cycle of investigation, but unlike the earlier work at the site, this phase of research involves

no shovels or bulldozers. The work in this volume is a concerted effort to revisit earlier work done at the site equipped with new sets of questions and theoretical perspectives and several decades of new archaeological data from the sites surrounding Pottery Mound Pueblo.

Most of the earlier work at the site was undertaken by field school students, young scholars learning their craft on the job. The list of field school participants reads like a who's who of southwestern archaeology, but as one might expect, the quality of the work products of these early excavations is quite variable. Having directed archaeology field schools for over two decades, I know all too well that field school research results vary depending on the year, the students, the site director, and the overall site research design. As discussed by Vivian (Chapter 2), the general lack of a problem-oriented research design during field school excavations at Pottery Mound is reflected in the students' field notes. Most student observations discuss context but not the rationales for excavation. Accurate measurements of rooms and features and scale maps are not consistently recorded in the field notes, a reality of the Pottery Mound field schools that is as true 50 years ago as it is today. There are some outstanding reports that describe entire blocks of architectural features, but significant insights still remain to be teased out of these resources.

Excavation strategies employed during the University of New Mexico's field school work at Pottery Mound (1954–1961) focused on room and kiva excavations, with a parallel strategy of slicing long, narrow test trenches through the site to locate deeply buried features (Vivian, Chapter 2). A single large bulldozer cut exposed the midsection of the site and is discussed later in this chapter. The choice of which rooms to excavate during each field school appears to have been made largely on the basis of assumed deposit depth, since rooms with sufficiently deep deposits would ensure an entire season's worth of work for a single field school student. This "find deep rooms" strategy commonly resulted in the complete excavation of one or more clusters of contiguous rooms each field season. These excavation clusters are labeled by year excavated (see Figure 1.3 and Appendix A).

I have not worked at the site, so my observations on Pottery Mound architecture represent somewhat of an "outsider's view." I have reviewed a significant portion of the field notes, maps, and photos presently available at the University of New Mexico's Hibben Center. This includes all of the available publications and unpublished typed reports on the site and approximately two-thirds of the field notebooks, most of which came from the early field school projects during the 1950s. Since my focus is on architecture, I made copies of pertinent site maps and recorded pertinent information from the field notes directly onto each map. Based on these maps and the overall site map compiled by David Phillips (see Figure 1.3), I've compiled a database of architectural data to allow comparisons of Pottery Mound architecture with other contemporaneous sites in the region (Appendix B). Even with these collaborative efforts there still remains a wealth of additional information buried in the field notes, site photos, and maps archived at the University of New Mexico.

In contrast to my archive-based approach to Pottery Mound, the comparative data from Hummingbird Pueblo is based on several years of excavation and mapping at that site (Adler 2001; 2002; Eckert 2003). The architectural data from Hummingbird are complementary to what we know from Pottery Mound, largely because of the dissimilar field methodologies used at the two sites. While Hibben's work at Pottery Mound emphasized the discovery and excavation of kiva and surface room features with only partial exposure of surface roomblocks, research at Hummingbird Pueblo has focused on the complete exposure of entire roomblocks and only limited excavations and testing in surface and subsurface architectural features. This is a beneficial contrast, given that those aspects of architectural variability informing our interpretations at Pottery Mound can guide future investigations at Hummingbird Pueblo, just as the understandings we have gained at Hummingbird can help structure ongoing inquiries into Pottery Mound's past.

Hummingbird Pueblo Architecture from a Comparative Perspective

As discussed in his 1986 report "Salvage Operations at Pottery Mound, 1977–1985," Frank Hibben (1986:3; 1975) considered Hummingbird Pueblo to be the "companion" or "sister" site to Pottery Mound.[3] Hummingbird Pueblo (LA 578) is located on a private ranch 36 km west of Albuquerque and approximately 32 km northwest of Pottery Mound (Figure 3.1). Archaeological investigations at the site over the past several years indicate extensive deep archaeological deposits at the site, allowing for stratigraphic interpretation of site occupation history. The main feature of the site is a rubble mound of fallen masonry architecture rising up to 6 m (19.8 ft) above the surrounding landscape (Figure 3.2). A single bulldozer trench cuts through the rubble-covered mound, an unfortunate legacy of an early owner of the site. Test excavations in the bulldozer trench exposed cultural deposits that reach 8 m (26.4 ft) deep in this part of the site. Based largely on the seriation of glaze-painted ceramic wares at Hummingbird, the site was occupied between about A.D. 1275 and 1450. This would put the founding of Hummingbird approximately three-quarters of a century earlier than the founding of Pottery Mound, since Eckert (Chapter 4) dates Pottery Mound's beginning to approximately A.D. 1350, and Curtis Schaafsma proposes A.D. 1370 (Appendix D). The occupations at the two sites both appear to end during the fifteenth century. Eckert (Chapter 4) estimates that Pottery Mound may have been occupied as late as A.D. 1500, while Schaafsma puts the occupational end point at A.D. 1450, contemporaneous with the end of permanent occupation at Hummingbird Pueblo.

Site Size and Architectural Layout at Pottery Mound Pueblo

My analysis of Pottery Mound architecture starts at the settlement scale and moves in from there. I begin with an assessment of the overall size and layout of the settlement, a "big picture" view of the site that is in reality a mosaic of many small, detailed insights. Hibben (1955:179) originally estimated the site size as 2 acres, but in subsequent publications his estimate of the overall site area increases to about 7 acres (1966:522; 1975:6–8). Hibben does not mention actual room counts, though J. J. Brody (1985) does mention an estimate of 500 total rooms in an unpublished manuscript. It is not clear whether this is Brody's estimate or a room count estimate given to him by Hibben.

According to David Phillips's composite site map, approximately 261 surface rooms have been excavated, exposed through surface scraping, or encountered in the extensive trenching at the site (see Figure 1.3). This does not include several of the buried rooms encountered in the lower levels of the bulldozer trench, rooms that underlie later architectural features at the site, or the rooms in the "Swan Unit" salvaged by Hibben and his coworkers. Given that multiple-story architecture was built in some parts of the site (see following), it is not unreasonable to estimate 400–600 total surface rooms at the site. Bear in mind that this estimate is not sufficiently reliable to stand as a proxy for prehistoric settlement population size given our lack of data to assess the contemporaneity of most of the site's surface structures.

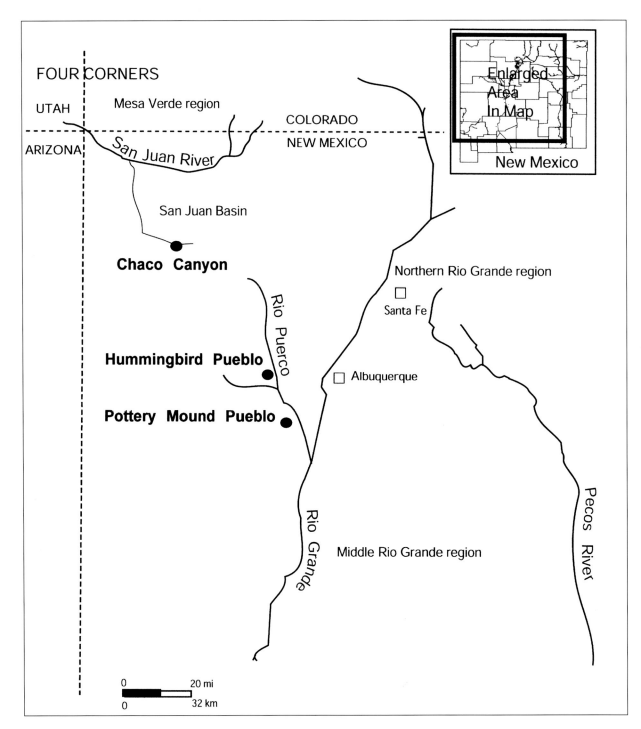

FIGURE 3.1
Location of Pottery Mound and Hummingbird Pueblo.

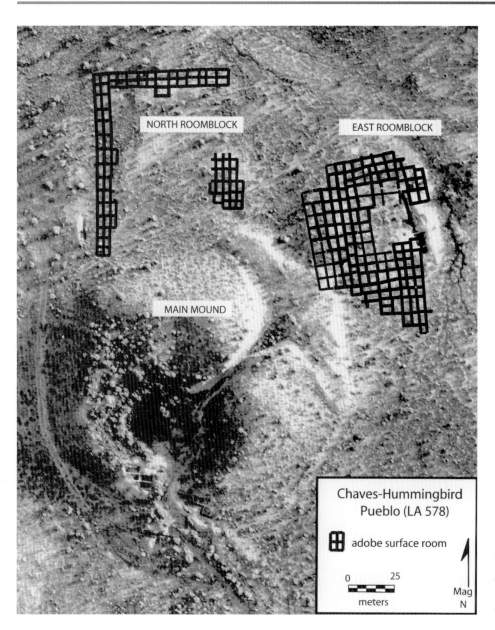

FIGURE 3.2
Aerial photo of
Hummingbird Pueblo
with roomblocks.

In contrast to the Pottery Mound archaeological record of extensive excavations in surface rooms and only limited knowledge of the spatial extent of major roomblocks, we have accurate maps of surface architectural features across most of Hummingbird Pueblo but only limited testing inside individual rooms at the site. Surface clearance work at Hummingbird has uncovered and mapped over 170 adobe surface rooms in the northern and eastern parts of the site (see Figure 3.2). We have not yet completed a parallel clearance program on the large architectural mound at Hummingbird largely

because of the difficulties in exposing the masonry walls that comprise most of the architecture in this part of the site. Based on overall site area and room density, the site contains an estimated 300–400 ground-floor rooms, with an additional 100–150 rooms in the multistory portions of the site. This overall site size estimate of 400–550 rooms at Hummingbird is commensurate with Pottery Mound, though we must be cautious given the dearth of absolute dates from both sites. We have only a small suite of absolute dates for the construction and occupation of the three major architectural complexes at Hummingbird, and most of the dates cluster between about A.D. 1325 and 1450, indicating rough contemporaneity of the various architectural components at the site. Hopefully a future suite of dates from curated materials at Pottery Mound will provide comparable temporal control.

For the sake of comparison, this estimate of Pottery Mound room counts falls comfortably within the range of room count estimates for relatively contemporaneous aggregated settlements in other parts of the Ancestral Pueblo realm. Prior to the fourteenth century, aggregated Pueblo III (A.D. 1150–1275) settlements rarely exceeded about 700 total rooms, with a few early large settlements exceeding 1,000 rooms in the Zuni region (Adler 1996:7, 106; Kintigh 1996). Pueblo IV period (A.D. 1275–1450) villages are larger on average than their Pueblo III predecessors, with average settlement sizes ranging between about 300 and 800 rooms in the Rio Grande region (Adams and Duff 2004:Table 1.1).

Plaza Space

Hibben (1975:6) describes the overall layout of Pottery Mound as one organized around four large plaza areas, "a plan [that is] usual at Pueblo IV sites." It is clear that plaza space played an important role in the overall site layout at both settlements. Plaza areas were created by leaving relatively large areas free of surface architecture, but given the lack of large block excavations and spotty nature of wall clearing at the site we cannot be sure to what extent the Pottery Mound plazas were truly enclosed by the surrounding roomblocks.

Plaza space also provides an important structuring element in the overall site layout at Hummingbird Pueblo. Based on the exposure of the northern and eastern roomblocks, Hummingbird Pueblo clearly follows a "plaza-oriented" site plan. The northern rooms form a large L-shaped set of contiguous adobe rooms, with one smaller, less linear roomblock in what would have been the southeast part of the complex (see Figure 3.2). These structures define a large plaza area, with a probable opening on the northeast corner of the room complex.

Like the northern roomblock, the eastern roomblock at Hummingbird is also bounded on three sides but is also distinctive in its own right. The northern and eastern roomblocks are comprised nearly entirely of coursed adobe architecture, but unlike the northern roomblock, the eastern complex of rooms is significantly "deeper" in terms of the number of rooms that separate

the plaza from the exterior of the roomblock. While most of the northern roomblock is two rooms deep, the eastern roomblock varies from five to seven rooms deep from plaza to back rooms. Like the northern roomblock, the eastern complex of rooms surrounds a well-defined plaza but there is clearly a significant difference in the sizes of these two public spaces. The plaza of the northern roomblock covers roughly 1,500 m², while the eastern roomblock plaza covers only about 170 m², about 12 percent the size of the northern plaza.

Given what we know of plaza space and site layout, Pottery Mound and Hummingbird Pueblo both conform best to the "plaza-oriented" layout, the most common village pattern in large, aggregated Pueblo IV period settlements in the Rio Grande region. Roomblocks in plaza-oriented pueblos are built to enclose open plaza spaces. This contrasts with what Reed (1956) described as "front-oriented" pueblos in which surface architectural units tend to face the same direction. Front-oriented architectural layouts create long, linear open spaces in between the roomblocks, somewhat like streets between housing clusters. The front-oriented settlement layout is common in the Four Corners area prior to its abandonment in the late thirteenth century. Scholars have linked the transition from front-oriented to plaza-oriented pueblos during the fourteenth to fifteenth centuries to several different factors, including the spread of the katsina belief system (Adams 1991), defense against outside attack (LeBlanc 1999), and a decreasing autonomy of households within the increasingly larger Ancestral Pueblo settlements of this time period (Lipe and Lekson 2001; Lipe and Ortman 2000). While it is possible that Pottery Mound incorporates both front- and plaza-oriented layouts in various parts of the site, the fact that plaza spaces at the site appear to have surface architecture on three or four sides points to a greater reliance on a plaza-oriented layout.

Hibben's excavations at Pottery Mound indicate that the differentiation of public plaza space and domestic surface architectural space may not have been static across time at the site. Kivas, commonly understood as civic structures used by suprahousehold societies and ritual groups, are located in plaza areas at Pottery Mound and other plaza-oriented pueblos. At least three kivas (3, 13, 14) were built over by later surface room architecture, indicating that surface architecture encroached on what was formerly plaza and kiva construction space. It may be the case that available plaza space may have decreased in extent over the course of the site's occupation. This possible decrease in plaza space may have been offset by limiting construction and reconstruction of later buildings in other parts of the site, but we can't assess this given the limited clearance of roomblock areas mentioned above. Both roomblock construction locations and plaza areas may well have shifted across the site through time, but to what extent we can attribute settlement layout to "horizontal stratigraphy" at Pottery Mound can't be addressed without more stratigraphic control and ceramic assemblage data from beneath room floors and in room fill.

In sum, the overall layout and differentiation of civic and domestic space at Pottery Mound and Hummingbird Pueblo does not set either site apart from other contemporaneous villages across the Rio Grande region and the Upper Rio Puerco (Baker and Durand 2003). The prevalence of plaza-oriented roomblock areas on both sites contrasts with areas to the west, such as the Four Corners region, a possible source of immigrant populations during the thirteenth and fourteenth centuries. At the same time, we need to bear in mind that Ancestral Pueblo communities in the Cibola and the Upper Little Colorado regions, possible source areas for migrants during this time, also relied on plaza-oriented site layouts to structure the organization of civic and domestic space.

Surface Architecture: Construction Techniques and Room Size

Construction techniques and the scale of surface architectural space comprise another data realm that archaeologists have utilized in comparing Ancestral Pueblo social organization, structure function, and population migration. By construction techniques I refer to the means by which rooms and room suites were added to the settlement. Cameron (1999) has assessed regional differences in roomblock construction techniques across the Southwest, showing that the means by which roomblocks were built are the primary influences on room size (as measured by floor area) across both historic and prehistoric pueblo sites. In general, Cameron shows that larger average floor areas are found in those settlements where roomblocks were built in large single-construction events. Roney (1996) and Cordell (1996) identify these large singular construction units as "ladder-type" buildings where two or more long, parallel walls are constructed. The space in between the walls is then subdivided by shorter walls to make a series of contiguous walls. Dean (1996)

describes Kayenta region examples of this same pattern. His "spinal" roomblocks commonly form the architectural cores of larger roomblocks onto which smaller, later sets of rooms are appended.

Scholars commonly interpret the construction of these large ladder or spinal roomblocks as one line of evidence for immigration of groups into a settlement. The rational is that immigrations of groups significantly larger than a single household would require the simultaneous construction of a large suite of domestic spaces. This is consistent with ethnographic data collected on migration demographics. Robert Netting and Glenn Stone observed this phenomenon among the Kofyar of Africa, where initial migration to a new agricultural region was undertaken by multihousehold groups (Glenn Stone, personal communication 1999).

As mentioned above, large areas of completely exposed wall tops are present at Pottery Mound, but unfortunately few of the available maps depict bonding and abutting patterns in the surface architecture. Even without bonding and abutting information, estimated floor areas gleaned from field school student notes and orientation of surface rooms depicted on the various Pottery Mound maps allow some generalizations about room construction techniques. Nearly all of the major roomblock exposures at Pottery Mound show some form of ladder construction, though maps vary in accuracy. Most of these construction units are three to four rooms long, though there are indications of longer ladder construction units in Unit C that are five or more rooms long. At this point there are not sufficient data to assess the overall percentage of rooms built in large-scale construction events relative to smaller, accretional construction events at the site, but future work at Pottery Mound could expose this information.

Construction techniques correspond in general with variations in room floor area averages at Pottery Mound. Based on available notes and maps, room size and feature information is available for 79 adobe surface rooms at Pottery Mound (summarized in Appendix B). The average floor area for excavated or surface-mapped Pottery Mound surface rooms is 6.1 m² (Table 3.1). Larger floor areas tend to be associated with suites of rooms built with ladder construction, though in some cases the average floor area is lowered by what appears to have been the later subdivision of certain rooms in a ladder-constructed room series (Rooms C9, C10, and C27, for example).[4]

The nearly complete clearing and mapping of room walls across the northern and eastern roomblocks at

Table 3.1. Room Dimension Data for Pottery Mound Surface Architecture

Roomblock	Average Room Floor Area (m^2)	Standard Deviation Floor Area (m^2)	Coefficient of Variation (CV)	Number of Measurable Rooms
Unit A (Duck Unit)	7.8	2.5	31.8	20
Unit B	4.6	1.3	26.6	17
Unit C	6.6	0.8	12.3	9
Unit D	6.6	1.7	25.2	18
Unit A with Unit D rooms	6.9	1.5	14.5	28
Unit D without Unit A rooms	7.8	0.7	9.0	10
Entire Site	**6.1**	**2.4**	**38.6**	**65**

Hummingbird allow comparisons of construction techniques. The ladder construction sections of adobe rooms at Hummingbird, most of which are found in the north roomblock and in parts of the eastern roomblock, include from 4 to 12 rooms built in a single event. These large construction events form the core components of both the northern and eastern adobe roomblocks. Though these patterns are not unequivocal evidence of immigration into the site, we shouldn't overlook their potential importance for addressing the addition of multifamily units into the settlement.

As Cameron (1999) has documented at other settlements, ladder-constructed rooms at Hummingbird are larger on average than those rooms that were built accretionally onto existing rooms. Floor areas of surface rooms in the northern roomblock range from 4.4 to 14.5 m^2, averaging 6.9 m^2 (SD = 1.68 m^2). The eastern roomblock surface rooms ranged between 2.5 and 13.2 m^2, with an average floor area of 5.8 m^2 (SD = 1.6 m^2). The larger number of rooms in the eastern roomblock (n = 95) does not appear to create a sampling bias. The eastern roomblock structures average 15 percent less floor area per room than surface rooms in the northern roomblock. The eastern roomblock also contains a larger number of accretional room construction events relative to the northern roomblock.

There are several other potential reasons for the consistently smaller floor area in the eastern roomblock. First, the two architectural blocks may not be contemporaneous, and room size may be related to changes in the use of interior space through time at the site. Assemblages of decorated ceramics excavated from the eastern and northern roomblocks do not show any significant differences, arguing for relative contemporaneity.

Second, room size may be influenced by the amount of open plaza space available within the complex. It appears from bonding and abutting relationships that rooms were added to both the front and back of a long row of rooms in the eastern roomblock. If plaza space was a determinant in how much space could be covered by subsequent architectural features, rooms may have been built on a more economic scale than elsewhere in the site.

Finally, it also may be the case that construction materials are the primary influence on room size. The length and width of surface rooms cannot exceed the maximum length of roofing beams. If there were fewer long timbers available in the site vicinity during the construction of the eastern roomblock, there would have to have been a concomitant decrease in the size of structures that could be roofed. This resource-related explanation would only hold if the rooms in the eastern block were the last to be constructed at the site.

Whatever the case, it is important to point out that the average surface room sizes at both sites are quite small from a regional perspective. Floor areas at Pottery Mound (6.1 m^2) and the northern and eastern roomblocks at Hummingbird (6.9 m^2 and 5.8 m^2, respectively) are well below most Pueblo IV period sites in the Southwest. In Cameron's (1999:Table 8) summary of room floor area size in Ancestral Pueblo settlements, the only room floor area averages falling below these averages were at Homol'ovi I (5.7 m²) and Mariana Mesa Site 616 (5.6 m²). Reasons for small floor area may relate to social organization, resource access, or other factors. On the social organizational side, Baldwin (1987) has argued that average room sizes below 10 m² are associated with matrilineal Puebloan groups, while average size above 10 m² is generally associated with patrilineal groups. It is also possible that this patterning may have less to do with postmarriage residence patterns than with available resources such as roofing timbers and construction materials. Large floor areas require large roofing beams, and the lowland settings of both sites may have meant reduced access to large upland tree species such as Ponderosa pine.

At this point in the analysis, room size and construction patterns provide potential lines of evidence for immigrant group movement into either settlement, but these patterns are somewhat equivocal. This does not mean we should cease looking for such patterning. As mentioned previously, there is a dearth of information on bond-about relationships at Pottery Mound, mostly due to the level of detail in student field observations. At the same time, excavations generally left walls intact, so future work at Pottery Mound should be able to uncover roomblocks and record architectural data that will allow more detailed comparisons between Pottery Mound and other Ancestral Pueblo sites. Field notes do describe subflooring operations that destroyed room floor surfaces, but significant data can still be recovered from excavated rooms. I turn now to a consideration of construction materials utilized at these two Rio Puerco settlements, specifically the use of adobe to construct surface and subsurface features.

Fabricating the Village: Coursed Adobe Architecture at Pottery Mound and Hummingbird Pueblos

Ancestral Pueblo reliance on coursed adobe was widespread across the Southwest, found as far south as Mexico and as far north as central Utah (Judd 1916; Moquin 1992). Unlike other sites in the vicinity where both masonry and adobe were utilized, there is no masonry architecture that has been uncovered to date at Pottery Mound. Surface and subsurface architectural features at Pottery Mound are constructed with coursed adobe.[5] Coursed adobe

walls are built up in layers or courses, with each course generally 12–18 in high. Though early analyses of coursed adobe architecture at places like Casa Grande (Mindeleff 1891) assumed that frames or molds were used in building up each successive wall course, Pottery Mound builders likely used a stiff adobe mixture patted into place by hand to build their walls. Each successive wall course was allowed to dry sufficiently in order to support the compressive weight of the next layer built on top of it.

Pottery Mound's location on the floodplain of the Rio Puerco makes the use of adobe a logical choice. The closest geologic outcrops of building stone are located nearby in the foothills and mountains to the west of the site, but a reliance on masonry construction would have required trips of several kilometers to and from quarry areas. The proximity of building materials, however, is not always a determining factor in Ancestral Pueblo construction strategies. Summaries by Cameron (1999) and Tsesmeli (2002) indicate that building choices were influenced by resource availability as well as the cultural preferences of the builders.

The reliance on coursed, rather than brick, adobe architecture at these two settlements is worth mention. Recent work by Gann (1995) documents that the use of adobe brick architecture in the Southwest began as early as A.D. 750. Later use of form-molded adobe bricks has been recorded in thirteenth- and fourteenth-century sites in Colorado, Arizona, and western New Mexico (Gann 1995:26). One area of significant use of form-molded adobe bricks included the settlements in the Homol'ovi site cluster near Winslow, Arizona—sites with strong ancestral ties to several modern Hopi communities. Adobe brick construction at Homol'ovi I and Homol'ovi III is important given the continued scholarly interest in possible links between Pottery Mound and probable ancestral Hopi settlements in the Lower Little Colorado River region, Antelope Mesa, and other areas. Given Cameron's (1998) proposal that coursed adobe architecture may have been an architectural choice influenced by the ethnic affiliation of the builders, we need to assess whether adobe brick architecture might also be a marker of group identity. Since there appears to be no reliance on adobe brick architecture farther east than Mariana Mesa (McGimsey 1980, cited in Gann 1995:22), this building technology might relate to the mobility of Ancestral Pueblo groups across the western reaches of the Ancestral Pueblo world.

Recent research on the topic of adobe technology at Hummingbird Pueblo may hold some promise for assessing the relationship between construction techniques and cultural group identity. As argued by Clark (2001) in his study of Tonto Basin migrations, immigrants may attempt to minimize physical visibility of their own technical styles so that they can better "fit in" to host communities. With this in mind, a multidisciplinary study of compositional differences in adobe construction material was undertaken at Hummingbird Pueblo. Adobe samples from exposed wall tops in the eastern and northern roomblocks were assessed using diffuse reflectance spectrophotometry (Balsam et al. 2002). This method provides a general compositional fingerprint of the adobe using spectral data from the near ultraviolet through the near infrared of the electromagnetic spectrum (250–850 nm) and at the most basic level compares whether different varieties of clay-rich soils were used in constructing the many rooms in this complex. Though not all room walls have been analyzed, our preliminary data indicate four primary adobe "recipes" were used in the eastern and northern roomblocks (see Figure 3.2). It is significant that these different "recipes" are, for the most part, found in spatially distinct parts of the roomblocks. Our preliminary interpretation is that these different adobe mixtures might well relate to the use of different adobe sources immediately surrounding the site. Not only might the differential use of adobe source areas account for these variations, it also may be the case that these recipes represent different technical styles used by migrant groups constructing domestic housing at the site during the fourteenth and fifteenth centuries A.D. This same analytical approach could be applied to adobe walls at Pottery Mound, providing insights into construction episodes and resource use.

As mentioned, there is a significant reliance on masonry construction in the main mound portion of Hummingbird Pueblo. We presently have only a relatively small sample of excavated contexts from this portion of the settlement, but our preliminary data indicate that this elevated portion of the settlement may contain some of the latest occupation components at Hummingbird. If this is indeed the case, we have to consider whether these latest masonry additions to the site are another line of evidence of extralocal populations moving into the site during the latter stages of occupation at the settlement. Given that the ceramic assemblages at Hummingbird do not appear to postdate the mid-fifteenth century, the masonry components at the site could date to between A.D. 1400 and 1450.

Rooms with a View: Multiple-Story Architecture at Pottery Mound and Hummingbird Pueblos

Adobe architecture presents us with challenges and benefits. The overall fragility of adobe architecture has its benefits because as unoccupied settlements melt away, the upper portions of the adobe structures collapse into the ground-floor rooms, encasing and preserving the lowest segments of the walls and floors. So the site's deterioration ensures the site's long-term preservation. Fortunately the preservation of surface room walls is sufficiently robust to allow insights into the number of architectural stories at both Pottery Mound and Hummingbird.

Hibben (1975:8) estimated that "in several sections the buildings were three to four stories high." He based his interpretation on stratigraphic evidence for multiple rebuilding episodes found across much of the site. This is problematic in that the number of reconstruction events and use surfaces observed in the site's stratigraphy has nothing to do with estimating the total number of stories, since each of these surfaces represents a rebuilding of ground-floor rooms. Estimating stories can be done by assessing evidence for upper-story architecture in the fill of ground-floor rooms (Creamer 1993) and the height of the standing walls.

These two lines of evidence indicate that parts of Pottery Mound Pueblo reached two to three stories in height, while other parts of the site were probably only a single story high. The first line of evidence, the presence of upper-story room components and their contents in the fill of ground-level rooms, is noted in field school notes and maps. Hearths, ceramic containers, roof components, and other materials are described in room fill, indicating not only that two or more stories of architecture were present, but that some upper-story rooms still contained features and artifacts when the architectural complexes began to decay and collapse. In a few instances field notes mention holes remaining in some of the best preserved walls where roofing vigas had either rotted away or been pulled out of place during structure collapse. These viga holes indicate at least two stories of architecture in parts of the site.

A second source of evidence for multistory architecture at Pottery Mound is the height of adobe surface room wall remnants in those portions of the settlement where surface architecture collapsed in place. Room wall height information is available for some of the excavated rooms at Pottery Mound, but for the purpose of this chapter, I have used the sample of walls exposed in the bulldozer trench that bisects the site (Appendix C). A total of 44 wall segments are mapped in the north wall of the 551-foot-long trench. The average wall height in this sample is 1.25 m. The central part of the site has the lowest walls primarily because of the razing and leveling associated with rebuilding episodes. In those parts of the stratigraphic profile where little to no rebuilding occurred, wall heights reach 2–2.5 m.

Similar patterns uncovered at Pot Creek Pueblo, a large thirteenth- to fourteenth-century pueblo located near Taos, New Mexico, make it likely that Pottery Mound's adobe architecture reached two and possibly three stories in parts of the site. Based on the Pot Creek Pueblo evidence, the wall remnants of single-story surface rooms generally don't exceed 1 m in height. Each additional story of architecture adds approximately 1 m of fill to the lowest-story room, increasing the height of the preserved walls by that same amount. Wall heights at Pot Creek Pueblo rarely exceed 2.5 m and are found only in those parts of the site where three stories of architecture had stood.

More detailed work with Pottery Mound field notes and maps should yield additional information on the height of preserved walls and character of room fill. A promising line of evidence for assessing construction height is the presence of functioning hearths recorded in Pottery Mound surface rooms. Hearths tend to be built in the uppermost story of multistory architecture, since the smoke from the fire has to exit out of a roof chimney or vent (Creamer 1993; Crown et al. 1996). The preliminary data from Pottery Mound show hearths in a number of room floors (30.4 percent of the sample), so single-story architecture may have comprised a third or more of Pottery Mound's architectural configuration.

Multistory architecture was also present at Hummingbird Pueblo but was more spatially distinct than at Pottery Mound. Test excavations in both adobe roomblocks support the presence of multistory architecture in the eastern roomblock but not the northern room complex. All of the rooms in the northern room complex appear to have been only a single story in height, another potential reason for these rooms being larger on average than those in the eastern roomblock. Whether this difference has to do with social differences in the occupants of the two roomblocks or with the construction history of each roomblock remains to be seen.

Room Features at Pottery Mound and Hummingbird Pueblos

In his discussion of ethnic group differences in the Tonto Basin region, Clark (2001) proposes that variation in less publicly visible aspects of architecture might correlate with differences in social group identity. One promising line of evidence for discerning social group differences in our Rio Puerco sites is the location, size, and formal characteristics of internal hearths, a relatively common feature in Pottery Mound and Hummingbird surface rooms. In those rooms where floor contexts were described or mapped (n = 79), 24 rooms (30.3 percent of total) had at least one formal hearth. Some rooms had multiple hearths, though it was not clear from the field notes whether all of the hearths were in use or whether some had been taken out of use by capping them with adobe.

Though not yet quantified, there may be some patterning in these features across the site. For example, of the four hearths that had size data in Area B, three (Rooms 2, 3, and 4) shared the exact same dimensions (13 x 22 in), while the fourth (Room 20) was nearly the same size (12 x 23 in). Unfortunately, most of the hearths reported in the field notes or maps were not sufficiently well described to expand this sample, but this is due in part to my not having read all of the available field notes in the archives of the Hibben Center.

Similar patterning has been noted in the limited number of surface rooms excavated at Hummingbird Pueblo. Hearth location, form, and size are highly regular at Hummingbird Pueblo, with hearths constructed against room walls using carefully shaped sandstone slabs, adobe mortar, and vessel support stones. At this juncture, then, it is not possible to assess the similarities and differences between internal room features at Pottery Mound, Hummingbird Pueblo, or other contemporary sites in the region. But the promise of meaningful patterning makes this a worthy topic of continued research.

Kiva Architecture at Pottery Mound

Ritual architecture and the organization of ceremonial space are likely contexts for encoding cultural similarities and differences, not only in construction technology but also overall size and layout. Recognizing that difficulties exist in the identification of architectural spaces that housed ritual activities, materials, and religious societies (Adler 1993; Peckham 1979; Smith 1952), there are regularities in Ancestral Pueblo ritual architecture that are, nonetheless, potentially informative (Adler and Wilshusen 1990). For example, Herr's (2001) survey of ritual architecture in the Mogollon region details variability through time and space that may well relate to localized group identities long before European contact in the Southwest. There are no comparative data on kivas from Hummingbird Pueblo, so this discussion focuses solely on Pottery Mound kivas.

Thanks to Helen Crotty's (1995; Chapter 6, this volume) syntheses of Pottery Mound kiva architectural features, these subterranean features may well hold some of the more compelling lines of evidence for the spatial, architectural, and iconographic manifestations of group identity and differentiation at Pottery Mound. Then again, they might not. In this section I discuss patterning in Pottery Mound kiva architecture, contrasting it with local and regional insights into this important form of Puebloan built space.

First we must address kiva shape. While there is some ambiguity surrounding the location and contents of Kiva 17 at Pottery Mound, there is no doubt that 16 of the 17 excavated kivas at Pottery Mound are rectilinear, ranging in shape from rectangular to square (see Figure 1.3). While this approximates dominant temporal and regional trends in kiva layout in some portions of the Ancestral Pueblo world, it is not the norm for most of the rest of the northern Rio Grande region.

Prior to the Pueblo IV period, most northern Rio Grande kivas are circular, with square or rectangular kivas more commonly utilized in Pueblo IV settlements (Lakatos 2003; Peckham 1979; Smith 1998). Lakatos (2003) has recently summarized variability in northern Rio Grande pit structures constructed between A.D. 600 and 1200. During this period the modal pit structure is circular, with an axis of orientation (the alignment from the hearth through the ventilator shaft) facing east to east-southeast and an average floor area of 18 m². The consistent patterning in these early pit structures argues for a strongly indigenous tradition in the region. Lakatos proposes that the relatively unvarying pit structure architectural footprint throughout the region indicates that the population increase documented for the northern Rio Grande during this time period was comprised primarily of local populations rather than immigrants from outside the region. Based on his regional sample, Lakatos sees little support for the movement of western San Juan region populations into the Rio Grande prior to the thirteenth century A.D.

Lakatos's perspective assumes that migrant groups were not quickly assimilated into extant communities in such a manner as to make them archaeologically invisible. In the case of subsurface architecture, his interpretation is likely to be correct given the increasingly ritual role that these features assume through time across the Ancestral Pueblo world (but see Lekson 1988 for a counterargument). Pit structures, many of which serve as the ritual and integrative facilities labeled as "kivas" probably "conveyed canonical information about ethnicity or cultural identity" (Lakatos 2003:54) and served to symbolize cultural identity that connected "past to present and present to the past" (Lakatos 2003:54) during the spread of Puebloan groups throughout the Rio Grande.

Based purely on the predominance of rectilinear pit structures (kivas) at Pottery Mound, site architecture diverges strongly from the centuries of reliance on circular pit structure construction in the northern Rio Grande. While the patterning in Pottery Mound kiva architecture is not unequivocal evidence for immigration of non–Rio Grande populations into the settlement, I think it is reasonable to argue that the architectural patterns reference two significantly different regional architectural traditions.

In her recent comparison of kiva architecture in the northern San Juan and northern Rio Grande regions, Smith (1998) established "modal" kiva characteristics for each region during the period spanning A.D. 1150–1350, basically taking up where Lakatos's synthesis ends. Focusing first on the sample of kivas from the northern Rio Grande, Smith synthesized data on 44 kivas from sites located between Santa Fe on the south to the Jemez and Taos regions on the north. Throughout the two centuries studied, the majority of northern Rio Grande kivas are built as circular features with east-facing ventilator systems and a median floor area of 14 m².

Lipe (1989) notes parallel trends in his synthesis of kiva architecture in both precontact and postcontact Pueblo communities. Specifically, Lipe documents a reliance on fewer, larger kivas in the Eastern Pueblo region in comparison to their Western Pueblo counterparts. Lipe argues that this trend is due in part to the greater reliance on moiety organization among the Eastern Pueblos. These larger social groupings would rely on fewer, larger integrative facilities compared to the smaller clan and medicine society organizations prevalent among Western Pueblo groups.

Turning back to Pottery Mound, the predominance of smaller rectilinear kivas makes the site different from

Ancestral Pueblo communities farther to the north that were included in Smith's study. The single circular kiva (Kiva 10) is the closest analogue to the modal pattern in the northern Rio Grande. While rectilinear kivas do appear with greater frequency through time, at no time do they outnumber circular kivas in Smith's (1998:107) regional sample. Rectilinear kivas are both more common and numerous in communities located to the west such as the ancestral Zuni and Hopi regions.

The predominance of rectilinear kivas at Pottery Mound relative to the patterns described by Lakatos (2003) and Smith (1998) may be due in part to the sequential nature of the various architectural samples. Both Lakatos and Smith summarize kiva architecture prior to A.D. 1350, the approximate start date for the primary occupation at Pottery Mound. Though Peckham (1979) discusses various characteristics of Classic period kivas, there is no summary of post–A.D. 1350 kiva architecture comparable to the syntheses by Lakatos and Smith. Peckham does note that the use of smaller, rectilinear kivas follows an architectural history that is distinct from round kivas in the northern Rio Grande. In particular, rectilinear surface rooms with kiva features are built into roomblocks throughout the region beginning during the eleventh and twelfth centuries. He notes that these "roomblock kivas" are most common in the northern half of the northern Rio Grande, but he admits to a small sample (Peckham 1979:68–69). As is evident (see Figures 1.3 and 3.3), the structures identified by Hibben as kivas are all located in plaza areas, spatially separated from the surrounding roomblocks. In fact, there is a relatively consistent placement of kivas along two alignments trending roughly north-northwest to south-southeast, with a bimodal spatial distribution of kivas with south- and east-facing ventilator systems along these alignments. It is possible that the general orientation of these two kiva alignments is an artifact of sampling bias at Pottery Mound, but this bias is difficult to assess given Hibben's general lack of discussion of excavation strategies at the site. Hibben's exploratory trenches clearly focus on plaza areas, but there are also significant gaps between trench alignments that may still conceal the remains of buried kivas. The pattern of kiva cluster alignment may be real, however, given that the two linear kiva clusters parallel the main orientation of most surface rooms. References in field notes describe surface wall alignments of the surface rooms falling between 20 to 25 degrees west of true north, approximating these

two kiva structure alignments. Investigations of the overall orientation of room walls, integrative architecture, and plaza space will have to be considered in more detail by future work focusing not only on individual structures but on the site as a whole.

Given that the occupation at Pottery Mound is estimated to have spanned 100–150 years, there is sufficient time for temporal changes in kiva form to have influenced the strong preference for rectilinear kivas at the site. An alternative (but not mutually exclusive) explanation is that regional cultural variation may be the key to the reliance on rectilinear kivas at Pottery Mound. In his concluding observations on rectilinear kiva form in the northern Rio Grande, Peckham (1979:72) notes that "the distribution of Classic Period rectangular kivas generally matches that of the Tiwa-speaking pueblos along the Rio Grande Valley and on the east side of the central mountain chain." He also notes that the distribution of rectangular "big kivas" (such as Kiva 5 at Pottery Mound) "coincides with the prehistoric territorial extent of the Southern Tiwa" (1979:78). It is not clear how Peckham defines the prehistoric distribution of Southern Tiwa peoples, but it is clear that he attributes kiva form to linguistically distinct cultural groups in the region.

If we follow Peckham, then, kiva form at Pottery Mound links the occupants of the site to Southern Tiwa–speaking communities such as Isleta and Sandia. This linkage to a linguistically homogeneous grouping is complicated, however, in light of the variation in kiva orientations at Pottery Mound. I refer specifically to the strongly patterned spatial distribution of kiva orientations for the 17 kivas at Pottery Mound. The axis of orientation is the alignment of the kiva's ventilator shaft, deflector, firepit, and (often) the *sipapu*. As Helen Crotty (Chapter 6) explains, alignment of the ventilator/deflector/firepit axis generally runs east-west (or southeast-northwest) in Rio Grande–region kivas. In contrast, the main axis of this same complex of features in northern San Juan, Kayenta, Hopi, and other Western Puebloan kivas tends to be oriented north-south.

Nine of the 17 (53 percent) kivas at Pottery Mound were built with a north-south axis orientation, while the remaining eight kivas (47 percent) are oriented east-west (Figure 3.3).[6] These kiva orientations are not randomly distributed within the two major kiva clusters. All but one of the kivas in the southwestern alignment have north-south alignments, the exception being Kiva 14, the largest kiva in that cluster. Similarly, only one kiva in the

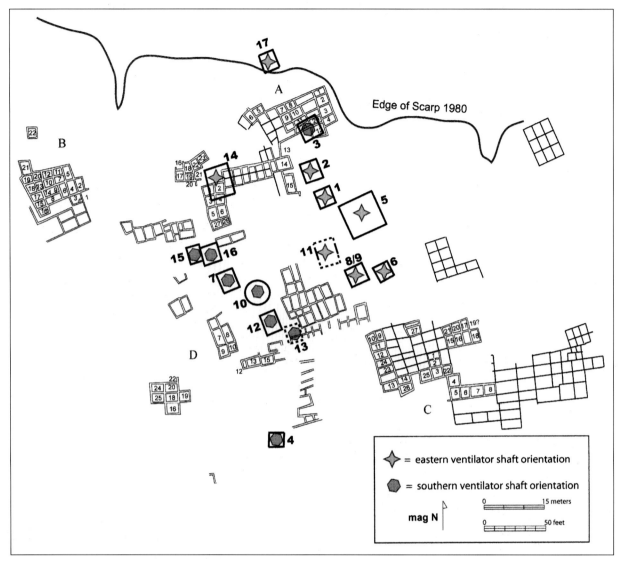

FIGURE 3.3
Kiva orientations at Pottery Mound Pueblo. (For an alternative location for Kiva 17, see Figure 1.3.)

northeastern cluster has a southern ventilator/deflector/firepit axis (Kiva 3), while the other seven share the east-west orientation.

Though we have only limited temporal control of structure use and abandonment sequences in the Pottery Mound kivas, it does not appear that kiva axis orientation is due to temporal differences alone. Only a few kiva structures were built over by later surface roomblocks (Kivas 3, 13, and 14, for example), so it is quite possible that many of the structures may have been in use at the same time during the occupation span of Pottery Mound Pueblo.

With respect to kiva orientation, Smith (1998:121–122) documents an increasing presence of south-facing kivas during the later thirteenth and early fourteenth centuries. At the same time, though, these south-facing kivas are spatially distinct in her sample. All south-facing kivas built after A.D. 1300 were located in the Chama subregion while all the east-facing kivas were found in the Santa Fe subregion. While we cannot simply link kiva orientation at Pottery Mound to distinct Ancestral Pueblo populations, these spatial patterns in orientation do support regional norms in the construction of these special

Table 3.2. Kiva-Related Features Found in Pottery Mound Surface Rooms

Room Number	Loom Anchor Holes	Banquette	Ventilator/ Deflector	Altar	Painted Plaster Wall
A3	X				
A24			X	X	
B2		along S wall			
B3		along E wall			
B6			X		
B10	X				
C3	X				X (wavy parallel lines)
D19			X		

Note: X = presence of feature in notes or field map.

features. So while I would agree that the presence of a south-facing kiva in the Santa Fe subregion during the fourteenth century does not provide unequivocal support for an immigration of Chama peoples into the area, we cannot ignore the possibility that this alignment might be due to a shift in population from one region to another.

We should not overlook the unique patterning in the Pottery Mound kiva sample. First, nearly all of the Pottery Mound kivas are rectilinear, straying significantly from the northern Rio Grande pattern that Lakatos and Smith document over several centuries of occupation in the region. Second, the nearly equivalent reliance on eastern and southern kiva orientations at Pottery Mound, while not unique on a regional level, is unique on the site level. Across the Eastern and Western Pueblo areas kiva orientations tend to be relatively homogeneous within individual settlements. This heterogeneity in kiva patterning at Pottery Mound may well indicate the presence of two or more belief systems, each with its own regional source area, in use during the site occupation.

It is tempting to assign this duality in kiva orientation to a moiety social organizational scheme at Pottery Mound. Moiety organization is well documented among historic Pueblo communities, tending to be the dominant organizational strategy among Eastern Pueblo groups compared to their Western Pueblo counterparts. While I certainly wouldn't want us to discount this possibility out of hand, we need to consider other lines of evidence that might bolster this interpretation. One logical avenue that

Crotty and others are investigating is the relative frequencies of design styles, motifs, and iconography in the two kiva orientation classes. Crotty's summary of Sikyatki designs or motifs (Chapter 6) does not indicate any significant differences in the presence of Sikyatki designs or motifs between the two clusters when we compare absolute frequencies, types of motifs, or percentages of painted layers with Sikyatki motifs. Perhaps the continued study of the unpublished mural drawings will yield patterning that has not yet been addressed.

Houseblock Kivas and Other Possible Ritual Architecture at Pottery Mound Pueblo

Though Crotty (Chapter 6) notes a possible lack of "Zuni-type houseblock kivas" at Pottery Mound, the strength of this statement depends in large part on how we identify these features. In fact, we may have some "Rio Puerco versions" of the houseblock kiva at Pottery Mound. For the sake of discussion I've compiled a list of rooms with features associated with subterranean kivas, including loom anchor holes, banquettes or raised floor areas, ventilator/deflector features, altars, and plastered walls with painted designs (Table 3.2). It is possible that some of these features or modifications could have been put into or on the walls of these structures after their period of primary use. Several rooms at Pottery Mound contain one or more such features, but there are no surface rooms that contain more than two of these features or modifications (Table 3.2). I would note that a single possible houseblock kiva was partially excavated at Hummingbird Pueblo, identified as such based on the presence of a ventilator/deflector system (oriented north, interestingly enough). I will leave the meaning of these features in surface rooms for future consideration given the small and disparate nature of the sample.

The Pyramidal Structure at Pottery Mound Pueblo

Finally, this discussion of architectural patterns at Pottery Mound would be incomplete without a consideration of the "pyramidal mound" feature that underlies much of the architectural remains at the site. Cordell (2004) has provided an informative synthesis of the published and unpublished descriptions of this purported mound feature, and I draw heavily on her observations here.

During his extensive field school excavations at Pottery Mound, Hibben uncovered a deeply buried stratum that he argued to have been an early pyramidal mound constructed on the Rio Puerco floodplain prior to large-scale construction at the site (Hibben 1966). As shown in the profile map of the bulldozer trench that spans most of the central portion of the site (Appendix C), the basal levels do contain a significant stratum labeled as "red clay" on most of the profile map sections. The deposit rises 1–2 m above the floodplain deposits depicted on the eastern and western margins of the profile. Excavating on the margins of the elevated feature, Hibben (1966; 1967) identified a number of purported cultural features, including footing trenches, use surfaces, and pits excavated into this red clay feature. He even argues to have found the remains of steps cut into the side of the feature, allowing easy access to this raised feature from the surrounding floodplain (1966:524–525). He attributed the presence of the feature to the same extralocal influences that introduced Mesoamerican iconography into the famed kiva murals unearthed at Pottery Mound (Hibben 1975).

If the feature was, indeed, constructed by human labor, it would represent a monumental investment in earth modification by a group of people for which we have no intact archaeological record at Pottery Mound. As Cordell (2004:6) notes in her review of the evidence, the mound described by Hibben covers approximately 4,900 m². A platform averaging 1.5 m in height would require 7,350 m³ of earth, a massive amount of dirt to pile up using only digging sticks, baskets, and human labor. This is not out of the realm of possibility given that earthen structures of similar scale are found in the Hohokam region (Elson 1998; Lindauer 1992) and in northern Chihuahua (Di Peso 1974:Volume 1).

More problematic than the scale of the feature is its proposed early construction date. Hibben proposes that this massive foundational structure was put in place by a community of thirteenth-century Ancestral Pueblo people. The material evidence for this community is comprised only of a limited presence of black-on-white ceramics on and around Pottery Mound Pueblo, ceramic assemblages dating primarily to the twelfth and thirteenth centuries in the Rio Puerco region. Hibben does not address where these earlier people lived during the construction of the feature, nor is there any explanation of the source of the mound fill or the methods used to construct such a significant platform.

This is not to say that anthropogenic factors did not contribute to the height of the site's elevation above the Rio Puerco floodplain The sheer mass of adobe comprising the walls, ceilings, and floors of the architectural features at Pottery Mound would have contributed as much or more material to the site's formation than the purported platform mound itself. If we assume an average wall thickness of 35 cm, average surface room size of 2 x 3 m, and wall heights of 2 m per room, 500 rooms in an aggregated roomblock configuration would contain between 5,000 and 6,000 m³ of adobe depending on the overall form of the roomblock. Adding in roof and floor components and multiple-story construction in some parts of the site would easily yield another 1,000 m³ of material. We cannot assume that all of Pottery Mound's adobe construction material remains on-site, particularly in light of the highly erosive history of the Rio Puerco floodplain (Bryan 1928; Love and Young 1983). At the same time, the gridlike form of surface pueblos traps a significant amount of blowing and flowing sediment over the course of site deterioration. My main point is that a very large mound of adobe would result from 100–150 years of construction, reconstruction, and ultimate destruction of the site of Pottery Mound.

I agree with Cordell (2004:13) that there is no good evidence for the construction of a major platform mound that serves as the foundation for the subsequent architectural features at Pottery Mound. One could provide additional conjecture about this feature, but the data to either support or negate Hibben's explanation are simply not available unless we are able to expose these deposits once again. Once exposed the test for differentiating an anthropogenic construction feature from a natural flood-plain landform would be straightforward. Natural deposition of sands, silts, and clays would be evident in patterns of upward fining of sediments and directional layering of deposits. In contrast, anthropogenic construction of a large earthwork would show up as unsorted basket loads of redeposited sediments, artifacts, and other associated materials across a large area.

Conclusions

This investigation of material patterning in architectural features at Pottery Mound and Hummingbird Pueblo addresses archaeological evidence that might inform the occupational histories of these two complex sites. A particular focus here is the question as to whether the architectural remains at these sites might inform on differences in past group histories at the site, including the immigration of nonlocal populations into these communities. Recent research on the archaeology of migration, group identity, and ethnicity has established that multiple lines of evidence are essential to archaeological inquiries into group identity and social interaction.

Consistent with the interpretations of other aspects of Pottery Mound's material record detailed in this volume, the architectural patterning at the site exhibits an amalgamation of attributes that are common to ancestral settlements across both the Eastern and Western Pueblo regions. Multiple lines of evidence support this amalgamation, including site size, use of plaza space, room floor area, architectural fabric, roomblock layout, internal features, and ritual structures. As a general observation, aspects of surface architecture provide evidence that the growth of settlements was not simply the result of natural population growth over the course of occupation at both sites. More specifically, the reliance on ladder construction techniques at both settlements might well be the result of multihousehold groups moving into these large aggregations during the fourteenth and fifteenth centuries A.D.

The surface architectural patterns are also ambiguous in many respects, with several lines of evidence that remain equivocal with respect to migration and social group difference, including site size, overall site layout, and surface room floor area. Both Pottery Mound and Hummingbird fall comfortably into the range of variation in settlement size documented for Pueblo IV period sites

across the northern Southwest (Adams and Duff 2004). Both settlements employ the plaza-oriented site layout that is characteristic of Pueblo IV villages across much of the Pueblo world, though there may be some significance to the differences in overall plaza space documented at Pottery Mound and Hummingbird Pueblo.

The large sample of surface rooms at both sites clearly shows the rooms to be on the smaller side relative to sites elsewhere in the Southwest, but again there are also significant differences between roomblocks sampled at the sites. For example, if the Unit B rooms (4.6 m² on average) were the only ones excavated at Pottery Mound, we could entertain parallels between Pottery Mound and some of the thirteenth- to fourteenth-century Homol'ovi sites (I and IV) in Arizona. On the other hand, the sample of Duck Unit rooms (7.8 m² on average) at Pottery Mound puts the site on par with most Pueblo IV sites in the Eastern Pueblo region for which floor area is available (Cameron 1999:Table 8). Similarly, there are significant differences in the average floor areas of rooms when we compare the northern and eastern roomblocks at Hummingbird Pueblo. These differences may stem from building strategies (ladder versus accretionary construction), availability of structural supports, differences in social group composition, or aspects of all of these variables.

The spatial clustering of kiva orientation patterns at Pottery Mound remains the most robust line of evidence for the coresidence of local and nonlocal populations at this site. At this point I think it is too simple to attribute the eastern-oriented kivas to a "Rio Grande" population at Pottery Mound and the southern-oriented kivas to immigrants from points farther west. It's a possibility, but these formal characteristics in integrative architecture can also be part of the larger spread of concepts and codes associated with religious system change across the Southwest during this period (Adams 1991; Cordell 1995; Crown 1994). I'm confident that if we continue to expand our ongoing cross-pollination research into Pottery Mound ceramic technology, iconography, and design motifs, we'll begin to tease out complementary and contrasting patterns in both surface and subsurface architectural contexts at Pottery Mound.

For me the larger question still remains what, in particular, can we say is significantly different or similar when we compare archaeological classifications like "ancestral Eastern Pueblo" and "ancestral Western Pueblo"? We are still at the most basic level of compiling data on regional, local, and site-level variability. Because our primary lines of evidence for assessing the dynamics of past group interactions and identity formation come from site-based research, we need to continue building multi-site comparisons of ceramics, architecture, site layout, and other potentially meaningful information (Ferguson and Anyon 2001). Pottery Mound, Hummingbird Pueblo, and other settlements within and outside of the Rio Puerco drainage hold significant promise for yielding important insights into the complex historical foundations of contemporary Native American societies in the Southwest.

ACKNOWLEDGMENTS

Unearthing evidence of a site's past archaeological investigations is often more challenging than the original excavations since one is never certain what is missing from the maps, field notes, and curated artifacts. Gratitude goes first to Polly Schaafsma for bringing all of the authors of this volume together at the School of American Research in 2004 to discuss Pottery Mound Pueblo. The two days of discussion, debate, and collaboration set the stage for a new phase of understanding the past half century of research at this unique site. This foray into the archives of Pottery Mound research has benefited from several guides, and to these guides I owe a debt of gratitude. None of this would have been possible had it not been for David Phillips's careful reconstruction of the overall Pottery Mound plan map of excavations (see Figure 1.3). David provided constant updates as maps and important site summaries from Dr. Hibben's personal archive were cataloged into the Maxwell Museum collections. My thanks also to Matthew Dawson, assistant curator at the Maxwell, for his assistance in error-checking my digital version of the bulldozer trench profile map (Appendix C) against the original version of the profile. I have personally benefited, as have all the authors in this volume, from the thorough history of excavations at the site compiled by Gwinn and Patricia Vivian. Thanks also to Paul Kay for his personal accounts of work at the site and his gracious sharing of photos, maps, and thoughts pertaining to Pottery Mound.

NOTES

1. Hummingbird Pueblo is also known as Chaves-Hummingbird Pueblo, in honor of the present landowner's father, Nickodemus Chaves. I use "Hummingbird Pueblo" in this paper to make it consistent with Frank Hibben's early research at Hummingbird Pueblo.

2. The only other person sharing this distinction is Dr. Linda Cordell at the University of Colorado.

3. Hibben excavated at Hummingbird Pueblo for several years, particularly during the 1980s, until the former landowner requested that he no longer dig at the site. The materials excavated from Hummingbird by Hibben are now curated at the University of New Mexico's Hibben Center.

4. There are also floor area averages that pool room sizes from spatially distinct areas. This includes the eight rooms listed under Unit D (D1–D6, D26, D27) that should probably be included in the Duck Unit sample (Unit A). The resulting statistics increase the Unit D room size average, but this is an admittedly small sample of rooms that are likely not part of a contiguous roomblock (see Table 3.1).

5. Coursed adobe is also referred to as "cob" (Gann 1995:11; Moquin 1992) or "pisé" (Judd 1916:247).

6. In this kiva count total, Kivas 8 and 9 are treated as individual kivas even though Kiva 8 is built over Kiva 9.

REFERENCES CITED

Adams, E. Charles

1991 *The Origins and Development of the Katsina Cult.* University of Arizona Press, Tucson.

Adams, E. Charles, and Andrew Duff (editors)

2004 *The Protohistoric Pueblo World, A.D. 1275–1600.* University of Arizona Press, Tucson.

Adler, Michael

1989 Ritual Facilities and Social Integration in Nonranked Societies. In *The Archaeology of Social Integration in the Prehistoric Pueblos,* edited by William Lipe and Michelle Hegmon, pp. 35–52. Crow Canyon Publications in Archaeology No. 1. Crow Canyon Archaeological Center, Cortez, Colorado.

1993 Why is a Kiva? New Interpretations of Prehistoric Social Integrative Architecture in the Northern Rio Grande Region of New Mexico. *Journal of Anthropological Research* 49(4):18–27.

2001 Report of Investigations at Hummingbird Pueblo, 2001 Field Season. Report submitted to the Center for Field Research, Earthwatch Institute. Manuscript on file, Department of Anthropology, Southern Methodist University, Dallas, Texas.

2002 Architecture and Ancestral Pueblo Migrations: Recent Research at Hummingbird Pueblo (LA 578). Paper presented at the Pecos Archaeological Conference, Pecos, New Mexico.

Adler, Michael (editor)

1996 *The Prehistoric Pueblo World, A.D. 1150–1350.* University of Arizona Press, Tucson.

Adler, Michael, T. Van Pool, and B. Leonard

1996 Ancestral Pueblo Population Aggregation and Abandonment in the North American Southwest. *Journal of World Prehistory* 10(3):375–438.

Adler, Michael A., and Richard H. Wilshusen

1990 Large-scale Integrative Facilities in Tribal Societies: Cross-Cultural and Southwestern US Examples. *World Archaeology* 22(2):133–46.

Aldenderfer, Mark, and Charles Stanish

1993 Domestic Architecture, Household Archaeology, and the Past in the South-Central Andes. In *Domestic Architecture, Ethnicity, and Complementarity in the South-Central Andes,* edited by M. Aldenderfer, pp. 1–12. University of Iowa Press, Iowa City.

Baker, Larry L., and Stephen R. Durand

2003 *Prehistory of the Middle Rio Puerco Valley, Sandoval County, NM.* Special Publication No. 3. ASNM, Albuquerque, New Mexico.

Baldwin, Stuart

1987 Roomsize Patterns: A Quantitative Method for Approaching Ethnic Identification in Architecture. In *Ethnicity and Culture, Proceedings of the Eighteenth Annual Conference of the Archaeological Association of the University of Calgary,* edited by R. Augher, M. Glass, S. MacEachern, and P. McCartney, pp. 163–74. University of Calgary, Alberta.

Balsam, Bill, Michael Adler, and Robert Deaton

2002 Analysis of Adobe Wall Composition at the Hummingbird Site, NM by Diffuse Reflectance Spectrophotometry. Poster paper presented at the Geological Society of America National Meeting, Denver.

Brody, J. J.

1964 Design Analysis of the Rio Grande Glaze Pottery of Pottery Mound, New Mexico. Unpublished Master's thesis, Department of Anthropology, University of New Mexico, Albuquerque.

1985 Pottery Mound—Stabilization and Research Proposal. Draft submitted to the Board of Archaeologists, February 20, 1985. Manuscript on file, Maxwell Museum of Anthropology, University of New Mexico, Albuquerque.

Bryan, K.

1928 Historic Evidence on Changes in the Channel of the Rio Puerco, a Tributary of the Rio Grande in New Mexico. *Journal of Geology* 36:265–82.

Cameron, Catherine M.

1995   Migration and the Movement of Southwestern Peoples. *Journal of Anthropological Archaeology* 14:104–24.

1998   Coursed Adobe Architecture, Style, and Social Boundaries in the American Southwest. In *The Archaeology of Social Boundaries*, edited by Miriam Stark, pp. 183–207. Smithsonian Institution Press, Washington, D.C.

1999   Room Size, Organization of Construction, and Archaeological Interpretation in the Puebloan Southwest. *Journal of Anthropological Archaeology* 18:201–39.

Clark, Jeffery

2001   *Tracking Prehistoric Migrations: Pueblo Settlers among the Tonto Basin Hohokam*. University of Arizona Press, Tucson.

Cordell, Linda

1995   Tracing Migration Pathways from the Receiving End. *Journal of Anthropological Archaeology* 14:203–11.

1996   Big Sites, Big Questions: Pueblos in Transition. In *The Prehistoric Pueblo World, A.D. 1150–1350*, edited by Michael Adler, pp. 228–40. University of Arizona Press, Tucson.

2004   Advanced Seminar on Pottery Mound, School of American Research, May 11–12. Manuscript on file, School of American Research, Santa Fe, New Mexico.

Creamer, Winifred

1993   *The Architecture of Arroyo Hondo Pueblo, New Mexico*. School of American Research Press, Santa Fe, New Mexico.

Crotty, Helen

1995   *Anasazi Mural Art of the Pueblo IV Period, A.D. 1300–1600: Influences, Selective Adaptation, and Cultural Diversity in the Prehistoric Southwest*. University Microfilms, Ann Arbor.

Crown, Patricia L.

1994   *Ceramics and Ideology, Salado Polychrome Pottery*. University of New Mexico Press, Albuquerque.

Crown, Patricia, Janet Orcutt, and Timothy Kohler

1996   Pueblo Cultures in Transition: The Northern Rio Grande. In *The Prehistoric Pueblo World, A.D. 1150–1350*, edited by M. Adler, pp. 188–204. University of Arizona Press, Tucson.

Dean, Jeffrey

1996   Anasazi Settlement Transformations in Northeastern Arizona, A.D. 1150–1350. In *The Prehistoric Pueblo World, A.D. 1150–1350*, edited by M. Adler, pp. 29–47. University of Arizona Press, Tucson.

Di Peso, Charles C.

1974   *Casas Grandes: A Fallen Trading Center of the Gran Chichimeca*. Vol. 1–3. Amerind Foundation, Dragoon, Arizona.

Dittert, Alfred

1959   Culture Change in the Cebolleta Mesa Region, Central Western New Mexico. Unpublished Ph.D. dissertation, Department of Anthropology, University of Arizona, Tucson.

Duff, Andrew

2002   *Western Pueblo Identities: Regional Interaction, Migration, and Transformation*. University of Arizona Press, Tucson.

Eckert, S. L.

2003   Social Boundaries, Immigration, and Ritual Systems: A Case Study from the American Southwest. Unpublished Ph.D. dissertation, Department of Anthropology, Arizona State University, Tempe.

Elson, Mark D.

1998   *Expanding the View of Hohokam Platform Mounds: An Ethnographic Perspective*. Anthropological Papers of the University of Arizona No. 63. University of Arizona Press, Tucson.

Ferguson, T. J., and Roger Anyon

2001   Hopi and Zuni Cultural Landscapes: Implications of History and Scale for Cultural Resources Management. In *Native Peoples of the Southwest: Negotiating Land, Water, and Ethnicities*, edited by Laurie Weinstein, pp. 99–122. Bergin & Garvey, Westport, Connecticut.

Gann, Douglas

1995   The Adobe Pueblo Site: Investigations in Pre-Hispanic Adobe Brick Architecture. Unpublished Master's thesis, Department of Anthropology, University of Arizona, Tucson.

Herr, Sarah
2001 *Beyond Chaco: Great Kiva Communities on the Mogollon Rim Frontier.* University of Arizona Press, Tucson.

Hibben, Frank
1955 Excavations at Pottery Mound, New Mexico. *American Antiquity* 21:179–80.
1960 Prehispanic Murals of Pottery Mound, New Mexico. *Archaeology* 13:267–74.
1966 A Possible Pyramidal Structure and Other Mexican Influences at Pottery Mound, New Mexico. *American Antiquity* 31:522–29.
1967 Mexican Features of Mural Paintings at Pottery Mound, New Mexico. *Archaeology* 20(2):84–87.
1975 *Kiva Art of the Anasazi at Pottery Mound.* KC Publications, Las Vegas, Nevada.
1986 Report on the Salvage Operations at the Site of Pottery Mound, New Mexico during the Excavation Seasons of 1977–1985. Originally written in 1985. Manuscript on file, Maxwell Museum of Anthropology, University of New Mexico, Albuquerque.

James, Steven
1994 Regional Variation in Prehistoric Pueblo Households and Social Organization: A Quantitative Approach. Unpublished Ph.D. dissertation, Arizona State University, Tempe.

Jones, Siân
1997 *The Archaeology of Ethnicity: Constructing Identities in the Past and Present.* Routledge, London.

Judd, Neil
1916 The Use of Adobe in Prehistoric Dwellings in the Southwest. In *Holmes Anniversary Volume: Anthropological Essays Presented to William Henry Holmes in Honor of His Seventieth Birthday, December 1, 1916.* J. W. Bryan Press, Washington, D.C.

Kintigh, Keith
1996 The Cibola Region in the Post-Chacoan Era. In *The Prehistoric Pueblo World, A.D. 1150–1350,* edited by Michael Adler, pp. 131–44. University of Arizona Press, Tucson.

Lakatos, Steven A.
2003 Pit Structure Architecture of the Developmental Period (A.D. 600–1200). In *Anasazi Archaeology at the Millennium: Proceedings of the Sixth Occasional Anasazi Symposium,* edited by Paul F. Reed, pp. 49–54. Center for Desert Archaeology, Tucson, Arizona.

LeBlanc, Steven
1999 *Prehistoric Warfare in the American Southwest.* University of Utah Press, Salt Lake City.

Lekson, Stephen
1988 The Idea of the Kiva in Anasazi Prehistory. *Kiva* 53(1):213–34.

Lindauer, Owen
1992 Architectural Patterning and Variation among Salado Sites. In *Proceedings of the Second Salado Conference, Globe, AZ, 1992,* edited by Richard C. Lange and Stephen Germick, pp. 50–56. Arizona Archaeological Society Occasional Paper. Arizona Archaeological Society, Phoenix.

Lipe, William D.
1989 Social Scale of Mesa Verde Anasazi Kivas. In *The Architecture of Social Integration in Prehistoric Pueblos,* edited by W. D. Lipe and M. Hegmon, pp. 53–71. Occasional Papers No. 1. Crow Canyon Archaeological Center, Cortez, Colorado.

Lipe, William, and Stephen Lekson
2001 Mesa Verde Pueblo Migration and Cultural Transformations, A.D. 1250–1350. Paper presented at the 66th Annual Meeting of the Society for American Archaeology, New Orleans.

Lipe, William, and Scott Ortman
2000 Spatial Patterning in Northern San Juan Villages, A.D. 1050–1300. *Kiva* 66(1):91–122.

Love, D. W., and J. D. Young
1983 Progress Report in the Late Cenozoic Geologic Evolution of the Lower Rio Puerco. *New Mexico Geological Society Guidebook: 34th Field Conference,* pp. 277–84. New Mexico Geological Society, Socorro, New Mexico.

Luhrs, Dorothy
1937 The Identification and Distribution of the Ceramic Types in the Rio Puerco Area, Central New Mexico. Unpublished Master's thesis, Department of Anthropology, University of New Mexico, Albuquerque.

McGimsey, Charles R.
1980 *Marianas Mesa: Seven Prehistoric Settlements in West-Central Arizona. A Report of the Upper Gila Expedition.* Papers of the Peabody Museum of American Archaeology and Ethnology Vol. 72. Harvard University, Cambridge, Massachusetts.

Mills, Barbara
1999 The Reorganization of Silver Creek Communities from the 11th to the 14th Centuries. In *Living on the Edge of the Rim: Excavations and Analysis of the Silver Creek Archaeological Research Project, 1993–1998,* edited by B. J. Mills, Sarah Herr, and S. Van Keuren, pp. 505–11. Arizona State Museum Archaeological Series 192, Vol. 2. Arizona State Museum, University of Arizona, Tucson.

Mindeleff, Victor
1891 *A Study of Pueblo Architecture: Tusayan and Cibola.* Bureau of American Ethnology Eighth Annual Report, pp. 3–228. Smithsonian Institution, Washington, D.C.

Moquin, Michael
1992 From Bi Sa Ani to Picuris: Early Pueblo Technology of New Mexico and the Southwest. *Traditions: The Adobe Journal* 8:10–27.

Olzak, Susan
1992 *The Dynamics of Ethnic Competition and Conflict.* Stanford University Press, Stanford, California.

Peckham, Stewart
1979 When is a Rio Grande Kiva? In *Collected Papers in Honor of Bertha Pauline Dutton,* edited by Albert Schroeder, pp. 55–86. Papers of the Archaeological Society of New Mexico No. 4. Archaeological Society of New Mexico, Albuquerque.

Reed, Erik
1956 Types of Village-Plan Layouts in the Southwest. In *Prehistoric Settlement Patterns in the New World,* edited by G. R. Willey, pp. 11–17. Viking Fund Publications in Anthropology No. 23. Johnson Reprint Corp., New York.

Roney, John
1996 The Pueblo III Period in the Eastern San Juan Basin and Acoma-Laguna Areas. In *The Prehistoric Pueblo World,* A.D. 1150–1350, edited by Michael Adler, pp. 73–85. University of Arizona Press, Tucson.

Ruppé, Reynold
1990 *The Acoma Culture Province: An Archaeological Concept.* Garland Publishing, New York. (Originally the author's Ph.D. dissertation, Harvard University, 1953.)

Smith, Rachel
1998 Kivas of the Northern San Juan and the Northern Rio Grande Regions, A.D. 1150–1350: A Comparative Analysis. Unpublished Master's thesis, Department of Anthropology, Washington State University, Pullman.

Smith, Watson
1952 *Excavations in Big Hawk Valley, Wupatki National Monument, Arizona.* Museum of Northern Arizona Bulletin No. 24. Northern Arizona Society of Science and Art, Flagstaff.

Spielmann, Katherine (editor)
1998 *Migration and Reorganization: The Pueblo IV Period in the American Southwest.* Arizona State University Anthropological Research Papers No. 51. Arizona State University, Tempe.

Tainter, Joseph A., and Bonnie Bagley Tainter
1996 Riverine Settlement in the Evolution of Prehistoric Land-Use Systems in the Middle Rio Grande Valley, New Mexico. In *Desired Future Conditions for Southwestern Riparian Ecosystems: Bringing Interests and Concerns Together.* USDA Forest Service, General Technical Report RM-GTR-272, Fort Collins, Colorado.

Tsesmeli, Lia

2002 Sifting through Mudbricks and Masonry in New Mexico, A.D. 750–1500. Paper presented at the 67th Annual Meeting of the Society for American Archaeology, Denver.

Voll, Charles B.

1961 The Glaze Paint Ceramics of Pottery Mound, New Mexico. Unpublished Master's thesis, Department of Anthropology, University of New Mexico, Albuquerque.

Wendorf, D. F., and E. Reed

1955 An Alternative Reconstruction of Northern Rio Grande Prehistory. *El Palacio* 62(5–6):131–73.

Wilcox, D. R., and J. Haas

1994 The Scream of the Butterfly: Competition and Conflict in the Prehistoric Southwest. In *Themes in Southwest Prehistory*, edited by G. Gumerman, pp. 211–38. School of American Research Press, Santa Fe, New Mexico.

CHAPTER FOUR

Understanding the Dynamics of Segregation and Incorporation at Pottery Mound through Analysis of Glaze-Decorated Bowls

Suzanne L. Eckert

Archaeologists familiar with the material culture of Pottery Mound have speculated that immigrants from the Western Pueblo region moved into the village. Soon after the first season of excavation, Hibben (1955:179) discussed the Hopi influence on pottery design and kiva mural decoration and noted that there was a "strong possibility of an intrusion from the west of a large group of Hopi peoples." Since then, numerous researchers have noted the influence of Hopi and Zuni styles on both pottery and kiva mural decoration at Pottery Mound (Brody 1964; Crotty 1990; Vivian 1961; Voll 1961). Based on ceramic and architectural evidence, I (2003:53–87) recently argued that immigrants from the Hopi and Zuni areas were living with indigenous residents in the village. Although the presence of immigrants has been considered, little attention has been devoted to understanding the effects immigrants and their descendants would have had on intra- and intervillage social dynamics once they made Pottery Mound their new home. I argue here that detecting immigrants living within a village is important in that it directs our attention toward understanding the tensions of segregation and incorporation that are a core aspect of Pueblo social dynamics. Various factors could have determined the form incorporation or segregation of immigrants took in prehispanic Pueblo villages including: the reason for immigration; the size of the immigrating group; expectations of returning to the homeland; and whether or not immigrants were recruited to move by indigenous groups. Immigrant and indigenous residents made decisions based upon these factors, decisions that were made while negotiating their position in a new social environment. In this paper, I examine social segregation and incorporation, in the context of immigration into Pottery Mound, through analysis of change and continuity in pottery styles on glaze-decorated bowls.

Incorporation, Segregation, and Immigration in the Pueblo World

Previous Research

In the ideal modern Pueblo world, successful operation of society requires "some degree of consensus and cooperation" among different social groups (Hegmon 1989:9). One way to create such cooperation is by incorporating individuals from diverse groups into a greater, unified whole such as a community, village, or religion. Much attention has been given to the role of Pueblo ritual, especially the katsina religion, in creating an arena where incorporation can be negotiated and maintained (Adams 1991; Bunzel 1932; Crown 1994; Parsons 1939; Potter 1997). Modern Pueblo ritual organizations build social networks and loyalties that help to crosscut kinship lines. For example, integration of Zuni clans is achieved through individual membership in various ceremonial organizations including curing societies and kiva groups (Ferguson 1989; Kroeber 1917; Parsons 1939). These various ritual organizations incorporate individuals into being "Zuni" by creating non-kin-based relationships and obligations that need to be respected to preserve proper balance in both Zuni society and the cosmos. Another important aspect of Pueblo religion is its public ceremonies (Adams 1991). Participants in such ceremonies are able to reaffirm their shared socio-ritual identity to other participants as well as to village members who are observing the event. Among modern Pueblo groups,

many of these ceremonies are concerned with rain and community well-being (Bunzel 1932).

Although much of the Pueblo ritual system may be focused on incorporation of individuals into Pueblo society as a whole, the potential for conflict is also inherent in the system. In many villages, different ceremonies and ritual knowledge may be ranked (Brandt 1994; Ortiz 1969). Not only can ritual knowledge be ranked, but within some modern Pueblo villages, certain kin-based groups are also associated with specific ceremonies (Dozier 1966; Eggan 1950; Mindeleff 1891; Parsons 1939; Sando 1982). Further, Brandt (1977; 1994) has stressed the secretive nature of Pueblo ritual and its role in village social hierarchies: power lies in who has sacred knowledge (see also Bunzel 1932). During "good times" the complexities and power structure of Pueblo ritual work to keep harmony in a village. However, during periods of social stress brought on by any number of internal or external factors, the ritual system adds another layer of tension to an already divided community prone to segregation and factionalism. If a village begins to fracture, individuals may be forced to choose between competing ritual and social obligations based upon their perceptions of which obligations benefit them the most. As such, the ritual system may become a source of underlying social tension as well as, or rather than, a source of incorporation.

Factionalism among historic Pueblo groups sometimes resulted in the splintering of a village, with part, or all, of its residents emigrating (Herr and Clark 1997; Levy 1992). Ritual practice played a role in determining where some of these migrants moved. There are historical cases of villages fissioning "through the movement and recruitment of religious groups . . . to other villages" (Brandt 1994:17). Similar recruitment may have occurred in the prehispanic era. For example, ritual practitioners in the fourteenth-century Upper Little Colorado River area appear to have been actively recruited by residents of the Hopi and Zuni regions (Duff 2002). Duff (2002) speculates that these recruits were incorporated into their new village with a certain amount of social power associated with their unique ritual ceremonies. As immigrants moved into new villages, either as a result of ritual recruitment or some other social process, negotiations would begin anew between segregation and incorporation in a social context changed by the immigrants' presence.

Migration is one of the most important concepts of modern Pueblo thought (Naranjo 1995:247) and social tensions between immigrant and local groups have become part of Pueblo identity and oral tradition (Edelman 1979; Ellis 1979; Nequatewa 1936; Parsons 1926; 1939; Stanislawski 1979; Strong 1979). There is archaeological evidence for group migrations over much of the Pueblo landscape in the prehispanic era (Beal 1987; Cameron 1995; Duff 1998; 2002; Haury 1958; Lindsay 1987; Plog 1979). If identity based on migration was as important to prehispanic Pueblo groups as it is among many of their descendants, then prehispanic immigrants would have been hard pressed to be completely incorporated into a new identity. As such, migration is one important context in which to understand the mechanisms of segregation and incorporation within a village.

The incorporation or segregation of immigrants in their new home varies from village to village among historic and modern Pueblo groups. At least 52 migrations have been documented among the historic Rio Grande pueblos (Herr and Clark 1997). Although many of these migrations were a consequence of the Pueblo Revolt of 1680, factionalism was also a common cause and disputes sometimes resulted in part, or all, of a community migrating to another village. In a few cases, immigrants were either completely incorporated or segregated; more commonly, though, immigrants were able to negotiate social acceptance somewhere between these two extremes (Brandt 1979; Ellis 1979; Lange 1979; Parsons 1928; 1939; Schroeder 1979). For example, at Jemez Pueblo, the descendants of Pecos immigrants segregate themselves by owning specific ritual artifacts and being members of a specific ritual society (Sando 1979; Schroeder 1979). At the same time, they have been incorporated as fully recognized residents of the village with all the privileges and obligations such membership entails. As this example illustrates, it is important to consider incorporation and segregation not as mutually exclusive social dynamics, but as two ends of a spectrum. It is within the full range of this spectrum that village residents base their daily decisions while negotiating identity within their social environment.

Examining Incorporation and Segregation at Pottery Mound

Examining segregation and incorporation in the archaeological record is not straightforward. Not only are segregation and incorporation the two extremes of a single range of behaviors, but also individuals within a village may make seemingly contradictory decisions that attempt to embrace both extremes. Depending on the social context, an individual may perceive benefits from emphasizing his

or her village-wide unity or his or her historical uniqueness. In this paper, I analyze aspects of both technological and decorative style on glaze-decorated bowls to interpret changes in incorporation and segregation of immigrants and local groups at Pottery Mound through time. Because technological and decorative styles on glaze-decorated bowls involve different social contexts and have different degrees of visibility, they provide complementary kinds of information concerning daily decisions made by those who produced and used the vessels.

A technological style is a suite of technological attributes that is characteristic of a specific body of information and practice used to manufacture vessels (Rice 1987:201). Lechtman (1977) has argued that technological style is the result of more than simply the natural constraints inherent in working with a specific material such as stone, metal, or clay. Rather, technological style is also the result of certain social behaviors such as organization of production, cultural attitudes toward material resources, and ritual systems (Lechtman 1977:6). In other words, it is the result of constraints imposed both by the natural properties of materials as well as cultural views concerning those materials. Technological style probably reflects both the active and passive aspects of a shared learning environment. Although new techniques can be learned, potters in traditional manufacturing societies are usually very conservative in adopting such changes into their production process (Arnold 1985; Cancian 1980).

A decorative style is a suite of design attributes that is characteristic of a specific way of decorating a vessel. Because decorated vessels are often used in public contexts, it is not unreasonable to assume that a decorative style can impart important cultural meaning to those who view it (Costin 1998; Hodder 1982; Wiessner 1983; Wobst 1977). Different social groups who wish to maintain their separate identities may consciously choose to emphasize difference by promoting group membership with a decorative style (Wiessner 1983). However, decorative style may convey less specific meanings, by providing daily reminders of the social structure through culturally loaded symbols, or by providing important cues to people in specific social contexts (Goffman 1974). On the other hand, similarity in decorative style could be used in some social contexts to intentionally blur distinctions between different groups who have been incorporated into a larger identity, such as village membership or shared religion.

Based upon analyses of a suite of different technological and decorative attributes, I (2003:53–87) have argued elsewhere that two groups of immigrants, one from the Zuni region and one from the Hopi Mesas, lived at Pottery Mound with indigenous groups. Throughout the remainder of this chapter, I assume that this previous argument is correct and I am working under the assumption that at least two groups of immigrants moved into Pottery Mound. However, even if the residents of Pottery Mound were different local groups with different histories, the issues of segregation and incorporation are still pertinent.

The issue I explore here is not one of whether immigrants lived in the village, but how their presence affected village social dynamics in terms of incorporation and segregation. Following Hegmon and colleagues (1998), I assume that the residents of Pottery Mound used or interpreted similar styles to indicate social sameness. Conversely, residents would have used or interpreted different styles to indicate social diversity. I assume that homogeneity in styles through time reflects an adherence to rules of social conformity by all members of the village, immigrant and indigenous alike (Hegmon et al. 1998:157), while heterogeneity in styles through time reflects changes in the social makeup of the village. Depending on the nature of the heterogeneity, I further assume that diversity of styles reflects the intentional decision by potters to segregate themselves into different social units based upon migration histories.

The Glaze-Decorated Bowls of Pottery Mound

The Data Set

Data for this study come from Linda Cordell's 1979 test excavations in the trash midden located immediately northwest of the mounded portion of Pottery Mound (see Figure 1.3 and Appendix A, tile NC, p. 256).[1] Cordell's work resulted in 17 arbitrary excavation levels through 3.4 vertical meters of stratified trash. Using a combination of seriation and mean ceramic dating, I (2003:31–52) determined that these 17 levels have a date range of approximately A.D. 1350–1450. If these 17 levels are assumed to have covered this entire date range, and if depositional processes remained consistent throughout time, then it can be assumed that each level represents approximately six years of accumulation. No cultural material recovered from the site suggests that it dated any earlier than A.D. 1350. Ceramic types collected from the surface, however, indicate that the

17 levels examined here do not include material from the latest occupation of the site, which may have lasted until as late as A.D. 1500.

Glaze technology was introduced into the Lower Rio Puerco region, in which Pottery Mound is located, sometime in the late 1200s or early 1300s (Eckert 2006). The production of red-slipped, glaze-painted pottery was a dramatic shift from the previous white ware tradition. This shift required changes in firing technology, paint recipe, and design layout on the part of local potters. Residents of Pottery Mound appear to have settled the village with a complete understanding of these techniques. The majority of decorated vessels at the village are glaze painted, with no evidence of an earlier white ware–producing occupation (Brody 1964; Eckert 2003; Voll 1961). The glaze paint on vessels is well controlled, with no evidence of experimentation and very few misfires. Glaze-painted ceramic types unique to the site, as well as local material used as temper, indicate that the majority of decorated pottery recovered from the site was locally produced.

The current study is focused on the 2,299 glaze-decorated bowl sherds recovered from Cordell's work for two reasons.[2] First, decorated bowls throughout much of Pueblo prehistory were used in both domestic and ritual contexts (Crown 1994; Hegmon 1995; Spielmann 1998). Second, unlike jars, bowls have both a "private" and a "public" surface for decoration. Although the exterior of a bowl can be seen from across a public space, the interior of a bowl can be seen only by those in close contact with it. As such, decoration on bowls may articulate with the complex social signaling of those who produced and used the vessels. The two surfaces could be used to incorporate different social information to be interpreted either in different social contexts, or by different individuals within the same social context.

The Analysis

TEMPER

Temper choice is examined as an attribute that reflects technological style. Temper would have been visible only during the initial production of a vessel. As such, it reflects behavior and potential signaling within a very narrow social context, that of the pottery production group. At Pottery Mound, these production groups are assumed to have been small groups of related women. Ethnographic studies among Pueblo potters have shown

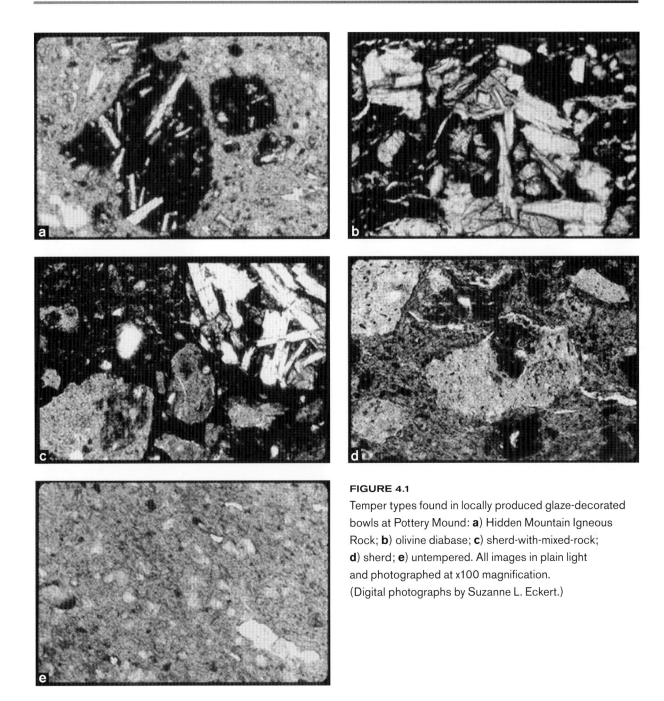

FIGURE 4.1

Temper types found in locally produced glaze-decorated bowls at Pottery Mound: **a**) Hidden Mountain Igneous Rock; **b**) olivine diabase; **c**) sherd-with-mixed-rock; **d**) sherd; **e**) untempered. All images in plain light and photographed at x100 magnification. (Digital photographs by Suzanne L. Eckert.)

that temper choice is one aspect of production technology that is considered important to conserve (Capone 1998; Lewis et al. 1990). Further, Capone (2006) has noted that temper choice among some early historic Rio Grande pueblos is strikingly consistent over time despite changes in other aspects of ceramic production technology. She argues that this consistency reflects a shared conception among potters within a village concerning the type of temper that is appropriate, and may reflect the signaling of social identity to some degree. With these studies in mind, I argue that differences in temper choice at Pottery Mound reflect different production groups, and may further reflect different social identities associated with indigenous and immigrant groups.

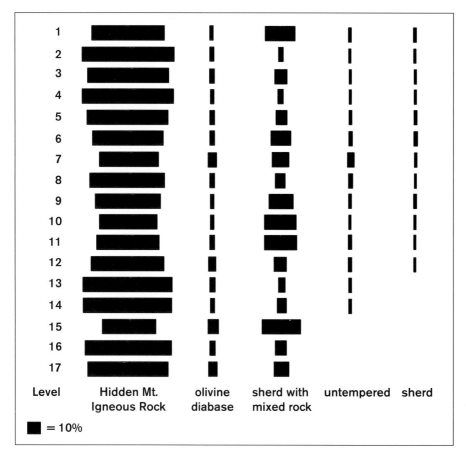

FIGURE 4.2

Stratigraphic changes in temper found in locally produced glaze-decorated bowls at Pottery Mound.

Through analysis of 78 petrographic thin sections of sherds recovered from Pottery Mound, five local temper types have been identified in glaze-decorated bowls (Figure 4.1; Eckert 2003:250–261): Hidden Mountain Igneous Rock, olivine diabase, sherd-and-mixed-rock (including various igneous and metamorphic rocks), sherd, and untempered.[3] Hidden Mountain Igneous Rock and olivine diabase have both been sourced to Hidden Mountain, a basalt outcrop approximately 3 km west of the village. Although from the same source, these two temper types reflect differences in collection techniques. Hidden Mountain Igneous Rock is a combination of igneous rocks that have the same chemical composition but different textures. Most examples of this temper within sherds show a high degree of weathering. This temper type was probably collected from the debris at the base of Hidden Mountain, where a mixture of eroded rock types and weathered material would accumulate. Olivine diabase, on the other hand, has the same chemical composition as other Hidden Mountain Igneous Rock

but reflects a single texture. Examples of this temper within sherds are often fresh and angular, with relatively little evidence of weathering. This temper type was probably collected from a fresh rock face at a specific location on Hidden Mountain. Similarly, the differences between sherd-and-mixed-rock and sherd temper are believed to reflect differences in either clay collection or material processing techniques (Eckert 2003:258–261).

Temper choice in glaze-decorated bowls becomes more diverse through time at Pottery Mound (Figure 4.2). Initially, potters were selecting from one of three temper choices: Hidden Mountain Igneous Rock, olivine diabase, or sherd-and-mixed-rock. These three temper choices reflect technological traditions that go back to at least A.D. 900 in the Lower Rio Puerco region (Durand and Hurst 1991; Eckert 2003; Warren 1982). Although these temper types continue to dominate the glaze-decorated bowl assemblage throughout time, two new temper choices are evident within the first half of Pottery Mound's occupation: untempered vessels begin to appear in Level 14, and

Table 4.1. Slip and Paint Color Combinations for Locally Produced, Glaze-Decorated Bowls at Pottery Mound

Ceramic Type	Vessel Interior		Vessel Exterior	
	slip color	paint	slip color	paint
early Rio Grande Glaze-on-red	red	black to brown glaze	red	black to brown glaze, if present
early Rio Grande Glaze Polychrome	yellow-buff to yellow-gray	black to brown glaze	red	black to brown glaze, if present
early Rio Grande Glaze-on-yellow	yellow-buff to pale yellow	black to brown glaze	yellow-buff to pale yellow	none
Pottery Mound Polychrome	yellow-buff	black to brown glaze and matte red paint	red	black to brown glaze, if present
Hidden Mountain Polychrome	red	black glaze, if present	bright white	black to green glaze

Zuni Glaze Ware, local copies

Ceramic Type	Vessel Interior		Vessel Exterior	
Heshotauthla Polychrome	red	black to green glaze	red	white matte paint, sometimes black glaze
Kwakina Polychrome	bright white	black to green glaze	red	white matte paint, sometimes black glaze

sherd-tempered vessels begin to appear in Level 12. These two temper types reflect new temper choices at the village and imply the presence of two immigrant pottery production groups. Although sherd temper is common throughout various parts of the Pueblo Southwest, I (2003:79–81) have associated the sherd temper identified at Pottery Mound with immigrants from the Zuni region based on stylistic similarities noted in the decorated wares. Similarly, I (2003:81–83) have associated untempered pottery with immigrants from the Hopi Mesas. The low frequency of these new temper types throughout the remainder of Pottery Mound's occupation suggests that immigrants and their descendants segregated themselves, at least in terms of pottery production groups, throughout their residence at the village.

CERAMIC TYPE

Change in ceramic types is examined as a reflection of decorative style. Although ceramic typologies are an archaeological construct, the types used here are defined by slip and paint color combinations. These attributes, especially slip color, would have been visible in a number of social contexts and could have been used to signal social

information to members within the same social group, or to members in different social groups (Carlson 1982; Crown 1994; Snow 1989). At Pottery Mound, village members could have divided themselves into any number of groupings based upon kin relations, religious affiliations, similar migration histories, or membership in the same exchange networks. Further, membership in these different groupings could have crosscut one another. Visual clues on pottery would not have created such social divisions. However, such clues could have been used to emphasize differences between groups by incorporating designs and colors that reminded viewers of such differences, or they could have been used to blur such boundaries by incorporating designs and colors that stressed village membership. Alternatively, potters could have incorporated diverse, potentially contradictory information in their designs. As noted above, bowls have both an interior and exterior space that can be decorated. These different spaces create the potential for potters to signal different information to different audiences using the same vessel.

Six common glaze-decorated ceramic types have been identified at Pottery Mound: early Rio Grande Glaze-on-red (including Agua Fria Gl/r), early Rio Grande

a.

b.

c.

FIGURE 4.3
Design layouts (after Eckert 2003) on locally produced glaze-decorated bowls at Pottery Mound: **a**) symmetrical layout on bowl interiors common to early Rio Grande Glaze Ware types and local copies of Zuni Glaze Ware types; **b**) asymmetrical layout on bowl interiors common to Pottery Mound Polychrome; **c**) banded layout on bowl exteriors common to Hidden Mountain Polychrome.

Glaze-on-yellow (including Cieneguilla Gl/y), early Rio Grande Glaze Polychrome (including San Clemente Polychrome), locally produced copies of Zuni Glaze Ware types, Pottery Mound Polychrome, and Hidden Mountain Polychrome.[4] In general, these types have different combinations of slip and paint colors (Table 4.1). However, local copies of Zuni Glaze Ware types have similar slip and paint color combinations as the early Rio Grande Glaze Ware types. Despite such similarities, they are separated because the Zuni Glaze Ware types have a distinct *bright* white slip, green glaze, and well-polished surfaces. Visually, sherds classified as local copies of Zuni Glaze Ware types look and feel identical to sherds found on contemporaneous sites in the Zuni region. Although only sherds are used in the current analysis, examination of whole vessels and large sherds from Pottery Mound and the nearby Hummingbird Pueblo (Eckert 2003:98–103) have shown that these six common glaze-decorated types are consistent in their design layouts. Early Rio Grande Glaze Ware and local copies of Zuni Glaze Ware vessels have banded, normally symmetrical designs on the interior of bowls. Pottery Mound Polychrome vessels have asymmetrical designs, reminiscent of contemporaneous Hopi Yellow Ware vessels, on the interior of bowls. Hidden Mountain Polychrome vessels have designs focused on the exterior (Figure 4.3). These differences in design layouts strengthen the argument that differences in color and paint combinations may have imparted information to those viewing decorated vessels.

Locally produced glaze-decorated bowl types become more diverse through time at Pottery Mound (Figure 4.4). Initially, only early Rio Grande Glaze-on-red and Glaze Polychrome were being produced. The presence of these two types, in varying proportions, is fairly typical of fourteenth-century central Rio Grande sites (Creamer and Renken 1994; Shepard 1942; Snow 1989; Warren and Snow 1976). These two types continue to dominate the Pottery Mound decorated-bowl assemblage throughout time. However, as with temper, new glaze-decorated bowl types begin to be produced early in the village's occupation: early Rio Grande Glaze-on-yellow and Pottery Mound Polychrome appear in Level 14, Hidden Mountain Polychrome appears in Level 12, and local copies of Zuni Glaze Ware appear in Level 11.[5] These are the same levels where new temper choices appear and, not surprisingly, there is a strong relationship between new temper and new pottery types (Eckert 2003). Specifically, although Pottery Mound Polychrome and early Rio Grande Glaze-on-yellow

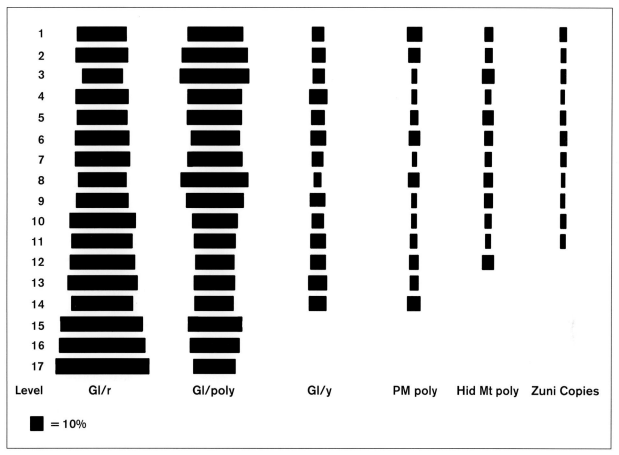

FIGURE 4.4

Stratigraphic changes in locally produced glaze-decorated bowl types at Pottery Mound.

tend to be tempered with Hidden Mountain Igneous Rock, these two types have the highest frequency of untempered glaze-decorated bowls. It is possible that Hopi potters found that they could not work well with local untempered clay and turned to local potters for advice. As a result, they incorporated rock temper into their production process when necessary. Locally produced copies of Zuni Glaze Ware types and Hidden Mountain Polychrome are always tempered with sherd, the temper choice associated with Zuni immigrants and their descendants (Eckert 2003:79–81). Further, bright white slips are used only on these types. The temper and ceramic type data, combined, suggest that migration history was an important factor in group identity from the time of an immigrant group's arrival to the end of the village's occupation.

Immigrants appear to have been signaling their unique migration histories on two different levels. Early

Rio Grande Glaze-on-yellow and Hidden Mountain Polychrome are the only two glaze-decorated bowl types that do not have a red-slipped exterior. These vessels would have been noticeably different from the more typical bowls with a red exterior, even from across a room, kiva, or plaza space. Because of this public distinctiveness, it seems reasonable that the scale of signaling by these vessel types would have been below the scale of the village, but above the scale of the immediate family. Local copies of Zuni Glaze Ware and Pottery Mound Polychrome, on the other hand, do have red-slipped exteriors. Only people within the immediate vicinity of a glaze-decorated bowl would notice the unique decoration on the interior of these vessels. As such, the exterior of these bowls may have been signaling membership on the village-wide level, while the interior was signaling group affiliation to people who were probably members of

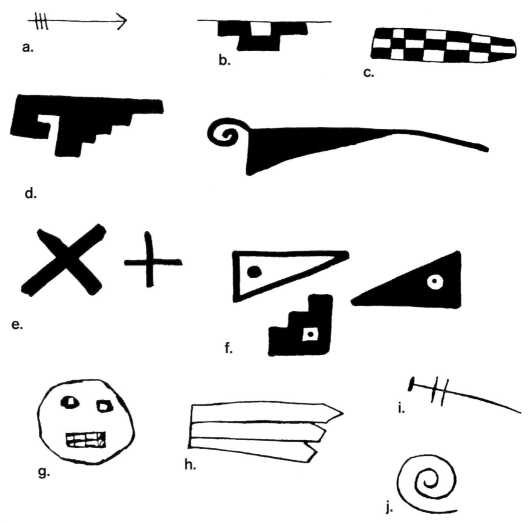

FIGURE 4.5

Examples of icons found on locally produced glaze-decorated bowl types at Pottery Mound.
(Drawing by Suzanne Eckert.)

the same intimate social group. Bowl interior decoration may have served to remind members of their group obligations and reaffirm their group's unique heritage.

ICONS

Icons are representations of identifiable objects (such as birds or clouds) portrayed, in this instance, on pottery. Graves and I (1998) found that Rio Grande Glaze Ware bowls have a specific suite of icons regularly portrayed on them that is different than the suite of icons portrayed on contemporaneous white ware and biscuit ware bowls. We argue that glaze-decorated vessels were used to convey information concerning belief in a regional religious sect. As part of our analysis, we analyzed whole glaze-decorated bowls from Pottery Mound and found that the same suite of icons appears on these vessels as on glaze-decorated bowls in the Rio Grande region. Crown (1994) has associated many of these icons with a pan-southwestern ideology emphasizing fertility, rain making, and community well-being.

Graves and I considered icons on whole vessels, often with little to no provenience information. As such, it was difficult for us to consider changes through time in iconic representation and associated ideology. However, Clark

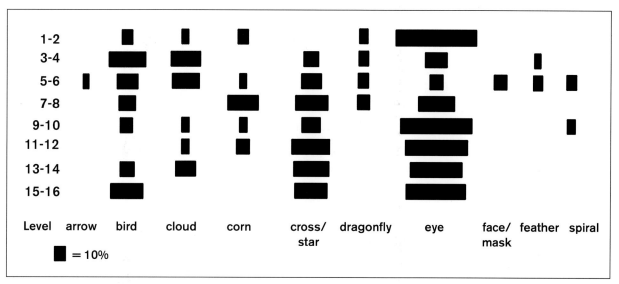

FIGURE 4.6

Stratigraphic changes in icons found on locally produced glaze-decorated bowl types at Pottery Mound.

and I (2004) have recently examined the avifaunal assemblage through time at Pottery Mound and found that the proportion of certain nonfood bird species changes over the occupation of the village. We argue that the feathers of these nonfood bird species were collected for ritual use and that the changes in proportions over time may reflect modifications in the ritual system. The increased frequency of perching bird remains may indicate the introduction of new ritual paraphernalia that more extensively utilized the feathers of these birds. To explore changes in ritual practice and ideology at Pottery Mound further, I examine changes in iconic motifs over time on glaze-decorated sherds.

I use "iconic motif" to mean any image with formal similarities to a referent (Crown 1994:134). I do not attempt to interpret these images here but rather am looking to see if certain iconic motifs co-occur, or if some iconic motifs never occur together. However, I do recognize that naming such images "clouds" or "serpents" automatically dictates a certain interpretation. I use these terms as a way to remain consistent with previous research (Adams 1991; Crotty 1990; Crown 1994; Fewkes 1973; Graves and Eckert 1998). Although other iconic motifs were identified on ceramic sherds at Pottery Mound, I focus on what appear to be the most common in the assemblage as a whole.

Because the frequency of identifiable iconic motifs on sherds is relatively low, I combined level data to help control for sample size issues. However, only 128 sherds

had identifiable iconic motifs, and so the findings reported here are suggestive, but only tentative. Ten iconic motifs occur on locally produced glaze-decorated bowl sherds at Pottery Mound: arrows, birds, clouds, corn (checkerboard), crosses, dragonflies, "eyes," faces/masks, feathers, and spirals (Figure 4.5). The diversity of iconic motifs increases through time (Figure 4.6) but does not appear to correspond with the arrival of immigrants from Hopi (at Level 14) or Zuni (at Level 12). Also, iconic motifs crosscut all ceramic and temper types (Eckert 2003:109–12). This suggests that no iconic motifs were associated with a specific immigrant or indigenous group. The increased diversity of iconic motifs over time, however, may reflect modifications to the village's ritual system. What such modifications were is impossible to know, but they may have included the introduction of new ceremonies or the broadening of old ceremonies to incorporate new imagery and/or paraphernalia. Combined, the temper data, ceramic type data, and iconic motif data all show a pattern of increased heterogeneity in ceramic material culture over time. In the first half of the village's occupation, this heterogeneity can be explained by the arrival of immigrants. However, the continued heterogeneity throughout time implies that these immigrants were not completely incorporated into a village-wide identity. It appears that residents at Pottery Mound segregated themselves into social groups based, at least in part, on migration history.

Social Implications of Increased Diversity in Decorated Bowl Attributes

The above analysis has implications for three aspects of understanding the social dynamics surrounding immigration into Pottery Mound: the timing of migration, the size of immigrant groups, and the segregation and incorporation of immigrants within the village. It also has implications for studies of migration at other Pueblo sites, especially in terms of considering the gender of immigrants and changes in material culture.

Timing of Migration

Two different immigrant groups moved into Pottery Mound at two different times. If we assume that each excavation level covers approximately six years of occupation, then Hopi immigrants arrived approximately 18 years, and Zuni immigrants arrived approximately 30 years, after the village was established by local groups. In other words, immigrants at Pottery Mound did not help to establish the village. As immigrants moved into Pottery Mound, they had to negotiate their position in an established social system with its own recognized hierarchy, daily organization, preferred language, and calendar of events. Although we cannot know the specifics of how these negotiations were resolved, they appear to have been successful in the sense that immigrants, their descendants, and indigenous groups lived together in Pottery Mound for another 70 to 80 years.

Size of Immigrant Groups

If it is assumed that the percentage of new temper types or specific ceramic types reflects the percentage of immigrants living in Pottery Mound, then the scale of immigration was small. Untempered vessels, associated with Hopi immigrants, never comprise more than 8 percent of the glaze-decorated bowl assemblage. Sherd-tempered vessels, associated with Zuni immigrants, never comprise more than 2 percent of the assemblage. However, temper may be a poor proxy for immigrant group size: local clays are difficult to work without adding temper and so immigrant Hopi potters may have had to change their temper selection; the production choices that result in the difference between "sherd temper" and "sherd-with-mixed-rock temper" are not understood, and so some Zuni immigrant potters may have had vessels with mixed rock in them.

Ceramic type can also be used as a proxy for immigrant group size. Early Rio Grande Glaze-on-yellow and Pottery Mound Polychrome, both associated with immigrants from Hopi, comprise 10–20 percent of the glaze-decorated bowl assemblage. Local copies of Zuni Glaze Ware types and Hidden Mountain Polychrome, associated with immigrants from Zuni, comprise 3–12 percent of the assemblage. However, these types may not be an appropriate proxy for the size of an immigrant group for two reasons. First, in some contexts, immigrants may have attempted to minimize visible differences to "fit in" with their host community (Clark 2001). Technological evidence suggests that immigrant potters may have been making their own unique types *as well as* the more common early Rio Grande Glaze-on-red type (Eckert 2003:112–15). Another reason that ceramic type is not a good proxy is that some local potters may have produced types associated with immigrants. Many of the early Rio Grande Glaze-on-yellows have technological traits associated with local potters. This mixing of local and immigrant technological and decorative traits may be the result of intermarriage of groups throughout time. If any single immigrant group was never more than 20 percent of the population at Pottery Mound, then intermarriage between local and immigrant groups would have become unavoidable in the 100+ years of occupation of the site.

Segregation and Incorporation

Immigrant potters, whether they were from Hopi or Zuni, decorated their vessels in such a way as to signal their unique migration history. However, they were using glaze-decorated bowls to emphasize their heritage in two ways. Some bowls produced by immigrants had a red-slipped exterior similar to the vessels produced by local potters. As such, only people within the immediate vicinity of a bowl would notice the decoration on the interior. These vessels would have signaled contradictory types of information: to those viewing the vessels from a distance, these vessels signaled village-wide membership; to those viewing the vessels from nearby, these vessels signaled the potter's unique heritage. Immigrant potters also produced vessels that were distinct, even from across a room or plaza space. These glaze-decorated bowls had either a yellow- or white-slipped exterior. Because of this public distinctiveness, it seems reasonable that these vessels were used to emphasize a potter's unique heritage to those that were not part of her family group. Immigrants to Pottery Mound, then, were attempting to both incorporate and segregate themselves within the village. Although these behaviors may have been contradictory, both would have provided benefits that an immigrant would want to take advantage of.

Migration histories could have played an important role in various aspects of a potter's life, including defining potential marriage and exchange partners, access to natural and sociopolitical resources, and who could be called upon in times of economic needs. Immigrants' distinctiveness could have been reflected by differences in any number of aspects of daily living: language, oral tradition, making tools, forming a ceramic vessel, building or remodeling a roomblock. Ideological differences concerning the ritual calendar, marriage practices, or social etiquette may also have divided groups. As such, these different histories would have played a role in defining the social incompatibility and tensions within a village. Because immigrants at Pottery Mound wanted to hold on to some aspects of their unique heritage, only some aspects of social practice would have been negotiable to change. Potters, and their associated social groups, would have wanted to reaffirm their identity by keeping core practices that reflected "who they were." Part of this reaffirmation appears to have been visual reminders on pottery.

At the same time that immigrants would embrace their history, they also shared daily interactions with indigenous residents of Pottery Mound. Immigrants and locals alike would have struggled with the same daily issues: how to negotiate their identity within a new social context of immigration, environmental concerns stemming from being agriculturalists in an arid environment, keeping the cosmos in balance, and daily domestic concerns over sickness, childbirth, marriage, and death. These shared struggles, and the need to work together to overcome some of them, would have resulted in immigrant potters wanting to emphasize their village membership. By producing pottery with the same suite of icons, similar colored slips (at least on the exterior), and glaze paint, potters from diverse backgrounds would have been able to create a visual sense of unity and oneness.

Immigrants in the Pueblo Southwest

Pottery Mound was not the only prehispanic Pueblo village that had immigrant and indigenous residents living together. During the thirteenth and fourteenth centuries in the Pueblo Southwest, immigrant groups moved across much of the Pueblo landscape (Cameron 1995; Duff 1998; 2002; Lindsay 1987; Plog 1979). These migrations, like previous and later migrations, redefined group identity. In each village where immigrants arrived, issues of segregation and incorporation would have been negotiated as diverse social groups tried to find a way to live together. How these negotiations were played out would have varied by the timing of the migration, immigrant and local group size, reasons for migration, and the idiosyncrasies of the individuals involved. This study provides two factors to consider when studying immigration at other southwestern sites.

To begin with, this study (along with many others in Southwest archaeology) focuses on pottery production. It is generally agreed upon that, in the prehispanic Southwest, this was the realm of women (Shepard 1956). The current study traces the behaviors of immigrant potters, and therefore immigrant women. Immigrant men and women may have moved in different worlds. Although it is often assumed that migration occurred on the household level (Duff 1998), migration on a small scale could also have been the result of marriage practices. The immigrant groups at Pottery Mound were apparently small. The gender makeup of these groups, therefore, may have played an important role in how social negotiations were played out within each group, as well as between different immigrant and indigenous groups. To truly understand immigrant social behaviors, we need to track other aspects of material culture that may be either gender neutral or male-gender specific. Specifically, although women were making ceramic vessels, it can be reasonably assumed that both men and women were using the vessels. Understanding the social contexts in which different ceramic types associated with immigrants were used would be one step toward this endeavor.

This study also shows that the majority of glaze-decorated bowls produced by immigrants were not simply copies of pottery types that they had produced in their homeland. In this analysis, locally produced copies of Zuni Glaze Ware types comprise the lowest frequency of immigrant-produced pottery types. It appears that immigrant potters were *referencing* their homeland using specific decorative attributes. Zuni potters incorporated bright white slips on Hidden Mountain Polychrome, while Hopi potters incorporated yellow slips and asymmetrical design styles on Pottery Mound Polychrome. However, neither of these local types were produced in Zuni or Hopi. Hidden Mountain Polychrome incorporates a white slip and a design focus on the exterior, a practice not seen in the Zuni region. Pottery Mound Polychrome incorporates glaze paint and a red slip on the exterior, a combination not seen on the Hopi Mesas.

As such, archaeologists should not necessarily expect to find material traditions that can be traced directly back to an immigrant's homeland. Rather, immigrant material culture may combine their homeland traditions with local traditions to create a new suite of attributes.

Conclusions: Immigrants and Changing Social Dynamics

Archaeologists have tended to focus on detecting the presence of immigrants in prehispanic Pueblo sites rather than on the social consequences of immigration. Such consequences, however, played a role in social organization, ritual systems, production and distribution of material culture, and other aspects of behavior that archaeologists are concerned with. Prehispanic immigrants and indigenous groups needed to negotiate various social dynamics when living together, including redefining identity within a new social context. In some instances, immigrants would have found it beneficial to emphasize their unique migration history; in other instances, it would have been more beneficial to emphasize a unified village membership. Daily interactions with indigenous groups and other immigrants would have influenced these processes of segregation and incorporation. It is this aspect of immigration that I have focused on in this analysis.

I argue that we can begin to understand the dynamics of segregation and incorporation through analysis of material culture that articulates with various levels of social identity. The migrations that characterized the thirteenth- and fourteenth-century Pueblo Southwest involved more than a demographic reorganization; they resulted in changes in social identity as disparate groups began to live together within villages. Prior to immigration into Pottery Mound, local potters within the site produced a narrow range of glaze-decorated bowl types that were tempered with various local materials. These temper choices reflect different pottery production traditions that had long precedence in the region and do not reflect social groups who divided themselves by different migration histories. As immigrants moved into the village, new technologies and decorative attributes were introduced. The continued use of a diverse suite of temper choices throughout the occupation of the site suggests that immigrants and indigenous groups continued to separate themselves, at least during pottery production. The increased diversity in decorative attributes suggests that immigrants' migration history became an important component of residents' identity. However, the mixing of aspects of immigrant and local decorative traditions, as well as increased diversity of iconic representations, suggest that various aspects of social behavior may have been expanded during this period. Immigrant identity changed to allow for both an emphasis on migration history on some level, as well as the ability to embrace a village-wide identity on another level. This redefining of identity reflects the complex dynamics of incorporation and segregation that immigrants throughout the Pueblo Southwest would have negotiated in different ways, depending on time and place. ⁂

NOTES

1. Artifacts and documentation from Pottery Mound are curated at the Maxwell Museum, University of New Mexico, Albuquerque.

2. A sherd was identified as a bowl based upon curvature and the presence of two slipped surfaces. A sherd was identified as a glaze-decorated bowl upon the presence of glaze paint on one or both surfaces.

3. See Eckert (2003:252–61) for a discussion on how these various temper types were named and described by previous petrographers including Anna Shepard, Helene Warren, Elizabeth Garrett, Judith Habicht-Mauche, and Patricia Capone.

4. Agua Fria Gl/r, Cienguilla Gl/y, and San Clemente Polychrome are all Rio Grande Glaze Ware types that require the rim for identification. Since both body and rim sherds were used in this analysis, they have been included in a broader classification that uses slip and paint color combinations, but not rim form, for identification. These pottery types are described in detail in Eckert (2003).

5. Although Rio Grande Glaze-on-yellow is found throughout much of the Rio Grande area, the version produced at Pottery Mound has a distinctive yellow-buff color that appears to be unique to the Lower Rio Puerco area and is the same color as the yellow slip on the interior of Pottery Mound Polychrome. Due to the similarity in the yellow slip color, the similarity in tempers, and the similarity in the timing of their appearance, I believe that the same potters produced both wares.

REFERENCES CITED

Adams, E. C.
  1991 *The Origin and Development of the Pueblo Katsina Cult.* University of Arizona Press, Tucson.

Arnold, D. E.
  1985 Patterns of Learning, Residence and Descent among Potters in Ticul, Yucatan, Mexico. In *Archaeological Approaches to Cultural Identity*, edited by S. J. Shennan, pp. 174–84. Routledge, London.

Beal, John D.
  1987 *Foundation of the Rio Grande Classic: The Lower Chama River, A.D. 1300–1500.* Southwest Archaeological Consultants, Inc. Manuscript prepared for the Office of Cultural Affairs, Historic Preservation Division, New Mexico.

Brandt, E. A.
  1977 The Role of Secrecy in a Pueblo Society. In *Flowers of the Wind: Papers on Ritual, Myth and Symbolism in California and the Southwest*, edited by T. C. Blackburn, pp. 11–28. Ballena Press, Socorro, New Mexico.

  1979 Sandia Pueblo. In *Southwest*, edited by A. Ortiz, pp. 343–50. Handbook of North American Indians, Vol. 9. Smithsonian Institution, Washington, D.C.

  1994 Egalitarianism, Hierarchy and Centralization in the Pueblos. In *The Ancient Southwest Community: Models and Methods for the Study of Prehistoric Social Organization*, edited by W. H. Wills and Robert D. Leonard, pp. 9–24. University of New Mexico Press, Albuquerque.

Brody, J. J.
  1964 Design Analysis of the Rio Grande Glaze Pottery of Pottery Mound, New Mexico. Unpublished Master's thesis, Department of Art History, University of New Mexico, Albuquerque.

Bunzel, R. L.
  1932 *Zuni Ceremonialism.* University of New Mexico Press, Albuquerque.

Cameron, C. M.
  1995 Migration and the Movement of Southwestern Peoples. Special Issue: Migration and the Movement of Southwestern Peoples, edited by Catherine M. Cameron. *Journal of Anthropological Archaeology* 14(2):104–24.

Cancian, F.

1980 Risk and Uncertainty in Agricultural Decision Making. In *Agricultural Decision Making: Anthropological Contributions to Rural Development*, edited by P. Barlett, pp. 161–76. Academic Press, New York.

Capone, P.

1998 The Wright Collection of Southwestern Pottery: Perspectives in Pottery Making and Collecting. In *Makers and Markets: The Wright Collection of Twentieth-Century Native American Art*, edited by P. Drooker, pp. 35–84. Peabody Museum Press, Cambridge, Massachusetts.

2006 Rio Grande Glaze Ware Technology and Production: Historic Expediency. In *The Social Life of Pots: Glaze Wares and Cultural Dynamics in the Southwest, A.D. 1250–1680*, edited by J. A. Habicht-Mauche, S. L. Eckert, and D. Huntley, pp. 216–231. University of Arizona Press, Tucson.

Carlson, R. L.

1982 The Mimbres Kachina Cult. In *Mogollon Archaeology: Proceedings of the 1980 Mogollon Conference*, edited by P. H. Beckett and K. Silverbird, pp. 147–67. Acoma Books, Ramona, California.

Clark, J. J.

2001 *Tracking Prehistoric Migrations, Pueblo Settlers among the Tonto Basin Hohokam.* Anthropological Papers of the University of Arizona No. 6. University of Arizona Press, Tucson.

Clark, T., and S. L. Eckert

2004 The Ritual Use of Birds in 14th Century Central New Mexico. Poster presented at the 69th Annual Meeting of the Society for American Archaeology, Montreal.

Costin, C. L.

1998 Introduction: Craft and Social Identity. In *Craft and Social Identity*, edited by Cathy Lynne Costin and Rita P. Wright, pp. 3–18. Archeological Papers of the American Anthropological Association No. 8. American Anthropological Association, Arlington, Virginia.

Creamer, W., and L. Renken

1994 Testing Conventional Wisdom: Protohistoric Ceramics and Chronology in the Northern Rio Grande. Paper presented at the 59th Annual Meeting of the Society for American Archaeology, Anaheim.

Crotty, H. K.

1990 Protohistoric Anasazi Kiva Murals: Variation in Imagery as a Reflection of Differing Social Contexts. Manuscript on file, Maxwell Museum of Anthropology, University of New Mexico, Albuquerque.

Crown, P. L.

1994 *Ceramics and Ideology: Salado Polychrome Pottery.* University of New Mexico Press, Albuquerque.

Dozier, E. P.

1966 *Hano: A Tewa Community in Arizona.* Holt, Rinehart and Winston, New York.

Duff, A. I.

1998 The Process of Migration in the Late Prehistoric Southwest. In *Migration and Reorganization: The Pueblo IV Period in the American Southwest*, edited by K. A. Spielmann, pp. 31–52. Arizona State University Anthropological Research Papers No. 51. Arizona State University, Tempe.

2002 *Western Pueblo Identities: Regional Interaction, Migration, and Transformation.* University of Arizona Press, Tucson.

Durand, S. R., and W. B. Hurst

1991 A Refinement of Anasazi Cultural Chronology in the Middle Río Puerco Valley Using Multidimensional Scaling. In *Anasazi Puebloan Adaptation in Response to Climatic Stress: Prehistory of the Middle Río Puerco Valley*, pp. 233–55. Bureau of Land Management, Albuquerque, New Mexico.

Eckert, S. L.

2003 Social Boundaries, Immigration, and Ritual Systems: A Case Study from the American Southwest. Unpublished Ph.D. dissertation, Department of Anthropology, Arizona State University, Tempe.

2006   The Production and Distribution of Glaze-Painted Pottery in the Pueblo Southwest: A Synthesis. In *The Social Life of Pots: Glaze Wares and Cultural Dynamics in the Southwest, A.D. 1250–1680*, edited by J. A. Habicht-Mauche, S. L. Eckert, and D. Huntley. University of Arizona Press, Tucson.

Edelman, S. A.

1979   San Ildefonso Pueblo. In *Southwest*, edited by A. Ortiz, pp. 308–16. Handbook of North American Indians, Vol. 9. Smithsonian Institution, Washington, D.C.

Eggan, F.

1950   *Social Organization of the Western Pueblos.* University of Chicago Press, Chicago.

Ellis, F.

1979   Isleta Pueblo. In *Southwest*, edited by A. Ortiz, pp. 308–16. Handbook of North American Indians, Vol. 9. Smithsonian Institution, Washington, D.C.

Ferguson, T. J.

1989   Comment on Social Integration and Anasazi Architecture. In *The Architecture of Social Integration in Prehistoric Pueblos*, edited by W. D. Lipe and M. Hegmon, pp. 169–74. Occasional Papers of the Crow Canyon Archaeological Center No. 1. Crow Canyon Archaeological Center, Cortez, Colorado.

Fewkes, J. W.

1973   *Prehistoric Hopi Pottery Designs.* Dover Press, New York.

Goffman, E.

1974   *Frame Analysis: An Essay on the Organization of Experience.* Harper and Row, New York.

Graves, W., and S. L. Eckert.

1998   Decorated Ceramic Distributions and Ideological Developments in the Rio Grande Valley, New Mexico. In *Migration and Reorganization: The Pueblo IV Period in the American Southwest*, edited by K. Spielmann, pp. 263–84. Arizona State University Anthropological Research Paper No. 51. Arizona State University, Tempe.

Haury, E. W.

1958   Evidence at Point of Pines for a Prehistoric Migration from Northern Arizona. In *Migrations in New World Culture History*, edited by R. H. Thompson, pp. 1–6. University of Arizona Social Science Bulletin No. 27. University of Arizona Press, Tucson.

Hegmon, M.

1989   Social Integration and Architecture. In *The Architecture of Social Integration in Prehistoric Pueblos*, edited by W. D. Lipe and M. Hegmon, pp. 5–14. Occasional Papers of the Crow Canyon Archaeological Center No. 1. Crow Canyon Archaeological Center, Cortez, Colorado.

1995   *The Social Dynamics of Pottery Style in the Early Puebloan Southwest.* Occasional Papers of the Crow Canyon Archaeological Center No. 5. Crow Canyon Archaeological Center, Cortez, Colorado.

Hegmon, M., M. C. Nelson, and S. M. Ruth

1998   Abandonment and Reorganization in the Mimbres Region of the American Southwest. *American Anthropologist* 100(1):148–62.

Herr, S., and J. J. Clark

1997   Patterns in the Pathways: Early Historic Migrations in the Río Grande Pueblos. *Kiva* 62(4):365–90.

Hibben, F. C.

1955   Excavations at Pottery Mound, New Mexico. *American Antiquity* 21(2):179–80.

Hodder, I.

1982   *Symbols in Action: Ethnoarchaeological Studies of Material Culture.* Cambridge University Press, Cambridge.

Kroeber, A.

1917   *Zuni Kin and Clan.* Anthropological Papers of the American Museum of Natural History Vol. 18, Part II, pp. 39–204. New York.

Lange, C. H.

1979   Cochiti Pueblo. In *Southwest*, edited by A. Ortiz, pp. 366–78. Handbook of North American Indians, Vol. 9. Smithsonian Institution, Washington, D.C.

Lechtman, H.

1977   Style in Technology: Some Early Thoughts. In *Material Culture, Style, Organization, and Dynamics of Technology*, edited by H. Lechtman and R. S. Merrill, pp. 3–20. West Publishing, St. Paul, Minnesota.

Levy, J. E.

1992   *Orayvi Revisited: Social Stratification in an "Egalitarian" Society.* School of American Research, Santa Fe, New Mexico.

Lewis, L., E. Lewis Mitchell, and D. Lewis Garcia

1990   *Daughters of the Anasazi.* Produced and directed by John Anthony. 28 minutes. Second Sight Productions, Indianapolis, Indiana.

Lindsay, A. J.

1987   Anasazi Population Movements to Southeastern Arizona. *American Archaeology* 6(3):190–98.

Mindeleff, V.

1891   *A Study of Pueblo Architecture in Tusayan and Cibola.* Bureau of American Ethnology Eighth Annual Report, 1886–1887, pp. 13–228. U.S. Government Printing Office, Washington, D.C.

Naranjo, T.

1995   Thoughts on Migration by Santa Clara Pueblo. Special Issue: Migration and the Movement of Southwestern Peoples, edited by Catherine M. Cameron. *Journal of Anthropological Archaeology* 14(2):247–50.

Nequatewa, E.

1936   *Truth of a Hopi: Stories Relating to the Origin, Myths, and Clan Histories of the Hopi.* Northland Publishing, Flagstaff, Arizona.

Ortiz, A.

1969   *The Tewa World: Space, Time, Being and Becoming in a Pueblo Society.* University of Chicago Press, Chicago.

Parsons, E. C.

1926   *Tewa Tales.* University of Arizona Press, Tucson.

1928   The Laguna Migration to Isleta. *American Anthropologist* 30(4):602–13.

1939   *Pueblo Indian Religion.* University of Chicago Press, Chicago.

Plog, F.

1979   Prehistory: Western Anasazi. In *Southwest*, edited by A. Ortiz, pp. 108–30. Handbook of North American Indians, Vol. 9. Smithsonian Institution, Washington, D.C.

Potter, J. M.

1997   Communal Ritual, Feasting, and Social Differentiation in Late Prehistoric Zuni Communities. Unpublished Ph.D. dissertation, Department of Anthropology, Arizona State University, Tempe.

Rice, P. M.

1987   *Pottery Analysis: A Source Book.* University of Chicago Press, Chicago.

Sando, J. S.

1979   Jemez Pueblo. In *Southwest*, edited by A. Ortiz, pp. 418–29. Handbook of North American Indians, Vol. 9. Smithsonian Institution, Washington, D.C.

1982   *Nee Hemish: A History of Jemez Pueblo.* University of New Mexico Press, Albuquerque.

Schroeder, A. H.

1979   Pecos Pueblo. In *Southwest*, edited by A. Ortiz, pp. 430–37. Handbook of North American Indians, Vol. 9. Smithsonian Institution, Washington, D.C.

Shepard, A. O.

1942   *Rio Grande Glaze Paint Ware: A Study Illustrating the Place of Ceramic Technological Analysis in Archaeological Research.* Contributions to American Anthropology and History No. 39. Carnegie Institution of Washington, Washington, D.C.

1956   *Ceramics for the Archaeologist.* Carnegie Institution of Washington Publication No. 609. Carnegie Institution of Washington, Washington, D.C.

Snow, D. H.

1989   A Very Brief Overview of Rio Grande Glaze and Matte-Paint Ceramics. Manuscript prepared for New Mexico Archaeological Council, Rio Grande Ceramic Workshop, Santa Fe, New Mexico.

Spielmann, K. A.

1998 Ritual Influences on the Development of Rio Grande Glaze A Ceramics. In *Migration and Reorganization: The Pueblo IV Period in the American Southwest*, edited by Katherine A. Spielmann, pp. 253–61. Arizona State University Anthropological Research Paper No. 51. Arizona State University, Tempe.

Stanislawski, M. B.

1979 Hopi-Tewa. In *Southwest*, edited by A. Ortiz, pp. 587–602. Handbook of North American Indians, Vol. 9. Smithsonian Institution, Washington, D.C.

Strong, P. T.

1979 San Felipe Pueblo. In *Southwest*, edited by A. Ortiz, pp. 390–97. Handbook of North American Indians, Vol. 9. Smithsonian Institution, Washington, D.C.

Vivian, P. B.

1961 *Kachina: The Study of Pueblo Animism and Anthropomorphism within the Ceremonial Wall Paintings of Pottery Mound, and the Jeddito*. Unpublished Master's thesis, Department of Art, State University of Iowa, Iowa City.

Voll, C. B.

1961 *The Glaze Paint Ceramics of Pottery Mound, New Mexico*. Unpublished Master's thesis, University of New Mexico, Albuquerque.

Warren, A. H.

1982 Pottery of the Lower Rio Puerco, 1980–1981. In *Inventory Survey of the Lower Hidden Mountain Floodpool, Lower Rio Puerco Drainage, Central New Mexico*, edited by P. L. Eidenbach, pp. 139–68. Human Systems Research, Inc., Tularosa, New Mexico.

Warren, A. H., and D. H. Snow

1976 Formal Descriptions of Rio Grande Glazes from LA 70. In *Archaeological Excavations at Pueblo del Encierro, LA 70; Cochiti Dam Salvage Project, Cochiti, New Mexico: Final Report, 1964–1965 Field Seasons*, assembled by D. H. Snow, pp. C1–C34. Laboratory of Anthropology Notes No. 98. Museum of New Mexico, Santa Fe.

Wiessner, P.

1983 Style and Social Information in Kalahari San Projectile Points. *American Antiquity* 48:253–76.

Wobst, H. M.

1977 Stylistic Behavior and Information Exchange. In *Papers for the Director: Research Essays in Honor of James B. Griffin*, edited by C. E. Cleland, pp. 317–42. Anthropological Papers No. 67. Museum of Anthropology, University of Michigan, Ann Arbor.

CHAPTER FIVE

The Kiva Murals of Pottery Mound
A History of Discovery and Methods of Study: Kivas 1–10

Patricia Vivian

The scientific and public value of discovering and recording kiva murals at Pottery Mound was recognized by Frank C. Hibben as early as the 1954 summer field season at the University of New Mexico, and efforts were made in the following years to find additional kivas as sources of mural art. Sixteen kivas were located during the 1954, 1955, 1957, 1958, and 1961 field seasons, and most were excavated or partially cleared. It is not certain when Kiva 17 was discovered. It appeared on Hibben's 1975 map and must have been found sometime after 1966 because Hibben reported only 16 kivas at that time. Moreover, he commented in *Kiva Art of the Anasazi at Pottery Mound* that "as this is being written a dig at the seventeenth kiva is being conducted, an excavation made necessary in order to rescue its precious paintings from vandalism of careless artifact-hunters" (Hibben 1975:12). However, in 1987 he included Kiva 17 among the cultural features "doomed to destruction" because of their proximity to the eroding bank of the Rio Puerco (Hibben 1987:3). During these field seasons students were routinely assigned to work in the kivas where they carried out multiple tasks, including mural scraping and recording. On the other hand, their notes do not provide enough details of this work. The following includes information from students' reports on kivas located, excavated, and recorded.

Discovery: The Field Schools

Four kivas were discovered in 1954, but work apparently was only carried out in Kiva 1, which was found on June 21 shortly after the field season started. Three days later a student noted that "Henry, an Indian worker, started an accurate color painting, after we finished taking the project and still pictures." On July 6 a student reported that new paintings in this kiva had been uncovered, and other notes indicated that students Natalie Vytlacil, Gretchen Steiner, Harry Menagh, and Jerome (Jerry) Brody were recording exposed murals. Brody also produced a plan drawing of Kiva 1 and a scaled drawing of figures on the east wall, one of which was a kilted man holding a bird.

Brody's notes, moreover, included his observations on wall preservation and mural removal. He reported that some collapsed wall fragments found on the kiva floor had been jacketed and observed that some of the burlap backing on these fragments had to be reinforced because they had fallen out of the jacket. Standing wall murals were not jacketed, but Brody's notes suggested a method for removing them intact from the wall using tissue paper and plaster. He pointed out that the wall sections were too large to remove as a single unit but recommended creating "artificial breaks" in the wall to remove "a strip of painting 6 inches wide without losing more than a quarter of an inch of painting on either side of the break." In some respects, it may be unfortunate that his recommendations were not implemented.

Kiva 2 was probably opened this year also. Beverly Meeker referenced a "Painted Kiva #2," though a penciled revision (likely made by dig foreman Russell Schorsch) of Meeker's notes changed the kiva number to 3. This may be an error. Kiva 3 was not excavated until 1957, though a portion of it was found in 1954 below Room 12. Kiva 4 was discovered during trenching operations in the southern zone of the site (Lateral Southeast Trench), but it is not certain if it was opened in 1954.

No new kivas were located in 1955, but work continued on recording murals in Kivas 1 and 2, which at that time were referenced by Roman numerals, a system that was changed to Arabic by 1957. Work on murals in both kivas seems to have been started before the entire structures were excavated to the floor. Recording presumably was under the direction of Natalie Vytlacil, though John Vaughn may have assisted her. Student notes of 1955 indicate that at various times they were assigned to "scrape walls" in Kiva 1 where work was focused on the east, west, and south walls. At least seven layers were removed from the east wall,

when on July 20 Sofia Yen "drew the Tassel-like pattern in actual size on the board for our 'official artist' to record the design." On July 21 she reported a "Cerullian [sic] Blue design on the bottom." Work on the south wall was also carried out to at least the seventh layer. Pat Gerster reported a "blue layer" on the third layer of this wall. The west wall was scraped down to the fourth layer. At least one section of the north wall in Kiva 1 was jacketed because much of the wall had fallen into the kiva. Hibben (1975:18) attributed this loss to deliberate prehistoric destruction. Yen reported on July 22 that "since we decided to jacket the northeast corner of the (north) wall with a design of a man holding a bird in his arm, I continued to scrape the east corner of the South wall." James DeBolt reported that he spent two weeks "scraping walls" in Kivas 1 and 2, but no other students referenced work in Kiva 2.

In 1957 two new kivas, 5 and 6, were discovered during trenching operations. Kiva 1 had been completed, and work was carried out in Kivas 2, 3, 4, 5, and 6. Vytlacil continued to supervise mural recording in 1957, and Sandra Strong assisted her in Kiva 2. Ed Dobson also was "put to work in Kiva 2 on paints" (tempera in 1957), scraping walls, and, by July 17, "recording murals." At least five mural layers were exposed in Kiva 2 during this summer. Larry Hammack completed the excavation of Kiva 3 and made scaled plans of the floor. There are no student notes concerning recovery of murals from this kiva. Barbara Alaire's notes indicate that she worked in Kiva 4, which was completed on July 30, near the end of the scheduled field season. She reported red paint on the north wall but gave no other details. Pauline Dix (Polly Schaafsma) recorded a number of details in Kiva 5 including the discovery of two major roof supports ("huge cedar log support"), "a crude painting of what appears to be a feathered staff in red and white," and "signs of paint," black and red, extending along the north wall from the northeast corner.

The west wall of Kiva 6 was discovered in a trench late in the season of 1957 just prior to a student field trip to Chaco. Gwinn Vivian and Natalie Vytlacil recommended backfilling the trench to preserve the wall for work the following summer. Hibben, however, cleared most of this wall during the weekend while Vytlacil, Vivian, and the students were in Chaco. The exposed mural was recorded and a second (and possibly a third) layer was scraped and recorded before the end of the field season. During this work it was determined that the wall was extremely fragile because of the nature of wall construction. Unlike many kiva walls at Pottery Mound that were of adobe, Kiva 6 walls were basically of pole and adobe daub. A space for the kiva had been excavated into refuse deposits and the sides of this space were then lined with upright poles identified in the field as pine and juniper. A thick coating of adobe was applied over the poles and this coating served as a base for plastered layers with murals. As fill in the kiva was removed during excavation, the pressure of refuse behind the walls tended to force them into the void created by the open trench. The decision was made to jacket the exposed portion of the west wall at the end of the field season. However, during jacketing the additional weight of the plaster caused this section of the wall to lean forward more precariously. The jacketed section was braced with lumber from the field lab ramada and the open trench was backfilled. There is an error in Hibben's (1975) identification of the mural that appeared on the first layer of this wall. He incorrectly identified a mural that he called "soul faces" (and in 1957 called "the star people") as being on Layer 1 of the west wall (Hibben 1975:Figures 106–7). This particular mural was on the second layer and underlay a panel of alternating seated human figures and mountain lions. This panel is illustrated on the title page of Hibben's 1975 book. Hibben (1975:Figures 47–48) identified it as the "Council of the Mountain Lions" and did note in this figure label that the title-page panel was on Layer 1 of the west wall.

Student notes for 1958 from the University of New Mexico field school provide fairly good information on mural exposure and recording in Kivas 2, 5, 6, and 7 and good detail on the removal of jacketed murals from Kiva 6. At least three students (Anne Barnes, Dee Torres, and Dee Mullinex) continued to scrape and record murals in Kiva 2. Although specific walls were not indicated, work on Layers 19 and 21 was noted, which is interesting given the 1957 record of five layers being exposed in this kiva. Barnes also reported on July 3, "Put a face jacket on a section of Kiva 2 in the southeast corner." It was not indicated if this section of wall was removed or left in place. We know an attempt was made to remove some jacketed wall fragments from Kiva 6 in 1958, but it is not clear if jacketed fragments in other kivas were left permanently in backfill or removed to the laboratory in Albuquerque.

Details on work in Kiva 5 in 1958 are less specific, presumably reflecting the more limited exposures of murals. At least four students (Ronnie Morrison, Barnes, Maria Jorrin, and Mullinex) reported scattered paintings but did not give information on layers. Morrison referred

to this kiva as the "big kiva" or "great kiva" and noted "several spots of red and black paint close to the floor." This may be the same paint reported by Dix (Schaafsma) in 1957. Barnes produced a drawing of a "white animal outlined in black" on the north wall, and she noted that "it appeared to have solid black paws and was standing upright." Jorrin worked on the north, south, and west "wall paintings."

According to the most detailed mural notes in 1958 written by Barnes and Torres, work in Kiva 6 was focused on the north and west walls. Although most of the east wall had previously collapsed, Hibben (1975:Figure 54) illustrated a relatively large section of mural from Layer 10 of the east wall. Work to expose the south wall had not yet been started. As previously stated, in 1957 the west wall had been partially exposed, and the first two layers and possibly the third were recorded. The section of the west wall to the right of a doorway was jacketed and supported by lumber as a "preservation measure" and the trench in front of the wall was backfilled. Barnes reported in 1958 that on July 30, after opening the kiva again, "we leaned the west wall back and jacketed the wall that was on the left side of the doorway. Then we patched a few worn places on the leaned wall." Hibben (1960:270) illustrated students working on a wall in Kiva 6, which may have been the north half of the west wall or possibly the east half of the north wall. Barnes had previously noted that the doorway in the west wall was "cut away," presumably to facilitate jacketing of the southern half. Torres stated that this wall was constructed of poles ("most are juniper but some are pine") covered with adobe. She also indicated "twenty-three layers" on the wall—a figure seemingly derived from visible layers on its cut edge.

Because most of the east wall had previously collapsed, work was begun on the north wall, presumably Layer 1, of Kiva 6. This wall was in poor condition, again the result of the pole and adobe construction. However, Hibben (1975:16) stated that it "had also been destroyed, again apparently on purpose." Based on a field sketch by Torres, the exposed mural on Layer 1 was of human figures. Fragments of plaster were uncovered revealing parts of paintings. Human figures similar to those previously found on the first layer of the west wall were exposed. Hibben (1975:Figure 48) illustrated a seated human and "deer-like animal" on the north wall of Kiva 6 that might have been a part of the panel sketched by Torres. The attempt to jacket all remaining portions of the north wall resulted in more destruction. After completion

a.   b.   c.

FIGURE 5.1

The sequence of photographs showing students attempting to lift the jacked mural from Kiva 6 in 1958:
a) lifting (Hibben is to the right of the group); **b**) straining to carry the mural;
c) aftermath. (Photographs by Patricia Bryan Vivian.)

of the jacketing, a number of the more hefty male students attempted to move the east portion into a truck for transport back to the lab in Albuquerque. However, in the process, the plaster cast broke, an incident I recorded in a series of three black and white photographs (Figure 5.1). On the following day, students jacketed the two broken halves of the north wall and a small piece from its middle section. The casts were strengthened and reportedly one of the pieces was brought into the lab while the second was given to the Amerind Foundation. The other pieces may have been left in the kiva. It is also unclear whether remaining pieces of the west wall were reburied in the kiva, which was backfilled for the season.

Student notes indicate that at least three additional kivas, 7 and 8/9, were located and excavated in 1958. Both had multiple layers of murals. Kiva 8 was apparently built over and partially into Kiva 9. Three students (Charles Dustin, Patricia Bryan [Vivian], and Jorrin) spent a day or more in Kiva 7. Bryan (Vivian) reported working on Layers 1, 2, and 3 of the south wall, and Jorrin recorded murals on Layer 2 of an unidentified wall.

There was no field school in 1959, nor in 1960, the latter summer being devoted only to intensive mural work sponsored by the National Science Foundation. This work is described in the following pages. In the summer of 1961, the last field school season at Pottery Mound, Kivas 10 through 16 presumably were discovered. However, student notes only reflect mural recording in Kiva 10, the single circular kiva at the site. Rosemary Older reported on July 31 that "fallen painted plaster was located along the eastern area of the circular wall." She continued "scraping the fallen painted layer" on August 1 and the following day "finished locating the last of the painted plaster along the east wall." It is not known which layer Older was referencing. Polly Schaafsma (personal communication 2005) noted that "there were numerous painted layers" in Kiva 10. She further pointed out that "between Hibben 1975 and my partial review of records on file at the Hibben Center, I have records of paintings on layers 3, 4, 5, 6?, 8–11, 14–17, 21, 23, 29 31." Hibben illustrated a number of other paintings from Kiva 10 (1975: Figure 20 [Layer 5], Figure 21 [Layer 4], Figure 95 [Layer

10]). Moreover, Hibben (1975:61, Figure 44) illustrated Layer 29 from the east wall of Kiva 10 and also selected paintings from Layer 31 on the south and west walls of this kiva (1975:Figures 4, 6). It is uncertain when these additional layers were uncovered and recorded (see also Crotty, this volume).

Mistakes in judgment and various losses underscore the problems inherent in the methods used to preserve and record murals at Pottery Mound. According to Hibben (1975:14), when the Kuaua murals were removed, a technique was worked out by which individual layers of plaster with paintings on their surfaces could be stripped from the walls and remounted on wallboard. Reportedly, this method gave excellent results, but it proved slow and costly. Hibben also noted that because the paintings lost moisture, the color became quite dull. He may have been justifying his methods used at Pottery Mound, which meant scraping away and ultimately destroying the murals as opposed to attempting to preserve them such as at Kuaua. However, as I point out later when describing the methods used to reproduce the paintings at Pottery Mound in 1960, they lost moisture and faded quickly anyway.

Mural Work for the National Science Foundation: Summer 1960

After four years of summer field schools at Pottery Mound (1954, 1955, 1957, and 1958), Frank C. Hibben obtained a grant from the National Science Foundation in which he proposed to use the summer of 1960 for the sole purpose of continuing to uncover and study the site's rich store of kiva mural art. Before that time, the murals of Kivas 1 through 5 had been at least partially studied. Kiva 6 had been opened with some brief initial study, and several layers of Kiva 7 had been recorded. Now there would be an opportunity to record the kiva murals in a consistent and professional manner.

The following information about who worked at Pottery Mound during the summer of 1960 is based on slide and photographic records and my memory. The mural crew was composed of Stanley Bussey, Jim Faris, Chuck McDougal, Milton Newton, and Ron Provencher; the artists were Maria Jorrin, Ted Frisbie, Chris Pierce, Dennis Tedlock, Stanley Bussey, and myself (Patricia Bryan Vivian). Russell Schorsch was the foreman. Under orders from Frank Hibben, who was on safari in Africa for most of that summer, we were to reopen Kiva 6 and continue the work of uncovering the murals on the south

wall and recovering possible fragments left from the west wall. Moreover, we were to continue to uncover and record the murals on the walls of Kiva 7 and commence the mural study of Kiva 8.

Dennis Tedlock and I began by shoveling infill dirt out of Kiva 6 when the remaining south wall and leftover fragments of the west wall came down, necessitating a quick abandonment. That ended further work in Kiva 6.

Consequently, we moved to Kiva 8 to record the very first layer (Figure 5.2). We faced handsome male and female dancers and imposing, powerful bird and snake figures; our work had begun. I recorded in Kiva 8 for most of the remainder of that summer. According to my slide records, Tedlock joined Jorrin shortly in Kiva 7. Black and white photos show that Chris Pierce worked in Kiva 8 and also in Kiva 7. Ted Frisbie joined us later and worked in Kiva 7. Hibben (1960:271) wrote that "paintings were copied by two artists working independently." To the best of my recollection, while working on the murals in 1960, this did not occur. There were simply too many murals and too much work to have successfully carried out such a plan.

Notes written in 1958 reveal that work had already started in Kiva 7 on Layers 1, 2, and 3 of the south wall. My slide records indicate that in 1960 work continued on the south wall at Layer 8, on the west wall at Layer 1, and on the east wall at Layer 9. I cannot explain the gap between work on Layer 3 and Layer 8 of the south wall except for the probable sketchiness of notes and records and a lack of wise supervision. There is also the slim possibility that the layers between 3 and 8 were only plastered. The east wall of Kiva 7 did not have the abundance of paintings of the south and west. This could have been due to damage. I cannot recall any paintings uncovered on the north wall of either Kiva 7 or 8, nor do I have slide or photographic records. There are clear records for paintings on the east, south, and west walls of Kivas 7 and 8. At least 36 painted layers were recorded in Kiva 7 and 20 painted layers in Kiva 8. According to Hibben (1975:16), there was a remodeled version of Kiva 8, Kiva 9, with 10 painted layers. However, to the best of my knowledge we were only aware of working in Kiva 8 during the summer of 1960.[1]

Methods

The methods used during this summer to uncover, reproduce, and study the murals of Kivas 7 and 8 were slow, painstaking, and, as some would argue, ethically questionable. The first step was to take a small penknife and carefully scrape away a layer or more of white plaster

FIGURE 5.2

Working in Kiva 8, Pottery Mound, summer 1960. Left to right: Stanley Bussey, Ron Provencher, Chris Pierce. (Photograph by Patricia Bryan Vivian.)

until the first plastered and painted layer was revealed (unless the first layer was painted). At that point the entire painted layer was gently uncovered by scraping the remaining plaster away from the underlying painting. Luckily, there was almost always at least one layer of plain plaster in between the painted layers. Occasionally, the plastered layers were so thin that the painted layers seemed to be on top of one another. This was difficult work; often the knife would make scratches and nicks in some beautifully painted area, or a piece would fall off. Once the painting on an entire wall had been uncovered, a grid would be constructed with nails hammered 6 in apart around the edge on all four sides. String would be tied to connect the top and bottom nails and then the nails on the left and right sides, which made a series of 6 in squares over the painting area. This method allowed

more accuracy in the reproduction and enabled us to see and control how shapes and lines fit together in the total spatial composition. It also offered more ease of drawing. Unfortunately, as soon as these paintings were exposed to the light and air of the present day, the rich, warm colors began to fade quickly. This was especially true of reds and yellows, which was disconcerting.

We came prepared with what we thought would be the best way to reproduce these precious colors and textures. I had remembered seeing the flat, dull tempera-paint field reproductions made in 1957 of paintings in Kiva 2. Later, even the bright and beautifully rendered finished paintings of Octavio Romano reproducing the originals from the field of images moving around all four walls on Layer 1 in Kiva 2 seemed too flat and opaque. I had decided, after a short introduction to reproducing murals from Kiva 7 during the summer of 1958, that the medium of pastel would come closest to yielding not only those rich colors, but the depth and soft velvety texture of the surfaces. This decision would also eliminate the messy mixing of tempera in jars while trying to match the desired colors. Pastels could be "mixed" in squares on a sheet of paper designated for that purpose. Therefore, pastel was the chosen medium for the work of 1960. While the pastels yielded beautiful color areas and could reproduce prehistoric stippling, attempting to re-create dry brush strokes or the look of scraping presented a challenge. We had to use pointed or sharpened pastels and this work was painstaking because we could not actually drag a brush or use a scraper. Therefore, we had to try and "copy" what the results of such methods looked like. Whatever we tried pointed to the fact that these paintings could not truly be copied. After a pastel field reproduction was finished, it would be stabilized with a clear fixative and put away in a portfolio. In addition, we made notes about the prehistoric paintings and methods used to reproduce them. Also, slides and photographs were taken and labeled to complete the records.

Another unpleasant aspect of the mural studies was that as soon as the pastel reproductions were completed for one painted layer of any given wall, these paintings were scraped away with our penknives and destroyed forever. So far it is questionable that any study, final published report, or book has been made that would mitigate the use of these techniques.

The following summary of pigments used by the Puebloans to create the Pottery Mound murals is drawn from my (1994:83) prior analysis of the paintings.

For the most part, the pigments used were mineral in origin and undoubtedly were derived from natural deposits in the immediate physical environment such as clay or sandstone stained with minerals. Based on the Awat'ovi analysis (Smith 1952), I suggest that there was red iron oxide from hematite, azurite, malachite, limonite, uranium oxide, a yellow iron oxide, copper salts, carbon, white clay, and gypsum (a white chalk). The materials available gave the Pueblo artist a basic palette of red, yellow, green, blue, black, and white. The existing paintings show many variations of the primary hues.

As I (1961:76–78) noted in my MFA thesis, it appears that pigments were mixed for different combinations, creating secondary and tertiary colors and diversity within the value and chroma scales such as different greens, pinks, oranges, purples, maroons, browns, and grays. The

variations were probably the results of a sense of experimentation as well as some accidents from impurities. Black and white were used extensively. Sometimes the black had a bluish tone that gave it a quality of depth. The application of white varied from a thick impasto consistency to a thin, rather transparent wash. Sometimes colors were superimposed, also giving the effect of depth and transparency. In other cases, areas of the neutral wall surface were left unpainted but were integrated into the positive design itself. Moreover, these prehistoric artists apparently used pigment in different forms such as raw lumps as well as thin washes. There is a certain sophistication reflected in the many variations of painting techniques.

My previous analysis also considered binders and tools that probably were used at Pottery Mound.

> The raw pigments were probably ground with a mano on a metate and were then mixed with a vehicle and a binding medium to cause the paint to adhere to the wall surface. As Smith (1952:30–31) has noted, today the Pueblo method of painting masks, kachina dolls, and other paraphernalia will often combine the vehicle and binder by mixing the pulverized dry pigment into the saliva generated by chewing a variety of seeds, which secrete a vegetable oil. Sometimes, either pinon gum or the juice of boiled yucca plants or squash is used. It seems possible that the same methods were used in preparing mural paint. According to Hibben (1960:269), they could have also used a medium of water and animal grease.

> Judging by the existing material, it is probable that a variety of tools was used to apply the paint. The exact nature of their brushes is not known, but it appears that they had both soft and stiff types. In recent times, strips of yucca leaf have been used. These are chewed at one end to remove the pulp and to leave the bare fibers protruding in the form of a brush. Moreover, it is evident that the manner in which brushes were used at Pottery Mound varied a great deal. This can be detected by the dry and wet brush strokes, stippling, splattering, and other techniques. In addition, the surface paint textures found within the painting make it obvious that the brush constituted only one tool, other possible ones being knives, scrapers, and the fingers or the whole hand [Vivian 1994:83–84].

The following is a previously published discussion of the manner in which paintings were applied to the plastered walls. This discussion parallels my previous reference to the methods employed when removing multiple painted and unpainted layers of plaster.

> It seems that the paintings were done on dry plaster, in the manner called "fresco secco," in which the paint forms merely a surface film adherent to the plaster base. In true fresco the paint is applied to damp plaster, with the result that the color becomes permanently bonded to the wall. The "fresco secco" technique at Pottery Mound was used on thin layers of finely prepared adobe plaster, less than 1/8 inch thick. When a new painting was created, the preceding one was coated with a layer of plaster. Thus, the basic adobe wall structure of the ceremonial room would be covered with a series of plastered and painted layers [Vivian 1994:84].

Watson Smith's (1952:19) four reasons for the probable frequent renewal of wall plaster at Hopi sites seem equally applicable to the kivas at Pottery Mound. I (1994:84) have summarized Smith's explanations as follows: the occasional partial disintegration or collapse of parts of the wall or plastered surface; the desirability of refurbishing the surface in order to obliterate an existing layer that has been blackened by soot; a customary periodic renewal in the nature of "spring cleaning"; or, finally, the ceremonial necessity of obliterating or secreting a sacred object after it has served the religious purpose for which it was made, in this case a mural painting.

I (1994:84) have also noted that "based on ethnographic knowledge, we think that the prehistoric Pueblo Indian also followed a strict ceremonial pattern directly related to his calendar, or yearly seasonal cycle, which could relate to painted plaster renewals." We know, for example, that today the Hopi calendar based on a combination of solar and lunar observations determines a succession of ceremonies portraying religious events and featuring spiritual personages. After making a brief study of some of the murals of Kivas 1 through 6, and a more thorough analysis of those in Kivas 7 and 8 (Vivian 1961), I have concluded that these paintings probably portrayed personages and settings for events that were integrated into the total esoteric ritual system of Pottery Mound and mirrored the dwellers' spiritual worldview.

How these conclusions fit into Frank Hibben's reasons for excavating Pottery Mound, or his scholarly goals, is uncertain. Although he agreed to allow me to write my University of Iowa MFA thesis on the subject of the kiva murals, he did not discuss with me any ideas about either the site or what he wanted me to include in my investigations. After reviewing some of Hibben's (1960; 1966; 1967) published papers and his book (1975), I can only conclude that his academic goals in pursuing Pottery Mound studies were strongly guided by what he perceived as major Mexican influences. He believed that the "black and white" people (Pueblo III) built an imposing tall, flat pyramid at the site that could be seen for miles. Subsequently, the "glaze" people (Pueblo IV) built rooms and kivas over and around the pyramid, effectively burying this earlier structure. However, the paintings created in the kivas during the Pueblo IV period reflected these people's absorption of Mexican ritual practices. According to Hibben (1966; 1967; 1975), this could be seen in the portrayals of parrots and macaws, eagles and jaguars, horned and feathered serpents, as well as warriors with shields edged with bird feathers. On the other hand, my (1961; 1994) approach to the study of the Pottery Mound murals concentrated on the katsina cult and the Puebloan religious calendar or ritual system. Undoubtedly, the richness of these paintings reflects a vast spiritual and social complexity encompassing many influences.

We have only begun to put together meaningful studies of Pottery Mound. Excavations and recordings in the past have not been as organized or as careful as they should have been. Moreover, some published studies reveal a number of inconsistencies and inaccuracies, as well as statements made that cannot as yet be verified. Hopefully the painstaking and methodical work of creating a clearer picture of this important site will continue. ⁘

NOTE

1. Editor's note: Hibben is clearly in error here, as Kiva 9 was constructed first and therefore cannot be a remodeled version of Kiva 8.

REFERENCES CITED

Hibben, Frank C.

1960 Prehispanic Paintings at Pottery Mound. *Archaeology* 13:267–74.

1966 A Possible Pyramidal Structure and Other Mexican Influences at Pottery Mound, New Mexico. *American Antiquity* 31:522–29.

1967 Mexican Features of Mural Paintings at Pottery Mound. *Archaeology* 20(2):84–87.

1975 *Kiva Art of the Anasazi at Pottery Mound.* KC Publications, Las Vegas, Nevada.

1987 Report on the Salvage Operations at the Site of Pottery Mound, New Mexico during the Excavating Seasons of 1977–1986. Manuscript on file, Maxwell Museum of Anthropology, University of New Mexico, Albuquerque.

Smith, Watson

1952 *Kiva Mural Decorations at Awatovi and Kawaika-a with a Survey of Other Wall Paintings in the Pueblo Southwest.* Papers of the Peabody Museum of American Archaeology and Ethnology Vol. 317. Harvard University, Cambridge, Massachusetts.

Vivian, Patricia Bryan

1961 Kachina, The Study of Pueblo Animism and Anthropomorphism within the Ceremonial Wall Paintings of Pottery Mound and the Jeddito. Unpublished Master of Fine Arts thesis, Department of Art, University of Iowa, Iowa City.

1994 Anthropomorphic Figures in the Pottery Mound Murals. In *Kachinas in the Pueblo World*, edited by Polly Schaafsma, pp. 81–91. University of New Mexico Press, Albuquerque.

CHAPTER SIX

Western Pueblo Influences and Integration in the Pottery Mound Painted Kivas

Helen K. Crotty

Introduction

The most striking evidence of Western Pueblo influences at Pottery Mound is seen in the Sikyatki-style designs found on early layers of most of the painted kivas discovered to date. Western traits can be detected, as well, in the style and subject matter of certain other murals and in the architecture of the Pottery Mound kivas. Pottery types found at the site include wares from Hopi and the Zuni/Acoma area along with locally made imitations of them, as discussed by Eckert (this volume). It seems clear that the arts of Pottery Mound were influenced at least in part by the arrival of immigrants from the west, but Pottery Mound was not simply a Western Pueblo outpost, nor were the Western traits ever entirely submerged in the culture of the Rio Grande. Eastern and Western Pueblo traits persist throughout the mural cycle, and it appears that the preservation of both traditions was a deliberate accommodation among the diverse cultural groups who made Pottery Mound their home.

Pottery Mound is the richest Pueblo IV kiva mural site known in the Southwest, having yielded more murals than other recognized major sites such as the villages of Awat'ovi and Kawaika'a, on Antelope Mesa near the present Hopi reservation in Arizona (Smith 1952), and Kuaua,

85

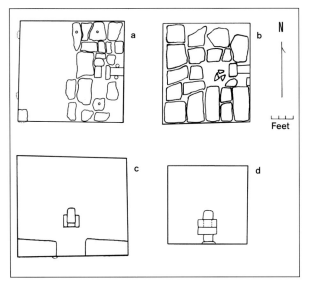

FIGURE 6.1a–d

Floor plans of Pottery Mound kivas: **a**) Kiva 1; **b**) Kiva 2;
c) Kiva 3; **d**) Kiva 4. Kivas 1 and 2 have eastern ventilators
and simple rectangular adobe deflectors; Kivas 3 and
4 have elaborate Rio Grande–style terraced three-sided
adobe altar/deflectors. Kiva 4 has a southern ventilator;
no ventilator was found for Kiva 3, but the location of the
altar/deflector and the divided bench on the south wall
suggest a ventilator to the south. (Drawings of **a**, **c**, **d** after
Bramlett [1963a]; drawing of **b** by Deborah Kelley from
student notes and photographs.)

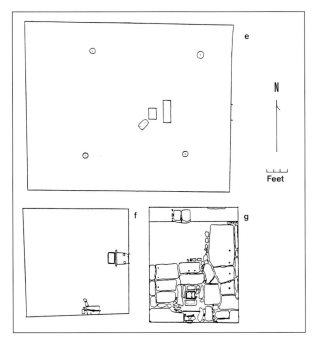

FIGURE 6.1e–g

Floor plans of Pottery Mound kivas: **e**) Kiva 5; **f**) Kiva 6;
g) Kiva 7. Kiva 5 is relatively large, with four-post roof
construction, adobe slab deflector, and eastern ventilator,
common features of Rio Grande "big" kivas. Kivas 6 and
7 both have stone slab deflectors and the remains of
flagstone pavement, but the ventilator of Kiva 6 is on the
east wall. Kiva 7 has a southern ventilator and the remnants
of flagstone pavement on its front bench. (After drawings
by Bramlett [1963a].)

on the Rio Grande near the town of Bernalillo, New
Mexico (Dutton 1963). Two other New Mexico sites have
yielded a lesser, but still significant, number of murals:
Picuris (Crotty 1999) and Mound 7 at Gran Quivira (or
Las Humanas) (Peckham 1981). Pueblo IV sites in Arizona
and New Mexico containing kivas with one or two murals
or only fragmentary remains of painted plaster are also
known (for summaries, see Crotty 1995; Smith 1952).

The Pottery Mound paintings were recorded by
student artists in some 800 field drawings comprising
approximately 375 murals, or fragments of murals, from
11 of the 17 kivas (P. Vivian, this volume). Frank Hibben's
1975 volume reproduces many, but by no means all, of
them. Research for this paper included examination of
the field drawings as well as other archival material now
available at the Hibben Center of the Maxwell Museum of
Anthropology at the University of New Mexico.[1]

The Kivas of Pottery Mound

My discussion begins with the kiva architecture because
integration is most easily seen here (Figure 6.1, Table 6.1).
The architecture and floor features of the Pottery Mound
kivas as a group diverge significantly from what might be
expected in a typical Rio Grande pueblo. Although kiva
features in the Rio Grande region tend to be more variable
than in the west, excavation reports for other fifteenth-
century Rio Grande kivas usually note that round, subterranean structures with floor features consisting minimally
of a west to east alignment of hearth, ash pit, deflector, and
ventilator are usual for the area (e.g., Baldwin 1988; Hayes
et al. 1981; Snow 1979; Vivian 1964). Rectangular kivas,
however, both surface and subterranean, are not rare in
Pueblo IV Rio Grande settlements southwest of Santa Fe.

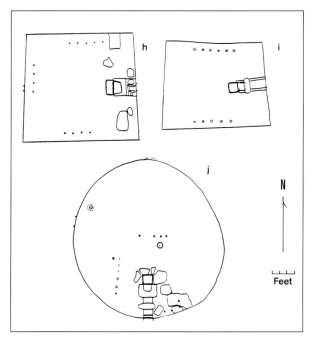

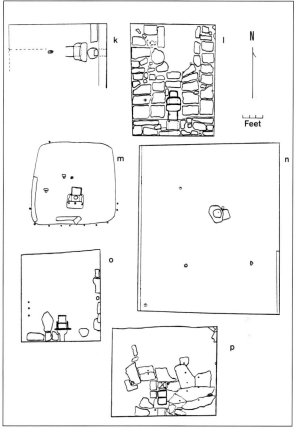

FIGURE 6.1h–j

Floor plans of Pottery Mound kivas: **h**) Kiva 8; **i**) Kiva 9; **j**) Kiva 10. Kiva 8 was constructed above Kiva 9, with the west and south walls coinciding but the north and east slightly expanded. Loom anchor holes in Kiva 9 are parallel with the firepit/deflector/ventilator axis as in Western Pueblo kivas, but Kiva 8 has an additional row along the front wall, more typical of Rio Grande kivas. Kiva 10, the only round kiva at Pottery Mound, has remains of flagstone pavement, southern ventilator, and three-sided adobe altar as well as a basalt deflector. There are two rows of loom holes, one parallel to and the other at right angles to the axis. (After drawings by Bramlett [1963a].)

FIGURE 6.1k–p

Floor plans of Pottery Mound kivas: **k**) Kiva 11; **l**) Kiva 12; **m**) Kiva 13; **n**) Kiva 14; **o**) Kiva 15; **p**) Kiva 16 (no plan currently available for Kiva 17). Kivas 11 and 12 have rear benches. Kiva 11, only partially excavated, has an ash pit and terraced adobe altar/deflector and eastern ventilator. Kiva 12, with Western Pueblo–style flagstone-paved floor and rear platform over southern ventilator, has Rio Grande–style ash pit and terraced three-sided adobe altar/deflector. Kiva 13 has rounded square shape with poles reinforcing the southern and southeastern walls. Kiva 14 lost some features along its northeastern wall. Three roof support posts remain, and the southeastern banquette section suggests its ventilator was on the east wall. By its size and features, it is a "big" kiva. Kivas 15 and 16 have southern ventilators and share parts of one wall. Kiva 15 has an unusual deflector consisting of three stone slabs, and Kiva 16 has an unterraced three-sided adobe altar/deflector. Both have the remains of flagstone pavement, and the scattered loom anchor holes in Kiva 16 suggest reused flagstones. A few loom anchor holes in Kiva 15 are parallel with the firepit/deflector/ventilator axis. (After drawings by Bramlett [1963a].)

Table 6.1. Architectural Features of the Pottery Mound Kivas

Kiva	#Plaster Layers/ #Painted Layers[a]	Approx. Shape	Construction	Area (m²)	Vent. Wall	Bench	Deflector	Niche	Ash Pit	Floor Treatment	Loom Anchor Holes	Reference
1	4/4	Square	Coursed adobe	21.6	E	¾	Adobe rectangle	2?, W, SW	√	Flagstones east third	Axis	Bramlett 1963a; 1963b
2	21/16	Square	Coursed adobe	n.i.	E	W	Adobe rectangle	W	√	Flagstones in center	n.i.	Bramlett 1963b
3	3/3	Irregular square	Adobe	20.6	S[b]	2 S	Terraced three-sided adobe	N	¾	n.i.	n.i.	Bramlett 1963a; 1963b; Meeker 1954
4	n.i./1	Square	Adobe	12.1	S	¾	Terraced three-sided adobe	¾	√	Adobe	n.i.	Bramlett 1963a; 1963b
5	3/3	Rectangle	Adobe four roof posts	58.4	E	¾	Adobe rectangle	W	¾	Adobe	n.i.	Bramlett 1963a; 1963b; Dix 1957
6	28/21	Square	Coursed adobe w/support poles	20.1	E	¾	Stone slab	n.i.	?	Remnants of flagstones	n.i.	Bramlett 1963a; 1963b
7	37/32	Rectangle	n.i.	19.0	S	N	Stone slab	n.i.	√	Flagstones	Axis	Bramlett 1963a; 1963b
8	19/18	Irregular square	Rubble masonry	19.2	E	¾	Adobe three sided, not terraced	W	√	Adobe with sporadic flagstones	Axis plus[c]	Bramlett 1963a; 1963b
9	23/13	Irregular square	Rubble masonry	13.9	E	¾	Adobe rectangle plus	W	√	Adobe with flagstones near center	Axis	Bramlett 1963a; 1963b
10	39/31	Circular	Rubble masonry	29.5	S	¾	Adobe three sided, not terraced basalt slab	N	√	Adobe with a few stones near firepit	Axis plus[c]	Bramlett 1963a; 1963b
11	n.i.		Adobe	12.5?	E	E	Terraced three-sided adobe	W	√	Adobe	n.i.	Bramlett 1963a; 1963b
12	25/5	Rectangle	Coursed adobe	18.2	S	S	Terraced three-sided adobe	N	?	Flagstone	?	Bramlett 1963a; Field Drawings
13	n.i./0	Rounded square	Adobe with support poles	10.5	S	W?	Terraced three-sided adobe	n.i.	¾	Adobe	¾	Bramlett 1963a; 1963b

Stewart Peckham (1979:71–72) suggests that their origins might have been to the west or south, or both, noting that their distribution "generally matches that of the Tiwa-speaking pueblos." He further observes that Classic period rectangular kivas in the general Albuquerque area bear "only superficial resemblance" to the Little Colorado style of kiva, lacking "the low broad bench spanning the narrow end of the structure."

At Pottery Mound, all but one of the excavated kivas are rectilinear in shape. Two of them, Kivas 7 and 12, are rectangular with the hearth-deflector-ventilator axis parallel with the longer walls in the Western Pueblo style; Kiva 12 even has a low, broad bench on its south wall that Peckham mentions as typical of the Little Colorado style. The other smaller rectilinear structures more closely approach square proportions. About half

Table 6.1. Architectural Features of the Pottery Mound Kivas

Kiva	#Plaster Layers/ #Painted Layers[a]	Approx. Shape	Construction	Area (m²)	Vent. Wall	Bench	Deflector	Niche	Ash Pit	Floor Treatment	Loom Anchor Holes	Reference
14	n.i./0	Rectangle	Adobe, four roof posts	48.1	E[d]	W and E?	None visible	n.i.	n.i.	Adobe	¾	Bramlett 1963a; 1963b
15	12/4	Square	Adobe	13.7	S	¾	three stone slabs, not terraced	?	√	Adobe (with flagstones under wall)	Axis	Bramlett 1963a; 1963b
16	11/11	Square	Coursed adobe and rubble	18.0	S	¾	Adobe three sided, not terraced	2, N, NW	√	Reused flagstones	?	Bramlett 1963a; 1963b
17	9/7	Square	Adobe	n.i.	E[e]	n.i.	n.i.	n.i.	n.i.	n.i.	n.i.	Hibben 1975; Field Drawings

Note: E = east; W = west; N = north; S = south; ¾ = absent; √ = present; ? = possibly present; n.i. = no information available.

[a]Information from field drawings and student notes. Layer numbers on field drawings include unpainted layers and are counted from the outside (or first) layer encountered in excavation, which was the last layer actually painted.

[b]Student notes state that there was no ventilator in Kiva 3, but the location of the altar/deflector and divided bench indicate that it would have been on the south wall.

[c]Loom anchor holes in Western Pueblo kivas are normally parallel with the firepit/deflector/ventilator axis; in Rio Grande kivas they may be placed perpendicular to the axis. In Kiva 8, two rows of loom anchor holes run parallel with the axis and another runs parallel to the west wall. In Kiva 10, one row runs parallel with the axis and one row perpendicular to it.

[d]Bramlett's notes provide little information about Kiva 14, the east wall of which had apparently been damaged. Since his floor plan shows a full bench on the west side and the finished edge of a partial bench on the southeast side, the ventilator would probably have been in the east wall.

[e]Except for a few field drawings, little is currently known about Kiva 17, which was excavated in a salvage operation sometime between 1961 and 1975. A note on one of the drawings (Maxwell Museum of Anthropology, University of New Mexico, catalog no. 76.70.737), however, indicates a niche on the west wall, which suggests that the ventilator was on the east wall.

of the Pottery Mound kivas have southern ventilators, as do most Western kivas, but the majority of them have massive adobe deflector/altars and ash pits, both of which are usually absent from contemporaneous Western kivas. Vertical flagstone slabs served as deflectors in the kivas of Awat'ovi and Kawaika'a (Smith 1972:120), and Kiva 7 has such a deflector. Deflectors made of rectangular slabs of adobe are recorded in Kivas 1, 2, and 5. Other Pueblo IV Eastern and Western preferences in overall size, type of wall construction, type of floor paving, presence or absence of benches or platforms, and alignments of loom anchor holes are also mixed. So far as I have been able to determine from the rather limited available literature, Pueblo

IV architectural features characteristic of Western Pueblo kivas occur with greater frequency at Pottery Mound than at any other prehistoric Rio Grande site.

Pottery Mound Kivas 5 and 14, both of which are large enough to have served as "big" kivas (Hawley 1950), are the most traditionally Rio Grande in architecture. "Big" moiety kivas are typical of Rio Grande pueblos but absent in the west, where clan-based social organization prevails (Eggan 1950). No paintings are reported from Kiva 14, which belongs to the earliest—apparently premural—occupation of Pottery Mound, but fragments of three painted layers are reported in Kiva 5 (Dix 1957; Maxwell Museum photo archives, PM Box 38, Slides 129, 138). This may be another example of deliberate integration, as it is the only Pueblo IV "big" kiva known to have contained mural decoration. Kiva 10, also quite large, is the single round kiva at Pottery Mound, but it was built with a southern ventilator. Although its murals are not well preserved, Kiva 10 has the most plaster layers (39) of any Pottery Mound kiva, and it is thought to have been in use when the site was abandoned.[2] Its murals are discussed below along with those of the other kivas of its era.

Kiva 12 is the most Western Pueblo in architectural features, including, as noted, a flagstone-paved platform over its southern ventilator (Figure 6.1*l*). Its only concessions to integration are an Eastern-style adobe deflector/altar and its ash pit. Kiva 12 is one of two Pottery Mound painted kivas that had no Sikyatki-style mural decoration. Western influences are plain, however, not only in its architecture, but also in its earliest mural, which depicts a painted textile organized as an offset quartered design familiar in the decoration of Pueblo III Kayenta pottery (see Webster, this volume, Figure 9.14*b*). Yet filler elements within the design appear to belong to later Pueblo IV styles of ceramic decoration common to both Sikyatki and glaze-painted pottery—perhaps a nod to integration. The second kiva in which no Sikyatki-style decoration is recorded is Kiva 15, from which only a few fragments of paintings were recovered from multiple layers in a cast preserved from fallen wall plaster.[3]

Newly available information about the ceramics found on the floors of the excavated Pottery Mound kivas permits a provisional chronology for them (Bramlett 1963a).[4] The earliest Pottery Mound kivas had no mural decoration. These are Kivas 11, 13, and 14; Bramlett (1963a) notes that Kivas 11 and 13 were found at the lowest level of the trenches that uncovered them and that only Glaze A ceramics were found on their floors. Kiva 14's stratigraphic position, Bramlett notes, was "not conducive to firm dating by that method" but pottery counts "are indicative of a strictly Glaze [A] use." Kiva 11 has an eastern ventilator; Kiva 13's is on a southern wall. Information is sketchy for Kiva 14, the eastern wall of which was damaged, but the remains of benches shown in the floor plan (Figure 6.1*n*) suggest that the ventilator was on the eastern wall.

Kivas 3, 4, 7, 15, and 16 were abandoned in Glaze B or very early Glaze C times. Only the fragmentary remains of painted plaster were recorded from Kiva 3 (Meeker 1954); like Kivas 13 and 14, it lay under a later roomblock. Traces of a band of red paint but no images are recorded

in Kiva 4. Kiva 7 has 37 recorded plaster layers, suggesting it may have been in use longer than any of the kivas at Pottery Mound except possibly Kiva 10. Its early murals, along with those of Kivas 10 and 15, are probably the first at the site and may slightly antedate the appearance of the fully developed Sikyatki style sometime around 1400. Like Kiva 12, it is rectangular rather than square in form; other Western influences are seen in its southern ventilator, flagstone-paved floor and front bench, and slab stone deflector. As Kiva 16 shares parts of a wall with Kiva 15, it is thought to have been built not long after Kiva 15 was abandoned, probably in early Glaze C times; Kiva 16 was also abandoned in early Glaze C times (Bramlett 1963a).

The remaining Pottery Mound kivas appear to have been abandoned later in the Glaze C period. Bramlett (1963a) suggests that Kivas 1, 2, 5, 9, and 12 were probably abandoned before the end of occupation and that Kivas 6, 8, and 10 may have been in use when the entire site was abandoned sometime around 1450/1475.[5] All of the kivas that had a showing of Glaze C ceramics on their floors had murals or traces of paint. The evidence thus indicates that mural art was not practiced during the initial occupation of Pottery Mound but was adopted after the arrival of immigrants from the Hopi area, which Eckert (this volume) estimates to have occurred some 18 years after the founding of the village by local peoples.

The Murals of Pottery Mound

A comparison of the murals of Pottery Mound with approximately contemporaneous paintings from Kawaika'a and Awat'ovi's intermediate occupation suggests to me that the artists were familiar with Rio Grande traditions as well as those of the west. If some of them had Western Pueblo roots, it does not appear that they were first-generation immigrants or visiting artists re-creating exactly the style and content of mural art of their homeland, although they were certainly conversant with it. It should be noted that the muralists of Pottery Mound created a lively and imaginative new iconography, building on these and perhaps other, unknown, sources, although only a few of the murals can be mentioned or illustrated here. Paintings in the Sikyatki style itself illustrate some of the ways that Pottery Mound murals differ from the Western Pueblo model (see Hays-Gilpin and LeBlanc, this volume). Mural versions of the fully developed Sikyatki style occur not at all at Kawaika'a and in only one Awat'ovi kiva, where they appear mainly on large, complex panels. At Pottery Mound we find not

Table 6.2. Sikyatki Designs or Motifs in Field Drawings from Pottery Mound Kivas

Pottery Mound Painted Kiva Number	1	2	6	7	8	9	10	12	15	16	17
Ventilator wall	E	E	E	S	E	E	S	S	S	S	E
Number of Painted layers in Kiva*	4	16	21	32	18	13	31	5	4	11	7
numbers below denote layer number											
Proto-Sikyatki decoration on shield(s)	0	0	0	36 35	0	12	15	0	0	0	0
Sikyatki design on shield	0	0	0	0	0	17	0	0	0	0	0
Sikyatki design as full panel	4 2	18[a] 12[a]	26 22 20 10 6	29 23	17	1	31[a] 30	0	0	9[a] 3[a]	9[a]
Sikyatki decoration on kilt	1	0	0	10	0	1[a,b]	21[a]	0	0	0	0
Sikyatki decoration of framing device	0	0	0	0	0	0	31 26 4[a]	0	0	0	0
Sikyatki motifs in decorative background	0	14	0	34 30	0	0	0	0	0	0	0
Sikyatki decoration of altar furniture	0	1	0	0	11 9[a,b]	0	0	0	0	0	0

Note: This information is more fully presented in Crotty (1995:Tables A.53–A.65). Unresolved discrepancies occur in the layer numbers noted on the field drawings; layer numbers given here are my best estimate and do not affect the relative chronology of mural art at the site.

*Total number of plaster layers exceeds number of painted layers.

[a]Denotes mural on wall opposite the ventilator. [b]Denotes niche indicated on field drawing.

only the panels—usually less flamboyant and more nearly symmetrical than the Awat'ovi examples—but elements of the style occur also in the decoration of shields, kilts, framing devices, background fillers, and painted altar furniture. Pottery Mound murals containing Sikyatki panels or elements are listed for each kiva in Table 6.2.

Table 6.3 shows iconography or stylistic conventions—in addition to the Sikyatki designs—that are found in both the Pottery Mound and the Antelope Mesa murals but not at Kuaua or other Rio Grande painted kivas, and Table 6.4 shows iconography or conventions found also at Kuaua or other Rio Grande mural sites but not in the Western Pueblo painted kivas.[6] The tables supplement the following discussion of the integration of Western Pueblo influences with Rio Grande traditions in selected kivas. As will be seen, both Western and Eastern traits persisted throughout the occupation of Pottery Mound.

The archaeological record suggests that Pueblo IV mural art began a little earlier at Awat'ovi than at Pottery Mound. The absence of formal composition in some of the first Awat'ovi murals is more reminiscent of rock art than anything seen at Pottery Mound. Development proceeds rapidly in the sequence of paintings in Awat'ovi's pre-Sikyatki kivas (Smith 1952: Figures 40–46). Representations of textiles, shields, and warriors occupy some of their early layers, and there are also panels utilizing Sikyatki-like motifs or certain compositional patterns that I will for convenience call proto-Sikyatki designs (Smith 1952:Figures 42a–d, 44b, 45b). Shields and warriors appear in the earliest Pottery Mound paintings from Kivas 7, 9, and 15, and some of the shields are decorated with proto-Sikyatki designs. A well-preserved example from Layer 36, the earliest painted layer of Kiva 7, is decorated with dart motifs similar

Table 6.3. Selected Iconography and Stylistic Conventions—Besides Sikyatki Designs—Shared by Pottery Mound and Antelope Mesa Pueblos

Pottery Mound Kiva Number	1	2	6	7	8	9	10	12	15	16	17
Ventilator wall	E	E	E	S	E	E	S	S	S	S	E
Number of Painted layers in Kiva*	4	16	21	32	18	13	31	5	4	11	7
numbers below denote layer number											
Frontal view of human or human-animal composite figure with unevenly bobbed hair and red lock	–	13 8	–	30 28	–	8 6 1	–	–	–	5	–
Profile view of human or animal-human composite figure with red lock in hair	–	2	1	21 18 3	–	8	–	–	–	–	–
Human figure with exaggerated shoulders	1	13 4 2 1	1	30 28 21 15 1	16 6 1	12 8 6 3	–	–	–	–	–
Legless human figure with bent elbows and open palms	–	8 2	–	30	–		–	–	–	–	–
"Rainbow" framing device	–	11 9 8 4	–	34 32 31 9	–	–	29	–	–	–	–
Mountain lion	4	–	–	36 28 11	7 5		18 15	–	–	9 8 6 5 4	5
Mountain lion paw with central void and whorled claws	–	–	1	–	5	–	–	–	–	–	–
Animal or human-animal composite passing through a shield	–	–	–	11	4	–	–	–	–	–	–
Depiction of altar furniture with cone-shaped symbolic corn ear	–	–	–	–	17	–	15	–	–	–	–

*Total number of plaster layers exceeds number of painted layers.

to those found in proto-Sikyatki panels from the early Awat'ovi kivas (Figure 6.2; cf. Smith 1952:Figure 42a–b).[7] The earliest of the Sikyatki-style panels in Kiva 7 occurs on Layer 29 (Figure 6.3). The mural fragment, as is typical of early Sikyatki panels at Pottery Mound, lacks the fluidity of the Awat'ovi Sikyatki examples, and it employs a rectilinear central image not seen in them (cf. Smith 1952:Figures 48a–b, 49a). It thus illustrates my reason for believing that the Pottery Mound muralists were neither newly arrived immigrants nor visiting artists from the west. On Layer 30, painted just before the Sikyatki panel

in Kiva 7, we can see that the muralists were familiar with Sikyatki imagery, but the motifs here have been placed in a seemingly casual and un-Sikyatki-like arrangement to which Rio Grande–style corn plants and stylized dragonflies have been added (Figure 6.4). The painting seems to express a symbolic relationship between corn, dragonflies, and Sikyatki motifs.

The central figures in the paintings illustrate stylistic features in the rendering of the human figure that the Pottery Mound murals share with those of Awat'ovi and Kawaika'a (see Table 6.3). They are depicted as legless

Table 6.4. Selected Iconography and Stylistic Conventions Shared by Pottery Mound and Kuaua

Pottery Mound Kiva Number	1	2	6	7	8	9	10	12	15	16	17
Ventilator wall	E	E	E	S	E	E	S	S	S	S	E
Number of Painted layers in Kiva*	4	16	21	32	18	13	31	5	4	11	7
numbers below denote layer number											
Frontal male figure with evenly cut long hair showing on both shoulders	–	–	–	–	16 15 1	–	–	–	–	–	–
Human figure with sloping shoulders	–	–	–	–	15 1	–	–	–	–	–	–
Human or composite human-animal figure wearing "warbonnet"	–	1	–	–	1	–	–	–	–	–	5
Flat-headed human or human-animal composite figure	–	13	–	–	–	–	–	–	–	–	–
Composition organized by midline band	–	–	–	–	14	–	39 37	–	–	–	–
Depiction of giant serpent	–	–	–	9	–	8	38 15	–	–	–	–
Lightning as crossed sticks	–	13	–	21 12	10 4 1	–	18 10A	–	–	–	–

*Total number of plaster layers exceeds number of painted layers.

torsos with arms bent upward at the elbows and open palms turned toward the viewer. There is an exaggerated swell where the shoulders emerge from the neck. The figures have asymmetrical haircuts with a red lock on the long side. In this case the hair is quite short, which seems to be the female version. Male figures have longer hair, but it is also cut to different lengths with a red lock on the longer side. Often a yellow or tan-colored square is painted over the eye on the side with the longer hair. Male figures shown in profile may also display the red lock and face paint. The exaggeration of the shoulders is found on most Pottery Mound figures and also at Awat'ovi and Kawaika'a, although human figures are less frequently portrayed at the latter sites and the upper bodies and heads are often missing in the eroded plasters. The truncated figure with upturned arms and open palms can be seen in several of the better preserved murals from Awat'ovi (e.g., Smith 1952:Figures 65a, 78b, 81a–b, 82a), and the asymmetrical haircut with a red lock and the male eye paint occurs in a frontal view of a row of male and female subjects in a mural from Kawaika'a (Smith

1952:Figure 67d). Whether the open-handed truncated figure, the exaggerated shoulders, or the eye paint and asymmetrical haircuts originated in the west or in the east, they are not seen in murals from Kuaua or other Rio Grande sites.

Another shared stylistic feature, a striped framing device with legless birds perched at the corners of a reserved square area, is seen on Layer 31 of Kiva 7 and in one of the pre-Sikyatki Awat'ovi kivas (Figure 6.5, see Table 6.3; cf. Smith 1952:Figure 70a). As I (1995:137–38, Figure 41) have argued elsewhere, the imagery appears to be derived from Smith's so-called bird perch motif in Pueblo III pottery of the Upper Little Colorado River area that, in a more abstract version, occurs in pottery decoration dating back to Pueblo II or even Pueblo I times in the San Juan region (Smith 1971:385, Figures 134a, 139j, 207a–i). In the examples illustrated by Smith, the birds all face in the same direction as a repeated motif around a central square, but a bowl found at Aztec Ruin and identified by Morris (1919: Figure 45b) as "a red bowl from the Little Colorado" shows pairs of birds facing one another as they do in the murals.

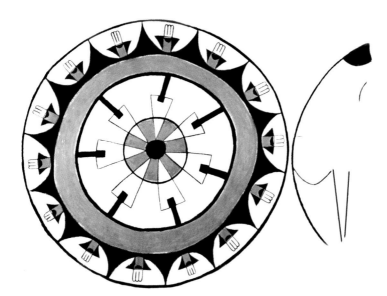

FIGURE 6.2

Shield decorated with "proto-Sikyatki" design, Kiva 7, Layer 36 or 37, southwest corner. (After field drawing by Ted Frisbie, courtesy of the Maxwell Museum of Anthropology, University of New Mexico, catalog no. 76.70.473.)

FIGURE 6.3

Sikyatki-style panel with unusual rectilinear central image, Kiva 7, Layer 29 or 30, southwest corner. (Digital composite after field drawings by Ted Frisbie, courtesy of the Maxwell Museum of Anthropology, University of New Mexico, catalog nos. 76.70.479, 480, 481.)

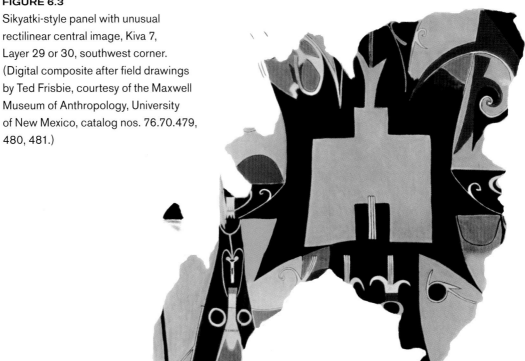

FIGURE 6.4
Partial female figures with uneven haircuts
and exaggerated shoulders, posed with bent
elbows and open palms, stylistic conventions
shared by Rio Grande and Antelope Mesa.
Casually placed Sikyatki motifs, along
with corn plants and stylized dragonflies
in background, Kiva 7, Layer 30 or 31,
on southeast and southwest ends of
south wall, flanking ventilator area.
(Digital composite after field drawings by
Ted Frisbie, courtesy of the Maxwell Museum
of Anthropology, University of New Mexico,
catalog nos. 76.70.470, 386, 387.)

FIGURE 6.5
"Rainbow" framing of miscellaneous feather
and dragonfly motifs with legless bird at corner,
Kiva 7, Layer 31, west wall. (After field drawing
by Liz Lapovsky, courtesy of the Maxwell
Museum of Anthropology, University of
New Mexico, catalog no. 76.70.472,
image from another layer deleted.)

Niche

FIGURE 6.6
Shield with Sikyatki-style decoration, Kiva 9, Layer 17, west wall. (After field drawing by Ted Frisbie, courtesy of the Maxwell Museum of Anthropology, University of New Mexico, catalog no. 76.70.785.)

The "rainbow" striping—to use another of Smith's terms—of the framing device and its right-angled movement to form a reserved square occur at Kawaika'a (Smith 1952: Figures 70b, 82b) and are frequently seen in the Pottery Mound kivas, although the birds at the corners are omitted in the later murals at both Pottery Mound and Kawaika'a.

Kiva 9, which lay beneath Kiva 8, has some of Pottery Mound's best-preserved murals on the later layers of its south and west wall, some of which extend to the ceiling. Like Kivas 7 and 15, it has representations of shields on an early layer. An example from Layer 17 of Kiva 9 exhibits the most fully developed Sikyatki design on a shield in the extant Pottery Mound murals. Broad lines set off the lower center segment as they do in many Sikyatki and proto-Sikyatki panels (Figure 6.6). A niche is indicated on the field drawing just below the shield. In this mural layer a shield with simple geometric decoration was preserved on the south wall, but it is the shield with Sikyatki-style decoration that is positioned directly over the niche on the west wall opposite the ventilator. As offerings are believed to have been placed in the niche, images represented near it were presumably to be objects of prayer or veneration. The composition of most murals in Pottery Mound kivas

with eastern ventilators is focused on the niche, with figures on the west and side walls, if preserved, turned toward it. Sikyatki-style designs or images decorated with Sikyatki elements are placed above or near kiva niches in several Pottery Mound murals (see Table 6.2), which suggests to me that the Sikyatki style had acquired a cosmological significance there that is not readily apparent in the murals of Awat'ovi and Kawaika'a.

On Layer 12 of Kiva 9, warriors are pictured on the south and west walls holding weapons and shields decorated with proto-Sikyatki designs (Hibben 1975:7, Figure 101).[8] The shields and warriors are followed by several unpublished complex and integrated compositions that have no visual counterparts in Pueblo IV mural art. Figure 6.7 is an outstanding example of a composition focused on the niche. A curved rainbow band bearing terraced pyramids adorned with feathered prayer sticks is supported by two ambiguous human-animal composites wearing headdresses composed of short yellow feathers encircling a spray of longer red feathers. Above the main composition with its elaborate bilateral mirror symmetry is a row of profile heads all facing in the same direction in serial repetition, a compositional form more

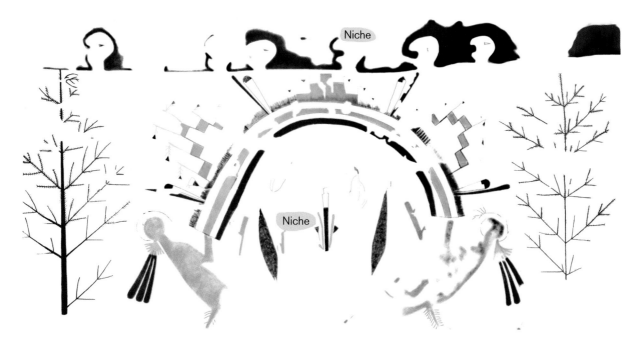

FIGURE 6.7

Rio Grande–style composition focused on the niche in west wall of Kiva 9, Layer 6. Composite human-animal figures wearing "feather bouquet" headdresses support a rainbow over the niche in bilateral mirror symmetry, but heads in upper register of the wall all face in the same direction in serial symmetry typical of Western Pueblo murals. Notes on the drawing state that the branches of the trees bore very fine leaves (needles?) in white—"possibly a fugitive organic green." (Digital composite after field drawings by Charles Welch and Chris Pierce, courtesy of the Maxwell Museum of Anthropology, University of New Mexico, catalog nos. 76.70.791, 792, 793, 794, 809.)

commonly found in the murals of Antelope Mesa than at Pottery Mound or Kuaua. Rainbows, on the other hand, appear less often in the west than they do in Rio Grande kivas, and they are particularly prominent at Picuris, where they are placed near subsidiary ventilators on the west walls opposite the main ventilator (Crotty 1995:277–78, Tables A.48–A.52; 1999:175–76, Figures 9.6, 9.7, 9.9, 9.10). The bouquetlike bundle of short yellow and long red feathers is found in a few contemporaneous Antelope Mesa murals, where it is pictured as embellishment at the end of a staff or as part of the feather decoration of a ceremonial shield (Smith 1952:Figures 50c, 54a, 56b, 73a). At Pottery Mound, it is pictured in several kivas, sometimes as a headdress, sometimes at the end of a staff, and sometimes apparently as altar furniture (see Table 6.3; Hibben 1975:Figures 61, 76, 86). It is not seen in the late Awat'ovi murals or at Kuaua or other Rio Grande sites. Human-animal composite figures occur in the Antelope Mesa murals (Smith 1952:Figures 49a, 55a, 65b, 69c, 80b)

but not so frequently, nor so imaginatively depicted, as at Pottery Mound (e.g., Hibben 1975:Figures 1, 2, 8, 12, 18, 19, 28, 37, 39, 56, 76, 78, 83, 86, 88). Only two examples occur in the Kuaua murals (Dutton 1963:Figures 63, 90).

Layer 1, the final layer of Kiva 9, seems to have been devoted to the Pottery Mound version of the Sikyatki style. The north and south walls are decorated with panels in which Sikyatki-like motifs are isolated in areas set off by a dramatic black zigzag line embellished with a stylized and symmetrical white plant form that produces a static effect quite unlike the predominately asymmetrical and curvilinear flow of motifs associated with the Awat'ovi Sikyatki murals (see Hays-Gilpin and LeBlanc, this volume, Figure 7.1; cf. Smith 1952:Figures 48a, 48b, 49a). Other examples of static Sikyatki designs from the probably contemporaneous Kiva 16 are illustrated by Hibben (1975:Figures 22, 51). On the west wall, flanking the niche, are two magnificent figures sporting squares of tan paint over one eye and asymmetrical haircuts with

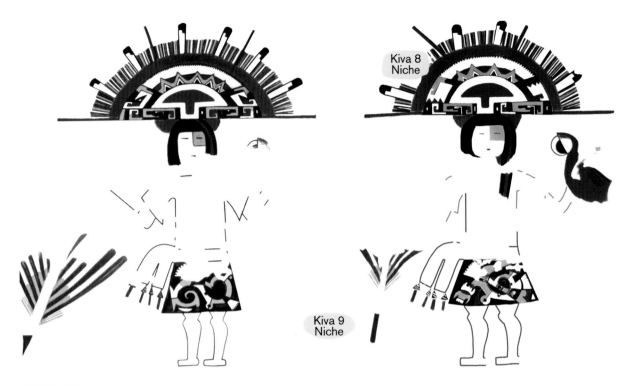

FIGURE 6.8

Pair of male figures wearing elaborate *tablitas* and kilts decorated with Sikyatki-style designs, Kiva 9, Layer 1, west wall. Each figure has a square of tan face paint over left eye and unevenly bobbed hair with red lock, stylistic details seen also in Antelope Mesa murals. Digital reconstruction shows the location of the Kiva 9 niche between figures and that of superposed Kiva 8 in the headdress of the right figure. (After field drawings by Chris Pierce and Ted Frisbie, courtesy of the Maxwell Museum of Anthropology, University of New Mexico, catalog nos. 76.70.742, 743, and photos of original paintings.)

a red lock and attired in elaborate *tablitas* and kilts decorated with Sikyatki motifs (Figure 6.8).

Kiva 8 is among the kivas thought to be in use when Pottery Mound was abandoned; it was built directly above Kiva 9 but slightly expanded. Perhaps because of its later date, some of the paintings are closer to Kuaua in style than are those from the other Pottery Mound kivas, but Western influences are still apparent. Unpublished field drawings of fragments of a Sikyatki panel on Layer 17 (Maxwell 76.70.287, 289) indicate a better understanding of the aesthetics and dynamics of Sikyatki design as expressed in Western Pueblo mural and pottery decoration than was demonstrated in the paintings mentioned above from Kivas 7, 9, and 16. Sikyatki designs are seen again on Layers 11 and 9 of the south and west walls, respectively, positioned in what appear to be painted representations of a structural rectangular space that

creates a large niche. Other examples of the painted structural niche occur in this kiva and in a more fragmentary form in Kiva 7. The Sikyatki elements are depicted as painted textiles arranged horizontally in the lower part of the rectangular space with vertical rows of beads hanging above (Figure 6.9). The painting on the south wall includes a representation of a white-on-black resist textile pattern, as seen in many Pottery Mound murals (see Webster, this volume), while that on the west wall, just above the niche, has a red and white ornament superimposed on the beads. Again in this kiva, Sikyatki designs are given a place of honor associated with both the real and the illusory niches.

On Layer 5 of Kiva 8, a ceremonial shield elaborately edged with multicolored feathers and decorated with the figure of a human-animal composite with a red lock in its hair is superimposed on the forequarters of two cougars

a.   **b.**

FIGURE 6.9

Representations of structural niches decorated with painted textiles and strings of black beads and white beads interspersed with red from Kiva 8: **a**) Layer 11, south wall showing beads above white-on-black patterned textile and a textile painted in the Sikyatki style. (After field drawing by Carolyn Pree, Maria (Jorrin) Martin, and Charles Welch, courtesy of the Maxwell Museum of Anthropology, University of New Mexico, catalog no. 76.70.324.) **b**) Layer 9, west wall, showing beads over textile painted in Sikyatki style and positioned above niche. (After field drawing by Chris Pierce, courtesy of the Maxwell Museum of Anthropology, University of New Mexico, catalog no. 76.70.340.)

(Figure 6.10). Animals or human-animal composites seemingly passing through shields or being transformed behind them occur also on Antelope Mesa (Smith 1952:Figures 47b, 56b, 89a) and in other Pottery Mound murals (see Table 6.3) but not at other Rio Grande sites. Of particular interest in this instance is the way the paws of the cougars are depicted with a negative space in the center of the paw and claws whorled around it. This conventionalized treatment of the paws of cougars or reptilian creatures appears in early Pueblo IV ceramic decoration of the Upper Little Colorado region and in Awat'ovi kiva murals of the early, middle, and late occupations, with the most exaggerated whorled claws seen in the pre-Sikyatki pottery and kivas (Crotty 1995:135–36; Smith 1952:203–4, Figures 41b, 43c, 55b, 71a). Numerous mountain lions are pictured in the Pottery Mound murals, especially in Kiva 16 (see Table 6.3), but the void-and-whorled-claw convention makes its appearance very late at the site, here on Layer 5 of Kiva 8 and in the last murals (Layer 1) from Kiva 6, another of the kivas

thought to have been in use at the time of abandonment (Hibben 1975:Title Page, Figures 47, 48).[9]

Despite the continuance of Western Pueblo iconography and conventions into the late murals of Kiva 8, figures rendered in a style very close to that seen in sixteenth-century murals from the Rio Grande pueblo of Kuaua occur both earlier and later (see Table 6.4). These similarities are perhaps most striking in the portrayal of the figure dubbed the "Man in the Moon" of Layer 1, the last mural, who strongly resembles Dutton's "Universal Deity" from Kuaua (Figure 6.11; cf. Dutton 1963:Frontispiece, Figure 54). Note that his shoulders are no longer exaggerated. His face is apparently masked; his forehead is covered by a warbonnet-like headdress, giving a flat-headed look; his mid-chest-length hair is evenly cut; and his hands are rendered as red handprints, just as they are at Kuaua. Many male figures in the Kuaua murals display long, evenly cut hair (Dutton 1963:Plates 14, 15, 16, 20, 24), and some wear the warbonnet-like headdress

FIGURE 6.10

Forequarters of two cougars emerging from behind a ceremonial shield edged with multicolored feathers and decorated with a composite human-rattlesnake figure with a red lock in its hair, Kiva 8, Layer 5, south wall. Paws of cougars exhibit Western Pueblo convention with circular void at center and whorled claws. (After field drawings by Patricia Bryan (Vivian) and Stan Bussey, courtesy of the Maxwell Museum of Anthropology, University of New Mexico, catalog nos. 76.70.318, 329, 330.)

FIGURE 6.11

"Man in the Moon" wearing mask, "warbonnet"-style headdress, chest-length hair, and with hands rendered as red handprints, strongly resembling Kuaua "Universal Deity" figure in pose and stylistic conventions, Kiva 8, Layer 1, east wall. (Field drawing by Stan Bussey and Pat Bryan [Vivian], courtesy of the Maxwell Museum of Anthropology, University of New Mexico, catalog no. 76.70.207.)

FIGURE 6.12

Mural from Kiva 2, Layer 13, west wall, exhibiting stylistic conventions of both east and west. A Western-style male figure with exaggerated shoulders, uneven haircut with red lock, holding a staff tipped with "feather bouquet" stands behind a ceremonial shield. He is flanked by Kuaua-style female human-bird composites whose flat heads balance jars from which stick lightning emanates. (After Hibben 1975:Figure 61.)

(Dutton 1963:Plates 10, 15, 24). The warbonnet-like head-dress is seen also in Rio Grande rock art.

Figure 6.12, from Layer 13 of Kiva 2, perhaps more than any single painting from Pottery Mound, combines the stylistic conventions of both east and west (see Tables 6.3, 6.4). Flat-headed female human-bird composites with paint applied to the upper portion of their faces are reminiscent of a figure portrayed in the Kuaua murals (Dutton 1963: Plate 16), as is the stick lightning springing from the black jars on their heads.[10] In contrast, the male central figure, with his exaggerated shoulders and uneven haircut, holding a staff topped with the "bouquet" of feathers, displays attributes seen in the Awat'ovi and Kawaika'a murals.

Kiva 10, the round kiva with the southern ventilator, had a relatively long occupation that is thought to have continued until the site was abandoned. Its earliest murals exhibit mostly Rio Grande affiliations. Layer 39, the oldest painted layer, is organized by what I have called a "midline" band (Figure 6.13). Rather than a broad black band, or dado, that serves as a ground line for the images, or a crenellated rainbow band that frames them, the midline band runs across the images. It occurs in some of the other Pottery Mound kivas (see Table 6.4) and also in a more sophisticated version at Kuaua (Dutton 1963:Plate 23), but never in the Antelope Mesa murals. Fragments of Kiva 10's Layer 38

show giant serpents with terraced pyramids—sometimes called cloud altars—on their backs (Figure 6.14). Giant horned serpents are also portrayed in Pottery Mound Kivas 7 and 9 (Hibben 1975:Figures 34, 42) and once or twice at Kuaua (Dutton 1963:49, Plate 13). They are found in Mimbres pottery decoration and Rio Grande and Jornada Mogollon rock art but are unknown in Western Pueblo rock art or murals (Crotty 1995:126–32).

Western influences appear on Layer 15 of Kiva 10 with the depiction of an assemblage of ritual objects, including artificial mound shapes, two of which are illustrated in Figure 6.15. Smith (1952:133–34, 233–34) discusses these "corn mountains" at length, and they are often seen in the virtually ubiquitous depictions of altar assemblages in the murals of Awat'ovi and Kawaika'a (Smith 1952:Figures 61a, 63a, 66d, 68c, 69b, d, f, 72a, 73c, 79b, 81a–b, 89c, 90c–d). This suggests to me that similar rituals were observed in Kiva 10. However, fragments of what appears to be a giant serpent are recorded on that same layer on another portion of the wall. While plaster losses make it impossible to determine what the relationship might have been if these are, indeed, parts of the same mural, it is clear that traditions of both east and west were being preserved and expressed in the ceremonies that took place here and in the other painted kivas of Pottery Mound throughout its occupation.

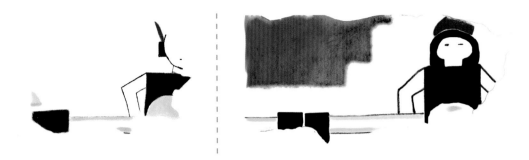

FIGURE 6.13

Rio Grande compositional device of midline band with human figures, Kiva 10, Layer 39, various wall sectors. Notes on the drawing indicate that the black stepped rectangle to the left of one of the figures was produced by cutting away the plaster of Layer 39 to reveal black paint on Layer 40 beneath. (Digital composite after field drawings by Ted Frisbie and Chris Pierce, courtesy of the Maxwell Museum of Anthropology, University of New Mexico, catalog nos. 76.70.26, 37.)

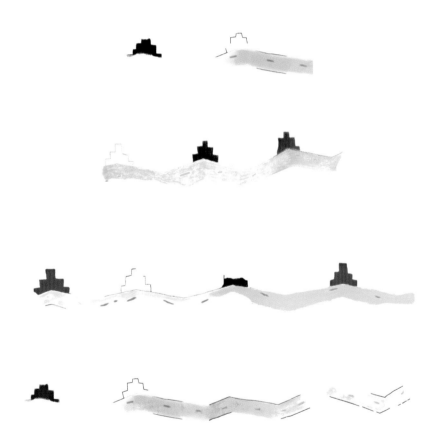

FIGURE 6.14

Giant serpent figures with terraced pyramids on their backs, Kiva 10, Layer 38, various wall sectors. (Digital composite after field drawings by Stan Bussey and Chris Pierce, courtesy of the Maxwell Museum of Anthropology, University of New Mexico, catalog nos. 76.70.35, 36, 76, 51, 40, 49, images from other layers deleted.)

FIGURE 6.15
Assemblage of ritual objects, including artificial "corn mountains," frequently portrayed in Antelope Mesa murals, Kiva 10, Layer 15, various sectors. (Digital composite after field drawings by Stan Bussey and Henry Perea, courtesy of the Maxwell Museum of Anthropology, University of New Mexico, catalog nos. 76.70.23, 39, 74.)

Summary and Conclusions

The painted kivas of Pottery Mound, together with those of Awat'ovi, Kawaika'a, and Kuaua, afford a rare opportunity to tease out the strands of different cultural traditions woven into a new social fabric in a Pueblo IV village. In an earlier work, I (1995:373) suggested that the initial Western Pueblo influences had dissipated over time at Pottery Mound, but as we have just seen, this was not the case. With a better understanding of the relative chronology of the various kivas and a closer examination of the imagery and stylistic conventions shared with the Antelope Mesa murals and absent at Kuaua or shared with Kuaua and absent at Antelope Mesa, it is possible to see that the artistic traditions of both east and west were preserved or renewed in the murals of even the last-inhabited kivas, whether their ventilators were situated on the east or the south walls. It seems reasonable to conclude from this that the people, however diverse their cultural origins, respected the traditions of their fellow villagers and integrated them into their communal religious observances.

The earliest settlers at Pottery Mound apparently did not practice mural art, but the varied architecture of early Kivas 11, 13, and 14 points to possible cultural diversity even in the earliest years. With the advent of the settlers with Western Pueblo origins, kiva architecture became even more diverse, and painted decoration of the walls was initiated. The mural art at the site seems to coincide closely with the emergence of the Sikyatki style of pottery decoration in the Hopi area around 1400, and murals inspired by the Sikyatki style appear quite early in nearly all of the painted kivas. The style is seen not only in abstract panels, as in the Awat'ovi examples, but on other pictured objects or figures in close proximity to the niches, suggesting its possible cosmological significance for the occupants. The generally static and angular quality of the early Sikyatki panels as well as the presence of Rio Grande iconography in many of the early murals, however, indicate that the Pottery Mound muralists were not first-generation immigrants from the Western Pueblos—although at least some were probably descended from them. The late appearance at Pottery Mound of the Western convention for depicting the paws of mountain lions points to continuing contact with the Hopi area, as does the presence of imported Sikyatki wares. Despite evident Western influences elsewhere, the treatment of human figures in the late murals of Kiva 8 approaches that seen in Rio Grande–style rock art as well as in the sixteenth-century murals of Kuaua. Figure 6.13 illustrates an earlier, well-integrated example from Kiva 2 where both figure styles are used in the same painting.

It is perhaps this joining of cultural traditions that tempts us to regard prehistoric Pueblo societies as mostly homogenous despite what we know about the diversity of languages and social systems and religious practices among modern Pueblo peoples. As Cordell and Plog (1979) long ago pointed out, normative generalizations about southwestern prehistory can be erroneous and misleading. Pottery Mound, with its abundant evidence of the apparently deliberate integration of separate traditions, has much to tell us yet. Further information about the painted kivas is still to be gleaned from the student notebooks and archival photographs newly deposited at the Hibben Center; this paper is only a first testing of the possibilities. ⁂

ACKNOWLEDGMENTS

I am deeply grateful once again to Deborah Kelley-Galin for her cheerful, untiring, and undercompensated work in preparing illustrations for my texts. For this volume, she has digitally tidied the slide images of the sometimes smudged and note-filled sheets of the field drawings and, when required, stitched together images from two or more field drawings to make a coherent composite. In addition, I acknowledge the courtesy of the Maxwell Museum Photographic Collections for making the images available for reproduction. My thanks also to the staff at the Hibben Center of the Maxwell Museum: to David Phillips, who first showed me the Bramlett notes; to Jean Ballagh, for calling my attention to student notebooks of particular interest; and to Catherine Baudoin for her assistance with the Hibben photo archives. I also want to acknowledge the help of Paul Kay, one of the student artists in the 1960s, who has provided much information over the years about the recording of the Pottery Mound murals as well as critical photos of the original paintings in situ, and of Bill Bramlett, another student researcher, who answered my many questions about his drawings and notes on the kiva architecture and chronology. I am most appreciative of the tireless efforts of Polly Schaafsma, whose vision and hard work have brought this volume to being, first in planning and bringing about the original seminar at the School of American Research, where the ideas and suggestions of the participants illuminated the questions to be researched; then in organizing a symposium at the Annual Meeting of the Society for American Archaeology in Salt Lake City, where revised papers were shared; and finally in serving as sharp-eyed editor of the draft chapters and somehow bringing all the diverse elements into a coordinated whole for publication.

NOTES

1. The field drawings of the murals were previously on file at the Maxwell Museum of Anthropology, University of New Mexico, but student notebooks and notes were transferred to the Maxwell following the death of Frank Hibben in 2002 and are newly available for study. Among them is an incomplete and unsigned manuscript by William O. Bramlett Jr. (personal communication 2005) dealing with the chronology of the Pottery Mound kivas and his assembled notes about their architectural features. This information was the basis for the drawings of kiva floor plans donated to the Maxwell in 1993 by Bramlett and provided most of the data for Table 6.1 and my proposed chronology of the murals. Bramlett's drawings of the floor plans have not yet been relocated and cataloged by personnel at the Hibben Center, but they are reproduced here as Figure 6.1.

2. The data concerning the number of plaster layers and mural layers published by Hibben (1975:Table 3) is not borne out by documentation. My discussion is based on information from field drawings and students' notes.

3. Two pages of field drawings from Kiva 15 have been on file at the Maxwell. Maxwell 76.70.186 indicates drawings from Layers 1–12 but illustrates just a portion of an animal tail, an outlined brown rectangle, and an unidentified outlined gray area. Maxwell 76.70.350 consists of shield designs with a notation that they appeared on Layers 3, 5, 6, and 7. Photos of these shields in the Maxwell Museum Photographic Collections (Box 47, Slides 43–46) indicates that the shields are much smaller in scale than those portrayed in other Pottery Mound kivas. Similarly small-scale representations are found in murals from fifteenth-century kivas at Gran Quivira (Crotty 1995; Peckham 1981).

4. The ceramics analysis available to Bramlett in 1963 was based on student identification of sherds and may not accurately reflect the chronology, as Pottery Mound Polychrome has been identified in sherds with Glaze A rims as well as in the more plentiful polychrome sherds with Glaze C rims (see Eckert, this volume). Additional evidence, however, such as stratigraphic location and the style and subject matter of the murals as compared with those from other Pottery Mound kivas and other sites lends support to the chronology proposed by Bramlett.

5. Except for a few field drawings, little is known about Kiva 17, which, according to Mathien (1982), was excavated by Kathy Weidner in salvage operations sometime in the summer of 1975. Sikyatki-style murals appear on its first and second painted layers, and a Kuaua-style headdress on a human-animal composite on its fourth, suggesting a fairly late date of abandonment. For additional details about its paintings, see Crotty (1995:Table A.62).

6. Although Dutton (1963:204) dates the Kuaua murals from the late fifteenth to the late sixteenth century, evidence suggests that they were actually painted some 100 years or more later (see Crotty 1995:61–64; Vierra 1987:8). By either reckoning, they are later than the last of the Pottery Mound murals, but they share many stylistic features with the murals of Pottery Mound's Kiva 8.

7. The student artists noted layer numbers on their drawings, but in Kiva 7, layer numbers for drawings from the southwest corner are often one digit higher than paintings on other walls that clearly belong to the same mural suite. In my text, therefore, I have used the layer number that agrees with the paintings on the other walls rather than the one that appears in the records.

8. The drawing illustrated by Hibben (1975:7) does not show the warrior's shield. It is visible in the original field drawing by Charles Welch (Maxwell 76.70.802). The niche is indicated on the lower right of the field drawing by Theodore Frisbie of the warrior on the west wall (Hibben 1975:7, Figure 101; Maxwell 76.70.789).

9. In Kiva 16, felines were painted on successive Layers 6, 5, and 4 in the same location (Maxwell 76.70.621, 622, 584). Charles Pierce observes on his drawing from Layer 5 that the same motif was repeated, "sometimes using the exact same lines" from one layer to the next. So far as I have been able to determine, this is the only known instance of repetition of motifs from one mural layer to another at Pottery Mound.

10. Only one of the presumably female figures portrayed in the Kuaua murals has survived with her head intact; the upper half of her face is painted yellow and she holds a narrow-necked jar and feather aspergillum (Dutton 1963:Plate 16, Figure 113). Crossed stick lightning, often associated with black jars, appears in most Kuaua murals (Dutton 1963:Plates 10, 11, 12, 16, 17, 18, 20, 21, 24).

REFERENCES CITED

Baldwin, Stuart
    1988   Studies in Piro-Tompiro Ethnohistory and Western Tompiro Archaeology. Manuscript on file, Department of Archaeology, University of Calgary, Alberta.

Bramlett, William O., Jr.
    1963a   Manuscript and notes on file, Maxwell Museum of Anthropology (Cat. No. 2003.31.5), University of New Mexico, Albuquerque.
    1963b   Drawings of Floor Plans of Pottery Mound Kivas. Manuscript on file, Maxwell Museum of Anthropology, University of New Mexico, Albuquerque.

Cordell, Linda S., and Fred Plog
    1979   Escaping the Confines of Normative Thought: A Reevaluation of Puebloan Prehistory. *American Antiquity* 44:405–29.

Crotty, Helen K.
    1995   *Anasazi Mural Art of the Pueblo IV Period, A.D. 1300–1600: Influences, Selective Adaptation, and Cultural Diversity in the Prehistoric Southwest.* University Microfilms, Ann Arbor.
    1999   Kiva Murals and Iconography at Picuris Pueblo. In *Picuris Pueblo through Time: Eight Centuries of Change at a Northern Rio Grande Pueblo,* edited by Michael A. Adler and Herbert W. Dick, pp. 149–187. William P. Clements Center for Southwest Studies, Southern Methodist University, Dallas, Texas.

Dix, Pauline
    1957   Student notebook from 1957 field school at LA 416, Pottery Mound. Manuscript on file, Maxwell Museum of Anthropology (Cat. No. 2003.37.12), University of New Mexico, Albuquerque.

Dutton, Bertha P.
    1963   *Sun Father's Way: The Kiva Murals of Kuaua, A Pueblo Ruin, Coronado State Monument, New Mexico.* University of New Mexico Press, Albuquerque.

Eggan, Fred
    1950   *Social Organization of the Western Pueblos.* University of Chicago Press, Chicago.

Hawley, Florence
    1950   Big Kivas, Little Kivas, and Moiety Houses in Historical Reconstruction. *Southwestern Journal of Anthropology* 6:286–302.

Hayes, Alden C., Jon N. Young, and A. Helene Warren
    1981   *Excavation of Mound 7, Gran Quivira National Monument, New Mexico.* Publications in Archaeology No. 16. National Park Service, Washington, D.C.

Hibben, Frank C.
    1975   *Kiva Art of the Anasazi at Pottery Mound.* KC Publications, Las Vegas, Nevada.

Mathien, Frances Joan
1982 Intermittent Excavations at Pottery Mound, June 7, 1980, through January 3, 1981. Manuscript on file, Maxwell Museum of Anthropology (Cat. No. 82.27.1), University of New Mexico, Albuquerque.

Meeker, Beverly
1954 Student notebook for 1954 field school at LA 416, Pottery Mound. Manuscript on file, Maxwell Museum of Anthropology (Cat. No. 2003.23.5), University of New Mexico, Albuquerque.

Morris, Earl H.
1919 *The Aztec Ruin.* Anthropological Papers of the American Museum of Natural History Vol. 26, Pt. 1. The Trustees of the American Museum of Natural History, New York.

Peckham, Barbara A.
1981 Pueblo IV Murals at Mound 7. In *Contributions to Gran Quivira Archaeology, Gran Quivira National Monument, New Mexico*, edited by Alden C. Hayes, pp. 15–38. Publications in Archaeology No. 17. National Park Service, Washington, D.C.

Peckham, Stewart
1979 When is a Rio Grande Kiva? In *Collected Papers in Honor of Bertha Pauline Dutton*, edited by Albert H. Schroeder, pp. 55–79. Papers of the Archaeological Society of New Mexico 4. Archaeological Society of New Mexico, Albuquerque.

Smith, Watson
1952 *Kiva Mural Decoration at Awatovi and Kawaika-a with a Survey of Other Wall Paintings in the Pueblo Southwest.* Papers of the Peabody Museum of American Archaeology and Ethnology Vol. 37. Harvard University, Cambridge, Massachusetts.

1971 *Painted Ceramics of the Western Mound at Awatovi.* Papers of the Peabody Museum of American Archaeology and Ethnology Vol. 38. Harvard University, Cambridge, Massachusetts.

1972 *Prehistoric Kivas of Antelope Mesa.* Papers of the Peabody Museum of American Archaeology and Ethnology Vol. 39, No. 1. Harvard University, Cambridge, Massachusetts.

Snow, David
1979 *Archaeological Excavations at Pueblo del Encierro, LA 70, Cochiti Dam Salvage Project, Cochiti, New Mexico, Final Report: 1964–1965 Field Season JC3580 (66), USNPS Southwest Region, Santa Fe.* Museum of New Mexico Laboratory of Anthropology Notes No. 78. Museum of New Mexico, Santa Fe.

Vierra, Bradley J.
1987 *Test Excavations at Kuaua Pueblo (LA 187).* Museum of New Mexico Laboratory of Anthropology Notes No. 396. Museum of New Mexico, Santa Fe.

Vivian, Gordon
1964 *Excavations in a 17th Century Jumano Pueblo, Gran Quivira.* Publications in Archaeology No. 8. National Park Service, Washington, D.C.

CHAPTER SEVEN

Sikyatki Style in Regional Context

Kelley Hays-Gilpin
Steven A. LeBlanc

Introduction

The Pottery Mound murals surely represent the great-est concentration of prehistoric paintings north of the ancient city of Teotihuacán. In spite of this, they remain largely unstudied. One of the most interesting ques-tions to be explored about them is how they related to the contemporary painted murals from Antelope Mesa, about 200 mi (330 km) away on the eastern edge of the Hopi Mesas in northern Arizona. Smith (1952; see also 1972) did an exhaustive study of the Antelope Mesa murals from the sites of Awat'ovi and Kawaika'a (some-times spelled Kawayka-a or Kawaikuh), which the Harvard Peabody Museum discovered in the 1930s. The Pottery Mound murals had not yet been discovered at that time, and Smith never had the opportunity to turn his keen analytical powers toward a comparison. The only in-depth, comparative study subsequent is that by Crotty (1995; 2001; this volume). But the corpus is large, the possible directions that can be investigated are broad, and much remains to be learned.

One of the most obvious and intriguing aspects of the murals in both areas is that they incorporate what is termed the "Sikyatki" design style. The asymmetri-cal, flamboyant, curvilinear, polychrome Sikyatki style, dominated by bird and feather motifs, is distinctive and unique in the greater Southwest. It appears in many

murals at Pottery Mound and a few at Awat'ovi. The style appears on a small amount of pottery at Pottery Mound and a great deal of Hopi pottery on Antelope Mesa and First Mesa. This uneven distribution suggests that the use and context of the style differed in the two at least partially contemporaneous settings.

This chapter focuses on murals, pottery, and other media that bear paintings in the Sikyatki style. Conventional archaeological wisdom identifies the Sikyatki style as Hopi, so the appearance of Sikyatki-style murals and pottery at Pottery Mound has been attributed to migrants from the Hopi Mesas. The situation may be more complicated. To unravel this problem we investigate the contexts of Sikyatki-style paintings in several media in both areas and query the cultural compositions, affiliations, and histories of the Pottery Mound and Antelope Mesa communities. We ask these questions: Where and when did this style develop? In what contexts does it appear? Did it develop first in murals, pottery, or textiles, or all of these at the same time? What accounts for the different distributions of this style in the Hopi murals and at Pottery Mound? Who painted in this style—everyone or just specialists? Men, women, other-gendered individuals, or some combination? What factors might account for its apparent rapid development and discontinuous spread? We cannot promise answers, but we hope the discussion will encourage scholars to think about Pueblo IV, cultural affiliation, specialization, and cross-media design studies in new ways.

Temporal-Spatial Setting

Murals

How common were murals in the prehistoric Southwest and when were they made? Crotty (1995) has summarized the known murals made prior to the Pueblo IV period. They tend to be rare, geometric, and monochromatic, with a few notable exceptions. A few Pueblo II–III murals in the Chaco and Mesa Verde areas have life-forms but closely resemble petroglyphs and rock paintings of static, frontal human figures, flute players in profile, and animals such as mountain sheep (Brody 1991:61–65). A polychrome geometric mural at Atsinna, near Zuni, dating between about A.D. 1275 and 1300, has a complicated pattern that resembles some of the geometric figures in later murals. In all cases, these murals are limited in number at any one locality and are very different from

the Antelope Mesa and Pottery Mound murals. We term these later murals "Pueblo IV style" to contrast them with earlier murals.

Based on murals found in the Homol'ovi sites in Arizona (Pond 1966) and our current understanding of when the Homol'ovi sites were depopulated, the Pueblo IV style mural tradition likely began sometime around A.D. 1375. The Homol'ovi sites probably did not last much beyond that time, and most of the murals found there seem less complex and probably predate the time the Pueblo IV style murals were being made. The one mural fragment described by Pond (1966) has the feet and legs of humanlike figures wearing kilts. This mural fits well within the Pueblo IV style tradition but lacks a ground line and other features that are common later. It also lacks Sikyatki-style elements. The Homol'ovi pottery assemblage lacks the fully developed Sikyatki style but includes some early elements of it, which we will discuss shortly. A beginning date of A.D. 1375 for the Pueblo IV style murals, a date closely coincident with the development of the Sikyatki style found in the Jeddito Yellow Ware ceramics (see following), seems reasonable. The remainder of this paper considers only the Pueblo IV style murals at Pottery Mound, Awat'ovi, and Kawaika'a.

Based on ceramics, it appears that Pottery Mound was founded in the 1300s and was depopulated by at least A.D. 1500 and most likely before. Based on the extreme rarity of Glaze C pottery (28 out of 44,527 painted sherds; see C. Schaafsma, Appendix C), and C. Schaafsma's (2002:195) estimated inception date of A.D. 1450–1460 for this type, an estimated terminal date for the site no later than A.D. 1475 would seem to be justified at this time. Kawaika'a was probably depopulated sometime between A.D. 1500 and 1540 (see following). But we know that painted Kiva 788 at Awat'ovi was deliberately filled with sand and a church was built over the kiva around A.D. 1630.[1] If the church was deliberately built over an important in-use kiva, as Montgomery and colleagues (1949) believed, it seems unlikely that the last murals in that kiva were painted much before A.D. 1625. Thus, the Pottery Mound paintings span 100–125 years at most, while the Antelope Mesa murals were being made for some 250 years (A.D. 1375–1625+), or for about twice as long.

Pueblo IV style murals also seem to be rather restricted in geographic space. In spite of considerable excavations of sites contemporary with these, no murals have been found in the Zuni area, the Silver Creek area (home of Fourmile Polychrome, discussed subsequently), the Salado and Hohokam Classic sites to the south, or Casas Grandes. Murals are rare but present in the remainder of the Rio Grande (see Chapter 8, this volume; Crotty 1995; Smith 1952:70–77), though none have been found at Hummingbird Ruin, which is quite near and partially contemporary with Pottery Mound. The notable exception is, of course, the murals in Kiva III at Kuaua (Dutton 1963).[2] As Webster (this volume) notes, these are very different from the Pottery Mound and Antelope Mesa murals in several important ways, including lack of Sikyatki-style imagery (therefore we do not discuss Kuaua here). Even on the Hopi Mesas, sites with murals seem to be rare. While much of the archaeological work there was early and not well documented, there have been excavations at Kokopnyama (including five kivas, one dating to A.D. 1380), Walpi, Pink Arrow (one kiva; at least part of the site dates to the late 1300s), Chakpahu, and Sikyatki. If murals like those at Awat'ovi or Kawaika'a had been found, we probably would know about them, but only a few tantalizing clues have emerged. Artist Fred Geary told architect Mary Colter that one of his paintings on an upper level of the Grand Canyon's Desert Watchtower was a copy of a mural excavated by an engineer named William Small "about 3/4 of a mile from Polacca" on First Mesa. The Sikyatki-style polychrome mural shows three feather motifs and three mountain peaks. Hopi painter Fred Kabotie told his son Michael that as a young child, he saw a mural depicting cranes at Old Soongopavi, below Second Mesa, when he accompanied his mother in searching the ruins for grinding stones to use. Kabotie said he always meant to paint it but never did (Welton 2006). The depiction of cranes recalls the crane mural at Pottery Mound (Hibben 1975:33).

Some of this absence of murals may be because the sites in many of these other areas were depopulated prior to A.D. 1400, about when the mural tradition was just taking off, although this is clearly not the case in all areas. The possible exception to the rarity of murals could be the Acoma area. Dating between the 1300s and 1600s, there are perhaps seven sites that might hold kivas with painted murals at and around Acoma Pueblo. Except for extremely limited excavations at Acoma itself (Ruppé 1953), no excavations have been done on any of these sites.

Sikyatki-style murals are much rarer than other kinds of Pueblo IV style murals, even though this style comprises a large proportion of known Hopi fourteenth- and fifteenth-century pottery assemblages. Sikyatki-style murals appear in most of the Pottery Mound kivas

in at least one mural layer (Figure 7.1), often more, but imported Hopi Yellow Ware is rare, comprising 2 percent of decorated sherds. Sikyatki Polychrome is particularly rare at Pottery Mound, and Pottery Mound Polychrome, a local glaze ware with Sikyatki-style designs, is also rare compared with other glaze ware types. Lacking further data, we cannot assess whether murals and pottery were contemporaneous. We have to look for other lines of evidence to evaluate whether Sikyatki style in Pottery Mound murals predates Sikyatki style in pottery in both areas. In our opinion, this is still an open question.

Sikyatki-Style Pottery

The Sikyatki style is named for the large site of Sikyatki, near First Mesa (Fewkes 1898; 1919), which probably had its primary occupation in the 1400s. Sikyatki style is usually associated with Sikyatki Polychrome ceramics made on or near the Hopi Mesas, although some bowls that would technically be classified as Jeddito Black-on-yellow have this style, and not all Sikyatki Polychrome vessels have what we would term Sikyatki style. The Sikyatki style has black and red on yellow colors; flamboyant bird and feather motifs (Figure 7.2); tapering spirals; flowers, butterflies, dragonflies, and katsinas; and spattered and engraved paint. Although they share some aspects with the much earlier Mimbres bowl paintings (Brody et al. 1983; LeBlanc 2004), Sikyatki designs seem to relate more to the designs on Fourmile Polychrome, Matsaki Polychrome, Ramos Polychrome, and some relatively rare ceramics from the Rio Grande, in particular, Pottery Mound Polychrome.

Pottery Mound's initial Glaze A ceramics were augmented by imported Sikyatki Polychrome and other Hopi types in the late 1300s–1400s and by a "local synthesis" (Figure 7.3)—glaze ware technology with Sikyatki-style decoration—called Pottery Mound Polychrome. Sikyatki style did not apparently develop in the ceramic medium at Pottery Mound because there are no intergrade styles between Glaze A types and Pottery Mound Polychrome, and Pottery Mound Polychrome designs appear to be much simpler than ones on Sikyatki-style Sikyatki Polychrome. Glaze A Black-on-red (Figure 7.4), the most frequent decorated type at Pottery Mound, usually has a paneled layout with geometric fill, often in an alternating pattern. Centers of bowls are not decorated. Exteriors have simple designs of paired lines or slashes. This style is very different from contemporaneous pottery in the fourteenth-century pueblos at Hopi (see Smith 1971), along the Rio Puerco of

FIGURE 7.1
Detail of Sikyatki-style mural at Pottery Mound, Kiva 9, Layer 1, south wall, right half.
(Courtesy of the Maxwell Museum of Anthropology, University of New Mexico, catalog no. 2005.59.8c.)

FIGURE 7.2
Sikyatki-style pottery jar.
(Photograph by Gene Balzer, courtesy of the Museum of Northern Arizona, catalog no. A5900.)

FIGURE 7.3
Pottery Mound Polychrome bowls from Pottery Mound. (Courtesy of the Maxwell Museum of Anthropology, University of New Mexico, catalog nos. 66.102.35, 87.50.16.)

the West and Little Colorado River (Adams 1991; Adams and Hays 1991; Hough 1901 on Stone Axe Pueblo), where banded bowl designs gave way to allover patterns hundreds of years earlier.

Sikyatki style may have developed in pottery on the Hopi Mesas, but not entirely from local traditions. The most frequent decorated pottery type on the Hopi Mesas in the mid-1300s was Jeddito Black-on-yellow (Figure 7.5). Massed red paint occurs after 1375 but remains rare till sometime in the 1400s. "Early" or "Jeddito-style" Sikyatki Polychrome never dominates assemblages, and it does not bear the distinctive Sikyatki style (Figure 7.6). It sometimes bears a few—but never all—of the stylistic features that appear on somewhat earlier pottery and on contemporaneous pottery from the Mogollon Rim area and even northern Chihuahua. Ceramic specialists generally agree that Fourmile Polychrome predates Sikyatki style on Jeddito Yellow Ware. Van Keuren (2001:17) writes, "Sometime in the 1320s, potters at a handful of villages in the Silver Creek drainage [near Show Low, eastern Arizona] began to alter the decorative configuration of White Mountain Red Ware, producing what is now

FIGURE 7.4
Glaze A Black-on-red bowl from Pottery Mound. (Courtesy of the Maxwell Museum of Anthropology, University of New Mexico, catalog no. 66.102.1.)

FIGURE 7.5

Typical Jeddito-style black-on-yellow bowls and a jar from the mid-1300s. (Photographs by Gene Balzer, courtesy of the Museum of Northern Arizona, catalog nos. A239, A725, A964, OC237, A760, A1567.)

FIGURE 7.6

Early-style Sikyatki Polychrome bowls. (Photographs by Gene Balzer, courtesy of the Museum of Northern Arizona, catalog nos. OC949 and OC307, from Kokopnyama on Antelope Mesa.) The bowl with the central spiral has been lost. It came from a painted kiva at Homol'ovi II. (Photograph by the late Gordon Pond, image on file at the Museum of Northern Arizona's Hopi Iconography Project and the Arizona State Museum's Homol'ovi Research Program.)

FIGURE 7.7
Fourmile Polychrome. (Photographs by Scott Van Keuren, courtesy of the Smithsonian Institution and Scott Van Keuren, U.S. National Museum of Natural History catalog nos. 177110, 177219, 177342, and 177393.)

known as Fourmile style."[3] The shift toward asymmetric, center-focused designs with spiral and feather motifs did not begin in the Hopi Yellow Ware until after 1350, and recognizable "flamboyant" Sikyatki style does not appear until sometime after 1400. Moreover, it seems that the Matsaki Polychrome at Zuni (Smith et al. 1966) and Pottery Mound Polychrome seem to be derived from Sikyatki-style Sikyatki Polychrome (rather than the earlier Jeddito-style Sikyatki Polychrome), based on use of interpenetrating negative and positive space, the forms of feather and spiral motifs, and divisions of the design field. Although Matsaki and Pottery Mound polychromes are in some ways "simpler" than the most elaborate Sikyatki Polychrome vessels, they were apparently made in more limited numbers and by less skilled painters than the most elaborate late or "flamboyant" style Sikyatki Polychrome from the Hopi Mesas. To be fair, a great deal of late style Sikyatki Polychrome from the Hopi Mesas is also rather simple and poorly executed, suggesting a range of skill levels among its makers. At any rate, if the Sikyatki style was a horizon style, Pottery Mound Polychrome and Matsaki Polychrome probably date to the 1400s.

In the Mogollon Rim area of Arizona, Fourmile Polychrome (Figure 7.7) developed when potters moved banded geometric designs to vessel exteriors and decorated bowl interiors with bold, asymmetric polychrome designs that included katsinas, serpents, birds, and abstract spirals and cloud terraces (Carlson 1971; Van Keuren 2001:189–92). Fourmile Polychrome prefigures many aspects of Sikyatki-style layout and iconography and, to some extent, division and framing of design fields and use of negative space. Fourmile colors, like those of other White Mountain Red Ware types, are black and white on red. The black- and red-on-buff or yellow color scheme appears in Kinishba Polychrome from south-central Arizona, which antedates Sikyatki Polychrome but is quite rare and lacks most of the other stylistic features of Sikyatki.

The one wild card is Ramos Polychrome from Chihuahua. While definitely not in the Sikyatki style, aspects of this tradition clearly relate to the Hopi Yellow Ware. Both Sikyatki and Ramos polychromes have black and red designs on a buff ground, some similar iconography, and bird effigy vessels. Both types depict birds, serpents, and masklike human faces, but overall styles, vessel shapes,

FIGURE 7.8

"Flying saucer"–shaped Sikyatki Polychrome jars with "flamboyant" style. The one on the left, with the bird and flower, has been restored, and the back part of the bird is in-painted. (Photograph by Gene Balzer, courtesy of the Museum of Northern Arizona, catalog nos. A2503 (left) and OC1820 (right).)

and layouts are distinct. Unfortunately, the dating of Casas Grandes/Paquimé is still under debate (e.g., Dean and Ravesloot 1993; LeBlanc 1980; Lekson 1984; Phillips and Carpenter 1999; Rakita and Raymond 2003; Ravesloot et al. 1995). However, all various chronologies have Ramos being produced earlier than Sikyatki. We do not pursue this possible linkage further here. Neither Fourmile nor Ramos provides a satisfactory antecedent for Sikyatki, but they are more plausible than the local Kayenta branch ceramic traditions of Hopiland (see, for example, Beals et al. 1945) or the widespread Pinedale style of the late 1200s and early 1300s (Carlson 1971; Lyons 2003).

Dating the beginning of Sikyatki style on Jeddito Yellow Ware is difficult. A small amount of early Sikyatki Polychrome appears at Homol'ovi I and II on the Middle Little Colorado River (see Adams and Hays 1991). A bowl looted from a painted kiva at Homol'ovi II (see Figure 7.6), and now lost, provides one of the best examples of an intergrade between Fourmile and Sikyatki (Pond 1966: Figure 4). It has a large, tapering, asymmetrical red and black spiral with two small eyes set into it. This figure takes up two-thirds of the design field, and a straight band partitions off the other third. The spiral is also a dominant motif on earlier Fourmile Polychrome and later Sikyatki Polychrome, and the 1/3 to 2/3 partitioning of the design field occurs in both types (see Lyons 2003:56). Placing two eyes on one side of a bird's head is a convention often

seen in Fourmile Polychrome, but less often in Sikyatki. The kiva in which this bowl was deposited was probably ritually closed around 1400 (Walker 1995:95, 101), when Homol'ovi II was depopulated (Adams 2001:246). Other vessels placed therein have typical Jeddito-style designs with a mix of apparently nonrepresentational bilateral, bifold, and asymmetrical center-focused designs typical of the 1350–1400 period in all the Homol'ovi collections.

Sometime after 1400, when the last of Homol'ovi's inhabitants had departed (many probably migrated to the Hopi Mesas), and before the probable abandonment of Kawaika'a around 1500, the following new stylistic attributes appear in Hopi Yellow Ware pottery: high shoulder and strongly incurved and recurved bowl rims, "flying saucer"–shaped jars (Figure 7.8), sharp increase in frequency of centered asymmetric motifs, especially spiral/bird forms, generous use of multiple pigments and paint treatments, and sharp increase in variety of framing treatments including no banding or framing lines, band without frame, frame without band, and a closely spaced band and frame treatment, as well as apparent persistence of the earlier format. A wider variety of painting techniques and colors appears, and we have the development of what Watson Smith called a "flamboyant" style. This is the Sikyatki style that appears in some of the kiva murals at Pottery Mound, Awat'ovi, and Kawaika'a and on a very limited number of pottery types outside the Hopi area:

Pottery Mound Polychrome and a Zuni buff ware type called Matsaki Polychrome (Smith et al. 1966).

No datable materials were collected in Fewkes's excavations of Sikyatki. Awat'ovi produced an abundance of tree-ring dates that establish occupation for hundreds of years from the 1200s to 1700, but repeated reuse of scarce wood resources has jumbled any helpful associations between pottery and wood samples. Therefore, dating the abandonment of Kawaika'a is extremely important to dating the beginning of Sikyatki style, because the style was well developed in pottery from its uppermost layers. Kawaika'a lies only a few miles from Awat'ovi on Antelope Mesa. It appears to have been founded at about the same time or a little later, in the 1200s, by people bearing a similarly diverse array of pottery types from the Kayenta, Kintiel-Klagetoh, Hopi Buttes, and other surrounding areas. A number of archaeologists excavated at Kawaika'a between 1900 and 1940, and some obtained datable materials. The latest reported tree-ring date of 1495 is from sample KAW-107, from a post in the talus slope near the southern set of graves. Douglass (1935) cites this date as evidence that Kawaika'a was occupied very close to the 1540 arrival of Coronado's expedition with Tovar and cites Luxan's 1582 journal describing a pueblo destroyed by Coronado's men in retaliation for injuries inflicted on the Spaniards. Some researchers and some Hopi historians feel that Kawaika'a, rather than Awat'ovi, was the first Hopi village encountered by Spaniards in 1540 and that at least a few people still lived there when Luxan arrived in 1582 (Hargrave 1951:23; Reed 1942; L. J. Kuwaniwisiwma, personal communication to Hays-Gilpin 2005). Brew (1941) argued against this view (Montgomery et al. 1949). According to tree-ring specialist Ahlstrom's (1998) records, however, sample KAW-107 was reexamined in 1965 and given a date of "1400vv," which means that an unknown number of outside rings was missing. The latest date reported in the reanalysis of all the 48 datable samples from the site is 1474vv, meaning the tree died any number of years after 1474.[4] Therefore, the occupation of Kawaika'a up to and beyond A.D. 1500 is not supported by the tree-ring evidence, which is, admittedly, meager. We find it implausible that a village could be continuously occupied for 100 years after its latest tree-ring date. Surely, some construction and at least repairs would have introduced more recent material. For this reason, and due to conflicting documentary accounts about which villages were occupied when Spaniards visited, we favor an end date of about 1500 for Kawaika'a at this time. Altogether,

the ceramic and tree-ring evidence suggests depopulation in the late 1400s.

In summary, there is a clear late thirteenth-century Western Pueblo pattern (dominated by Pinedale style) followed by a clear fourteenth-century pattern at Hopi (dominated by Jeddito style) followed by a great deal of diversity in the fifteenth century that includes but is not limited to Sikyatki style (see Lyons [2003] for a full description of the first two stages of the sequence). The flamboyant Sikyatki style appears at Hopi sometime after 1400, perhaps even after 1450. It was well developed by about 1500 and continued in use at Awat'ovi until the founding of the Spanish mission there in 1629. The style is most frequent on Antelope Mesa and First Mesa. Based on a cursory inspection of the Charles Owen collections at the Chicago Field Museum, vessels bearing this style were rare on Second and Third mesas. Pottery with this style rarely appears anywhere outside of the eastern Hopi Mesas. Pottery Mound and a few Zuni sites, such as Hawikku, are exceptions.

The Distribution of Sikyatki Designs on Murals

Murals with Sikyatki style are rare outside Pottery Mound and appear in only one kiva on Antelope Mesa (Awat'ovi T14 Room 3; Figure 7.9). Because many of the Pottery Mound murals depict kilts and blankets with Sikyatki-style designs, we suggest that the mode of transmission of this style was painted textiles, not murals or pottery. The loss of textiles from the archaeological record may account for the discontinuous distribution of this style on murals and pottery as much as any other factor. We will first explain why we think most of the Sikyatki-style murals at Pottery Mound represent textiles, then discuss a number of social factors that may be implicated in this style's distribution in time, space, and across media.

Sikyatki style's presence at Pottery Mound is particularly intriguing as it is rarely found on ceramics that might have been made at the site, and when it is used on ceramics it is used in a much more limited manner than is seen in the murals (Figure 7.10). Conversely, this style is quite common in the Pottery Mound murals. Excavations were conducted in 17 kivas at Pottery Mound. A few produced no painted murals or no records of them survived (K3, K4, K11, K13, K14), or murals were in such limited numbers or in such poor condition that little can be said about them that pertains to these issues (K5, K12, K15).[5] Therefore there

FIGURE 7.9
Sikyatki-style murals from Awat'ovi Test 14, Room 3. (Courtesy of the Peabody Museum of Archaeology and Ethnology, Harvard University.)

FIGURE 7.10
Sikyatki Polychrome bowls with elements similar to those in the murals illustrated in Figures 7.1 and 7.9 but with a more limited repertoire. (Courtesy of the Peabody Museum of Archaeology and Ethnology, Harvard University, catalog nos. 12529, 26886.)

are nine kivas that contain enough material to warrant further discussion (K1, K2, K6, K7, K8, K9, K10, K16, K17).

These kivas are far from identical and instead have a wide range of features (see Figure 6.1, Bramlett's drawings of kiva plans). These kivas can be broken down into round (Kiva 10) or rectangular (the remainder). Four kivas had air vent deflectors that were three sided without terraces, five deflectors were three sided with terraces, and five deflectors were straight. Eleven of these deflectors were made of adobe, three of stone. Two-thirds of the kivas had no benches, but three had benches behind the deflector, one had one on the opposite wall, and two had them on side walls. About half were oriented to the south and half to the east. One might expect such variation to reflect minor ethnic differences (for example, migrants from different areas), differences in ceremonial practice, or other social differences that might be reflected in their users' willingness to use Sikyatki designs in their murals. However, this is not the case. Each of these kivas has one or more usages of Sikyatki designs. To put this another way, Sikyatki style is ubiquitous at Pottery Mound.

At Antelope Mesa, good, clear Sikyatki style exists only in the murals of Kiva T14, Room 3 at Awat'ovi. No other kiva there, anywhere else on Antelope Mesa, or at any other Pueblo III or Pueblo IV site, including Kuaua, has murals that use this design style. We return to such comparisons later. But first we look at how the style is used in the murals. It is possible to place the designs into four broad categories. These are key to understanding what is being depicted and perhaps to how the designs were being used and transmitted. They are:

1. Designs on garments being worn. In particular, many figures wear kilts that seem to have been painted with Sikyatki designs (see Figure 6.8). As Webster has pointed out, textiles depicted on the murals, as well as those recovered archaeologically in the Southwest, show woven, embroidered, tie-dyed, and painted designs. All these techniques are used on kilts worn by people in the murals.

2. Designs on what appear to be blankets or mantas that are not being worn, or perhaps screens that hung or were propped behind altars (Figure 7.11). The designs appear to be painted on these objects. They have black borders that are wider than the black lines that outline figures or design elements. Sometimes there are double borders. These appear to be depictions of selvages or

FIGURE 7.11
Hanging textile with Sikyatki style. Detail of Pottery Mound mural from Kiva 2, Layer 1, north wall. (Courtesy of the Maxwell Museum of Anthropology, University of New Mexico, catalog no. 2005.59.2d.)

borders of blankets. They are rectangular. It is clear that blankets are shown in the murals with designs other than Sikyatki style, including blankets with small dot-in-square patterns that may depict tie-dye or another resist technique and blankets that appear to be painted with crisscrossing bands of typical Glaze A pottery designs. At least three panels at Pottery Mound show blankets hanging on walls. The clearest is a set depicted as if hanging from horizontal beams as a backdrop in the mural on Kiva 16, Layer 11 (Hibben 1975:122–23). Something similar is probably depicted in Kiva 2, Layer 1 (see Figure 7.11; Hibben 1975:32–33). Also, Kiva 10, Layer 10 (Hibben 1975:124) and Kiva 12, Layer 25 (Hibben 1975:125) surely must be depictions of textiles. Thus, we are sure textiles that are not being worn are being shown in the murals as if they were hanging on walls. We term these "blankets" in this paper to keep the nomenclature simple.

3. Designs that appear to be positioned behind people, but where there is no evidence they represent hanging textiles. For example, the corn maiden–like figures in Kiva 7, Layer 30 are surrounded by small, free-floating Sikyatki style spirals and feather, bird, and butterfly elements (see Figure 6.4). We use the term "background" for these images. These may be textile depictions that happen to be too fragmentary to be recognized as such.

4. Designs that are incorporated into complex panels, often in elements that frame central portions, and where the panels overall do not appear to represent textiles. While it is possible that these depictions were intended to represent textiles, this seems unlikely. See, for example, Kiva 10, Layer 31 (Hibben 1975:Figure 6).

5. Designs that appear to be painted on shields—for example Kiva 9, Layer 12 (Hibben 1975:Figure 101) and Layer 17 (Maxwell Museum Cat. No. 76.70.785) and Kiva 10, Layer 15 (Maxwell Museum Cat. No. 76.70.38).

6. Miscellaneous fragments that cannot be assigned any category, but which do not appear to comprise an additional category.

The distribution of these types of depictions is given in Table 7.1 for murals at Pottery Mound.

This is a conservative estimate of the number of Sikyatki-style blankets depicted because, as noted, some of the design panels that are listed under "background" may have represented blankets but edges were destroyed and no distinctive features remain to indicate that that they were actually blankets, so we have listed them as "background," "complex panels," or "miscellaneous." Ignoring the miscellaneous category, the majority of occurrences are either kilts, blankets, or shields—18 instances including questionable examples. Only seven instances are clearly not kilts, blankets, or shields, with another five or so that may or may not have been blankets. This is a rather extraordinary finding. About 60 percent and perhaps more of the Sikyatki images on the murals are shown as portable art. Blankets, kilts, and shields could have easily traveled between towns.

It is also true that ceramics are portable and that some Jeddito Yellow Ware definitely made its way from the Hopi Mesas to Pottery Mound. Bowls and jars provide many instances of Sikyatki style, but they contain only fragments or pieces of the complex designs seen on the murals or on the blankets or kilts depicted on the murals. Pottery painting has a narrower repertoire of icons than mural painting and, presumably, of painted textiles. Potters seem to have shared a vocabulary with mural painters but lacked the overall grammars and narratives of murals. The ceramics present pieces of the imagery. Single elements, or snippets, are what we see. These are often rendered very elegantly and so appear as coherent images, but when seen alongside the murals, it is clear that they are always just elements. If the same people painted in all media, they used very different combinations of, and settings for, the same images. It seems more likely to us that murals and pottery were not painted by the same individuals, who may have been divided by gender roles, sodality membership, or some other social distinction. Pottery painters may have viewed ceremonies and textiles in which Sikyatki-style murals and textiles were displayed, and from that imagery, they extracted pieces that they could remember and apply to pottery vessels. Pottery therefore was probably not the primary mode of transmission of the Sikyatki style between the Hopi Mesas and Pottery Mound. Rather, as Brody (1964:125) has already suggested, Sikyatki style in murals may have represented textiles.

Our first important conclusion is that if textiles were involved, we may be missing the bulk of the imagery being made at Pottery Mound and elsewhere. Elements of designs that were widely used on textiles may have been reproduced on ceramics and used on shields. It may be the case that occasionally these images were used in murals, most of the time depicting textiles, but sometimes they were used in complex panels or as backgrounds. Nevertheless, textiles, now lost to us, seem to have been the dominant medium. This has profound implications for how the style may have been transported and how it was used socially.

It is interesting that of all the textiles that have been recovered from Ancestral Puebloan sites, none

Table 7.1. Distribution of Sikyatki Design Elements in Pottery Mound Kivas

Kiva	Kilts	Blankets	Background	Complex Panels	On Shields	Miscellaneous
K1	1S	3N?	4N	–	–	–
K2	–	1N, 21W (same as 18W)	–	21-18W?	14?	–
K6	–	10E?, 6W?	6S?	–	–	22S, 20S?
K7	–	–	30S, 29W[a]	22E[a]	–	23W, 4W
K8	11S?	20S	–	–	–	–
K9	1W	1S (same as 20S), 1N	–	–	17W, 12W?	8E
K10	21	13, 31	–	–	15	6
K16	–	3E, 8N	2W?	–	–	–
K17	–	9W, 6W?	–	–	–	–

Note: Occurrences are listed by layer-wall. Question marks involve both uncertainty about designs, layers, or both. This table is based on our present knowledge about mural provenience. As the Maxwell Museum continues to study the site and excavation records, and as better data emerge, this list may change.

[a]May be blankets but no edge survived.

are clearly kilts. In fact only a couple of kilts have been found anywhere in the Southwest (Kent 1983). Yet, the early Spanish chronicles refer to kilt wearing in the Rio Grande, and they are commonly depicted being worn at both Pottery Mound and Antelope Mesa, and they also appear in Rio Grande–style rock art. This entire class of textiles is not found archaeologically, signifying just how much of the design environment may be missing to us due to poor preservation.

The quantities of these textiles could have been substantial. However, there is some divergent evidence on how common they were. The narratives of the Coronado expedition often state that certain pueblos did not grow cotton or that cotton textiles were few.[6] And the expedition collected 300 or more textiles from Rio Grande pueblos for winter clothing their first winter (Winship 1896:219). They apparently did the same thing the second winter. In each case, the seizure was met with great resistance implying that large textiles suitable for winter

clothing or bedding were scarce and valuable. Conversely, when the Espejo expedition reached Awat'ovi in 1583 they were given "six hundred pieces of cotton cloth, small and large, white and figured, so that it was a marvelous sight to behold" (Hammond and Rey 1966:190), and when Obregón described this same event he said the Hopi gave the Spaniards "a thousand cotton blankets" (Hammond and Rey 1928:329). We know from prehistoric examples that painted textiles were common (Kent 1983; Teague 1998). There is no means at present to estimate how many blankets would have been painted in Sikyatki style in various communities, but the numbers could have been substantial. Interestingly, Coronado sent to Mexico two textiles he had "painted with the animals which they have in this country, although, as I said, the painting is very poorly done, because the artist did not spend more than one day in painting it. I have seen other paintings on the walls of these houses which have much better proportion and are done much better" (Winship 1896:332). The implication seems to be that textiles were painted, there were artists who did this, and that they were not painted with representative art, as the artist was not facile in doing so. This seems to fit with what we know archaeologically. Moreover, blankets, and to a lesser extent kilts, are very observable. Whether being worn, hung over a beam in a house, or used ceremonially, they would have been visible. In contrast, bowls are relatively small and would often have been stored out of sight or filled with food when in use. If one was interested in signaling their belief system or their allegiance to a new religion, using designs on textiles would have been far more effective than using designs on ceramics (see Hays 1992 for further discussion of this issue). Visibility is also an important issue for understanding the murals. In large communities, only a fraction of the population is likely to have seen any particular mural because kivas are relatively small, dark rooms, and Pueblo people who still use kivas do so in small groups of initiated individuals. Noninitiates are prohibited from entry except during rare occasions. Murals were certainly not displayed as publicly as textiles would have been.

Sikyatki-Style Murals at Awat'ovi

As noted, the number of Sikyatki designs at Awat'ovi is actually quite limited in spite of the fact that the images there are quite spectacular. All convincing Sikyatki-style images were confined to Kiva T14, Room 3. Smith suggested that a few other designs in other kivas might have been in the Sikyatki style but none of these display enough distinctive features to convince us. There were no shields or kilts depicted that have Sikyatki designs, although some depicted kilts were very colorful and elaborate and possibly were painted kilts: for example, T5, Room 1, Layer 2 left (Smith 1952:Figure 67) and T14, Room 3, Layer 1 right (Smith 1952:Figure 51).

That leaves three major design panels in T14, Room 3 that had Sikyatki style: those on Layers 4–12, 9–16, and 11–18. The double numbers refer to images that spanned walls that had different layer numbering sequences. In particular, Layers 4 and 12 either represent the same painting episode or are only one layer apart. So, quite likely there were only three painting episodes that produced all the Sikyatki panels in this kiva. All these panels are quite similar. The details of using fine tick marks, very delicate scroll ends of elements, similarity in the use of large central circular emblems, very elaborate *tiponis* (perfect ears of corn or other items adorned in cotton,

feathers, and other materials that serve as a priestly leader's badge of authority), circles with interior boxes that have inwardly curved sides, and a heavy emphasis on tan, brownish-red, and black with very minor use of blue and gray all suggest painting by the same artist(s).

The panels are bounded on the bottom and at least one side (most on both sides) by thick black lines (no tops survived). These are not the very wide bands found at Pottery Mound, nor are they double framing bands. All three of these designs could be interpreted as textiles but not as convincingly as some of those at Pottery Mound. In particular the design in Kiva T14, Room 3, Layers 9 and 16 appears to depict an altar scene with piles of corn and two tiponis in a central location with two elaborate figures flanking it on either side (Figure 7.12). These figures are in Sikyatki style and conceivably could be depictions of textiles hanging behind the altar, but most likely they are background images like some at Pottery Mound.

Given the similarity of the three panel sets, and given that they really span Layers 4–11, which in turn could span perhaps seven years, these could easily have been painted by the same person(s). This kiva had a total of 34 plaster layers, of which not quite two-thirds were painted. If each layer represented a year, then a use-span of 34 years is indicated. Even if we double this, and assume two years between plasterings, the kiva would have had a 68-year use-life, which seems reasonable. With two years between painting events we still get only 14 years (seven layers) for the time in which the Sikyatki-style murals were painted. Thus, in all likelihood, the use of Sikyatki designs in the mural medium at Awat'ovi was restricted to one kiva in a very brief interval. The contrast with Pottery Mound is striking.

Equally intriguing is that Smith (1972) argued that all the kivas in the area termed T14 were occupied contemporaneously. Tree-ring dates from this kiva cluster range from the mid-1400s to 1493 (none are cutting dates). It is quite likely, then, that the Sikyatki murals at Awat'ovi were painted in the very late 1400s or early 1500s. This is about the time Pottery Mound was depopulated. Did a group move from Pottery Mound to Awat'ovi at that time? These murals could have been painted by a couple of men from such a group whose style then died out when they ceased to paint murals. We have been able to find nothing out of the ordinary about Kiva T14, Room 3 that would suggest that it was made by an immigrant group, but that would not be necessary for immigrants to have painted a few murals.

FIGURE 7.12
Awat'ovi mural that appears to depict an altar scene with piles of corn and *tiponi* in a central location with two elaborate figures in Sikyatki style flanking it on either side. Kiva T14, Room 3, Layer 16, east wall, Layer 9, north wall. (Smith 1952: Figure 59a. Courtesy of the Peabody Museum of Archaeology and Ethnology, Harvard University.)

Who's Who? Multiethnic Communities

Several social factors might account for the discontinuous patterning of Sikyatki style on pottery and murals at Hopi, Zuni, and Pottery Mound. The first is migration and preservation of social differences among people with different histories, the second is ritual specialization and sodalities, and the third is gender and craft specialization. We will discuss these factors in some detail in the remainder of this chapter. Our goal is to show that Sikyatki style need not have been associated with Hopi or any other extant ethnic or language group.

Migration

We are not ruling out one or more migrations to Pottery Mound from Antelope Mesa, as proposed by Crotty (1995), but we can also make a plausible case for at least one mural-painting immigrant to Antelope Mesa from Pottery Mound. Whichever way they were headed, east, west, or some of both, who were the migrants? Should we call them Hopi or Eastern Pueblo? Or are these present-day terms inappropriate?

The Sikyatki style is assumed to have developed on the Hopi Mesas, rather than at Pottery Mound or Zuni, because of the abundance of Sikyatki Polychrome pottery in Hopi Mesas sites, because it reaches its most elaborate expression there, and because the only plausible transitional styles and techniques are found in the

Jeddito Yellow Ware sequence (though these are not abundant), and not in the Zuni or Rio Grande pottery traditions. We have already discussed one problem with this scenario: although we have the Sikyatki style preserved in pottery and murals, the most likely mode of transmission for Sikyatki style was painted textiles, a highly portable and highly visible medium. Second, if the most plausible pottery antecedents of the Sikyatki style appeared in the Upper Little Colorado area on Fourmile Polychrome before they appeared at Hopi and Pottery Mound, then the style may have been developed by late fourteenth-century or early fifteenth-century immigrants to Hopiland, who are unlikely to have been Hopi speakers (Zunian or Keresan are perhaps more plausible). The problem we address in this section is the tendency for researchers to equate the geographic locality "Hopi Mesas" with "Hopi" as an ethnic identity.

Even today, to call Hopi a coherent ethnic group is a stretch. Since at least the late 1800s, Hopi people have described themselves as an aggregate of clan people with varied migration histories and varied linguistic, cultural, and geographic backgrounds. Judging by pottery and architecture styles as well as traditional histories, people living on the Hopi Mesas in the fifteenth century were certainly not ethnically homogenous; the murals and pottery in both areas are not homogenous, and even Jeddito Yellow Ware pottery is far from homogenous (Smith 1962; 1971). Our recent informal survey of thousands of whole Jeddito

FIGURE 7.13
Garfish in kiva mural at
Kawaika'a. (Smith 1952:
Plate D and Figure 60b,
T4 Room 4, right half,
bottom left.
Courtesy of the Peabody
Museum of Archaeology
and Ethnology, Harvard
University.)

Yellow Ware vessels in museum collections shows that the Sikyatki style, in its most elaborate and well-executed expressions between about 1450 and 1600, was not necessarily typical of pottery produced in the Hopi area during that interval. We tend to focus on the most spectacular examples for illustration and exhibit. The vast majority of fifteenth- to sixteenth-century Hopi Yellow Ware pottery was not so well executed or expertly conceived.

Archaeological evidence and traditional histories suggest that Awat'ovi and Kawaika'a were, like Pottery Mound and Hawikku, multiethnic communities where people with diverse histories lived together for a time. Traditional histories clearly state that Kawaika'a was a "Laguna village," that is, Keresan speaking (Stephen 1936:714), and many different people lived at Awat'ovi, including many Keresans (Courlander 1971:209, 268). The people at Sikyatki and many of the Antelope Mesa sites are said to have come from the "eastern pueblos" (Courlander [1971:150]; Hodge [1907:564]; when Hopi people refer to "eastern" pueblos they may include Zuni, which lies east of Hopi, although anthropologists classify Zuni as Western Pueblo). Our survey suggests that Awat'ovi, Kawaika'a, and Sikyatki have the most pottery with Sikyatki style. But as already noted, only a few murals at Awat'ovi and none at Kawaika'a have Sikyatki-style imagery.

Many murals in both sites, as well as at Pottery Mound and Kuaua, have a narrative style that depicts altarlike figures and supernatural personages. Many of these have pronounced Eastern Pueblo features and styles. A Kawaika'a mural, Test 4, Room 4, Layer 8, depicts a garfish (Figure 7.13; Smith 1971:Figure 60b), whose closest natural habitat probably would be the Rio Grande (see also P. Schaafsma, Chapter 8). Second, katsina depictions from the Hopi Mesas and other parts of Arizona in the 1300s are always depicted frontally, with an emphasis on the face, and other anthropomorphic figures are usually fairly simple. In contrast, some murals and a small number of Jeddito Yellow Ware pottery vessels from the 1400s include depictions of human figures in detailed ritual regalia, with chiseled profiles emphasizing the nose and chin (for example, University of Colorado vessel 3692 from Room 22, Kawaika'a; Figure 7.14; Smith [1952:Figure 27e–f, h–m, n–p]). These have no precedent in Arizona but do appear in the Jornada Mogollon rock art style and later in the Rio Grande style (Schaafsma 1992:Figures 78, 79, 94, 146; 2000:Figure 15a–e). Hairstyles depicted on many such figures are recognized by Hopi people today as Eastern Pueblo styles, not Hopi (E. Polingyouma, personal communication to Hays-Gilpin 2002; Figure 7.15), and a number of Hopi consultants have identified

FIGURE 7.14
Profile figure on Sikyatki Polychrome jar. University of Colorado vessel 3692 from Room 22, Kawaika'a. This vessel has been heavily restored, but we believe this portion to be mostly original. (Courtesy of the University of Colorado Museum. Profile figures from Antelope Mesa murals. From Smith 1952:Figure 27e–f, h–m, n–p. Courtesy of the Peabody Museum of Archaeology and Ethnology, Harvard University.)

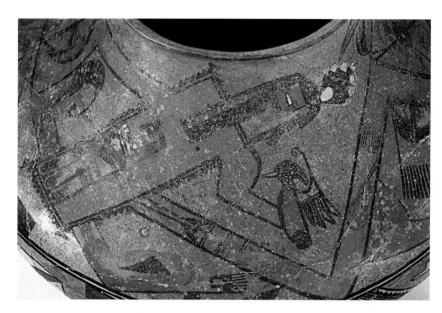

these murals as "Eastern Pueblo" in informal discussions about the images.

Therefore, when we suggest that Sikyatki style may have evolved at Hopi, we should not assume that its inventors spoke Hopi or that they had lived on the Hopi Mesas for more than a few generations, if that. Most important, we need to recognize that many different mural and pottery styles coexisted on Antelope Mesa. Some of these apparently did not evolve locally but had their origins as far east as the Rio Grande region, probably as far southeast as the Jornada Mogollon area (P. Schaafsma, Chapter 8). Others were probably developed by migrants who came from the south, on and below the Mogollon Rim. Some may have developed locally, such as the broad line geometric-style murals that resemble Tusayan Polychrome pottery (Smith's Layout Group I, for example, Smith 1952:Figures 83, 85). But this style also resembles exterior designs on many Galisteo Basin Rio Grande Glaze Ware bowls. When working only with mural fragments, it is impossible to adequately use overall layout and context to distinguish between styles that use similar elements.

Just as archaeology provides ideas and information that are of interest to some Hopi people today, Hopi oral traditions, used cautiously, provide ideas and information that can be useful to archaeologists (Bernardini 2002; Duff 2002; Lyons 2003). Traditional histories suggest that small groups migrated from village to village, sometimes staying and sometimes passing through, that

Pueblo people spoke different languages and had different ritual societies, and that the people we now call Hopi had origins in many different pueblos, as well as among the Paiute, Pima, Havasupai, and other tribes.

All Pueblos agree that all people emerged into this world through a series of previous underworlds. *Sipapu* or *shipap* is a Keresan language term used by both Hopi and Keresan-speaking pueblos. Many Hopi people identify the Sipapuni as a particular travertine dome in the Grand Canyon; other Hopi, especially those of First Mesa and their Keresan neighbors to the east in New Mexico, say its location has been forgotten. Voth relates two different versions of the emergence story in his 1905 compendium: in one, the narrator identifies the original language as Hopi, in the other, it is Keres. In both cases, as families emerge they prepare to disperse in different directions, and Mockingbird gives each group a different language (in some versions, the deity Màasaw gives out languages). They say the people emerged into this world through a series of previous underworlds, split up into small groups that traveled, leaving ruins, pottery fragments, and petroglyphs as their footprints. When they received signs that it was time to come together in the center place reserved for them, they turned toward the Hopi Mesas. The people who gathered there spoke different languages and had different ceremonies and different deities. They only "became clans" when they accepted a common identity, symbol, or totem, and only "became

FIGURE 7.15

Profile figures in Awat'ovi mural with "Eastern Pueblo" hairstyle. Detail of Awat'ovi Room 788, left wall, Layer 3. (See Smith 1952:Figure 80b. Courtesy of the Peabody Museum of Archaeology and Ethnology, Harvard University.)

Hopi" when they joined villages and became part of the Hopi ceremonial cycle and Hopi way of life (see especially Whiteley 2002).

In their migrations to the Hopi Mesas, clan traditions describe groups who split up to go separate ways, sometimes meeting again generations later, sometimes losing their relatives forever. Individuals married in and out of clan groups. Sometimes groups joined with others and traveled together for many generations, only to split up again and disperse to different villages when they reached the Hopi Mesas. They had to petition village leaders for entry to the Hopi villages. Already established villages wanted to recruit immigrants with important ceremonies that could bring rain. Some recruited warriors for protection. Undoubtedly, some leaders recruited immigrants to join their particular factions in times of social instability. Prospective immigrants without much to offer were turned away, but they sometimes returned later with new ceremonies or new and more prestigious social ties.

The name "Kawaika'a" is a Keresan word used by Hopi people today to refer to Laguna Pueblo. A number of other pueblos call Laguna village in New Mexico "Kawayka." The name probably refers to a group of people who speak Keres, not to a place. This is a fairly common practice in naming ancient village sites around the Hopi Mesas. For example, the name "Kokopnyama," a large Antelope Mesa site, means "Firewood clan's place."

Many traditional histories identify groups who lived on Antelope Mesa and First Mesa as Eastern Pueblos. First Mesa had many ceremonies with songs sung in Keresan and ritual sodalities that strongly resembled Keresan ones (Courlander 1971:268–69; Stephen 1936:578). The aforementioned Firewood clan came from the east, lived at Kokopnyama, then at Sikyatki. Other clans said to have lived at Sikyatki are identified with Jemez and other New Mexico villages. Many say the people who lived at Kawaika'a, the mural-rich site on Antelope Mesa, spoke Keresan. Courlander (1971:268) was told that Kawaika'a and nearby Mishiptonga were Eastern Pueblo people. In addition, Whiteley (2003:150–51) notes that many of the important ritual sodalities in Hopi villages are said to have been brought first to Awat'ovi by leaders who went to the Rio Grande to get them, or by Rio Grande immigrants, then they were dispersed to other villages by refugees from Awat'ovi's destruction in 1700.

No recorded traditions claim that anyone now living at Hopi is descended from people who lived at Kawaika'a, but many claim descent from Awat'ovi inhabitants. The Kawaika'a people may have simply joined Awat'ovi in the late 1400s, or they may have migrated somewhere else. Florence Hawley Ellis (1967:40) states that "there is a Hopi tradition of some of the Keres from their area having moved to Acoma, and our guess is that Pottery Mound, on the Puerco, became the home of these migrants who added Hopi pottery and Hopi style in kiva murals to the traits of the Acoma nucleus they were joining"; and, "When the Pueblo IV site of Kawaika in the Jeddito was abandoned, say the Hopi, its people migrated to Acoma country. Possibly they went to Pottery Mound to merge with the Keresans there." Laguna Pueblo, founded after the Pueblo Revolt of 1680, "had a Hopi Sun Clan, but that could have grown from no more than one female Hopi migrant" (Ellis 1979b:439).

Oral traditions say Awat'ovi was first settled by the Bow clan, but many other clans lived there, sometimes just passing through, sometimes staying. The Bow clan retained leadership into historic times; other Hopi villages were led by the Bear clan. Some traditions say Awat'ovi's inhabitants spoke Keresan, usually expressed at Hopi as "Laguna" or "Kawayka"; others simply indicate that a large number of Keresan speakers lived there. Some Hopi consultants told Courlander (1971) that "Lagunas and Acomas were at Awat'ovi." Voth (1905) says the Bow clan came from the southwest. It had Shalako, Tanki, Tukwunang, and Shawiki katsina, and the chief of the Bow clan had the Wuwutsim Society. Initiation songs for Wuwutsim and Two Horn societies are in sung in the "Laguna language" (Keresan), at least on First Mesa, in the late 1800s (Stephen 1936:260fn). Whiteley (2003) notes that Awat'ovi is said to have obtained its ritual knowledge from the Eastern Pueblos, though this could have taken place during the Pueblo Revolt period. We would suggest that exchange of ritual knowledge and personnel began in the prehistoric period and continued for centuries.

Everyone agrees that Awat'ovi's population was large and diverse and that a great many elaborate and important rituals were practiced there. A great deal can be said about the apparent "foreignness" of Awat'ovi and its power as a trade center and as a ritual center, and we will return to these topics shortly. In addition, large clay mines, coal mines, and huge pottery firing areas attest to the productivity of Awat'ovi's potters, as do the many vessels traded far and wide that have been chemically sourced back to Awat'ovi. Some yellow ware at Pottery Mound was sourced to clay found near Awat'ovi and some to Kawaika'a (Bishop et al. 1988).

Craft and Ritual Specialists

The second likely reason for the discontinuous distribution of the Sikyatki style is specialization. The most elaborate and flamboyant expression of the style in murals and on the most finely formed, finished, and painted pottery vessels probably reflects the work of craft specialists and ritual specialists. Some degree of craft specialization may be inferred from the high degree of control over paint recipes, line quality, labor input, and vessel forming and finishing. For murals, many of the same criteria apply, as well as access to a variety of pigments, including exotic materials. Ritual specialization may be inferred by the complexity of ritual iconography. The mural painters and probably some of the pottery painters may have been sodality members with esoteric knowledge. These individuals and their families apparently were dispersed among several distant communities. If they spoke Keres, they may have had ritual sodalities with Keresan origins. Christine Van Pool is presently exploring Sikyatki style in terms of shamanistic imagery (see, for comparison, her work on Ramos Polychrome [Van Pool 2003]). Shamanism, broadly defined, is a form of specialist ritual practice that has been documented for many Keresan pueblos, but not very much for Hopi. The Sikyatki style could plausibly have signaled membership in a shamanistic sodality like those that survived into historic times in some of the Eastern pueblos. If not shamanism, a sodality that was specially concerned with the upper world and bird imagery might be implicated. Members of such a sodality may have been present in both the Pottery Mound and Hopi areas. The pairing of textiles with colorful, curvilinear Sikyatki-style textiles with black and white textiles with rectilinear geometric motifs in one of the Pottery Mound murals is striking (Hibben 1975:122–23) and might suggest complementary roles for sodalities based on upper world and lower world imagery or summer and winter dual divisions, a pattern seen more often in Eastern pueblos (including Zuni) than at Hopi.

HOW MANY PAINTERS?

In order to try and put the murals into a social context, it is useful to speculate on how many people were mural painters at any one time. How many people were mural painters, and were the painters specialists? Understanding this helps us understand how conventions could have been transmitted and how mural painting may have related to other painting activities. We can approach this problem by imagining some plausible scenarios from the perspectives of both Antelope Mesa and Pottery Mound. The numbers of murals present and the span of occupation of the sites can be estimated based on existing excavation records, maps, numbers and sizes of known rooms, and our own site visits. Although the details are debatable and should be tested where possible, these parameters constrain the range of possible scenarios. These scenarios are not strictly testable as hypotheses, but they do help us sort out plausible from implausible scenarios.

At Pottery Mound 17 kivas were found; while they had a total of about 375 layers in all, about two-thirds (approximately 250 layers) were painted.[7] If we assume that half of all kivas have been found, then there were about 500 painting episodes during the life of the town. If these took place over the span of about a century, then five murals were painted each year. Two or three groups of men could easily have accomplished this task. Perhaps three men painted each kiva as a team, two masters and one apprentice at any given moment (or one master and two apprentices). As men grew older the apprentice would have graduated and a new apprentice appointed, so the teams could have had multigenerational continuity. Each group could have painted two or three murals per year. The alternative is that men from each kiva painted their own murals. If each kiva was used for 25 years, surely an underestimate, then about nine kivas would have been in use at the same time, and so each kiva would have been painted every other year. A team of painters painting every other year could have obtained and retained the skill to render these paintings. One model has 2 or 3 groups of contemporary painters, the other 9 or 10. The true number cannot be known but likely lies somewhere in this range. The models, as constrained by the available facts, suggest that if painters were part-time specialists, only a small proportion of the community painted murals.

The mural and architectural data from Awat'ovi and Kawaika'a on Antelope Mesa provide for somewhat different scenarios. Here 32 kivas were encountered and about 80 percent of these had some paintings on their walls. On average there were nine sets of murals (multiple walls painted at the same time) per kiva. A rough estimate from the site maps, site visits, and the proportion of the site that was tested or excavated suggests that about a third of the kivas on these sites were discovered (only 10 percent of Awat'ovi and a smaller proportion of Kawaika'a were excavated, but the Harvard team was making a special effort to find kivas). This estimate implies that in both towns combined there were about 80 kivas that were used at some time. All these kivas combined, if they had an average of nine painted layers each, would have witnessed about 720 painting events. This seems like a large number of paintings except that the tradition lasted almost

300 years. So only two or three mural paintings would have been executed per year for both towns, or one to two painting events per town, per year. This is a considerably lower number than the estimated five annual painting events at Pottery Mound.

It would have been easy for one multigenerational team in each town to have painted all the murals. Although there were 80 kivas total between the two towns, this would have resulted in seven contemporary kivas per town, a number not unlike that for Pottery Mound with an estimate of nine contemporary kivas. At Antelope Mesa each kiva would have been painted, on average, about every five years. This is less frequent than our estimate for Pottery Mound, and it is somewhat less likely that men from each kiva painted only their kiva, as it is harder to see how they could have maintained the skill if they painted so infrequently. Given the high skill level involved, it is likely that such a small group of men would have painted for many years. Such a group might slowly have evolved as men aged, died, and were replaced by their apprentices. It seems very unlikely that many such sets of men existed. If even as few as seven sets of such men were working at the same time, then each team would have painted only once every five years in order to account for all the murals.

In any case, the two Antelope Mesa towns in question had probably about 250 men resident in each, so this would mean if there was a specialist team that only 3 out of 250 men in each town would have been involved in mural painting in any given year. If each kiva had a different team then perhaps 20 men would have been kiva painters. This is still relatively specialized work even with this many painters.[8] Conversely, it is easy to envision itinerant painters, who would move between villages, painting several murals per year. This would seem more likely than many painters each working only very occasionally. Thus, the level of specialization among mural painters would have been many times greater than for the pottery painters or textile painters. Again, under such circumstances we would expect highly coherent styles and continuity (although with evolution) over time. This seems to be what we find.

Gender

A third factor that may account for the uneven distribution of the Sikyatki style is gender. We assume that men painted kiva murals because most (though not all) ritual sodalities that use kivas are limited to men and because painting ritual paraphernalia is associated with men's work in all the ethnographic records. But pottery painting is more complicated in the pueblos, where who paints pottery is more closely linked to the degree of productive specialization than to gender roles.

Clay is feminine in the Pueblo world and is mostly manipulated by women. Clay is the flesh of Clay Old Lady or Grandmother Clay, who gives her flesh to potters (Parezo et al. 1987). Potters in turn offer her food and promise to make her beautiful. Women use clay to make pottery and plaster house walls, floors, and hearths. Some men in the pueblos make pottery as well, but the activity itself, like all those involving clay, is generally considered feminine. Men build houses and kivas, but women do the plastering. Stephen (1936) describes kiva renovation at Walpi in the 1880s, noting that men built the walls and girls plastered them; sometimes boys made simple mural paintings. The associations between women, pottery, clay, and a feminine substance/supernatural being are very strong in all the pueblos, suggesting ancient roots.

Archaeological evidence also suggests that women made most of the pottery in the past. When pottery-making implements are found in graves, they occur with female-sexed skeletons. At least one image of a female making pottery has been identified on an eleventh-century Mimbres Black-on-white bowl. Therefore, the association between women and pottery making and the feminine gendering of clay is probably ancient, but we do not know whether women always painted their pottery (Hays-Gilpin 2000).

Craft specialization in many cultures entails transforming a traditional gendered division of labor (Senior 2000; see also Sundstrom 2002 for an example of craft specialization transforming the individual specialist's gender identity). Individuals or families who chose to devote more time and skill to these tasks did so at the expense of other activities such as farming, hunting, gathering, and even child rearing. Throughout Native North America, individuals who took on a nonconforming gender identity often became craft specialists and sometimes ritual specialists as well. More frequently, family members worked together. In the historic pueblos, men often painted pottery formed and fired by their wives. Maria and Julian at San Ildefonso and Nampeyo and Lesou at Tewa Village on First Mesa come to mind. Because so much detailed ritual iconography appears on some Sikyatki Polychrome pottery, it seems possible to us that some of it was made, or perhaps only painted, by male

sodality initiates, by older (postmenopausal) women who had significant ritual roles, by women potters who had specialized craft production and "nonfeminine" ritual roles (such as Nancy of Zuni, who wore men's clothes and danced katsina), or by males who did some women's work and some men's work in addition to special ritual roles (such as We'wha of Zuni; see Roscoe [1991]). As tentative evidence for this, note that some Sikyatki Polychrome pottery has the broken banding line, and some does not. Elsewhere, one of us (Hays-Gilpin in press) has used ethnographic evidence (from Stephen in Patterson 1994) to associate the broken banding line with women potters of childbearing age. Increasing frequency of pottery without the banding line might indicate increasing numbers of male pottery painters.

As noted previously, mural painters—and there were not many mural painters—probably were men rather than women. The association between paint, ritual roles, and men is strong but not absolute in the archaeological evidence. When prepared pigments or elaborately painted artifacts occur in burials, they usually, but not always, appear with adult males (Lewis 2002). Historically, men prepare and apply paint for prayer sticks, katsina regalia, and other ritual paraphernalia (Stephen 1936). The exception in both prehistoric and historic times is paint materials associated with pottery; these are associated with females. Therefore, the association between women and clay/pottery seems to override the association between men and paint except when family-level craft specialization appears and men take up pottery painting.

Suppose that both men and women painted pottery on Antelope Mesa, but only women did so at Pottery Mound, and that only male sodality members painted murals in both areas. That might account for the different proportions of Sikyatki-style murals and pottery vessels on Antelope Mesa and at Pottery Mound. Alternatively, we can suggest that a group of men migrated to Pottery Mound from Antelope Mesa, bringing along a few yellow ware vessels, but very few women potters. These few women might have made some Pottery Mound Polychrome using local techniques and materials, but it seems more likely that a few locally trained potters simply emulated the Sikyatki style. Alternatively, the Sikyatki style might have originated in male shamanistic (or other esoteric) ritual practice in either locality and was differentially transferred to pottery by a few gender-bending male painters and by women who incompletely emulated their iconographic repertoire.

Conclusion—Confusion

In summary, rather than viewing Sikyatki style in murals and pottery as a "Hopi" import to Pottery Mound, we suggest a regional stylistic synthesis initiated by innovations in the Western Pueblo (Hopi and Little Colorado River) area and accelerated by the multidirectional spread of religious organizations through migration, pilgrimage, intercommunity recruitment of specialists, portability and exchangeability of textiles used in ritual, changing gender dynamics, and emulation. We remain cautious about concluding which direction the flamboyant "late" Sikyatki style moved—Textiles to murals and pottery? Pottery to murals and textiles? Or murals first? East to west, or west to east?

Sikyatki style may have developed first in pottery, then mural painters and the painters of textiles could have expanded and elaborated it. Or the style could have developed first in textile painting (likely) or mural painting (possibly) then spread, albeit incompletely, to pottery. The first steps toward Sikyatki style, such as the distinctive red and black on yellow color scheme, asymmetry, and the centrality of bird and feather motifs, may have developed on Jeddito Yellow Ware pottery in the late 1300s and early 1400s via influences from Fourmile Polychrome and Chihuahua polychromes. Clearly, post-1400 mural painters, and presumably textile painters, used more elaborate and intricate compositions and a broader vocabulary of elements. Some of these elements may well have been borrowed back by potters who saw elaborate murals and textiles in ritual settings but recalled (or were allowed to use) only small parts of the whole compositions. Some Sikyatki Polychrome potters may have been specialist producers or members of family production teams in which those who painted the most elaborate pots had greater access to ritual knowledge and possessed authority to use ritually important motifs.

Sikyatki style could have developed on the Hopi Mesas as a result of elaboration of ritual iconography focused on katsinas and influences brought by immigrants from the south, particularly the Upper Little Colorado and Middle Little Colorado (Homol'ovi) areas. But the rapid development of the style, its focus on Antelope Mesa and First Mesa, and traditional histories suggest these were not the only important immigrants to this area. Eastern Pueblo people from the Rio Grande region undoubtedly joined Western Keres speakers in settling the eastern Hopi Mesas. The Hopi villages of the 1400s may have been no melting pot, but loose confederacies of clans and ritual sodalities that actively preserved individual histories, ritual practices, iconographies, and art styles. As in the historic pueblos, family ties across regions and language groups facilitated movement of family groups during times of hardship. Ritual ties among sodality members in different pueblos might have served much the same purpose in the past. Diverse art styles might have signaled exclusive or inclusive membership in diverse kiva societies and the more public, plaza-oriented katsina societies.

The question is where the Sikyatki style fits in each region. On Antelope Mesa, the style was widespread and visible on pottery vessels, both jars and bowls, and appeared rarely in kivas. At Pottery Mound, the style is rare on pottery, is not highly visible on bowl interiors, but is ubiquitous inside kivas. This suggests that the Sikyatki style signaled a fairly visible, public expression of ritual iconography on Antelope Mesa, but a restricted, private expression at Pottery Mound. If the style spread west to east, then the style and its iconography may have been carried by male initiates of a ritual society that was relatively egalitarian and open at Hopi (such as the katsina society) but became restricted when immigrants reached Pottery Mound. The style was there expressed in murals and textiles used in ritual and only marginally on local pottery by potters who saw and emulated only a small part of its repertoire. But if the style moved east to west, it may have been developed by men who migrated to Pottery Mound from the Upper Little Colorado area (see Eckert 2003 and this volume), bringing some of the aesthetics of Fourmile Polychrome, merging these notions with Southern Tiwa or other Jornada Mogollon–derived conventions in rock art and Chihuahuan pottery (P. Schaafsma, Chapter 8), and developing their own synthesis as a way to carve a niche for themselves in the elaborate ritual life of Pottery Mound. Some of these hypothetical migrants might not have stayed long at Pottery Mound, just one to several generations, but could have engaged in a "return migration" to the Hopi Mesas. All this is speculation, of course, but the notion of migrating and returning back to a center place is a common theme of Pueblo traditional histories, and the main point here is that Pueblo histories are indeed very complicated based on the archaeological evidence of material culture and the evidence of traditional histories as told by Pueblo people since the late 1800s.

Migrants out of Pottery Mound would not have been able to return to communities in the Upper Little Colorado region because these had been depopulated in the early 1400s. Hopi traditional histories (L. J. Kuwanwisiwma, personal communication to Hays-Gilpin 2005) say that residents of this area split up and relocated to the Hopi Mesas and Zuni. Suppose for a moment that Pottery Mound migrants also split and joined their relatives in these two areas. Family groups from Pottery Mound might have had initiates among them who knew the Sikyatki style from ritual performance that involved murals and textiles, and they might have had skilled potters. Migrants often find that they need to resort to craft specialization when joining a community that has already allocated the best farmland to those who arrived earliest (Arnold 1985:168, 196–99), so late arrivals to Awat'ovi and Kawaika'a may have produced a high proportion of late fourteenth-/early fifteenth-century pottery including Sikyatki Polychrome. Some of the basic stylistic conventions for painting pottery—particularly those derived from Fourmile Polychrome—may have been shared between immigrants and potters of the Hopi Mesas. Immigrants could have developed the elaborate Sikyatki style in pottery as a distinct, but not too distinct, contribution to the local mix. Likewise, Pottery Mound migrants who went to Zuni could have produced Matsaki Polychrome there (in this speculative scenario, the color scheme for Sikyatki and Matsaki Polychrome must be derived from a textile antecedent, rather than the base color of Jeddito Yellow Ware). The point is not whether all this happened, but that based on the data we have now, it could have happened. And so could a number of other scenarios.

We submit that without more precise chronologies, it is not possible to choose among the scenarios we have imagined here. Although large pueblo sites like Awat'ovi, Kawaika'a, and Pottery Mound appear to Euro-American eyes to be stable, long-lived communities, archaeology, ethnography, and traditional histories converge on the view that their populations were nonetheless highly mobile, with family groups moving from one village to another, even across regions and language groups. We may think of Pueblo history as braided streams rather than a flowing river, as Ferguson (2002) has suggested, and of Pueblo villages as leaky containers through which diverse groups passed over periods of one or several generations, as Bernardini (2002) has suggested (though not in exactly those words). Without good clusters of tree-ring dates clearly associated with murals and pottery, we are unable to discern movements and changes at the scale of a few generations. Datable beams were also highly mobile in large pueblos and were used and reused until few remained, and virtually none remained where first set into the roofs of buildings. Unfortunately, without data on the distribution of pottery types and styles in the fill of Pottery Mound kivas, even indirect dating seems unlikely at that site.

Perhaps our most important contributions are simply cautionary. Like Bernardini, Duff, Lyons, and many Pueblo cultural experts, we concur that long-term stability of population may well be an artifact of Spanish settlement, Navajo and Ute raiding, and other historic period constraints. Migrations need not have been one-way. Men, women, and people who crossed or combined gender roles may have produced different styles in different contexts, muddling our attempts to construct unilinear evolutionary sequences of artifacts, identifiable ethnic groups within pueblos, and evidence of distinct ritual sodalities and functions. Finally, the most important artifact class in reconstructing the story of Sikyatki style may be missing altogether from the archaeological record. We have only apparent depictions of painted textiles and no actual specimens with which to bolster our argument that textiles were the most likely mode of transmission of this style across the Southwest.

NOTES

1. We know that this kiva had some construction sometime after 1503 based on tree-ring specimens, but we don't know how much later.

2. There were also a few mural fragments in Kiva VI at Kuaua.

3. This A.D. 1320 date may be a bit early, as it leaves very little time for Pinedale Polychrome pottery to have been produced.

4. The report states that the latest date is 1469vv but lists a date KAW-151 of 1474++vv (Bannister et al. 1967).

5. For example, Kiva 12 had murals on at least four layers, but only one layer had a mural in good enough condition to determine whether it could have had Sikyatki style or not. Kiva 15 and Kiva 5 also had murals on several layers, but again they were too fragmentary to ascertain whether Sikyatki style was present. One of the Kiva 5 paintings can be identified as a feathered wand, and so may be Sikyatki style.

6. Editor's note: But see the introductory quote of Chapter 1.

7. Hibben and Crotty don't agree on the number of layers, and the number of layers on different walls of the same kiva is not always identical. Moreover, some layers had just scraps of paint and may never have had major full-wall paintings. Thus, determining the number of painted layers is more subjective and uncertain than it might appear. Since all these numbers are just broad estimates, no purpose is served in trying to refine these numbers for the present purposes.

8. If the population peak was closer to 2,000 people, then there may have been as many as 500 adult men (50 percent adults, half men and half women, or 25 percent of the total being adult men). Five hundred adult men implies even more specialization than proposed here.

REFERENCES CITED

Adams, E. Charles

1991 *The Origins and Development of the Pueblo Katsina Cult.* University of Arizona Press, Tucson.

2002 *Homol'ovi: An Ancient Hopi Settlement Cluster.* University of Arizona Press, Tucson.

Adams, E. C., and K. A. Hays (editors)

1991 *Homol'ovi II: The Archaeology of an Ancestral Hopi Village.* Anthropological Papers of the University of Arizona No. 55. University of Arizona Press, Tucson.

Ahlstrom, Richard V. N.

1998 Untitled and unfinished manuscript on Kawaika-a. Manuscript on file, Museum of Northern Arizona, Hopi Mural Project, Flagstaff.

Arnold, Dean E.

1985 *Ceramic Theory and Cultural Process.* Cambridge University Press, Cambridge.

Bannister, B., W. J. Robinson, and R. L. Warren

1967 *Tree-Ring Dates from Arizona J: Hopi Mesas Area.* Laboratory of Tree-Ring Research, University of Arizona, Tucson.

Beals, Ralph, George Brainerd, and Watson Smith

1945 *Archaeological Studies in Northeastern Arizona: A Report on the Archaeological Work of the Rainbow Bridge—Monument Valley Expedition.* University of California Press, Berkeley and Los Angeles.

Bernardini, Wesley

2002 The Gathering of the Clans: Understanding Ancestral Hopi Migration and Identity, A.D. 1275–1400. Unpublished Ph.D. dissertation, Department of Anthropology, Arizona State University, Tempe.

Bishop, R., V. Canouts, S. De Atley, A. Qöyawayma, and C. W. Aikens

1988 The Formation of Ceramic Analytical Groups: Hopi Pottery Production and Exchange, A.D. 1300–1600. *Journal of Field Archaeology* 15:317–37.

Brew, John Otis

1941 Preliminary Report of the Peabody Museum Awatovi Expedition of 1939. *Plateau* 13:37–48. Museum of Northern Arizona, Flagstaff.

Brody, J. J.

1964 Design Analysis of the Rio Grande Glaze Pottery of Pottery Mound, New Mexico. Unpublished Master's thesis, Department of Art, University of New Mexico, Albuquerque.

1991 *Anasazi and Pueblo Painting.* School of American Research Press, Santa Fe, New Mexico.

Brody, J. J., C. J. Scott, and S. A. LeBlanc

1983 *Mimbres Pottery: Ancient Art of the American Southwest.* Hudson Hills Press, New York.

Carlson, Roy

1971   *White Mountain Red Ware: A Pottery Tradition of East-Central Arizona and Western New Mexico.* Anthropological Papers of the University of Arizona No. 19. University of Arizona Press, Tucson.

Courlander, Harold

1971   *The Fourth World of the Hopis: The Epic Story of the Hopi Indians as Preserved in Their Legends and Traditions.* University of New Mexico Press, Albuquerque.

Crotty, Helen K.

1995   Anasazi Mural Art of the Pueblo IV Period, A.D. 1300–1600: Influences, Selective Adaptation, and Cultural Diversity in the Prehistoric Southwest. Unpublished Ph.D. dissertation, Department of Art History, University of California, Los Angeles.

2001   Shields, Shield Bearers, and Warfare Imagery in Anasazi Art, 1200–1500. In *Deadly Landscapes: Case Studies in Prehistoric Southwestern Warfare*, edited by G. E. Rice and S. A. LeBlanc, pp. 65–83. University of Utah Press, Salt Lake City.

Crown, Patricia

1994   *Ceramics and Ideology: Salado Polychrome Pottery.* University of New Mexico Press, Albuquerque.

Dean, J. S., and J. C. Ravesloot

1993   The Chronology of Cultural Interaction in the Gran Chichimeca. In *Culture and Contact: Charles C. Di Peso's Gran Chichimeca*, edited by A. I. Woosley and J. C. Ravesloot, pp. 83–103. Amerind Foundation and University of New Mexico Press, Dragoon, Arizona, and Albuquerque.

Douglass, A. E.

1935   *Dating Pueblo Bonito and Other Ruins of the Southwest.* Pueblo Bonito Series No. 1, Contributed Papers. National Geographic Society, Washington, D.C.

Duff, Andrew

2002   *Western Pueblo Identities: Regional Interaction, Migration, and Transformation.* University of Arizona Press, Tucson.

Dutton, Bertha P.

1963   *Sun Father's Way: The Kiva Murals of Kuaua.* University of New Mexico Press, Albuquerque.

Eckert, Suzanne

2003   Social Boundaries, Immigration, and Ritual Systems: A Case Study from the American Southwest. Unpublished Ph.D. dissertation, Department of Anthropology, Arizona State University, Tempe.

Ellis, Florence Hawley

1967   Where Did the Pueblo People Come From? *El Palacio* 74(3):35–43.

1979a   Isleta Pueblo. In *Southwest*, edited by Alfonso Ortiz, pp. 351–65. Handbook of North American Indians, Vol. 9. Smithsonian Institution, Washington, D.C.

1979b   Laguna Pueblo. In *Southwest*, edited by Alfonso Ortiz, pp. 438–49. Handbook of North American Indians, Vol. 9. Smithsonian Institution, Washington, D.C.

Ferguson, T. J.

2002   Academic, Legal, and Political Contexts of Social Identity and Cultural Affiliation Research in the Southwest. Paper presented at the Southwest Symposium, Tucson.

Fewkes, Jesse Walter

1898   *Archaeological Expedition to Arizona in 1895.* Bureau of American Ethnology Seventeenth Annual Report, 1893–1896, Part 2, pp. 519–742. U.S. Government Printing Office, Washington, D.C.

1900   *Tusayan Migration Traditions.* Bureau of American Ethnology Nineteenth Annual Report, 1897–1898, Part 2, pp. 573–634. U.S. Government Printing Office, Washington, D.C.

1919   *Designs on Prehistoric Hopi Pottery.* Bureau of American Ethnology Thirty-Third Annual Report, 1911–1912, pp. 207–284. Smithsonian Institution, Washington, D.C.

Hammond, G. P., and A. Rey (editors)

1928   *Obregons' History of Sixteenth Century Explorations in Western America, Entitled: Chronicle, Commentary, or Relation of the Ancient and Modern Discoveries in New Spain, New Mexico and Mexico, 1584.* Wetzel, Los Angeles.

1966 *The Rediscovery of New Mexico 1580–1594. The Explorations of Chamuscado, Espejo, Castaño de Sosa, Morlete, and Leyva de Bonilla and Humana.* University of New Mexico Press, Albuquerque.

Hargrave, Lyndon Lane

1935 The Jeddito Valley and the First Pueblo Towns in Arizona Visited by Europeans. *Museum Notes* 8(4):21.

1951 First Mesa. *Museum of Northern Arizona Reprint Series* 2:30–35. Reprinted from *Museum Notes of the Museum of Northern Arizona* 3(8):1–6. Museum of Northern Arizona, Flagstaff, 1931.

Hays, Kelley Ann

1992 *Anasazi Ceramics as Text and Tool: Toward a Theory of Ceramic Design "Messaging."* Ph.D. dissertation, Department of Anthropology, University of Arizona. University Microfilms, Ann Arbor.

Hays-Gilpin, Kelley A.

2000 Gender Ideology and Ritual Activities in the Ancient Southwest. In *Women and Men in the Prehispanic Southwest: A Gendered Perspective on Labor, Power, and Prestige*, edited by Patricia Crown, pp. 91–135. School of American Research Advanced Seminar Series, School of American Research Press, Santa Fe, New Mexico.

2007 Life's Pathways: Geographic Metaphors in Protohistoric Puebloan Material Culture. In *Archaeology without Borders: Contact, Commerce, and Change in the U.S. Southwest and Northwestern Mexico*, edited by L. D. Webster and M. McBrinn. University Press of Colorado, Boulder, in press.

Hibben, Frank

1975 *Kiva Art of the Anasazi at Pottery Mound.* KC Publications, Las Vegas, Nevada.

Hodge, Frederick Webb (editor)

1907 *Handbook of American Indians North of Mexico.* Bureau of American Ethnology Bulletin 30. Smithsonian Institution, Washington, D.C.

Hough, Walter

1903 *Archaeological Field Work in Northeastern Arizona: The Museum-Gates Expedition of 1901.* Report of the United States National Museum for 1901, pp. 279–358. Smithsonian Institution, Washington, D.C.

Kent, Kate Peck

1983 *Prehistoric Textiles of the Southwest.* School of American Research Press, Santa Fe, New Mexico.

LeBlanc, Steven A.

1980 The Dating of Casas Grandes. *American Antiquity* 45(4):799–806.

2004 *Painted by a Distant Hand: Mimbres Pottery from the American Southwest.* Peabody Museum Press, Cambridge, Massachusetts.

Lekson, Steven H.

1984 Dating Casas Grandes. *Kiva* 50(1):55–60.

Lewis, Candace K.

2002 Knowledge Is Power: Pigments, Painted Artifacts, and Chacoan Ritual Leaders. Unpublished Master's thesis, Department of Anthropology, Northern Arizona University, Flagstaff.

Lyons, Patrick D.

2003 *Ancestral Hopi Migrations.* Anthropological Papers of the University of Arizona No. 68. University of Arizona Press, Tucson.

Mindeleff, Victor

1891 *A Study of Pueblo Architecture in Tusayan and Cibola.* Bureau of American Ethnology Eighth Annual Report. Smithsonian Institution, Washington, D.C.

Montgomery, Ross Gordon, Watson Smith, and John Otis Brew

1949 *Franciscan Awatovi.* Papers of the Peabody Museum of American Archaeology and Ethnology Vol. 36. Harvard University, Cambridge, Massachusetts.

Morris, Earl H.

1928 Kawaikuh. Manuscript on file, Earl Morris Collection, University of Colorado Museum, Boulder.

Parezo, Nancy J., Kelley Hays, and Barbara Slivac

1987 The Mind's Road: Southwestern Indian Women's Art. In *The Desert is No Lady: Southwestern Landscape in Women's Writing and Art*, edited by V. H. Norwood and J. J. Monk, pp. 146–73. Yale University Press, New Haven, Connecticut.

Parsons, Elsie Clews

1932 *Isleta Pueblo*. Bureau of American Ethnology Forty-Seventh Annual Report. Smithsonian Institution, Washington, D.C.

1939 *Pueblo Indian Religion*. University of Chicago Press, Chicago.

Patterson, Alex

1994 *Hopi Pottery Symbols*. Based on the work of Alexander M. Stephen. Johnson Books, Boulder, Colorado.

Phillips, D. A., Jr., and J. P. Carpenter

1999 The Robles Phase of the Casas Grandes Culture. In *The Casas Grandes World*, edited by C. F. Schaafsma and C. L. Riley, pp. 78–92. University of Utah Press, Salt Lake City.

Pond, Gordon

1966 A Painted Kiva near Winslow, Arizona. *American Antiquity* 31:555–58.

Rakita, G. F., and G. R. Raymond

2003 The Temporal Sensitivity of Casas Grandes Polychrome Ceramics. *Kiva* 68(3):153–84.

Ravesloot, J. C., J. S. Dean, and M. S. Foster

1995 A New Perspective on the Casas Grandes Tree-Ring Dates. In *The Gran Chichimeca: Essays on the Archaeology and Ethnohistory of Northern Mesoamerica*, edited by J. E. Reyman, pp. 240–51. Aldershot, Avebury.

Reed, Erik

1942 Kawaika-a in the Historic Period. *American Antiquity* 8(1):119.

Roscoe, Will

1991 *The Zuni Man-Woman*. University of New Mexico Press, Albuquerque.

Ruppé, Reynold J.

1953 The Acoma Culture Province: An Archaeological Concept. Unpublished Ph.D. dissertation, Harvard University, Cambridge, Massachusetts. Published in 1990 as *The Acoma Culture Province: An Archaeological Concept*. Garland Press, New York.

Schaafsma, C. F.

2002 *Apaches de Navajo: Seventeenth-Century Navajos in the Chama Valley of New Mexico*. University of Utah Press, Salt Lake City.

Schaafsma, Polly

1992 *Rock Art in New Mexico*. Museum of New Mexico Press, Santa Fe.

2000 *Warrior, Shield, and Star*. Western Edge Press, Santa Fe, New Mexico.

Senior, Louise M.

2000 Gender and Craft Innovation: Proposal of a Model. In *Gender and Material Culture in Archaeological Perspective*, edited by M. Donald and L. Hurcombe, pp. 71–87. Macmillan Press, London.

Smith, Watson

1952 *Kiva Mural Decorations at Awatovi and Kawaika-a*. Papers of the Peabody Museum of American Archaeology and Ethnology Vol. 37. Harvard University, Cambridge, Massachusetts.

1962 School, Pots, and Potters. *American Anthropologist* 64(6):1165–78.

1971 *Painted Ceramics of the Western Mound at Awatovi*. Papers of the Peabody Museum of American Archaeology and Ethnology Vol. 38. Harvard University, Cambridge, Massachusetts.

1972 *Prehistoric Kivas of Antelope Mesa, Northeastern Arizona*. Papers of the Peabody Museum of American Archaeology and Ethnology Vol. 39, No. 1. Harvard University, Cambridge, Massachusetts.

Smith, Watson, Richard B. Woodbury, and Nathalie
F. S. Woodbury
1966 *The Excavation of Hawikuh by Frederick
Webb Hodge*. Contributions from the Museum
of the American Indian, Heye Foundation
Vol. XX. Heye Foundation, New York.

Stephen, Alexander
1936 *The Hopi Journals of Alexander Stephen*, edited
by Elsie Clews Parsons. Columbia University
Press, New York.

Sundstrom, Linea
2002 Steel Awls for Stone Age Plainswomen:
Rock Art, Women's Religion, and the
Hide Trade on the Northern Plains. *Plains
Anthropologist* 47:99–119.

Teague, Lynn S.
1998 *Textiles in Southwestern Prehistory*. University
of New Mexico Press, Albuquerque.

Van Keuren, Scott
2001 Ceramic Style and the Reorganization of
Fourteenth Century Pueblo Communities
in East-Central Arizona. Unpublished Ph.D.
dissertation, Department of Anthropology,
University of Arizona, Tucson.

Van Pool, Christine S.
2003 The Shaman-Priests of the Casas Grandes
Region, Chihuahua, Mexico. *American
Antiquity* 68(4):696–717.

Voth, H. R.
1905 *The Traditions of the Hopi*. Field Columbian
Museum Publication 96. Field Columbian
Museum, Chicago.

Walker, William H.
1995 *Ritual Prehistory: A Pueblo Case Study*. Ph.D.
dissertation, Department of Anthropology,
University of Arizona. University Microfilms,
Ann Arbor.

Welton, Jessica
2006 The Watchtower Murals: 1930s Paintings by
Fred Kabotie. *Plateau* 2(2):42–51. Museum of
Northern Arizona, Flagstaff.

White, Leslie
1932 *The Pueblo of San Felipe*. Memoirs of the
American Anthropological Association 38.
American Anthropological Association,
Menasha, Wisconsin.
1935 *The Pueblo of Santo Domingo, New Mexico*.
Memoirs of the American Anthropological
Association 43. American Anthropological
Association, Menasha, Wisconsin.
1942 *The Pueblo of Santa Ana*. Memoirs of the
American Anthropological Association 60.
American Anthropological Association,
Menasha, Wisconsin.

Whiteley, Peter
2002 Archaeology and Oral Tradition: The
Scientific Importance of Dialog. *American
Antiquity* 67(3):405–15.
2003 Re-imagining Awatovi. In *Archaeologies of
the Pueblo Revolt: Identity, Meaning, and
Renewal in the Pueblo World*, edited by
Robert W. Preucel, pp. 147–66. University
of New Mexico Press, Albuquerque.

Williams, Walter
1987 *The Spirit and the Flesh: Sexual Diversity
in American Indian Culture*. Beacon
Press, Boston.

Winship, G. P.
1896 *The Coronado Expedition, 1540–1542*. Bureau
of American Ethnology Fourteenth Annual
Report, 1892–1893, Vol. 1, Part 1, pp. 329–613.
U.S. Government Printing Office,
Washington, D.C.

CHAPTER EIGHT

The Pottery Mound Murals and Rock Art
Implications for Regional Interaction

Polly Schaafsma

Among the many impressive Pueblo IV period sites in the Rio Grande valley, Pottery Mound with its many painted kivas is distinctive. As noted elsewhere in this volume, no other site has yielded such a large number of paintings or painted kivas. The variety of subject matter and detail portrayed at Pottery Mound is rivaled only by that in the Hopi mural paintings from Awat'ovi and Kawaika'a on Antelope Mesa above Jeddito Wash (Smith 1952). In 1966, lacking any knowledge of rock art, Hibben asserted that the murals were "Mexican" in content in order to bolster his case for a constructed pyramidal mound underlying the site (see G. Vivian and Adler, this volume). More commonly it is proposed that the murals were introduced from the Western Pueblo region.

In the previous chapter Hays-Gilpin and LeBlanc discuss the possible social implications of the Sikyatki style at Pottery Mound, concluding that social mobility and ritual specialization were characteristic of the Pueblo IV period. In contrast, it is the purpose of this essay to examine the dominant style of the murals, which is non-Sikyatki in content, establishing its place within the broader context of the Pueblo IV Rio Grande style as represented in the rock art. Using the extensive rock art database available for comparison, it is clear that the Pottery Mound murals (with the Sikyatki exception) fit comfortably into the Eastern Pueblo iconographic milieu widely represented in landscape art between ca. 1325 and 1680 (all dates cited are A.D.). In turn, however, the social dynamism of the times, reflected in the multiethnic communities postulated by Hays-Gilpin and LeBlanc, may explain the Rio Grande style as manifested in the murals at Awat'ovi and Kawaika'a.

The stylistic features characteristic of Rio Grande Pueblo IV rock art have been discussed at length previously (Schaafsma 1980; 1992a). In general the style and content of both the murals and Pueblo IV rock art throughout the Rio Grande province describe the same conceptual world. Because rock art commands a broad regional base widely distributed throughout the landscape, it serves to define a territory in which shared ideas were held. By comparing general subject categories as well as specific elements and details featured in the murals with those in the rock art, the Pueblo regions ideologically closest to Pottery Mound can be identified.

Comparisons between mural art and visual imagery in other media have a limited history. While recent studies have addressed the relationships between kiva murals and rock art (Brody 1991; Schaafsma 2003), these works are preceded by scanty efforts along these lines. Noteworthy, however, is the appendix to Dutton's (1963) *Sun Father's Way* by Agnes C. Sims in which she details similarities between the Kuaua murals and petroglyphs in the Galisteo Basin, along the Santa Fe River, and as far south as Black Mesa in Socorro County. Sims (1963:216) expressed the idea that many of these same figures were incorporated into the Hopi pantheon following the Pueblo Revolt and the reestablishment of Spanish hegemony in New Mexico.

Sims's work notwithstanding (see also Sims 1948; 1949; 1950; Renaud 1938), it is important to note that during the late 1950s and early 1960s when the Pottery Mound murals were being recorded, rock art in the Rio Grande was poorly known, and Sims's observations were unheeded. Lacking sufficient knowledge of the regional rock art context, the murals stood out almost as curiosities and anomalies. To quote: "The investigations at Pottery Mound have revealed a number of features which are not typical of Rio Grande sites and are unexpected in the area. The most important discovery was a series of prehistoric paintings" (Hibben 1960:267). A context for the murals was provided primarily by the murals at Awat'ovi and Kawaika'a at Hopi and by those to the north at Kuaua, the Hopi murals being closer in spirit to the Pottery Mound work.

Rio Grande Pueblo IV Mural Sites

Painted kivas were widely distributed during Pueblo IV times in the Rio Grande valley and environs, but the collection of mural paintings from Pottery Mound comprises by far the richest, most diverse, and complex group of murals known to date. Although Frank C. Hibben (1975:14) lists 17 painted kivas, paintings in Kivas 4, 11, 13, and 14 were lacking. In 11 kivas (Kiva 1, 2, 6, 7, 8, 9, 10, 12, 15, 16, 17), multiple layers of elaborate paintings were well enough preserved to be recorded in detail. The walls of Kiva 5, a rectangular great kiva, and possibly Kiva 3 had only a few isolated designs. Except for a feathered staff, the motifs in Kiva 5 were unidentifiable.

There are a number of Pueblo IV sites with painted rooms in the Rio Grande valley besides Pottery Mound and Kuaua, and they are widely distributed from the Northern Tiwa to the Tompiro districts (Figure 8.1). These have been summarized by various scholars (Crotty 1995; Smith 1952:68–78; Tichy 1947). In addition, early historic documents describe painted walls in Piro and Southern Tiwa pueblos (Hammond and Rey 1927:24–26; 1966:82; Villagrá in Espinosa 1933:132, 140). Kuaua, about 40 mi north of Pottery Mound on the Rio Grande, had one painted kiva (Kiva III). The paintings are considerably more limited in subject matter than the Pottery Mound murals and the compositions less complex. The many painted layers in Kiva III featured rain ceremonies with black-kilted ritual performers, a few animals, corn plants, birds, cloud terraces, and rain- and lightning-generating jars, or ollas (Dutton 1963). Simpler yet were kiva paintings at Picuris, featuring cloud terraces, again with lightning and maize plants, but without ceremonialists (Crotty 1999). Shield motifs were the dominant image on several layers of plaster in a round Keresan kiva at Pueblo del Encierro near Cochiti, ca. 1325–1700 (Schaafsma 1965). East of the Sandia Mountains, fragmentary remains of paintings were found at Paako (Tichy 1938), and kiva paintings at Gran Quivira (Las Humanas) are described by Peckham (1981). At the Northern Tewa site of Otowi (ca. 1325–1580) a solo mountain lion occurred on a kiva wall (Tichy 1947). Images on several layers from a kiva in Tijeras Pueblo (ca. 1325–1425; Cordell, ed. 1980:9–11), east of Albuquerque, were essentially undecipherable (Crotty 1995; Hyer 1976). Most recently in 2002, a round, east-oriented Southern Tewa painted kiva was excavated at San Lazaro in the Galisteo Basin (1325–1680; Fenn 2004:Plates 140–44). Star faces and narrow decorative bands with stepped cloud motifs,

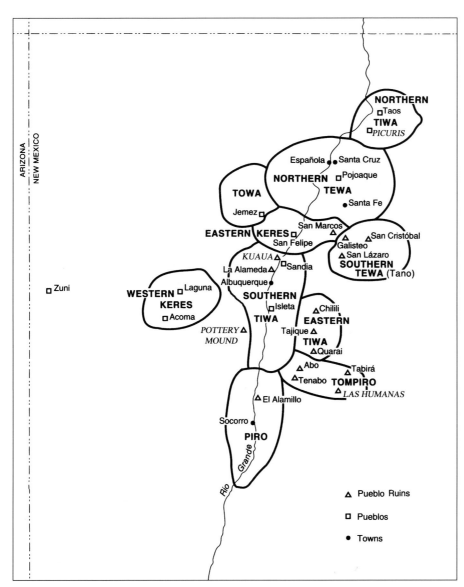

FIGURE 8.1
Rio Grande Pueblo linguistic divisions with contemporary pueblos and some Pueblo archaeological sites indicated. Major sites for which there is adequate documentation of kiva murals are noted in italics. Mural fragments have also been found in other sites in the Keresan and the Northern and Southern Tewa regions. (Adapted from C. Schaafsma 1994:Figure 11.1.)

spirals, and zigzag patterns were among the recognizable elements. Plaster fragments with finely delineated painted feathers were also discovered at Galisteo Pueblo.

Rock Art and Murals Compared

As indicated, Pottery Mound and other Pueblo IV mural sites in the Rio Grande are not islands of iconography within an otherwise sterile topography. Rather, mural art is embraced within a broader and more widely distributed graphic art form, that is, the rock art. Rio Grande Pueblo petroglyphs and rock paintings comprise a relatively continuous body of iconography, most of which is closely related to that found in the murals (Tables 8.1 and 8.2).

Before addressing the continuities, however, I discuss some of the fundamental differences between mural paintings and rock art, many of which relate to factors pertaining to context, place, and technical factors. Each of these broad contextual categories would have engendered the need for different emphases in subject matter, as appropriate to place and occasion. The social roles of the artists may have differed as well (Schaafsma 2003).

Table 8.1. Pottery Mound Murals and Rio Grande Rock Art: Detailed Shared Element List

ANTHROPOMORPHIC FIGURES

Masked figures:

Star katsina (probable in murals—head area missing)

Raptor katsina

Mask with downturned mouth

Mask with "eye-patch"

Profile figures: Warriors, raptor katsinas, and others

Other ritual figures:

War gods

Shield-bearing warriors

Other warriors with weapons

Transformational bird/humans or katsinas

Seated ritual performers

*Note: As in the murals, many of these figures in
Rio Grande rock art are fully defined, as opposed
to schematic.*

ATTIRE

Masks: bowl shaped, round
(see above for specific masks)

Feathered headdresses

Necklaces

Kilts and breechcloths:

Cloth and hide kilts

Kilts and breechcloths with tassels

Manta dresses

Mantas worn as shawls

Tasseled sashes, including colored tassels

White leggings with red fringe

Arm or leg ties

HELD ITEMS

Masks held in hand (rare)

Staffs, including feathered staffs

War clubs, including both blunt and bipointed axes (with
deer hoof on end—rare)

Bow and arrow

Other projectiles

Mountain lion skin quivers

SHIELDS AS INDEPENDENT ELEMENTS

Shield Features:

Eagle tail feather motif

Star motif

Line, hook, circle motifs

Face (sun?) as design motif

Scalloped edging

Turkey feather edging

LIFE FORMS–ANIMALS, BIRDS, INSECTS

Mountain lions:

Wearing ceremonial attire
(quivers, feathers)

Seated mountain lions

With game (rare)

As small fetishes (rare)

Spotted felines

Skunks

Macaws

Eagles

Swallows

Whooping cranes

Snakes (includes rattlesnakes),
star-faced snakes

Dragonflies

Butterflies (rare)

HORNED SERPENTS

With feathers

Associated with four-pointed star
or with cloud terrace

STAR

With face and/or with crown of
eagle tail feathers

Associated with Horned Serpent (see above)
or rattlesnake

METEOROLOGICAL ELEMENTS

Stepped cloud terraces
(most common)

Cumulus clouds
(curvilinear)

Lightning

Rainbow

POTTERY VESSELS

In hand of ritual performers,
spewing moisture

On head of female (rare)

PLANTS

Sunflower

Maize

Squash

Evergreen

Table 8.2. Tallies of Numbers of Sites with Selected Elements Shared between the Pottery Mound Murals and Rio Grande Rock Art in the Designated Linguistic Provinces

Pueblo Province (Element)	N Tiwa	N Tewa	W Towa	E Keres	S Tewa	S Tiwa	E Tiwa	Tompiro	Piro
Shield bearer (full)	–	3	–	2	4	1	–	1	3
Shield bearer (schematic)	–	9	1	7	4	4	–	1	3
Shields (independent)	–	5	4	6	6	4	–	1	1
Shield/predator complex	–	1	1	–	2	1	–	2	–
Raptor katsina	–	1	–	1	6	4	1	1	2
Star katsina	–	–	–	–	4	3	1	1	–
Stars: super-naturals, shield design, independent	–	4	–	1	8	7	1	13	2
Star/snake conflations	–	–	–	1	2	1	–	–	–
War gods	–	2	1	2	4	1	–	–	3
Supernatural mountain lion	–	–	–	3	3	–	–	2	1
Horned Serpent (one horn)[a]	1	4+	–	3	7	3	–	4	1
Conflated figures	–	1	–	2	5	4	–	1	1
Eye-patch mask	–	–	–	3	4	3	–	2	1?
Masks: downturned mouth	–	–	–	–	–	–	–	2	2

Note: [a]See also Figure 8.19

The linguistic districts delineated in Figure 8.1 and named in this table (Table 8.2) are those of historic Rio Grande Pueblos. The late prehistoric linguistic boundaries are believed, however, to approximate the historic ones. Although some ambiguity may be present regarding the exact locations of Southern Tiwa, Keresan, and Northern Tewa borders, this does not pose a significant problem here.

The figures selected for distributional analysis are figures that also occur in the Pottery Mound murals. The numbers in the table designate the number of sites in each region in which a given element is found, not the number of figures. However, the actual number of a selected element occurring in any given region is reflected in the site count. The purpose of this study is to illustrate the broader context for the murals and their relationships within the Pueblo area in general, but more specifically within the Rio Grande. As stated in the main text, masks as such, generalized ceremonial figures, clouds, and dragonflies are so pervasive that I have not included them here.

The number of rock art sites noted should be regarded as a rough sample. A major problem with listing numbers of sites lies in defining site boundaries. In the Rio Grande valley, boulder fields with petroglyphs can extend for several miles. For example, within the 17 mi of the West Mesa Southern Tiwa escarpment, only six "sites" are recognized here, although the petroglyphs themselves cluster into many more potential site groupings.

The temporal factor is another aspect of these data that is difficult to control within certain limitations. The elements under consideration are thought to be roughly contemporary with the Pottery Mound murals, although the prehistoric rock art may have a somewhat broader chronological scope (ca. ±100 years) in some cases.

These problems notwithstanding, Table 8.2 shows the general distribution of mural-related elements in Pueblo rock art, thereby indicating the cultural/geographic patterning of the larger iconographic matrix of which Pottery Mound was a part.

Table 8.3. Selected Points of Dissimilarity between the Pottery Mound Murals and Rio Grande Rock Art

Murals	Rock Art
Sikyatki designs: complex and in most kivas	Sikyatki motifs: rare and isolated
Ceremonial scenes: complex	Ceremonial scenes: limited
Female ceremonialists common	Female ceremonialists rare
Women wearing kilts	No females with kilts identified
Tie-dye or negative painting: common on kilts and mantas	Tie-dye or negative painting: blankets rare
Asymmetrical hairstyles common	Asymmetrical hairstyles rare
Masks as separate element: limited to three—all handheld	Masks as separate element: extremely common—bowl shaped, square, round, triangular, profile
Macaws numerous	Macaws occasional
Altar paraphernalia with maize ears, pahos, slab pahos	Altar paraphernalia rare
Containers: bowls and jars common	Containers rare
Flute players rare	Flute players occasional
Stars: with faces, feathers	Stars: with faces, feathers, talons, and projectiles
Sun shields: feathered	Sun shields: serrated edges
Two-horned serpents: none	Two-horned serpents: commonly found in northern Pueblo rock art sites

Kiva wall paintings, by virtue of the fact that they embrace a flat wall, display a number of formal spatial and compositional strategies not employed in rock art. The decorative field may be covered by overall patterning, as in the case of the Sikyatki-style paintings, or it may be filled by well-composed paintings, often narrative in content, portraying ongoing ritual performances. Participants may stand in rows, and a ground line is often established. More rarely, a centered dominant heraldic figure may prevail. There are other artistic conventions such as figures rising from bands.

In contrast, rock art commands irregular spaces on often rough surfaces and boulders, a situation that favors isolated, scattered icons or small figure groups at best (see Schaafsma 2003). Ground lines are usually absent. As petroglyph artists strived to economize the efforts

needed to produce images pecked in stone, abstraction and simplification were the rule, and usually only selected elements that would convey essential meanings were pictured. While a few of the more complete carvings approach the complexity found in the kiva art, rock paintings, more easily rendered than images cut in rock, are more likely to share details with the kiva murals. Overall, however, technical restrictions characteristic of rock art limit the amount of information conveyed, and the metaphorical world that finds elaborate expression in the kiva murals is given abbreviated treatment.

Other differences between murals and rock art (Table 8.3) have to do with their contrasting types of locations—ceremonial rooms versus the cultural landscape—and the symbolism ascribed to these locations. Hence, the purposes for which rock art was made and the functions it served would have differed from those of kiva paintings, even if both served ritual functions. Sikyatki designs, as they embrace the Pueblo cosmos, may have been an appropriate backdrop for ceremony, but unimportant in rock art, for example.

The katsina mask as an independent element is the hallmark of Pueblo IV rock art sites in the Rio Grande valley (Schaafsma 1992a), and its ubiquity in the landscape may have a functional significance that pertains specifically to location (Schaafsma 2003). The mask may stand for the katsina spirit itself rather than a katsina impersonator. Articulated with the landscape, the mask image may be perceived as having the power to attract rain clouds, as many images are regarded as prayers for rain (Stephen 1936:211). In contrast, the mask never occurs as an *isolated* element in kiva art and only as an *independent* element in two, or possibly three, instances at Pottery Mound—in the hand of a katsina impersonator who appears to have removed his mask (Crotty 1995:Figure 69; Hibben 1975: Figure 67). Interacting groups of figures wearing mantas, kilts, breechcloths, and other ceremonial attire are fewer in rock art. Often in rock art, masked figures are represented individually and not as part of a narrative or group scene. When narrative or ritual scenes do occur, they usually consist of a line of small figures, as in Tompiro and Piro paintings.

A number of elements occurring in rock art are absent or extremely rare in the murals, differences that are difficult to explain. Chronological and functional concerns do not seem to account for such discrepancies. A case in point is the age-old flute player, whose place on the rocks is legend, but who rarely appears at Pottery Mound (Kiva 9, Layer 8, Hibben Center Photo Archives, Albuquerque, New Mexico). The Hand, Somaikoli, and Shalako katsinas, frequent in rock art and thought to be contemporary with Pottery Mound, are absent in mural paintings. The serrated-edged shield and sword swallowers are among other rock art subjects that fall in this category.

These disparities, however, are eclipsed by the likenesses in that a basic cast of characters, similarly attired, appear with all the familiar symbols of Pueblo cosmology in both media. Although modifications toward simplicity are observable in most of the rock art, especially the petroglyphs, both art forms derive from a common cosmovision and religious ideology, expressed by means of an established vocabulary of symbols and visual metaphors rendered in accordance with standard stylistic norms.

Analysis of Elements and Stylistic Features: Pottery Mound and Pueblo IV Rock Art

The Pueblo IV rock art and kiva mural iconography includes ceremonial figures, often richly attired (see Webster, this volume), or personages that combine human aspects with those of birds and animals. Katsinas are a part of this package, along with shield-bearing and other warriors with weapons and horned and feathered serpents. Raptor katsinas and Morning Star icons with a strong Eastern Pueblo distribution may have been derived in part from contact with Western Plains groups. Feathers and feather fans play a major role throughout this visual text—as headgear, in the hands of ceremonial participants, and as attachments to shields and other paraphernalia. The significant role of feathers in kiva murals and rock art is repeated in ceramic designs of the period, and notably so in the Sikyatki style.

Selected content of the Pottery Mound murals is compared with its distribution in Pueblo IV rock art sites (see Table 8.2). Via this exercise, the regions most closely related to the Pottery Mound murals are made evident. It should be noted that in addition to generalized ceremonial figures, elements related to the rain-making complex, such as katsina masks, the stepped cloud terrace, and dragonfly, are so pervasive that I have not included them in this distributional inventory. South of the Northern Tewa province, masks are represented in high proportions and large numbers—often in the hundreds—in nearly all Pueblo IV and Jornada sites. This geographic distribution, in turn, involves stylistic and contextual continuities (see also Saville 2003). These data refute the idea that the katsina cult entered the northern Rio Grande from the Western Pueblos (Adams 1991).

In regard to the Horned Serpent, I have extended the inventory to the Jornada region. This continuity reinforces Jornada relationships and precedents for certain aspects of Pueblo IV art and ideology, following and including the Classic Mimbres (1000–1150; Schaafsma 1980; 1992a; 1994; Schaafsma and Wiseman 1992; Stewart et al. 1990). The total picture of graphic art and its associated cosmology in Pueblo IV cannot be understood without taking the Mimbres and Jornada and even the Casas Grandes regions into consideration, regions that are commonly ignored to the detriment of an understanding of the history of Pueblo religion.

The data in Table 8.2 embrace only a representative sample of the sites containing the elements selected.

FIGURE 8.2
Southern Tewa paired shield bearers in the Galisteo Basin, New Mexico, in the context of other war-related figures including stars. Each shield bearer holds a war club, ca. A.D. 1325–1525. (Photograph by Curtis Schaafsma.)

In terms of what is "out there," the rock art is, of necessity, underrepresented. While the data offered here are limited, and because a larger sample would result in vastly higher site counts, it is anticipated that the proportion of sites represented in a region would remain roughly the same. The data used to compile Table 8.2 were retrieved from the author's extensive rock art slide collection, plus numerous published sources (Boyd and Ferguson 1988; Cole 1992; Dongoske and Dongoske 2002; Marshall and Walt 1984; Schaafsma 1968; 1975; 1980; 1990; 1992a; 1997; 2000; Slifer 1998; among others).

The War Complex
Overall, the war-related elements in the Pottery Mound murals, such as shields, shield-bearing warriors, warriors with weapons, war gods, star katsinas, stars and serpents, and predator animals, are closely related to those pictured in Eastern Pueblo IV rock art. Moreover, the closest parallels between these iconographic sets are found in the central part of this area embracing the Southern Tewa, Southern Tiwa, and Tompiro linguistic regions, herein referred to as the "core area" (see Table 8.2 and Figure 8.1). The rock art figures of these regions are often the most complete and detailed and, therefore, most closely approximate their mural counterparts. This is especially true in regard to warriors—with and without shields—stars and star-related supernaturals, and predatory

animals. The war complex is discussed in detail in the work of Schaafsma (2000).

Both fully defined and schematic shield bearers are concentrated in large numbers in the northern Rio Grande (see Table 8.2). Schematic figures have sticklike appendages and face frontally. Of primary interest are a number of large, lifelike shield bearers, akin to those portrayed in the Pottery Mound murals (Figures 8.2–8.5). In particular, the Southern Tewa sites in the Galisteo Basin—Comanche Gap #1 (Schaafsma 1992b), Largo Spring, and a painting at the mouth of Shé Canyon—comprise a focus of shield bearers and other warriors comparable to those at Pottery Mound. Most have profile faces, and some look like toothless old men (compare Figures 8.3 and 8.6). The war club with deer hoof (Figure 8.6) occurs as a separate item in a Southern Tiwa petroglyph. A few Northern Tewa fully defined, shield-bearing warriors, including one wearing a predator bird mask (see Figure 8.4, Figure 8.7), however, warn against an exclusive Southern Tewa geographic relationship between Pottery Mound and rock art warriors.

As for shields as separate icons, the focus remains in the north where large shields are featured in the rock art of the Northern Tewa and also in at least some Western Towa sites, Tovakwa (LA 481) being a case in point. Shields are, nevertheless, widely distributed throughout the Pueblo Rio Grande (see Table 8.2).

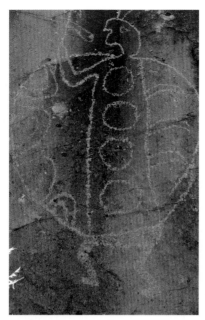

FIGURE 8.3
Shield bearer with a toothless profile holding a feathered projectile, Galisteo Basin, ca. A.D. 1325–1525. (Photograph by Polly Schaafsma.)

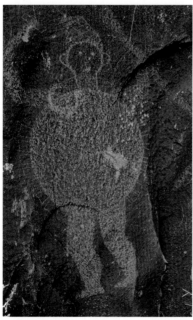

FIGURE 8.4
Northern Tewa shield bearer wearing netted war god cap with eagle feathers. The shield is edged with turkey feathers. (Photograph by Polly Schaafsma.)

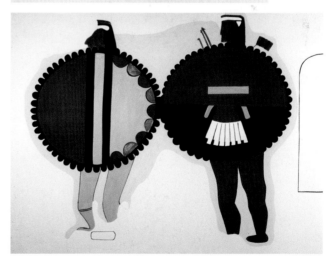

FIGURE 8.5
Lifelike shield bearers, Kiva 2, Layer 3, Pottery Mound. Scalloped edges may indicate that they are of buffalo hide manufacture. (Courtesy of the Maxwell Museum of Anthropology, University of New Mexico, catalog nos. 76.70.635, 639, 640.)

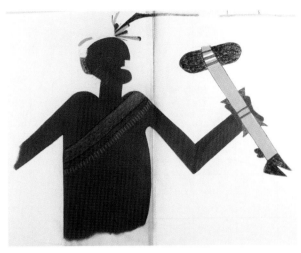

FIGURE 8.6

Toothless warrior with bandoleer and war club, Kiva 9, Layer 12, Pottery Mound. (Courtesy of the Maxwell Museum of Anthropology, University of New Mexico, catalog no. 76.70.802.)

FIGURE 8.7

Northern Tewa shield-bearing bird warrior with knife. Hispanic Christian crosses, lower right, were added historically. (Photograph courtesy of Barbara Alpert.)

Some motifs on shields such as the star with four expanding points occur in rock art from the Northern Tewa south into the Piro region as well as at Pottery Mound (see Figure 8.5). This star, rare in Western Pueblo art, also shows up on shields in the Hopi murals (Smith 1952:Figures 40*a* and 56*b*). Vertically divided shields with "hooks" and circles (see Figure 8.3, 8.5 [Hibben 1975:132–33]) occur north of Pottery Mound in the rock art of the Western Towa and Southern Tewa. Although this shield design occurs at Pottery Mound, to date it has not been documented in the southern Pueblo rock art. Turkey feather and scalloped shield edging are predominantly Rio Grande features and are absent or rare (Smith 1952:Figure 47*e*) in the Western Pueblo art.

Shield/predator complexes that unite the power of felines and eagles or other raptors with warfare are pictured in both murals and rock art (see Table 8.2). The feline/shield relationship evolves into a sophisticated unified symbolic complex in mural art, both at Pottery Mound and in the Jeddito murals (see Figure 6.10; Schaafsma 2000:Figures 3.32, 3.38), but in rock art this relationship takes the abbreviated form of simple juxtapositioning and is somewhat rare at that. Shield-bearing eagle warriors, however, as exemplified by the Northern Tewa example figure (see Figure 8.7), are present in petroglyphs in the Southern Tewa and Tompiro regions.

The raptor-headed shield-bearing warrior is thought to be conceptually related to the raptor-headed katsina depicted in the context of warfare iconography in rock art and at Pottery Mound (Figures 8.8–8.9). Raptor-headed katsinas, pictured as whole figures or by mask only, are widely dispersed and well represented in the Rio Grande but undocumented in the Jeddito murals and rock art sites. In the Rio Grande region, they occur in significant numbers in the Southern Tewa and Tiwa landscapes (see Table 8.2). Examples in the Galisteo Basin are comparable to the mural images in their large size and full definition.

Warrior katsinas include star katsinas. Ceremonial figures in the murals with feathered kilts and stars painted on their torsos are probably star katsinas, although due to erosion their heads are missing (Hibben 1975:Figures 25–26). Rock art star katsinas, sharing formal qualities with mural renditions, wear kilts or breechcloths and carry weapons in Southern Tewa, Southern Tiwa, and Tompiro rock art sites (Figure 8.10).

In the Rio Grande, stars are subject to complex metaphorical treatment, and they are often identified as the Morning Star and always relate to war (Schaafsma

FIGURE 8.8

Drawings of Southern Tewa petroglyphs of persons wearing raptor masks, Galisteo Basin, ca. A.D. 1325–1525. (Adapted from drawing by Tamara Wiggans Desrosiers.)

2000:144–54). Eastern Pueblo depictions may have projectiles in their headgear, eagle-tail fan headdresses, and talons (Figure 8.11). The conflation with eagle attributes compounds the star's symbolic qualities that include that of a scalper. Stars are found in the greatest numbers in the rock art of the core area (see Table 8.2; Baldwin 1992; Schaafsma 2000:144–49) where they are frequently pictured with faces in addition to avian accoutrements. At Pottery Mound (Figure 8.12), stars are found in a variety of contexts—as a shield motif, clustered together, or painted on the torso, kilt, or leggings of a performer (Hibben 1975:Figures 2, 25–26, 32, 34, 106–7). Stars or star shapes are rare in the Jeddito murals where they tend to be schematic and lack elaborations (Smith 1952:Figures 40a, 41d, 48a, 49a, 56b).

FIGURE 8.9

Raptor katsina holding double-bitted ax, Kiva 7, Layer 10, Pottery Mound. (Courtesy of the Maxwell Museum of Anthropology, University of New Mexico, catalog nos. 76.70.369, 371, 370.)

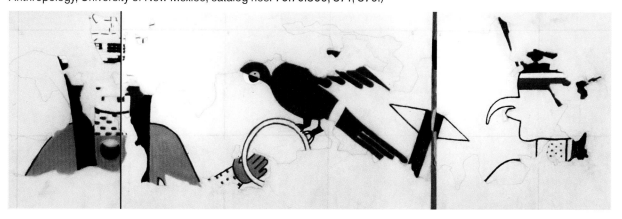

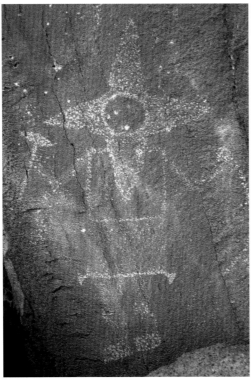

FIGURE 8.10
Southern Tiwa star katsina, Petroglyph National
Monument, Albuquerque, ca. A.D. 1325–1600.
(Photograph by Polly Schaafsma.)

FIGURE 8.11
Southern Tiwa star with face, eagle tail fan, talons,
and projectile in headdress, Petroglyph National
Monument, Albuquerque, ca. A.D. 1325–1600.
(Photograph by Polly Schaafsma.)

FIGURE 8.12
Star with face from Pottery Mound, Kiva 6,
Layer 6, with feather inserted in nose septum.
(Courtesy of the Maxwell Museum of Anthropology,
University of New Mexico, catalog no. 76.70.570.)

FIGURE 8.13

Star-faced rattlesnake, Kiva 8, Layer 7, Pottery Mound. (Courtesy of the Maxwell Museum of Anthropology, University of New Mexico, catalog no. 76.70.205.)

The metaphorical star/serpent complex is less common but maintains a central Rio Grande focus (see Table 8.2). Horned serpents or rattlesnakes associated with stars—in spatial proximity or with stars for faces—are scattered among Eastern Keres, Southern Tewa, and Southern Tiwa sites. The closest likeness to the star-faced rattlesnakes in Kiva 8, Layer 7 at Pottery Mound occurs in a West Mesa Southern Tiwa site (Figures 8.13, 8.14).

War Gods, identified via their pointed caps and weapons, sometimes carry shields. They are pictured in rock art from the Western Towa, Northern, and Southern Tewa regions along the Rio Grande south to the Piro district, with most in Galisteo Basin sites (see Table 8.2). An important attribute of this figure is the cap. The pointed, and often netted, War God cap is seen in Kiva 2, Layer 1 at Pottery Mound (Figure 8.15; Hibben 1975:Figure 17) and in a Northern Tewa site, where two eagle feathers are attached to the apex of the cap (see Figure 8.4). A War God in the Awat'ovi murals and another in a Galisteo Basin petroglyph share a more extreme version of this hat, which resembles a star point (Schaafsma 2000:Figure 3.16*b*; Smith 1952:Figure 65*a*), a feature that appears to symbolize their relationship to the Morning Star (Young 1992). Other probable star-related, skin-kilted figures with upright feather headdresses, but lacking the four-pointed star face, at Piedras Marcadas in Petroglyph National Monument are repeated at Pottery Mound (Hibben 1975: Figure 57). In the murals, their faces are black, a common feature of warriors.

Other details in regard to war-related persons are shared between the Pottery Mound murals and the petroglyphs at Comanche Gap #1. In Kiva 2, Layer 1 (see Figure 8.15) the treatment of the paunchy figure with serrated

FIGURE 8.14

Southern Tiwa star-faced snake with eagle feather headdress, Petroglyph National Monument, Albuquerque, ca. A.D. 1325–1600. (Photograph by Polly Schaafsma.)

a.

b.

FIGURE 8.15
Field drawing of ceremonial procession of warriors and related figures, lefthand section, Kiva 2, Layer 1, Pottery Mound. **a)** shows the left hand sheet of the drawing, which continues on **b)** right hand sheet. Frontal figure with asymmetrical hairdo appears to be a transgendered warrior prevalent in Pueblo oral history. Drawing by John Vaughn. (Courtesy of the Maxwell Museum of Anthropology, University of New Mexico, catalog nos. 76.70.668, 665.)

FIGURE 8.16
Seated sword swallower in profile, Southern Tewa, ca. 1325–1525. (Photograph by Curtis Schaafsma.)

edging (left) specifically resembles the manner in which sword swallowers are depicted at Comanche Gap #1 (Figure 8.16). Further, the transgendered warrior figure on this same layer (third from right) is also pictured as a katsina at Comanche Gap #1.

It is important to note that specific identities are found between the murals and Southern Tiwa rock art as well, although these are fewer in number and less dramatic. The conflated snake/star figures are described above.

The mountain lion, whose supernatural powers were valued in war and the hunt, was considered in the shield/predator discussion. This feline, often ritually attired, is commonly portrayed in the Pottery Mound and Antelope Mesa murals and widely in Rio Grande rock art (Figure 8.17). Along the Rio Grande, from the northernmost part of Keresan territory south to the Piro and Tompiro provinces, the mountain lion may be shown with a quiver, wearing a pointed cap, or with various other accoutrements as well as seated (Baldwin 1986; Schaafsma 1975: Figures 53, 71; see Table 8.2). Seated in human poses,

FIGURE 8.17
Piro mountain lion petroglyph, ca. A.D. 1300–1400.
(Photograph by Polly Schaafsma.)

mountain lions at Pottery Mound (Kiva 6, Layer 6) wear arrow-filled quivers and feathers on their heads (Hibben 1975:Frontispiece). In addition, spotted felines also occur in kiva murals at Pottery Mound (Kiva 6, Layer 6 and Kiva 17) and Kawaika'a (Smith 1952:Figure 56*b*), and in Rio Grande rock art (Schaafsma 2000:Figure 3.23*d*). Paws of the mountain lion with whorled claws around a circular foot are not only portrayed in the Pottery Mound and Jeddito murals (see Crotty, this volume), but also in Rio Grande rock art. This widespread convention (see Smith 1952:204) is common in Piro petroglyphs at Cerro Indio, the primary occupation of which dates between ca. A.D. 1300 and 1400 (Marshall and Walt 1984:147–50). Puma paws with whorled claws are also pictured in Tompiro rock art near Tenabo (Schaafsma 1992:Figure 120), although in this case a more specific temporal ascription is impossible due to the longevity of the site (ca. 1325–1672).

In regard to feline hunting prowess, and of specific interest in this review, are two paintings: one at Pottery Mound, Kiva 16, Layer 4, and another on the rocks in the Tompiro region (Figures 8.18 and 8.19). Both cats are similarly pictured with large game animals flung upside down over their backs. Small mountain lion fetishes also occur twice in Kiva 16 and in Tompiro rock art (Baldwin 1986:Figure 2).

In summary, the varied images that comprise the war complex at Pottery Mound are well represented in the Rio Grande Pueblo landscape, with the greatest likenesses being found in the core area, especially in regard to the stars and raptor-headed katsinas. Shield bearers

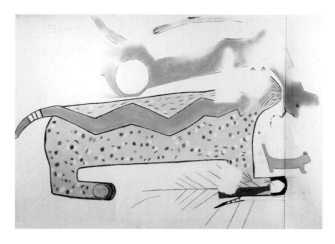

FIGURE 8.18
Feline with antelope flung over its back. Note small mountain lion hunting fetish pictured in front. Pottery Mound, Kiva 16, Layer 4. (Courtesy of the Maxwell Museum of Anthropology, University of New Mexico, catalog no. 76.70.584.)

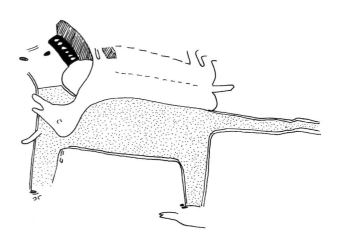

FIGURE 8.19
Tompiro rock painting of mountain lion with game, probably a deer over its back. The mountain lion is yellow, outlined in white, with a headdress in two shades of red. The deer is white. There are suggestions of red ties, perhaps with feathers affixed above the mountain lion's feet, ca. A.D. 1325–1672. (Drawing by Polly Schaafsma.)

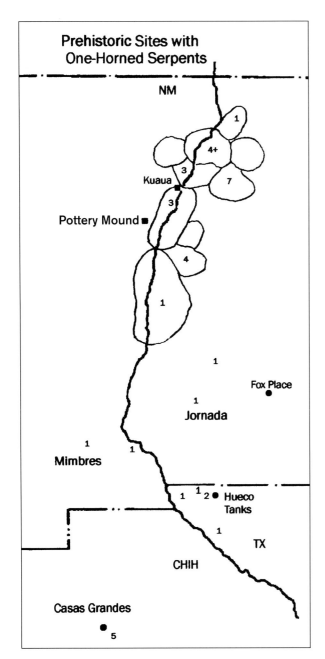

FIGURE 8.20

Map showing the distribution of the Horned Serpent in rock art sites from Taos, New Mexico, to Paquimé, Chihuahua. The numbers indicate the number of sites at which these figures occur, not the numbers of Horned Serpents pictured. At the Fox Place, a green Horned Serpent was painted on the wall of a room, dated at A.D. 1250 (Schaafsma and Wiseman 1992).

comparable to Pottery Mound depictions are focused in the Galisteo Basin, although, as previously noted, shields in general are common throughout the Northern Tewa and Western Towa regions. The significant number of Southern Tewa war personages with parallels at Pottery Mound raises the question of whether or not close social ties existed between the Southern Tewa war societies responsible for these images and Pottery Mound.

The Horned Serpent

This multifaceted supernatural (Schaafsma 2001) with a single horn is widespread in rock art from Paquimé in northern Chihuahua to Taos, New Mexico (Figure 8.20, see Table 8.2). Because of the historical importance of its distribution in general, as well as its implications for Pottery Mound specifically, I have noted all known rock art sites where this deity is pictured in the Southwest. A single thick, usually forward-pointing horn distinguishes this being, although backward horns occur regionally. Regional differences are also found in feather arrangements. This figure is to be distinguished from two-horned serpents frontally depicted in rock art of the northern Rio Grande Pueblos.

At Pottery Mound the Horned Serpent is depicted as a full-fledged serpent (Figure 8.21*a*), a lightning puppet (Kiva 8, Layer 1, Hibben Center Photo Archives, Albuquerque, New Mexico), a masked impersonator (Figure 8.21*b*), and a cloud serpent (see Figure 6.14). In the last example, no head is shown, and the snake, bearing stepped clouds, encircles the room. The masked impersonator also has a stepped design on its back, inside the "hump." Meteorological phenomena are aspects of this deity (Schaafsma and Taube 2006). In Pueblo rock art, it is pictured frequently by the Southern Tewa (Figure 8.22), although elaborate portrayals are also found in Tompiro rock art. To date, it has not been documented from secure prehistoric contexts in Western Pueblo art (see following).

Feathers are the most common additional attribute of the Horned Serpent, but its meanings may also be compounded with the addition of teeth, a tongue, drops of moisture or feathers emitting from the mouth, checkerboard necklaces, and the above mentioned cloud terrace. These details are most commonly portrayed in, but not limited to, the rock art of the central Pueblo Rio Grande. The association of this ophidian with four-pointed stars at Pottery Mound and in Southern Tiwa and Tewa rock art is discussed in connection with Venus symbolism and warfare with roots in Mesoamerica (Schaafsma 2000:152).

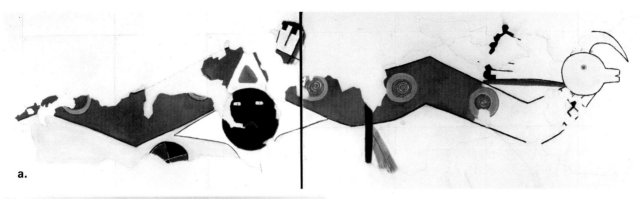

a.

b.

FIGURE 8.21

a) Horned and Feathered Serpent with Morning Star icon, Kiva 7, Layer 9, Pottery Mound. Drawing by Dennis Tedlock. (Courtesy of the Maxwell Museum of Anthropology, University of New Mexico, catalog no. 76.70.408.) **b**) Horned Serpent impersonator, Kiva 7, Layer 21, Pottery Mound. (Courtesy of the Maxwell Museum of Anthropology, University of New Mexico, catalog no. 76.70.487.)

FIGURE 8.22

Pair of Horned Serpents, Southern Tewa, ca. A.D. 1325–1680. (Photograph by Polly Schaafsma.)

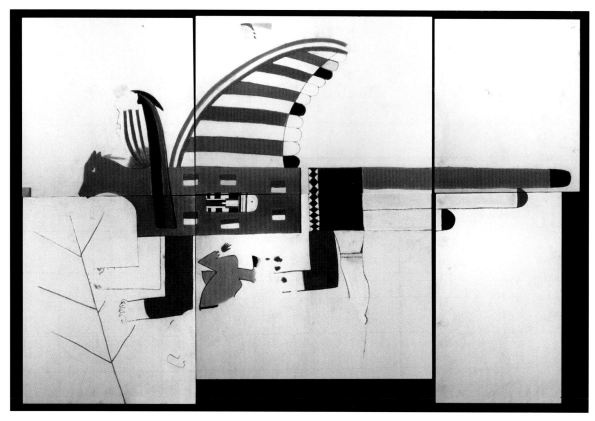

FIGURE 8.23

Human/bird/feline supernatural, Kiva 9, Layer 3, Pottery Mound. (Courtesy of the Maxwell Museum of Anthropology, University of New Mexico, catalog nos. 76.40.574–76, 76.40.578–579, 76.40.581.)

FIGURE 8.24

Masked animal wearing a kilt and sash, Petroglyph National Monument, Albuquerque. (Photograph by Polly Schaafsma.)

The Horned Serpent is found on rocks in southern New Mexico and Chihuahua near Paquimé (Schaafsma 1997; 1998:Figures 11–13). It is also pictured on ceramics beginning with Mimbres bowls (1000–1150) and on later Ramos Polychrome vessels (ca. 1200–1425; Schaafsma 1998:36–40). On three Mimbres bowls, a person in a Horned Serpent costume performs beheadings (LeBlanc 1999:Figure 2.7). It is not known, however, if the decapitees are victims of hostile encounters.

Pertinent to this discussion is the close iconographic resemblance between the Ramos Polychrome horned serpents (Schaafsma 1998:37–40) and those in the Pottery Mound murals. In both cases, showy feather fans project backward behind the horn, and snouts are sharply squared off. Although Horned Serpent rock art iconography is abundant, especially in the northern Rio Grande, serpents with this kind of feather fan headdress have not been documented in any Pueblo site outside of Pottery Mound. Furthermore, in the Southwest, *Horned Serpent impersonators* are known from only the Mimbres bowls, the Casas Grandes region, and Pottery Mound (Schaafsma 1998:Figure 13; Van Pool 2003:Figure 2D, Color Photo 2).

Other Ceremonial Participants

There remain many other ritual persons portrayed in the Pottery Mound murals and Rio Grande rock art. Important among these are supernatural beings with attributes of more than one species. Some are masked. Conflated images involving people and animals—mountain lions, eagles, bears, snakes, and insects—are pictured frequently and more elaborately at Pottery Mound than anywhere else in Pueblo IV art (Hibben 1975:Figures 1, 2, 4, 5, 8, 12, 18, among others). In the murals, sometimes more than one animal species is combined with human traits. Human legs, heads, and kilts may signal the human component of the being involved (Figure 8.23; see also Smith 1952:Figure 49a for a comparable figure at Awat'ovi). In rock art (see Table 8.2), among the most complex of these synthetic figures are the Tewa predator bird warriors already addressed (see Figures 8.7, 8.8). Also notable is a Southern Tiwa petroglyph of a masked animal wearing a kilt and sash (Figure 8.24).

Details of ceremonial attire

Numerous items of attire are depicted rather universally in the kiva murals (see Webster, Chapter 9). Some of these occur in Rio Grande rock art, although because simplification is the trend in rock art, such details are often missing. When articles of costuming are included, as in the

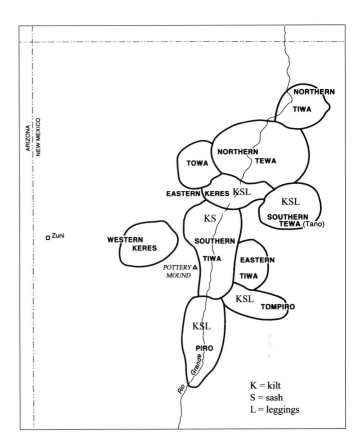

FIGURE 8.25

Map showing the distribution of kilts, sashes, and leggings (i.e., ceremonial attire exclusive of masks, headgear, and shields) pictured in Rio Grande rock art. (Adapted from C. Schaafsma 1994:Figure 11.1.)

FIGURE 8.26
Southern Tiwa katsina with an "eye-patch" mask.
A looped necklace and kilt are also delineated,
Petroglyph National Monument, Albuquerque.
(Photograph by Polly Schaafsma.)

small and detailed rock paintings of the Tompiro and Piro regions, they are similar to those in the murals. Figure 8.25 shows the distribution of the most obvious items of dress: kilts, sashes, and leggings. Buckskin leggings with fringes are found in both rock art and in the Pottery Mound murals but not in Western Pueblo art.

Manta dresses fastened over one shoulder are pictured in at least one Tompiro rock painting. The related shoulder capes or blankets (see Webster, Chapter 9), often with undulating lower borders, are specifically delineated (Schaafsma 2000:55, Figure 3.17e–f) or implied in Shalako figures that occur widely in the rock art throughout the Keresan, Southern Tewa, and Southern Tiwa regions.

Handheld items pictured in Rio Grande rock art most commonly include feathered and plain staffs, evergreen boughs, blunt and bipointed war clubs, quivers, bows, and arrows. Crooked prayer sticks, a bullroarer, yucca whips, and swallowing swords occur in the hands of ritual practitioners in rock art but not in the kiva murals. Female figures balancing pots on their heads occur in Keresan rock art, at Pottery Mound (see Figure 6.12), and at Kawaika'a (Smith 1952:Figure 67d).

As previously noted, masks in Pueblo IV (and in Jornada-style) rock art and the sites in which they occur are so numerous they preclude tallying in this context. While the murals are easily regarded as the "mother lode" repositories of iconography, in something of a reversal, masks as individual icons are never subjects of mural paintings. In the Pottery Mound murals, the rare portrayals of handheld masks were mentioned earlier. One of these is an "eye patch" mask (Crotty 1995:Figure 69).

Rock art masks display seemingly limitless variation and patterning that often appear to be idiosyncratic. There are, however, a couple of repeated types of masks shared by both the murals and rock art that are worth singling out in addition to the profile raptor katsina mask discussed earlier. Ceremonial participants wearing masks with an "eye patch" (or "eye paint," see Chapter 6) occur at Pottery Mound, in the Jeddito murals (Smith 1952: Figure 67d), and in Rio Grande petroglyphs (Figure 8.26). At Pottery Mound and at Kawaika'a, masks of this type are sometimes associated with asymmetrical hairdos, a hairstyle pictured only rarely in Rio Grande rock art. "Eye patch" masks are found on occasion in Southern Tewa, Southern Tiwa, and Keresan sites (see Table 8.2). A few "eye patch" masks are known from Western Pueblo rock art contexts (see Cole [1992:Figure 5.9] for a petroglyph at Homol'ovi; Hays [1994:Figure 6.10] for another depicted on a post-1450 Jeddito yellow sherd from Tsukuvi [or Chukubi] ruin on Second Mesa [Mindeleff 1891:58–59]).

Masks with small, downturned mouths have a southern distribution, occurring in Tompiro and Piro sites (see Table 8.2). It is noteworthy that they also are found in Jornada sites beyond the Pueblo area. In the Pottery Mound murals, these sinister mouths, often red and toothed, are portrayed on star faces and other war-related persons (see Figure 8.21; Hibben 1975:Figures 55, 59, 105). A detailed petroglyph mask from the Piro site of Cerro Indio, with a toothed mouth, horn, and eagle feathers (Figure 8.27) shares this and other attributes with the Pottery Mound star faces.

Sunflowers

Flowers are relatively uncommon in Pueblo art (see Smith 1952:Figures 76a, 79a, b; Hibben 1975:Figure 4 [possible stacked blossoms]). Sunflowers alone, although rare as well, have a broad southern Pueblo distribution in Pueblo IV rock art and one example also occurs in a Jornada-style petroglyph site in Lincoln County. The delicate rendering of sunflowers in Kiva 1, Layer 1 (Hibben 1975: Figure 8) is repeated in Piro and Tompiro rock art—as a petroglyph at Tenabo and painted in an overhang at Cerro Indio (Brody 1991:Plate 1.35). From further afield, similar sunflowers are rendered on a Sikyatki Polychrome bowl from Awat'ovi (Smith 1952:Figure 17f).

Summary

It is clear from the foregoing analysis that the iconography in the Pottery Mound murals has a strong regional artistic context within the Puebloan Rio Grande. The same icons and metaphorical complexes seen in the murals are widely distributed in landscape art throughout the Rio Grande valley. Some of these same specific traits are shared with the Jeddito murals that in general are stylistically the same as the Pottery Mound murals. The closest relationships between the murals and rock art is with the Southern Tewa, Southern Tiwa, and Tompiro sites. Warfare iconography at Pottery Mound has strong parallels in Southern Tewa rock art, a factor that could denote a social tie between war societies at Pottery Mound and the Galisteo Basin. No linguistic affiliation for Pottery Mound is suggested on the basis of the art. On the whole, the murals contain visual metaphors that crosscut linguistic boundaries within the Rio Grande valley, communicating a common worldview beyond the spoken language. Thus the visual text of murals and rock art functioned to bind Pueblo communities together, if not politically and economically, then with a unified cosmology.

The Broader View: Looking West

With the contextual relationship between the Pottery Mound murals and the Rio Grande valley Pueblos well established via the rock art, the broader picture needs to be examined via rock art elsewhere, given the close relationship between the Pottery Mound murals and those of the Jeddito. This is necessary in order to at least propose potential social interactions Pottery Mound may have had with the Western Pueblos. Also remaining for consideration are the Sikyatki paintings that comprise

FIGURE 8.27
Although lacking the points of a star, this Piro mask shares the crown of eagle feathers and downturned toothed mouth with star icons. (Photograph by Polly Schaafsma.)

an important minor component of the Pottery Mound murals (see Crotty, this volume, Table 6.2; Hays-Gilpin and LeBlanc, this volume).

Western Pueblo IV Rock Art

In terms of rock art, a boundary between the Eastern or Rio Grande Pueblos and the Western Pueblos falls immediately to the west of the Rio Grande valley proper. This discontinuity suggests a social boundary of some kind, irrespective of the pottery trade into Pottery Mound from the west (see Eckert, this volume).

The image complex that distinguishes the Rio Grande style is not present in rock art of the Rio San José, Middle Rio Puerco, and in the Cebolla Canyon system west of Acoma as far as we know. Dittert (1998:86) makes the case that Acoma's most important outside contacts between 1275 and 1500 were to the west with Zuni. He also notes: "Many places of major religious importance are located there [from St. Johns to Springerville in Arizona and in New Mexico, south of Zuni] and are still visited today." These observations are consistent with the rock art evidence.

Most importantly for the focus of this paper, in general Western Pueblo rock art has significantly less connection with the kiva murals than does Eastern Pueblo rock art (see Cole 1992; McCreery and Malotki 1994; Schaafsma 1994:76–77; Schaafsma and Young, in press; Scott 1997; Young 1988). The entire symbolic repertoire is simplified, elements of the war complex are notably rare, and rock production is less overall. With the seeming exceptions of a few katsina performers, masks, masked birds, and stepped cloud terraces, Rio Grande–style rock art is relatively meager prehistorically at Zuni. Large shields at Dowa Yalanne are likely historic in origin (Schaafsma and Young, in press; Young 1988).

Early Pueblo IV petroglyphs in the Upper and Middle Little Colorado date between ca. 1275 and 1400 (Cole 1992:120; McCreery and Malotki 1994:58; Scott 1997; Stephenson et al. 1997) and, therefore, possibly overlap the Pottery Mound murals by several decades. A recent survey at Bigelow Crossing (Scott 1997) and a review of the entire suite of petroglyphs (CD-ROM, courtesy of Charles Hoffmann, Northern Arizona University) documented a few masks or masklike faces interspersed with an iconography more in keeping with Pueblo III.

> In the Palavayu area [see McCreery and
> Malotki 1994:Figure 1.2], rock art of this style
> differs from the eastern expression in both
> subject matter and manner of portrayal. . . .
> Missing are the stars and star faces, intricately
> patterned masks and headgear, one-horned
> snakes, fish, badgers, and skunks . . . , and
> only six examples of shields or shield-bodied
> figures have been found. The "cloud terrace,"
> a stepped pyramid, is occasionally seen.
> Masks are usually simple in design, . . .
> A few full-bodied masked figures are found,
> but only two at the same site (Figure 2.19) are
> adorned with the sash and ceremonial attire
> [McCreery and Malotki 1994:55–56].

These last mentioned petroglyphs, however, are unlike Rio Grande–style katsina depictions. McCreery and Malotki (1994:56) observe that katsina iconography is "thinly scattered." In Figure 4.3 they illustrate 84 masks and masked figures that comprise a nearly total inventory from the area surveyed (1994:Figure 4.3; Malotki, personal communication 2003).

Although a terminal date around 1400 surely accounts for discrepancies between this rock art and that in the Rio Grande, the continuously occupied Zuni region, does not pick up the difference.

Rock Art on Antelope Mesa at Hopi

If one were asked, "With what body of graphic art do the Pottery Mound murals share the closest resemblances?" the answer would be, without hesitation, the kiva murals of Awat'ovi and Kawaika'a. In regard to figure types, the painstaking detail, and the variety of subject matter and the complexity of the visual metaphors portrayed, the kiva art of both localities is comparable.

In light of this, a review of the rock art of Antelope Mesa is critical in order to evaluate the graphic art context in the immediate vicinity of the Western Pueblo murals. How does it compare with Pueblo IV rock art located within a 200-mile-long corridor in the Rio Grande valley and nearby related provinces to the east of the river? The petroglyphs between Awat'ovi and Kawaika'a were recorded by Cindy Dongoske in conjunction with research sponsored by the Hopi Cultural Project Office (Dongoske and Dongoske 2002:Figures 8.2–8.8). Historic rock art could date as recently as the twentieth century, as farmlands continued to be cultivated below the western escarpment by Hopi clans from both First and Second Mesa (Brew 1979:515, Figure 1). Awat'ovi itself was occupied from ca. 1200 to 1700 (Dongoske and Dongoske 2002:120). Thus while it is clear that some of the petroglyphs on the Antelope Mesa cliffs both predate and postdate the murals, the majority are probably contemporary with the wall paintings. Limited inspection by the author of rock art directly below Awat'ovi itself indicates that this is true for the sites reviewed. The Dongoskes (2002:123) note that the largest and most complex petroglyph sites occur within a half mile or less of Awat'ovi.

In general, the Antelope Mesa petroglyphs attributable to Pueblo IV manifest a more limited visual vocabulary than the Rio Grande work. However, it may be argued that these figures were strongly influenced by Rio Grande norms, if not actually manufactured by Rio Grande immigrants themselves, although the repertoire of elements is notably more sparse. Rare among the Antelope Mesa petroglyphs is the variety of full-figured ceremonial participants: raptor katsinas, conflated ceremonial participants, seated ceremonialists, and figures wearing cloth or skin kilts, tasseled sashes, and other costuming details. The many distinctive profile faces—masked and unmasked—are also limited in number in Antelope Mesa rock art. Stars are rarely pictured, and stars with faces, feathers, talons, and arrows—in other words, the Morning Star complex—is nearly absent. The general prolific variability displayed in Rio Grande masks is lacking on the cliffs of Antelope Mesa, although some of the same figures—borderless masks, masks with horns, and square-toothed mouths—are represented in both regions. Katsina masks in the rock art are mostly round in shape, and bowl-shaped masks are rare (Dongoske and Dongoske 2002:Figure 8.3). In some respects, including the boldness of execution, a number of the masks below Awat'ovi most closely resemble masks from Southern Tewa sites in the Galisteo Basin. This cursory evaluation and the implications thereof need to be explored further in light of what is known about migrations into the Hopi region from the east.

Among the Antelope Mesa petroglyphs there are a few additional figures with a peculiarly Rio Grande cast. These include the previously discussed Horned Serpent and a few shield designs, neither of which appear in the Jeddito murals. The widely distributed serpent (see Figure 8.20) with the distinctive, large, tapered, forward-reaching horn (Dongoske and Dongoske 2002:Figure 8.2) is present in First Mesa rock art (Stephen 1936:Figures 494, 496b) but has not been documented elsewhere in the entire Western Pueblo region (see McCreery and Malotki 1994; Schaafsma and Young, in press; Young 1988). In one case below Awat'ovi, the snake is juxtaposed with a rectangular element with a dot pattern inside (Cindy Dongoske, personal communication 2002). The latter resembles a resist-dyed textile represented in Rio Grande Keresan rock art (see Schaafsma 1975:Figure 49). Other images of the Horned Serpent on First Mesa typically have snipe tracks along the body, and the horn is very small, consistent in form with that of the contemporary Hopi Horned Serpent effigy (Stephen 1936:Figures 496a, 504, 505).

A number of shields pecked on the cliffs below Awat'ovi have designs similar to those found in the Rio Grande (Dongoske and Dongoske 2002:Figures 8.3, 8.4, 8.7). Probably not coincidentally, one four-pointed star occurs beside a shield bearer whose shield design is a distinctly Northern Tewa pattern (Dongoske and Dongoske 2002:Figure 8.3, right). In the Rio Grande valley, the horizontally divided shield with downward projecting triangles is nearly exclusive to the Northern Tewa region, where variations on this basic layout are found repeatedly (Schaafsma 2000:Figure 3.8a, b). More prevalent on Antelope Mesa is a vertically divided shield decorated with two or three circles on one side and tapered, curved elements on the other. Several variations of this shield pattern occur on the cliffs below Awat'ovi and in the Rio Grande valley. This shield motif is widely distributed in the Rio Grande from the Western Towa and Southern Tewa regions to Pottery Mound (Hibben 1975:Figures 103–4; Schaafsma 2000:Figure 3.8c–f) and is not, therefore, distinctive to any particular linguistic group. In addition, in the Jeddito sites there are occasional masks pecked on rock angles (Dongoske and Dongoske 2002:123). This is a common phenomenon throughout Rio Grande and Jornada rock art sites, a practice apparently introduced to the Jeddito from the Eastern Pueblos. In summary, as far as is known to date, the rock art complex below Awat'ovi, predominantly Rio Grande in character albeit somewhat simplified, is limited in its distribution in the Western Pueblo region.

Finally, an interesting piece of evidence for east to west communication exists in the murals themselves—in the freshwater long-nosed gar at Kawaika'a (Smith 1952:Figure 60b). A long-nosed gar was also represented at Pottery Mound (Kiva 10, Layer 11, Hibben Center Photo Archives, Albuquerque, New Mexico). This fish was still present in the Rio Grande valley in the nineteenth century and occurs in archaeological assemblages from Pueblo III and Pueblo IV sites (Akins 2003:21; McNew and Loendorf 1997:97). Gar scales from Pueblo del Arroyo in Chaco Canyon indicate that this fish was traded in from the Rio Grande (Judd 1959:127–28). In the Pueblo IV murals it appears to have had watery symbolic connotations.

In conclusion, the Jeddito murals and even the rock art stand out as something of an anomaly in the prehistoric Western Pueblo region. Lacking the broad *regional* contextualization provided by rock art enjoyed by the Pottery Mound murals, the Antelope Mesa murals along with the associated rock art appear to be a Rio Grande import. If so, a proposed influx from the Rio Grande implies a network of social exchange between Antelope Mesa and Rio Grande pueblos, possibly Pottery Mound specifically. Given this scenario, the apparent absence of Rio Grande ceramics on Antelope Mesa (see Smith 1971) suggests that one needs to be cautious about drawing conclusions about social dynamics on the basis of ceramics alone.[1] In this case the picture is richly complicated by the mural paintings and to a lesser degree by the rock art.

Social Dynamics, Cultural Exchange, and the Sikyatki Issue

Following a model suggested by Jeffrey Clark (2001), I suggest that the complexity of the Jeddito murals, predominantly Rio Grande in content, is indicative of actual migration by Eastern Pueblos into the eastern Hopi Mesas, rather than simple emulation by Hopis of Rio Grande concepts. Further, the archaeological evidence for immigrants from the Rio Grande to the eastern Hopi Mesas is supported by oral tradition that includes accounts of long visitation relationships (Parsons in Stephen 1936:xxx–xxxi; see also Whiteley 2002:151).

Ethnographic models provide some insight into how individuals or kiva groups may have communicated, shared, or passed on rituals and ceremonies. Relocation of village segments or kin groups into other villages often involved contributions of ritual knowledge and efficacious ceremonies, these being part of the qualification for acceptance (Parsons 1932:349; Titiev 1944:120). As a result, ritual knowledge passed from one village to another (see Stevenson [1904:567] for a graphic account of this process between Hopi and Zuni). Use of Keresan songs in Hopi ceremonies suggests Keres groups contributed to the ritual legacy of these Western Pueblos (Stephen 1936:713). Eastern Hopi also have a substantial relationship with the Tewa. Visitation relationships between Pueblos, including visitation between the Rio Grande Pueblos and Hopi, apparently common in the historic period, were possibly based in prehistoric precedents and had a direct influence on ceremonialism (Parsons in Stephen 1936:xxx–xxxi). New ceremonies and rituals would have demanded the use of the "correct" visual text or iconography. Thus the reservoir of iconographic resources of any one village would have been amplified here and there and from time to time by an incoming group or visitations. The close connection between the Antelope Mesa and the Pottery Mound murals on numerous fronts seems to imply such relationships.

Social exchange or factors involving immigration between the Rio Grande and the Jeddito region, in turn, has implications for Pottery Mound itself. The small percentages of Hopi Yellow Wares found at the site (see Eckert, and Appendix D, this volume) appear to substantially exceed those documented for other contemporaneous nearby Rio Grande pueblos (Franklin 1996; Marshall 1987:65–81) and provide supporting evidence for relationships between Pottery Mound and the eastern Hopi region.

In turn, the Sikyatki-style murals at Pottery Mound have generated enormous interest and complicate this discussion. At Hopi itself, the style reached an apex of development as a ceramic design style (Fewkes 1973). At Pottery Mound, in every painted kiva from which multiple layers of paintings were recorded, there were one or more layers with abstract decorative panels painted in Sikyatki style (see Crotty, Table 6.2, and Hays-Gilpin and LeBlanc, this volume). In contrast, Sikyatki murals per se were found in only one room at Awat'ovi (Test 14, Room 3; Smith 1952:Figures 48, 49*a*). In addition, at Pottery Mound Sikyatki motifs are found sporadically on shields, kilts, headdresses (Crotty 1995:Tables A.53, B.1; Webster, this volume), and as separate designs in association with Rio Grande elements. Although Sikyatki elements occur on very rare occasions in rock paintings and petroglyphs in the Rio Grande, rock art does not provide a larger context for Sikyatki mural paintings anywhere. The only comprehensive set of Sikyatki-like drawings were recorded from the late Pueblo *cavate* structures on the Pajarito Plateau (Chapman 1938).

The social history of the Sikyatki style appears to be complex. Its origins are still open to discussion. The suggestion by Hays-Gilpin and LeBlanc (this volume) that painted textiles may have been a primary medium for this art and responsible for its spread is worthy of considerable thought. Their proposal that the Sikyatki style was utilized primarily by small, widely dispersed groups of ritual specialists may explain its distribution as well as its importance at Pottery Mound. Webster (this volume) notes that painted cotton cloth is prevalent in the Pottery Mound murals. Was cloth painted with Sikyatki designs traded from Pottery Mound to the Western Pueblos rather than vice versa (but see Webster, this volume)?

Concluding Remarks

Shared iconography and visual metaphors, along with artistic conventions, are viewed as extremely sensitive indicators of social relationships. It is also apparent that the iconography of the murals and rock art contains information that is not necessarily present in data provided by broken dishes—either technically or in ceramic design programs. In other words, the graphic art of murals and rock drawings is a facet of the prehistoric record that derives from a vastly different functional category of behavior based in ritual performance and cosmological beliefs—one which significantly broadens, complicates, and even frustrates perceptions of the past based on more traditional archaeological data.

This comparative review has shown that the Pottery Mound murals were predominantly part of a widely distributed Rio Grande art complex and ideological sphere that prevailed during Pueblo IV. While within the Rio Grande region itself no linguistic affiliation of Pottery Mound can be suggested on the basis of rock art/mural relationships, it is important to note that the closest relationships between the murals and rock art fall within the glaze ware regions. Specific shared items in the rock art have been detailed from the Southern Tewa through the Tompiro and Piro linguistic provinces. The warfare content of the murals has some provocative analogues with the Southern Tewa rock art, leading to the suggestion that some war societies may have been shared between the Southern Tewa and Pottery Mound. This is an area that needs further examination in the future.

Although a Keresan affiliation was previously suggested for Pottery Mound (Hibben 1975:54), with specific ties to Acoma, such a relationship is not well borne out by the rock art. As noted previously, Dittert's (1998) contention that Acoma's primary relationships lay to the west concurs with the pattern observed in the rock art. The significance of Acoma/Zuni Glaze Wares at Pottery Mound (Eckert 2003; Hibben 1987; Voll 1961) needs to be evaluated in the context of these data.

In conclusion, it is essential to not lose track of the fact that the representational content—which comprises the majority of the Pottery Mound murals—along with Rio Grande–style rock art is part of a wider ideological and strong artistic tradition in the Rio Grande corridor of New Mexico. It is necessary to look *beyond* the perimeters of the Pueblo sphere to the Jornada Mogollon, the Plains, and ultimately Mexico to fully understand the origins, cosmology, and content of Pueblo IV art. These associations have been detailed elsewhere (Schaafsma 1980; 1992a; 1994; 1999; Schaafsma and Schaafsma 1974; Schaafsma and

Taube 2006). Predator bird warriors and the Morning Star with its associations with arrows, war, and sacrifice, as previously discussed, have a strong *Eastern* Pueblo distribution and occur in both the murals and rock art. It is possible that both Pueblos and Plains groups derived similar ideas from Mexican sources and/or that ideas were communicated between Western Plains groups and the Eastern Pueblos (James Brown, personal communication 2004). The social mechanisms accounting for this kind of interaction have not been examined, an endeavor quite beyond the scope of this discussion.

All in all, the graphic vocabulary and quantities of rock art and kiva murals indicate that during early Pueblo IV, the Rio Grande valley overall was the forefront of religious and ceremonial vigor. Katherine Spielmann's (1998a) study, which addresses bowl diameters and jar forms of Rio Grande Glaze Wares, suggests that this dynamism was associated with communal feasting and water-related rituals. She concludes that communal feasting was more heavily emphasized in the Rio Grande than elsewhere in the Southwest (1998a:259). These findings imply a high degree of ritual exchange within the Rio Grande itself and support the implications suggested in general by the murals and rock art. The many painted kivas may indicate Pottery Mound's role as a prestigious religious center and focus of long-distance ritual exchange as well (see Spielmann 1998b:15). In the likely scenario that this was the case, then Pottery Mound may have been the focus of ritual dialogue with Western Pueblo groups, and with Hopi in particular, thus explaining the connectivity between Pottery Mound and Antelope Mesa, in the absence of an equivalent rock art contextual milieu for the Jeddito murals.

The excavation of more late fourteenth- to fifteenth-century kivas in the Rio Grande will someday put the site of Pottery Mound in better perspective.

ACKNOWLEDGMENTS

I would like to take this opportunity to thank numerous persons for various suggestions and ideas that have contributed to this paper. These include the authors of this volume who have communicated their expertise and various perspectives throughout the seminar and subsequent writing process. Catherine Baudoin of the Maxwell Museum of Anthropology provided untiring assistance with the Pottery Mound photographs and drawings, and Chris Millington scanned slides for publication. In addition, Tamara Wiggans Desrosiers and Barbara Alpert each provided illustrations and their kind permissions to use this material, and members of the Santa Fe seminar reviewed this chapter and offered helpful comments. Research would be much more difficult without the help of librarians Mara Yarborough and Minnie Murray at the Museum of Indian Art and Culture/Laboratory of

Anthropology. Liz Nichols and the late Charles Hoffmann provided detailed documentation of rock art in the Upper Little Colorado River drainage. Cindy Dongoske shared information on the rock art below Awat'ovi and Kawaika'a, and Joe Day graciously spent a day guiding us to these sites. Curt Schaafsma provided technical assistance and was willing to read and comment on various drafts of this manuscript. All photographs in this chapter are by the author unless stated otherwise. Any errors or shortcomings are, of course, my responsibility.

NOTES

1. The ceramics of Awat'ovi other than those of the earlier Western Mound (Smith 1971) have yet to be studied.

REFERENCES CITED

Adams, E. Charles

1991   *The Origin and Development of the Pueblo Katsina Cult.* University of Arizona Press, Tucson.

Akins, Nancy J.

2003   An Analysis of Faunal Remains from the Midden of the Artificial Leg Site 12, Bernalillo County, New Mexico. In *Climbing the Rocks: Papers in Honor of Helen and Jay Crotty*, edited by Regge N. Wiseman, Thomas C. O'Laughlin, and Cordelia T. Snow, pp. 17–24. Papers of the Archaeological Society of New Mexico No. 29. Archaeological Society of New Mexico, Albuquerque.

Baldwin, Stuart J.

1986   The Mountain Lion in Tompiro Stone Art. In *By Hands Unknown: Papers on Rock Art and Archaeology in Honor of James G. Bain*, edited by Anne Poore, pp. 8–17. Papers of the Archaeological Society of New Mexico No. 12. Ancient City Press, Santa Fe, New Mexico.

1992   Evidence for a Tompiro Morning Star Kachina. *Artifact* 30(4):1–14. El Paso Archaeological Society, El Paso, Texas.

Boyd, Douglas K., and Bobbie Ferguson

1988   *Tewa Rock Art in the Black Mesa Region.* Cultural Resources Investigations, Velarde Community Ditch Project, Rio Arriba County, New Mexico. Bureau of Reclamation, Southwest Region, Amarillo, Texas.

Brew, J. O.

1979   Hopi Prehistory and History to 1850. In *Southwest*, edited by Alfonso Ortiz, pp. 514–523. Handbook of North American Indians, Vol. 9. Smithsonian Institution, Washington, D.C.

Brody, J. J.

1964   Design Analysis of the Rio Grande Glaze Pottery of Pottery Mound, New Mexico. Unpublished Master's thesis, Department of Art, University of New Mexico, Albuquerque.

1991   *Anasazi and Pueblo Painting.* A School of American Research Book. University of New Mexico Press, Albuquerque.

Chapman, Kenneth M.

1938   Pajaritan Pictography—The Cave Pictographs of the Rito de los Frijoles. Appendix I in *The Pajarito Plateau and its Ancient People*, by Edgar L. Hewett. Handbooks of Archaeological History. School of American Research, Santa Fe and the University of New Mexico Press, Albuquerque.

Clark, Jeffrey J.

2001   Migration, Enculturation, and Ethnicity. Paper presented at the Mogollon-Zuni Advanced Seminar, Museum of Northern Arizona and Center for Desert Archaeology, Flagstaff.

Cole, Sally J.

1992   *Katsina Iconography in Homol'ovi Rock Art, Central Little Colorado River Valley, Arizona.* The Arizona Archaeologist 25. Arizona Archaeological Society, Phoenix.

Cordell, Linda S.
1980 University of New Mexico Field School Excavations at Pottery Mound, New Mexico, 1979, Preliminary Report. Manuscript on file, Maxwell Museum of Anthropology, University of New Mexico, Albuquerque.

Cordell, Linda S. (editor)
1980 *Tijeras Canyon: Analyses of the Past*. Maxwell Museum of Anthropology Publication Series. University of New Mexico Press, Albuquerque.

Crotty, Helen K.
1995 *Anasazi Mural Art of the Pueblo IV Period, A.D. 1300–1600: Influences, Selective Adaptation, and Cultural Diversity in the Prehistoric Southwest*. Ph.D. dissertation, University of California, Los Angeles. University Microfilms International, Ann Arbor.
1999 Kiva Murals and Iconography at Picuris Pueblo. In *Picuris Pueblo through Time: Eight Centuries of Change at a Northern Rio Grande Pueblo*, edited by Michael Adler and Herbert W. Dick, pp.149–88. William P. Clement Center for Southwest Studies, Southern Methodist University, Dallas, Texas.

Dittert, Alfred E.
1998 The Acoma Culture Province during the Period A.D. 1275–1500: Cultural Disruption and Reorganization. In *Migration and Reorganization: The Pueblo IV Period in the American Southwest*, edited by K. A. Spielmann, pp. 81–90. Arizona State University Anthropological Research Papers No. 51. Arizona State University, Tempe.

Dongoske, Kurt E., and Cindy K. Dongoske
2002 History in Stone: Evaluating Spanish Conversion Efforts through Hopi Rock Art. In *Archaeologies of the Pueblo Revolt: Identities, Meaning, and Renewal in the Pueblo World*, edited by Robert W. Preucel, pp. 114–31. University of New Mexico Press, Albuquerque.

Dutton, Bertha P.
1963 *Sun Father's Way*. University of New Mexico Press, Albuquerque.

Eckert, Suzanne L.
2003 Social Boundaries, Immigration, and Ritual Systems: A Case Study from the American Southwest. Unpublished Ph.D. dissertation, Arizona State University, Tempe.

Espinosa, Gilberto (translator)
1933 *History of New Mexico by Gaspar Perez de Villagrá*. Quivira Society IV, Los Angeles.

Fenn, Forrest
2004 *The Secrets of San Lazaro Pueblo*. One Horse Land and Cattle Company, Santa Fe, New Mexico.

Fewkes, Jesse Walter
1973 *Designs on Prehistoric Hopi Pottery*. Dover Publications, New York.

Franklin, Hayward H.
1996 Valencia Pueblo Ceramics. With a Petrographic Analysis by Betty Garrett. Unpublished manuscript, Office of Contract Archaeology, University of New Mexico, Albuquerque. Manuscript on file, No. P.2785, Laboratory of Anthropology, Santa Fe, New Mexico.

Hammond, George P., and Agapito Rey
1927 The Gallegos Relation of the Rodriguez Expedition to New Mexico (1581–1582). *New Mexico Historical Review* 2:239–268.
1966 *The Rediscovery of New Mexico, 1580–1594*. Coronado Historical Series No. 3. University of New Mexico Press, Albuquerque.

Hays, Kelley Ann
1994 Kachina Depictions on Prehistoric Pueblo Pottery. In *Kachinas in the Pueblo World*, edited by P. Schaafsma, pp. 47–62. University of New Mexico Press, Albuquerque.

Hibben, Frank C.
1960 Prehispanic Paintings at Pottery Mound. *Archaeology* 13(4):267–74.
1966 A Possible Pyramidal Structure and Other Mexican Influences at Pottery Mound, New Mexico. *American Antiquity* 31(4):522–29.
1975 *Kiva Art of the Anasazi*. KC Publications, Las Vegas, Nevada.
1987 Report on the Salvage Operations at the Site of Pottery Mound, New Mexico during the Excavating Seasons of 1977–1986. Manuscript on file, No. P2662, Library of the Laboratory of Anthropology, Museum of New Mexico, Santa Fe. (Date approximate, some copies have minor revisions.)

Hyer, S.

1976 Wall Paintings from a Kiva in Tijeras Canyon, New Mexico. Manuscript in possession of the author.

Judd, Neil M.

1959 *Pueblo del Arroyo, Chaco Canyon, New Mexico.* Smithsonian Miscellaneous Collection 138(I). Smithsonian Institution, Washington, D.C.

LeBlanc, Steven A.

1999 *Prehistoric Warfare in the American Southwest.* University of Utah Press, Salt Lake City.

McCreery, Patricia, and Ekkehart Malotki

1994 *Tapamveni: The Rock Art Galleries of Petrified Forest and Beyond.* Petrified Forest Museum Association, Petrified Forest, Arizona.

McNew, Judie, and Larry L. Loendorf

1997 Pups, Suckers and Cats: Fish on the Rocks in Doña Ana County, New Mexico. In *American Indian Rock Art* 23, edited by Steven M. Freers, pp. 95–101. American Rock Art Research Association, Tucson, Arizona.

Marshall, Michael P.

1987 *Qualacu.* U.S. Fish and Wildlife Service and Office of Contract Archaeology, University of New Mexico, Albuquerque.

Marshall, Michael P., and Henry J. Walt

1984 *Rio Abajo: Prehistory and History of a Rio Grande Province.* Historic Preservation Division, New Mexico Historic Preservation Program, Santa Fe.

Mindeleff, Victor

1891 *A Study of Pueblo Architecture, Tusayan and Cibola.* Bureau of American Ethnology Eighth Annual Report, 1886–1887. Smithsonian Institution, Washington, D.C.

Parsons, Elsie Clews

1932 *Isleta, New Mexico.* Bureau of American Ethnology Forty-Seventh Annual Report, 1929–1930, pp. 193–466. U.S. Government Printing Office, Washington, D.C.

Peckham, Barbara

1981 Pueblo IV Murals at Mound 7. In *Contributions to Gran Quivira Archaeology,* edited by Alden C. Hayes, pp. 15–38. Publications in Archaeology No. 17. National Park Service, Washington, D.C.

Renaud, E. B.

1938 *Petroglyphs of North-Central New Mexico.* Archaeological Survey Series, 11th Report. University of Denver, Denver, Colorado.

Saville, Dara

2003 Rock Art, Kachinas, and the Rock Art at Cerro Indio. In *Climbing the Rocks: Papers in Honor of Helen and Jay Crotty,* edited by Regge N. Wiseman, Thomas C. O'Laughlin, and Cordelia T. Snow, pp. 177–88. Papers of the Archaeological Society of New Mexico No. 29. Archaeological Society of New Mexico, Albuquerque.

Schaafsma, Curtis F.

1994 Pueblo Ceremonialism from the Perspective of Spanish Documents. In *Kachinas in the Pueblo World,* edited by Polly Schaafsma, pp. 121–38. University of New Mexico Press, Albuquerque.

Schaafsma, Polly

1965 Kiva Murals from Pueblo del Encierro (LA 70). *El Palacio* 72(3):7–16.

1968 The Los Lunas Petroglyphs. *El Palacio* 75(2):13–24.

1975 *Rock Art in the Cochiti Reservoir District.* Papers in Anthropology 16. Museum of New Mexico Press, Santa Fe.

1980 *Indian Rock Art of the Southwest.* School of American Research, Santa Fe and the University of New Mexico Press, Albuquerque.

1990 The Pine Tree Site: A Galisteo Basin Pueblo IV Shrine. In *Clues to the Past: Papers in Honor of William M. Sundt,* edited by Meliha Duran and David T. Kirkpatrick, pp. 239–58. Papers of the Archaeological Society of New Mexico No. 16. Archaeological Society of New Mexico, Albuquerque.

1992a *Rock Art in New Mexico.* 2nd edition. Museum of New Mexico Press, Santa Fe.

1992b Imagery and Magic: Petroglyphs at Comanche Gap, Galisteo Basin, New Mexico. In *Archaeology, Art, and Anthropology: Papers in Honor of J. J. Brody,* edited by Meliha S. Duran and David T. Kirkpatrick, pp. 157–74. Papers of the Archaeological Society of New Mexico No. 18. Archaeological Society of New Mexico, Albuquerque.

1994   The Prehistoric Kachina Cult and Its Origins as Suggested by Southwestern Rock Art. In *Kachinas in the Pueblo World*, edited by P. Schaafsma, pp. 63–80. University of New Mexico Press, Albuquerque.

1997   *Rock Art Sites in Chihuahua, Mexico.* Archaeology Notes 171. Office of Archaeological Studies, Museum of New Mexico, Santa Fe.

1998   The Paquimé Rock Art Style, Chihuahua, Mexico. In *Rock Art of the Chihuahuan Desert Borderlands*, edited by Sheron Smith-Savage and Robert J. Mallouf, pp. 33–44. Center for Big Bend Studies, Occasional Papers No. 3. Sul Ross State University and Texas Parks and Wildlife Department, Alpine, Texas.

1999   Tlalocs, Kachinas, and Sacred Bundles and Related Symbolism in the Southwest. In *The Casas Grandes World*, edited by Curtis F. Schaafsma and Carroll L. Riley, pp. 164–92. University of Utah Press, Salt Lake City.

2000   *Warrior, Shield, and Star.* Western Edge Press, Santa Fe, New Mexico.

2001   Quetzalcoatl and the Horned and Feathered Serpent of the Southwest. In *The Road to Aztlan: Art from a Mythic Homeland*, edited by V. M. Fields and V. Zamudio-Taylor, pp. 138–49. Los Angeles County Museum of Art, Los Angeles.

2003   Landscape and Painted Walls: Images in Place. Manuscript submitted to the Mural Project, Museum of Northern Arizona, Flagstaff.

Schaafsma, Polly, and Curtis F. Schaafsma

1974   Evidence for the Origins of the Pueblo Kachina Cult as Suggested by Southwestern Rock Art. *American Antiquity* 39:535–45.

Schaafsma, Polly, and Karl A. Taube

2006   Bringing the Rain: An Ideology of Rain Making in the Pueblo Southwest and Mesoamerica. In *A Pre-Columbian World: Searching for a Unitary Vision of Ancient America*, edited by Jeffrey Quilter and Mary E. Miller, pp. 231–86. Dumbarton Oaks Research Library and Collection, Washington, D.C.

Schaafsma, Polly, and Regge N. Wiseman

1992   Serpents in the Prehistoric Pecos Valley of Southeast New Mexico. In *Archaeology, Art, and Anthropology: Papers in Honor of J. J. Brody*, edited by Meliha D. Duran and David T. Kirkpatrick, pp. 175–84. Papers of the Archaeological Society of New Mexico No. 18. Archaeological Society of New Mexico, Albuquerque.

Schaafsma, Polly, and M. Jane Young

2007   Rock Art of the Zuni Region: Its Cultural-Historical Implications. In *Zuni Origins: Anthropological Approaches on Multiple Americanist and Southwestern Scales*, edited by David A. Gregory and David R. Wilcox. University of Arizona Press, Tucson, in press.

Scott, Eric

1997   Mogollon Rock Art at Bigelow Crossing: An Inter-Regional Comparison. *American Indian Rock Art* 23, edited by Steven M. Freers, pp. 121–26. American Rock Art Research Association, Tucson, Arizona.

Sims, Agnes C.

1948   An Artist Analyzes New Mexico's Petroglyphs. *El Palacio* 55:302–9.

1949   Migration Story in Stone. *El Palacio* 56(67–76).

1950   *San Cristóbal Petroglyphs.* Southwestern Editions, Santa Fe, New Mexico.

1963   Rock Carvings: A Record of Folk History. In *Sun Father's Way*, by Bertha P. Dutton, pp. 214–20. University of New Mexico Press, Albuquerque.

Slifer, Dennis

1998   *Signs of Life: Rock Art of the Upper Rio Grande.* Ancient City Press, Santa Fe, New Mexico.

Smith, Watson

1952   *Kiva Mural Decorations at Awatovi and Kawaika-a.* Papers of the Peabody Museum of American Archaeology and Ethnology Vol. 37. Harvard University, Cambridge, Massachusetts.

1971   *Painted Ceramics in the Western Mound at Awatovi.* Reports of the Awatovi Expedition 8. Papers of the Peabody Museum of American Archaeology and Ethnology Vol. 38. Harvard University, Cambridge, Massachusetts.

Spielmann, Katherine A.

1998a Ritual Influences on the Development of Rio Grande Glaze A Ceramics. In *Migration and Reorganization: The Pueblo IV Period in the American Southwest*, edited by K. A. Spielmann, pp. 253–61. Arizona State University Anthropological Research Papers No. 51. Arizona State University, Tempe.

1998b The Pueblo IV Period: History of Research. In *Migration and Reorganization: The Pueblo IV Period in the American Southwest*, edited by K. A. Spielmann, pp. 1–29. Arizona State University Anthropological Research Papers No. 51. Arizona State University, Tempe.

Stephen, Alexander M.

1936 *The Hopi Journal of Alexander M. Stephen*, edited by Elsie Clews Parsons. 2 vols. Contributions to Anthropology 23. Columbia University, New York.

Stephenson, Christine, Suzanne DeRosa, Cathy Evans, and Charles A. Hoffman

1997 Bigelow Crossing: A Survey of Rock Art. Manuscript on file, Library of the Laboratory of Anthropology, Santa Fe, New Mexico.

Stevenson, Matilda Coxe

1904 *The Zuni Indians*. Bureau of American Ethnology Twenty-Third Annual Report, 1901–1902. Smithsonian Institution, Washington, D.C.

Stewart, Joe D., Paul Matousek, and Jane H. Kelley

1990 Rock Art and Ceramic Art in the Jornada Mogollon Region. *Kiva* 55(4):301–19.

Tichy, Marjorie F.

1938 The Kivas of Pa-ako and Kuaua. *New Mexico Anthropologist* 2(4–5):71–80.

1947 A Painted Ceremonial Room at Otowi. *El Palacio* 54(3):59–69.

Titiev, Mischa

1944 *Old Oraibi: A Study of the Hopi Indians of Third Mesa*. University of New Mexico Press, Albuquerque.

Van Pool, Christine S.

2003 The Shaman-Priests of the Casas Grandes Region. *American Antiquity* 68(4):696–717.

Voll, Charles

1961 The Glaze Paint Ceramics of Pottery Mound. Unpublished Master's thesis, University of New Mexico, Albuquerque.

Whiteley, Peter

2002 Re-imagining Awatovi. In *Archaeologies of the Pueblo Revolt: Identity, Meaning, and Renewal in the Pueblo World*, edited by Robert W. Preucel, pp. 147–66. University of New Mexico, Albuquerque.

Young, M. Jane

1988 *Signs from the Ancestors: Zuni Cultural Symbolism and Perceptions of Rock Art*. University of New Mexico Press, Albuquerque.

1992 Morning Star, Evening Star: Zuni Traditional Stories. In *Earth and Sky: Visions of the Cosmos in Native American Folklore*, edited by Ray A. Williamson and Claire R. Farrer, pp. 75–109. University of New Mexico Press, Albuquerque.

CHAPTER NINE

Ritual Costuming at Pottery Mound
The Pottery Mound Textiles in Regional Perspective

Laurie D. Webster

Introduction

Few archaeological textiles have been recovered from late precontact sites in the Rio Grande valley, and those that have lack evidence of decoration. Fortunately, the Pueblo IV murals from Pottery Mound, Kuaua, Awat'ovi, and Kawaika'a, with their rich depictions of ritual dress, offer a rare glimpse into the ritual costuming of past Pueblo societies. In this chapter, I briefly explore the archaeological and historical roots of these ritual clothing traditions and examine variability in Pueblo IV costuming on a regional scale.

The murals provide information about not only specific articles of clothing, but complete costume assemblages. They reveal how particular styles of garments were worn and how they were used relative to each other. One only has to attend a contemporary Pueblo dance at Hopi, Zuni, or one of the Rio Grande pueblos to appreciate the importance of textiles in the scheme of the performance. Much of the iconography displayed at the ceremony is expressed through ritual dress. The choice of garment, and the prescribed manner in which each piece is worn, is dependent on the type of ceremony and the participant's role in the ritual. Although ritual clothing styles and designs have become less diverse during the past 150 years, regional differences in clothing conventions still

FIGURE 9.1
Buffalo Dancers by Crescencio Martinez, San Ildefonso Pueblo, 1918, showing men's and women's dance regalia worn in the Buffalo Dance. (Courtesy of the School of American Research, catalog no. IAF.P19 [detail]. Photograph by Lynn Lown.)

persist. The mural paintings suggest that such differences were even more pronounced in the prehispanic past.

Given that some readers may be unfamiliar with Pueblo textiles, I begin with a brief review of the most common components of historic Pueblo ritual dress (Figure 9.1). The major components of Pueblo male ceremonial attire are the kilt—a rectangular piece of fabric that encircles the hips—and one or more sashes, used to secure the kilt in place. Sometimes the kilt is replaced by a breechcloth that passes between the legs, and sometimes a shirt or tunic is worn. Men often wear leggings with ties or garters. Female ceremonial attire typically includes a blanket worn wrapped around the body, commonly referred to as a manta dress, and a sash to hold the dress in place. Sometimes a second blanket or manta is worn over the shoulders. Men wear elements of the female costume when impersonating female beings, and women wear elements of the male costume for certain ceremonies (for example, a kilt over the shoulders). For a more detailed discussion of historic Pueblo ritual dress, see Kent (1983a), Fox (1978), and Roediger (1941).

The Archaeological and Historical Roots of Pueblo IV Ritual Clothing

Just as the U.S. Southwest represents the northern extent of a Middle and South American loom-weaving tradition (Kent 1983b; King 1979:275; Teague 1998), and as Pueblo IV kiva murals are related in some way to Mesoamerican mural painting, so too, in my view, does Pueblo IV ritual costuming represent the northern fringe of a widespread Mesoamerican ritual clothing tradition. Evidence of this influence is apparent in Hohokam and Mimbres societies by A.D. 1000 and in Ancestral Pueblo ("Anasazi") societies of the southern Colorado Plateau slightly later. As I will discuss, the Pueblo IV costume repertoire reflects a broad emulation of Mesoamerican garment styles and incorporates many of the same or similar symbolic elements. Pueblo ritual garments vary considerably from their Mesoamerican counterparts, however, in terms of their symmetry relationships and designs (Teague 1998:151). Unfortunately, except for some costume depictions on Ramos Polychrome ceramics (King 1974), little is known about late precontact ritual styles of dress in southern

a.

b.

c.

d.

FIGURE 9.2

Kilts worn by male deities or deity impersonators in the Mesoamerican codices, with Awat'ovi figure shown for comparison: **a**) Aztec figure of the rain god Tlaloc, *Codex Magliabechiano*; **b**) Borgia Group figure of Tlaloc, *Codex Laud*; **c**) Mixtec figure of Tlaloc, *Codex Vindobonensis*; **d**) Awat'ovi figure wearing kilt, Room 788. (**a**, **b**, **c** from Anawalt [1981:Examples 2o, 11u, 8n, respectively], courtesy of the University of Oklahoma Press; **d** from Smith [1952: Plate I], courtesy of the Peabody Museum of Archaeology and Ethnology, Harvard University.)

Arizona and New Mexico or the U.S.-Mexico borderlands. Before ritual clothing relationships between Mexico and the U.S. Southwest are fully understood, more research is needed on ritual costume depictions on ceramics and other media from Durango, Zacatecas, and other parts of northern Mexico, where few actual textiles have survived. In the meantime, our best information about precontact and early postcontact Mesoamerican ritual clothing comes from Anawalt's (1981) comprehensive study of costume depictions in the Aztec, Tlaxcalan, Tarascan, Mixtec, Borgia Group (unknown provenience), and Lowland Mayan codices, the source I have used for this brief comparison of Mesoamerican-southwestern ritual dress.

Kilts

THE MESOAMERICAN CODICES

Anawalt (1981:182) identifies the kilt as one of five draped garment styles featured in the Mesoamerican codices and notes that "since male kilts usually appear on deities or their impersonators, it must have been a special-purpose garment limited to ceremonial contexts" (see also 1981:33, 106, 156–58, 182, 209–11, Charts 1 and 2, Examples 2o, 8n–p, 11q–u, Charts 2o and 8n; Figure 9.2). In several depictions discussed by Anawalt (nine from the Borgia Group, one from a Mixtec codex, and one from an Aztec codex), kilts are worn by the rain god Tlaloc or his impersonator (see Figure 9.2a–c). In the Mixtec codices, kilts are also associated with priests and with humans and deity figures playing the ritual ballgame. In the Borgia Group and Lowland Maya codices, they are also associated with the death god.

Female kiltlike garments or skirts, *cueitl* in Nahuatl (Anawalt 1981:33), are often worn by female deities and their impersonators. Those associated with female figures in the Aztec and Tlaxcalan codices from central Mexico (e.g., Anawalt 1981:Figure 12, Examples 2p, 5m; Figure 9.3a, b) are more highly decorated than any of the kilts

a.　　　　　　　　　　　　　　　　b.

c.

FIGURE 9.3

Decorated wraparound skirts (*cueitl*) worn by female deities and deity impersonators in the Mesoamerican codices, with Pottery Mound figure shown for comparison: **a**) Aztec priest wearing flayed skin of human impersonator of a fertility goddess, *Codex Borbonicus*; **b**) Tlaxcalan earth-mother goddess Ixnextli, *Tonalamatl Aubin*; **c**) Pottery Mound figure wearing possible resist-dyed skirt or kilt, Kiva 1. (**a**, **b** from Anawalt [1981:Examples 2p and 5m, respectively], courtesy of the University of Oklahoma Press; **c** from Hibben [1975:Figure 92], courtesy of KC Publications.)

worn by males from all regions. In terms of their allover patterning and diverse decorative styles, including bordered designs and those suggestive of negative painting or resist-dye techniques, they more closely resemble the Pueblo IV kilt styles in the northern Southwest (e.g., Figure 9.3c) than do any of the male Mesoamerican kilts.

ARCHAEOLOGICAL EVIDENCE IN THE
U.S. SOUTHWEST AND U.S.-MEXICO BORDERLANDS

Archaeological evidence of the kilt does not appear in the Southwest until the mid- to late A.D. 1200s. Although no kilts were identified in the poorly preserved Paquimé textile assemblage (King 1974), they are worn by human figures on Ramos Polychrome jars, including a front-facing human with feathered elbows (Townsend 2005: Plate 55a) and two flying human figures (Figure 9.4a).

Kilts or skirts are also depicted on male and female figures on Ramos Polychrome effigy vessels (King 1974:84–85, Figures 79-8.1, 80-8).

The only definite archaeological examples of prehispanic kilts from the U.S. Southwest come from Sinagua and Salado sites dated between A.D. 1200 and 1450, and they exhibit considerable variability (Kent 1983b:237). All are made of cotton. The one from Hidden House is decorated with tapestry insets (Figure 9.4b), the one from Camp Verde has an openwork design worked in gauze weave, and the one from Tonto Ruins is undecorated. The general absence of the kilt style from Pueblo III sites on the Colorado Plateau led Kent (1983b:237) to interpret the kilt as a non-Pueblo southern style that reached the northern Southwest sometime around A.D. 1300. Its widespread depiction in the Pottery Mound, Awat'ovi, and

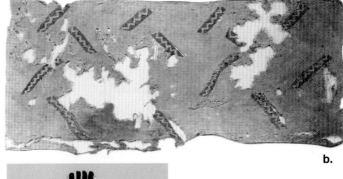

FIGURE 9.4

Archaeological evidence of kilts in the U.S. Southwest and northern Mexico:
a) Ramos Polychrome jar with human flying figure wearing kilt, northern Chihuahua, ca. A.D. 1200–1450; **b**) kilt from Hidden House, central Arizona, ca. A.D. 1200–1275; **c** and **d**) Pottery Mound depictions of male dancers wearing kilts, Kiva 8 and Kiva 1, respectively, ca. A.D. 1400–1500. Kilt on left may depict a resist-dye technique, kilt on right a tapestry-weave design. (**a** photograph by Virginia Shields, courtesy of the National Museum of Natural History, Smithsonian Institution, catalog no. A-323868; **b** courtesy of the Arizona State Museum, University of Arizona, catalog no. ASM 20493; **c** and **d** from Hibben [1975:Figures 75 and 72, respectively], courtesy of KC Publications.)

Kawaika'a murals establishes this garment as an integral component of Pueblo male ceremonial dress by the A.D. 1400s (e.g., Figure 9.4c, d).

Sashes and Breechcloths

THE MESOAMERICAN CODICES

The basic item of clothing worn by all Mesoamerican males was the loincloth, or maxtlatl. This long, narrow piece of fabric was wrapped around the hips, passed between the legs, and tied at the waist. The ends of the garment were worn in one of two ways, either tied in a knot at the front of the body or allowed to hang with one panel in front, the other in back. In the latter style, the sashlike ends of the garment were often decorated. Gods and god impersonators in the codices consistently wear the latter style, suggesting it as the older and more prestigious of the two (Anawalt 1981:21–24). All of the kilt-wearing figures from the Borgia Group illustrated by Anawalt (1981:Example 11q–u) wear long pendant loincloths with one end hanging in back, the other to one side (see Figure 9.2b). The figures are shown in profile and depict either a weapon-wielding Tlaloc or the death god Mictlantecutli. The Mixtec codices also depict figures in profile wearing kilts with long pendant loincloths (Anawalt 1981:Examples 8n–p; see Figure 9.2c). Their stances and the way in which the kilts and sashlike loincloths are worn are highly reminiscent of some of the figures in the Pueblo IV kiva murals, especially the warrior or hunter images (see Figure 9.2d; see also Figures 9.5e, 9.10d).

ARCHAEOLOGICAL EVIDENCE IN THE U.S. SOUTHWEST

Both the Pueblo sash and breechcloth appear to share a historical stylistic relationship with the Mesoamerican maxtlatl. The earliest sashes in the prehispanic Southwest are 2/2 (over two, under two) braided sashes from late Basketmaker II and early Basketmaker III sites (e.g., Kent 1983b:60–62). Significantly, the braiding technique itself spread into the Southwest from Mexico. Several braided sashes from Basketmaker sites and an early Mogollon site are woven of dog or other mammal-hair yarn (Hough 1914:72; Kent 1983b:Figure 25). The use of this fiber is rare in Basketmaker and Mogollon textiles and suggests that these animal-hair sashes played a special, if not ritual, role in these early agricultural societies. Perhaps their long pendant fringes conveyed a similar meaning as those on modern Hopi ceremonial sashes, which are said to symbolize falling rain (Kent 1983a:82).

The 2/2 weave structure predominated until Pueblo IV, when 3/3 (over three, under three) braided sashes, probably made by a frame-braiding technique, appeared in the Upper Little Colorado and Hopi areas (Kent 1957:602). Fragments of 3/3 braided sashes were recovered from both the Awat'ovi and Hawikuh assemblages (Webster 1997; 2000:Table 10.2). Braided sashes appear to be the most common sash style depicted in the Pueblo IV murals.

The other major style of sash known archaeologically in the late prehistoric Southwest is the warp-faced belt. These belts are made by a loom-woven technique that also spread into the Southwest from Mexico. Warp-faced belts are present in southern and central Arizona by A.D. 1100 and the Hopi region sometime after A.D. 1300 (Teague 1998:184). Examples of warp-float patterned weaves are known from Tonto Ruins (Kent 1983b:Figure 111) and Awat'ovi (Webster 2000:Table 10.2) and appear to be depicted on effigy vessels from Paquimé (King 1974:88, Figure 85-8.1), as well as in the Pueblo IV murals.

Sashes with decorated ends are shown on male human figures in Mimbres pottery (Brody 2004:Figure 30, Plate 2). Although no archaeological examples have survived, woven breechcloths with decorated front panels are known from Pueblo III sites on the Colorado Plateau (Kent 1983b:243). A decorated breechcloth is also depicted on an early historic Tabira Black-on-white canteen (Brody 2004:Figure 45). Breechcloths and decorated sashes are represented in the Pueblo IV murals, and their postcontact descendents—embroidered breechcloths and Hopi

brocaded sashes—are important components of historic Pueblo ceremonial clothing assemblages.

Shirts and Tunics

THE MESOAMERICAN CODICES

The Pueblo ceremonial shirt is another garment that seems to derive from a widespread Middle and South American template. Anawalt (1981:9) differentiates between Mesoamerican slip-on garments lacking underarm seams, open-sewn garments worn as sleeveless vests, and closed-sewn garments seamed along the sides below the armholes. The only slip-on garment identified by Anawalt in the pan-Mesoamerican costume repertoire is the quechquemitl, a woman's garment. The open-sewn sleeveless vest (xicolli) was a high-status male garment, worn by priests, gods, and god impersonators (Figure 9.5c). Virtually all Mesoamerican closed-sewn sleeved shirts and sleeveless tunics were identified by Anawalt (1981:211, Charts 4, 22) as quilted body armor (ichcahuipilli), based on their association with figures holding shields, lances, and other weapons (Figure 9.5a, b). The Nahuatl word "ichcahuipilli" translates as "cotton armor for war" (Anawalt 1981:39). Anawalt (1981:214) states that the only sleeved garments worn in all of Mesoamerica were those associated with special-purpose warrior costumes. The presence of this warrior costume style in the Aztec, Tlaxcala, Tarascan, Mixtec, and Lowland Mayan codices attests to its widespread nature.

ARCHAEOLOGICAL EVIDENCE IN THE U.S. SOUTHWEST

Archaeological examples of cotton shirts or tunics appear in the Southwest as two main styles: shirts worked in openwork weaves and plain-weave shirts decorated with painted or resist-dye techniques (Kent 1983b:230–32, Figure 137; Figure 9.6a–c). Based on the discovery of openwork fragments at Hohokam and Mimbres sites and depictions of openwork shirts on Classic Mimbres pottery (Kent 1983b:153; Teague 1998:Figure 3.23; Figure 9.6c), openwork shirts appear to be the earlier style, occurring as early as A.D. 1000 in southern Arizona and New Mexico. Post–A.D. 1200 examples of openwork shirts include a white sleeveless interlinked shirt from the vicinity of Tonto Cliff Dwellings (the famous "Tonto shirt"; Figure 9.6a) and a white braided shirt with sleeves from White House in Canyon de Chelly (Kent 1983b:Figures 30, 34, 137i, j).

After A.D. 1250, plain-weave shirts with painted or resist-dye designs are found in the Kayenta area. Examples

  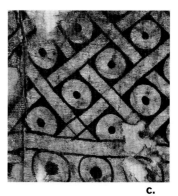

a. b. c.

d. e.

FIGURE 9.5
Closed-sewn quilted body armor (*ichcahuipilli*) worn by Aztec warriors in the Mesoamerican codices, with Kuaua and Awat'ovi figures shown for comparison, and detail of an Aztec vest (*ixcolli*): **a**) Aztec warrior, *Codex Azcatítlan*; **b**) Aztec warrior, *Codex Vaticanus*; **c**) detail of an Aztec negative-painted vest (ixcolli) from the Templo de Mayor at Tenochtitlán (Mexico City); **d**) Kuaua "universal deity" figure wearing tunic and carrying bow and quiver, Kiva III; **e**) Awat'ovi warrior figure wearing tunic and carrying bow and quiver, Room 529. (**a** and **b** from Anawalt [1981:Figure 4e, f], courtesy of the University of Oklahoma Press; **c** adapted from Mastache [2005:20]; **d** from Dutton [1963:Cover], courtesy of the University of New Mexico Press; **e** from Smith [1952:Figure 53b], courtesy of the Peabody Museum of Archaeology and Ethnology, Harvard University.)

a.

b.

c.

d.

FIGURE 9.6

Archaeological examples of shirts in the Southwest: **a**) openwork shirt, vicinity of Tonto Ruins, Arizona, ca. A.D. 1300–1450; **b**) negative-painted or resist-dyed shirt, Poncho House, northeastern Arizona, ca. A.D. 1250; **c**) Mimbres figure wearing openwork shirt, A.D. 1000–1200; **d**) Pottery Mound figure wearing openwork shirt, Kiva 1, ca. A.D. 1400–1500; **e**) Kawaika'a figure wearing openwork shirt, Test 5, Room 2, ca. A.D. 1375–1500; **f**) Awat'ovi figure wearing negative-painted or resist-dyed shirt, Room 788, ca. A.D. 1500–1630. (**a** courtesy of the Arizona State Museum, University of Arizona, catalog no. ASM 13400; **b** from Guernsey [1931:Plate 63], courtesy of the Peabody Museum of Archaeology and Ethnology, Harvard University; **c** from Teague [1998:Figure 3.23], courtesy of the University of Arizona Press; **d** from Hibben [1975:Figure 60], courtesy of KC Publications; **e** and **f** from Smith [1952:Figures 66c and Plate F, respectively], courtesy of the Peabody Museum of Archaeology and Ethnology, Harvard University.)

e.

f.

include a sleeveless cotton shirt with a painted design from Painted Cave (Haury 1945; Kent 1983b:Figure 137*g*) and a negative-painted (or resist-dye) sleeved shirt from Poncho House (Guernsey 1931:52, 102–3, Plate 63; Kent 1983b:Figure 122; Figure 9.6*b*). Farther south, Pond (1966:557, Figures 1, 2) reported a long tunic with a "negative square and black dot" design from a fourteenth-century painted kiva at Homol'ovi II.

Negative painting and tie-dye involve two different processes. Negative-painted textiles are produced by covering one surface of a light colored fabric with pigment except in areas where the design is intended to show through. As in negative-painted pottery, it is the uncolored areas of the fabric that carry the design. Some of the textiles that Kent (1983b:195–98) described as negative painted may have been treated with some kind of resist material before the color was applied. The exact method of producing these textiles is still to be determined.

Tie-dye, on the other hand, is a resist-dye technique that entails binding a section of the fabric and then immersing the textile in dye. Typically, the technique produces a series of squares or diamonds, or occasionally circles, each with a small dot at the center. This dot-in-a-square motif (see, for example, Figures 9.7*b*, 9.8*d*, *e*) appears on ceramics and other media as well as textiles and seems to be part of a widespread Middle American iconography related to serpents, rain, fertility, and maize (Webster et al. 2006). The tie-dye technique itself has antecedents in Mexico and Peru.

No examples of tie-dye shirts have been identified in the U.S. Southwest, but tie-dyed cotton fabrics are known from 11 southwestern sites, all but two in the Kayenta and Sinagua regions (Kent 1983b:192–95; Webster et al. 2006: Table 1). Except for a complete tie-dyed blanket discussed in a following section, all are small fragments, and some might be the remains of shirts. Farther south, shirts or ponchos decorated in what appears to be tie-dye or another resist-dye technique are worn by human figures on some Ramos Polychrome effigy vessels (King 1974: Figure 83-8; Moulard 1984:Plate 81).

A few textile fragments from the Kayenta area have their dot-in-a-square motifs produced by negative painting, rather than tie-dye (Kent 1983b:Figure 133*b*). These "imitation tie-dye" fabrics are easily distinguished from tie-dye because in the former technique, the color is applied to just one surface, whereas in tie-dye the color completely penetrates the cloth. A resist-dye technique such as batik might also have been used to produce the dot-in-a-square motifs or the solid lines, circles, and bars that appear on textiles in the kiva murals, but no archaeological examples of this technique have been identified.

The most significant archaeological shirt from the perspective of the Pueblo IV kiva murals is the one from Poncho House (Figure 9.6*b*). Made from four pieces of plain-weave cloth, the shirt lacks underarm seams and is constructed in the same manner as historic Pueblo shirts. Its brown negative-patterned design bears a striking resemblance to several of the shirts, tunics, and kilts depicted in the Pueblo IV murals (e.g., Hibben 1975: Figures 30, 74; Smith 1952:Plate F, Figure 50*c*; see, for example, Figures 9.6*f*, 9.7*a*, *c*, 9.8*f*). The white circles depicted on the shirt are also a prominent motif in the murals (see, for example, Figures 9.4*c*, 9.7*c*, 9.8*a*, 9.14*d*).

The strong relationship seen between shirts/tunics and warfare in the Mesoamerican codices is echoed in the Pueblo IV murals, where shirt- or tunic-clad figures are frequently associated with bows, arrows, quivers, and other images of hunting and warfare (e.g., Dutton 1963: Figure 54; Hibben 1975:Cover image; Smith 1952:Plate A, Figures 53*b*, 61*b*; see Figure 9.5*d*, *e*). The Pueblo III individual from Poncho House with whom the aforementioned painted or resist-dyed shirt was found was likewise accompanied by a full-sized bow and arrows (Guernsey 1931:52, 102–3, Plate 63). Of the Mesoamerican examples illustrated by Anawalt, it is the Aztec shirts, with their overall patterning, that bear the closest resemblance to the decorated shirts in the Pueblo IV kiva murals, a correlation noted also between the skirts of central Mexico and the Pueblo IV kilts. Of particular interest are Anawalt's Aztec Example 4f (see Figure 9.5*b*), which appears to be decorated in a resist-dye technique (compare with Figure 9.6*f*), and a sleeveless vest (xicolli) recovered from the Templo Mayor at Tenochtitlán, decorated in negative painting (Mastache 2005:20; see Figure 9.5*c*).

In postcontact Pueblo societies, shirts are usually associated with males. Wright (1979:34), however, describes the use of a sleeveless tunic by the chief priestess of the Mamzrauti Society, and a sleeved shirt is also worn by what appears to be a female figure at Pottery Mound (Hibben 1975:Figure 60; Figure 9.6*d*).

Blankets and Manta Dresses
THE MESOAMERICAN CODICES

The shoulder blanket, or tilmatli, was the most important visual symbol of male dress in central Mexico, one that provided immediate recognition of an individual's class,

a.
b.
c.

d.
e.

FIGURE 9.7

Conventions shared by the Pottery Mound and Antelope Mesa murals: **a–b** show garments patterned in negative-painted or resist-dye techniques, **a**) Pottery Mound, Kiva 7, ca. A.D. 1400–1500, **b**) Awat'ovi, Room 529, ca. A.D. 1400–1550; **c–d** show female figures in the frontal position with wraparound garment tassels on the wearer's right (viewer's left), sashes tied on the wearer's left (viewer's right), **c**) Pottery Mound, Kiva 8, ca. A.D. 1400–1500, **d**) Awat'ovi, Room 788, ca. A.D. 1500–1630; **e–f** show blankets depicted on walls, **e**) Pottery Mound, Kiva 10, ca. A.D. 1400–1500, **f**) Kawaika'a, Test 5, Room 2, ca. A.D. 1375–1500. (**a**, **c**, **e** from Hibben [1975: Figures 30, 74, and 95], courtesy of KC Publications; **b**, **d**, **f** from Smith [1952:Figure 51c, Plate I, and Figure 74c, respectively], courtesy of the Peabody Museum of Archaeology and Ethnology, Harvard University.)

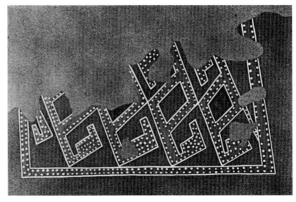

f.

rank, and status (Anawalt 1981:27–33). During the Aztec reign, the only persons permitted to wear decorated cotton blankets were nobles and leaders of high rank or warriors who earned the right to wear them through military deeds. All others wore yucca blankets. The most highly decorated examples illustrated by Anawalt (1981:Cover, Example 2k; 1990) appear to be decorated in resist-dye designs, but other decorative techniques, such as positive and negative painting, were also used (Anawalt 2000:218).

Although most of these tie-dyed capes or mantles are long in length, short capes are also depicted in the codices. The small shoulder blankets depicted in the Pueblo IV kiva murals (see Figure 9.2d) show their closest resemblance to Anawalt's (1981:103, 154) Borgia Group and Mixtec examples. In all of these cases, the capes are short and cover either just the chest or the back and shoulders. In the Mesoamerican codices, they are worn by male deities but only occasionally in conjunction with the kilt and sashlike loincloth (Anawalt 1981:Example 20; see Figure 9.2a). Most Aztec examples of short capes appear to reflect a secular use.

ARCHAEOLOGICAL EVIDENCE IN THE U.S. SOUTHWEST

The remains of large white plain-weave cotton blankets have been found at most Ancestral Pueblo, Salado, Sinagua, and Hohokam sites where textiles were preserved. Decorated blankets, however, are far less common. Ancestral Pueblo weavers on the southern Colorado Plateau produced most of their intricate designs by weaving striped patterns in simple twills (Kent 1983b:156, Plate 14) or by coloring plain-weave fabrics with tie-dye or negative painting (Kent 1983b:192–98). One exceptional blanket from Grand Gulch is exquisitely worked in diamond-twill tapestry (Kent 1983b:Plate 10). In central and southern Arizona, weavers tended to execute their designs in more complex weaves, such as weft-wrap openwork, gauze, and supplementary weft (Kent 1983b; Teague 1998).

One complete tie-dyed blanket is known from a site in Lake Canyon, Utah, north of the San Juan River (Kent 1983b:Figures 120, 121). Unlike the dynamic, asymmetrical arrangements of negative-patterned elements found on the Pottery Mound, Antelope Mesa, and Kuaua textiles, the dot-in-a-square motifs on the Lake Canyon blanket are evenly distributed into five symmetrical rows. Fragments of tie-dye from Kayenta sites south of the San Juan River, however, suggest an asymmetrical arrangement of motifs (Kent 1983b:Figures 122, 133a, Plate 16). It is these fabrics that appear to be antecedent to the tie-dye-like garments and blankets depicted in the Pottery Mound, Awat'ovi, and Kawaika'a murals.

Examples of negatively painted cotton blankets with geometric designs are known from Painted Cave (see Figure 9.14a) and White House in the Kayenta area, Hidden House in the Verde Valley, and a few other sites (Kent 1983b:192–98). Another painted cotton textile from the Pinaleño Mountains in southern Arizona might have been made by Kayenta migrants.[1] Based on the present distribution, northeastern Arizona appears to have been a center for this technique. Given the fact, however, that few decorated fabrics have survived at Pueblo III sites in the San Juan Basin and none at all at Pueblo IV sites in the Rio Grande, it is impossible to know the actual distribution of these painted blankets prior to their appearance in the Pueblo IV murals.

All large painted blankets in the Southwest with reconstructed designs have their solid and decorated bands arranged in an offset-quartered layout (e.g., Kent 1983b:Figures 123, 132, Plate 17; see Figure 9.14a). Haury (1945:29) attributed the roots of this design scheme to the quartered layouts on Hohokam Red-on-buff pottery. The design bands of the black-and-white Hidden House blanket are perpendicular to the edges of the cloth, whereas the more colorful examples from White House and Painted Cave have their design panels oblique to the warp and weft (Kent 1983b:Plate 17, Figure 124; see Figure 9.14a). This latter orientation is the same way in which the offset-quartered designs are depicted in the Pottery Mound murals (Hibben 1975:Figures 94, 96; see Figure 9.14b). Fragmentary depictions of other painted blankets show the motifs obliquely arranged (Hibben 1975:Figure 95; Smith 1952:Figures 44c, 45a, c; Figure 9.7e, f). Other murals may depict painted blankets with abstract Sikyatki designs (Brody 1964:123–125; Smith 1952:Figures 44b, 48b, 49a), but no archaeological examples of fabrics with these designs are known.

Summary

Most styles of ritual clothing depicted in the Pueblo IV murals appear to have antecedents in Mesoamerican ritual costume traditions. Given the fact that these clothing styles were widespread throughout Mexico and Central America, it is not surprising that they would also extend into the U.S. Southwest, alongside a Middle American–derived loom tradition based on the production of fabrics with four complete selvages and an untailored clothing tradition based on the draping and tying of cloth around the human body.

The different styles of kilts, sashes, breechcloths, shirts, tunics, wraparound dresses, and shoulder blankets depicted in the Pueblo IV murals may have entered the U.S. Southwest as components of integrated costume repertoires, perhaps related to particular ceremonies, deities, or symbolic complexes. Certain styles of sashes and aprons might have had a ceremonial usage as early as Basketmaker times. Cotton shirts with openwork designs were present in Classic Mimbres and Hohokam societies by about the eleventh century, and shirts with openwork and painted or dyed designs were in use in the Kayenta region by the thirteenth century. Ethnographic analogy suggests that such shirts were worn by religious leaders. Archaeological evidence of kilts and large blankets, some probably worn as wraparound dresses, dates to the thirteenth century in the Western Pueblo region. Similar garments also appear to be depicted on ceramics from Paquimé.

Not only do Pueblo ceremonial garments have antecedents in Mesoamerican clothing complexes, they also share many conventions of use. The wearing of particular garment styles by deities and deity impersonators and warrior figures among the Lowland Maya, Mixtec, Aztec, and other groups echoes their presumed use at Paquimé and in the Pueblo IV murals. Also echoed are the profile stances of figures and the ways of wearing and combining particular articles of clothing. This suggests that these styles were not adopted piecemeal, but as coherent clothing assemblages that continued to evolve over time.

Although most ritual garments in the U.S. Southwest have precedence in the south, none are rubber-stamp copies of Mesoamerican ritual costumes. Southwestern communities reinterpreted these ideas according to local tastes, beliefs, and artistic conventions. An analogy may be seen in the ways nineteenth-century Hispanic, Zuni, and Navajo weavers emulated and developed their own variations of Mexican Saltillo serapes, the high-status garment of the time. Although inspired by the same template, the Saltillo-like weavings of each group are technologically distinguishable and stylistically distinct.

Regional Variability in the Costume Depictions from Pottery Mound, Antelope Mesa, and Kuaua

The Study Database

The present analysis is based on a sample of 149 costumed figures and 274 articles of clothing depicted in the murals of Pottery Mound, Kuaua, Awat'ovi, and Kawaika'a. Data were derived from published illustrations in Hibben (1975), Smith (1952), and Dutton (1963). The current data set includes only the most complete clothing depictions and excludes the unpublished images from Pottery Mound. The database could be expanded considerably, perhaps 30 percent or more, with the addition of all incomplete costume depictions, undecorated articles of clothing, and unpublished images from these sites. Of the 149 costumed figures in the study sample, 56 are from Pottery Mound, 18 from Kawaika'a, 43 from Awat'ovi, and 32 from Kuaua. I collected the following information for each clothing depiction: garment type, background color, probable raw material, probable weave structure, suggested method of decoration, design structure, presence/absence of contrasting selvage, tassel/fringe placement, and tassel/fringe treatment. I also recorded whether the figure was displayed in a profile or frontal position, the way each garment was worn on the body, and the gender of the figure, when obvious. Gender was often an ambiguous attribute, perhaps intentionally so.

Data were divided into two temporal groups, pre- and post–A.D. 1500, based on dates assigned to the kivas and wall paintings by Crotty (1995) and Smith (1972). The pre–A.D. 1500 data set includes all of Pottery Mound and Kawaika'a and seven rooms from Awat'ovi (Test 14, Rooms 2, 3, and 4, Kivas C–D, Room 218, and the early east wall of Room 529). I also included three Sikyatki pots from Awat'ovi with costume depictions (Smith 1952: Figure 17m, n, p) in the early Awat'ovi sample. Some of the Kawaika'a and early Awat'ovi depictions may extend into the early A.D. 1500s. The post–A.D. 1500 data set includes Room 528, the rest of Room 529, and Room 788 from Awat'ovi, and all of the Kuaua depictions. There are 96 figures (56 from Pottery Mound, 18 Kawaika'a, 22 Awat'ovi) in the pre–A.D. 1500 data set and 52 figures (21 from Awat'ovi, 31 Kuaua) in the post–A.D. 1500 data set. Table 9.1 summarizes the temporal distribution of the costume database, and Tables 9.2 through 9.6 summarize the results of the analysis.

Because the subject of this book is Pottery Mound, I focus this chapter on the Pottery Mound assemblage and discuss the other assemblages in relation to it. Table 9.2 provides a summary of the Pottery Mound costume assemblage. Before discussing the different garment classes, terminology used in the discussion and tables should be explained. When I say that no tassels are depicted, I mean that both sides of a garment are visible and the garment

Table 9.1. Composition and Temporal Distribution of the 274 Articles of Clothing in the Pueblo IV Costume Database

| | Pre–A.D. 1500 | | | Post–A.D. 1500 | |
	Pottery Mound	Kawaika'a	Awat'ovi (Test 14, Rooms 2, 3, 4; Kivas C–D; Room 218, early component of Room 529)	Awat'ovi (Rooms 528, 788, late component of Room 529)	Kuaua
Kilts	43	7	10	11	31
Sashes	43	10	10	16	33
Shirts and tunics	9	2	4	4	6
Manta dresses and other wrapped blankets	10	8	6	11	0
Total	**105**	**27**	**30**	**42**	**70**

Table 9.2. Summary of the 105 Articles of Clothing with 56 Costumed Figures in the Pottery Mound Sample

	Number of items in sample	% of assemblage
Garment styles		
Kilts	43	41.0
Sashes	43	41.0
Shirts/tunics	9	8.6
Mantas tied over one shoulder	7	6.6
Garments wrapped around torso	2	1.9
Shoulder blankets	1	0.9
Background color used		
Black	35 kilts, 7 mantas, 1 shoulder blanket	41.0
White	34 sashes, 1 shirt	33.3
Other colors	5 sashes, 5 shirts, 4 kilts	13.3
Bicolored	4 sashes, 1 kilt, 2 shirts	6.7
Multicolored (three or more colors)	3 kilts, 1 shirt, 2 garments around torso?	5.7
Suggested raw material		
Cotton	43 sashes, 38 kilts, 7 mantas, 2 garments around torso, 4 shirts, 1 shoulder blanket	90.5
Cotton, hide, or body paint?	5 shirts	4.8
Hide or fur	3 kilts	2.8
Feathers	2 kilts	1.9
Suggested weave structures of the 95 possible cotton garments		
Plain weave	37 kilts, 1 sash, 7 mantas, 2 garments around torso, 1 shirt, 1 shoulder blanket	51.6
Oblique interlacing (braiding)	41 sashes	43.2
Twill-tapestry weave	1 kilt, 1 shirt	2.1
Weft-wrap openwork	1 shirt	1.1
Netting or interlinking	1 shirt	1.0
Weft-faced plain weave	1 sash	1.0

Table 9.2 continued on page 180

Table 9.2 continued from page 179

Table 9.2. Summary of the 105 Articles of Clothing with 56 Costumed Figures in the Pottery Mound Sample

	Number of items in sample	% of assemblage
Suggested decorative techniques		
Solid color	41 sashes, 15 kilts, 3 mantas, 3 shirts, 1 shoulder blanket	60.0
Negative painting or resist-dye	15 kilts, 1 manta, 1 sash	16.2
Painted	7 kilts, 2 shirts, 2 garments around torso?	10.4
Negative painting/resist- + tie-dye	2 kilts, 3 mantas	4.8
Stripes	1 kilt, 1 shirt, 1 sash	2.8
Tapestry	1 kilt, 1 shirt	1.9
Openwork	2 shirts	1.9
Feathered	1 kilt	1.0
Feathers + painted	1 kilt	1.0
Tassel placement		
No tassels depicted	23 kilts, 9 sashes, 8 shirts, 5 mantas, 2 garments around torso, 1 shoulder blanket	45.7
Frontal view, wearer's right	9 sashes, 3 kilts, 2 mantas, 1 shirt	14.3
Profile view, in back	12 sashes	11.4
Frontal view, wearer's left	8 sashes	7.6
Profile view, in front	3 sashes, 2 kilts	4.8
Frontal view, one on each side	2 kilts	1.9
Unknown—section of painting missing	13 kilts, 2 sashes	14.3

lacks evidence of tassels (see, for example, Figures 9.10f, 9.11c). This differs from situations in which one or both corners of the garment are missing and the presence or absence of tassels cannot be determined (see, for example, Figure 9.12a, c). When I identify tassels or fringe as occurring on the right or left side, I am referring to the wearer's right or the wearer's left, rather than the viewer's.

Several murals depict females or dual-gendered figures with garments wrapped around their upper torsos and under their arms. Only the upper bodies of these figures are depicted (see, for example, Figures 9.7d, 9.9b–d). This makes it impossible to know if the artist was intending to depict a short kilt or large blanket. In these cases, I have classified the garment simply as a *wraparound garment*.

I have already described the decorative techniques of negative painting and tie-dye. For the purposes of this study, if a negative design consisted entirely of solid lines, circles, or other motifs worked in negative patterning,

I recorded this as *negative painting or resist-dye*, because the design could have been produced by either technique (e.g., Hibben 1975:Figure 75; Smith 1952:Figure 80b; see Figures 9.2d, 9.4c, 9.6d, f). As noted, although archaeological examples are lacking, it is entirely possible that a wax-resist technique like batik could have been used to produce these designs. Given that Kent (1983b:195–98) used the term "negative painting" to describe the archaeological painted blankets and textiles she analyzed, I retain her terminology here with the understanding that the exact method of producing these textiles is still to be determined.

If a negative design consisted entirely of a series of small squares, each with a dot at the center, I recorded this as *tie-dye* (e.g., Smith 1952:Figure 65a, right, 82a; Figure 9.8d). When both dotted squares and solid design elements co-occurred within a single garment, I recorded this as a combination of *tie-dye and negative painting/resist-dye* (e.g., Hibben 1975:Figure 100, right;

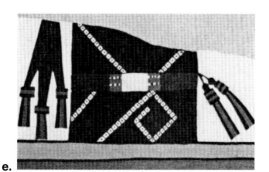

FIGURE 9.8

Types of garments decorated with resist-dye or negative-painted designs in the Pottery Mound and Antelope Mesa murals:
a) manta dress, Pottery Mound, Kiva 16, ca. A.D. 1400–1500; **b**) kilt, Pottery Mound, Kiva 2, ca. A.D. 1400–1500;
c) wraparound garment, Kawaika'a, Test 4, Room 4, ca. A.D. 1375–1500; **d**) wraparound garment, Awat'ovi, Test 14,
Room 2, ca. A.D. 1400–1550; **e**) tunic, Kawaika'a, Test 4, Room 7, ca. A.D. 1375–1550; **f**) tunic, Awat'ovi, Room 529,
ca. A.D. 1400–1550. (**a** and **b** from Hibben [1975:Figures 100 and 14, respectively], courtesy of KC Publications;
c–f from Smith [1952:Figure 52b, Plate E, Figure 88c, and Figure 50, respectively], courtesy of the Peabody Museum
of Archaeology and Ethnology, Harvard University.)

a.

b.

c.

d.

FIGURE 9.9

Ways of depicting female and dual-gendered figures in the Pottery Mound and Antelope Mesa murals: **a**) female figure with manta dress worn over one shoulder and under the other, Pottery Mound, Kiva 9, ca. A.D. 1400–1500; **b**) dual-gendered figure with garment wrapped around the torso and under the arms, Pottery Mound, Kiva 7, ca. A.D. 1400–1500; **c**) female figure with garment wrapped around the torso and under the arms, Awat'ovi, Room 788, ca. A.D. 1500–1630; **d**) female or dual-gendered figures with garments wrapped around their torsos and under their arms, Kawaika'a, ca. A.D. 1375–1500. (**a** and **b** from Hibben [1975:Figures 45 and 38, respectively], courtesy of KC Publications; **c** and **d** from Smith [1952:Figures 78b and 67d, respectively], courtesy of the Peabody Museum of Archaeology and Ethnology, Harvard University.)

Smith 1952:Figure 50c, 51c; see Figure 9.7a, c, Figure 9.8a, f). Because we lack archaeological examples of fabrics decorated with these motifs from Pueblo IV sites, the distinctions made here between tie-dye and negative painting/resist-dye are best interpreted as stylistic differences, rather than technological ones. Given the fact that Pueblo III textile producers are known to have mimicked the appearance of tie-dye motifs by other means, such as negative painting, it is impossible to know which

technique these mural artists were trying to depict, or if different regional conventions were used to render the same techniques.

Many of the kilts and other garments from the Antelope Mesa sites, and a few from Kuaua, have decorated borders that suggest embroidery or supplementary weft (Smith 1952:Figure 25; Webster and Loma'omvaya 2004; see Figures 9.2d, 9.5e, 9.7d, 9.10e, f). In embroidery, the decorative yarns are added to a finished piece of fabric, whereas in supplementary weft (also known as brocade), the contrasting yarns are incorporated during the weaving process, while the textile is still on the loom. Although no archaeological examples of cotton embroidery have been identified from Pueblo IV contexts, the remains of postcontact wool examples that I believe to be embroidery are known from seventeenth-century contexts at Awat'ovi, Hawikuh, Guisewa, Unshagi, Pecos, and San Lazaro pueblos (Fenn 2004:244–45; Webster 1997, 2000). In the chapter tables, I use the term "embroidery" to describe this style of decoration, while recognizing that the exact process used to produce these Pueblo IV designs remains open to question. It is entirely conceivable that such designs were produced by supplementary weft or brocade until the Spaniards introduced sheep wool and metal needles during the seventeenth century.

Although most of the costumes depicted in the murals were probably intended to represent woven fabrics of cotton, some appear to represent hide, and others may represent garments woven from other fibers, such as yucca. The only woven textile fragment I know of from Pottery Mound is made of a noncotton plant fiber (Webster 1997). Yucca and agave were widely used for weaving in southern and central Arizona and northern Mexico, and ethnohistorical accounts describe the importance of yucca in Zuni textile production at the time of contact (Webster 1997; 2000:193). The extent of its use at the other protohistoric Pueblo villages is yet to be determined.

Kilts and Breechcloths
KILT DEPICTIONS AT POTTERY MOUND
The 43 kilts in the Pottery Mound sample encompass a diverse assortment of colors, materials, and decorative techniques (Table 9.3). Most of the Pottery Mound kilts have black backgrounds and are either solid black (34.9 percent) or decorated with asymmetrical, negative-patterned designs (39.6 percent). Fifteen are decorated by negative painting or resist-dye (e.g., Hibben 1975:Figures 2, 14, 16, 47, 49, 60, 75, 86, 91, 93; see Figures 9.4c, 9.6d, 9.10a, b), and two combine negative painting/resist-dye and tie-dye (Hibben 1975:Figures 30, 92; see Figures 9.3c, 9.7a). Most of these designs are composed of hooklike elements, and some have solid white circles, lozenges, or bars. Four (9.3 percent) of the black-background kilts are decorated with contrasting selvage cords, two with red yarns along the lower edge that extend into the tassels (Hibben 1975:Figures 19, 39; see Figure 9.13b, c), and two

with alternating red and orange trim along the lower edge (Hibben 1975:Figures 47, 92; see Figures 9.3c, 9.13a).

Seven of the Pottery Mound kilts appear to be painted. Most are decorated with geometric motifs (e.g., Hibben 1975:Figures 7, 39), but two have similar Sikyatki designs (Hibben 1975:Figures 64, 65; see Figure 9.11c), and one has stylized birds (Hibben 1975:Figure 93). The assemblage also contains a multicolored kilt that may represent a tapestry or twill-tapestry technique with its motifs arranged in bifold rotation (Hibben 1975:Figure 72; see Figure 9.4d), a two-color striped kilt (Hibben 1975:Figure 49), three crescent-shaped hide or fur kilts (Hibben 1975:Figures 23, 57, 71; see Figure 9.11a), and two feathered kilts (Hibben 1975:Figures 25, 26), one of which displays a painted (?) star or Venus motif.

In approximately 19 percent of the Pottery Mound kilt depictions, the upper edge of the kilt extends above the sash (e.g., Hibben 1975:Figures 19, 39, 49; see Figure 9.13a–c). More than half of the Pottery Mound kilts lack tassels. Of the figures with complete kilt depictions, two are profile views showing the tassels worn in front (e.g., Hibben 1975:Frontispiece left, Figure 47; see Figure 9.13a), three are frontal views showing the tassels on the wearer's right (viewer's left; e.g., Hibben 1975:Figure 75; see Figure 9.4c), and two illustrate one on each side (Hibben 1975: Figures 39, 92; see Figures 9.3c, 9.13b). It is conceivable that these latter two might represent breechcloths instead of kilts. In contrast to kilts, which encircle the hips, breechcloths pass between the legs, then are folded over a belt. Since tassels occur at each corner of a fabric where the selvage cords are tied, breechcloths usually have a tassel visible on each side of the wearer. The only way that tassels can appear on both sides of a kilt is if a kilt is wrapped around the body in thirds and one tassel is allowed to protrude from the inner layer of wrapping.

A COMPARISON OF THE POTTERY MOUND, ANTELOPE MESA, AND KUAUA KILT DEPICTIONS
Pre–A.D. 1500 kilt depictions. Seven kilts from Kawaika'a and 10 from Awat'ovi fall within this time period (see Table 9.3). Unlike the strong emphasis on black negative-painted and tie-dyed kilts in the Pottery Mound sample (37.6 percent), only one kilt from Awat'ovi is decorated in this manner (Smith 1952:Figure 52a, left) and none at all from Kawaika'a. Rather, shirts, tunics, wraparound garments, and shoulder blankets are the usual garments decorated with these designs at the Antelope Mesa sites. Black is a much more common kilt background color at

Table 9.3. Kilt Depictions

| | Early Period | | | | | | Late Period | | | |
| | Pottery Mound N = 43 | | Kawaika'a N = 7 | | Awat'ovi N = 10 | | Awat'ovi N = 11 | | Kuaua N = 31 | |
	N	%	N	%	N	%	N	%	N	%
Background color										
Black	35	81.4	3	42.8	2	20.0	1	9.1	29	93.5
White	–	–	1	14.3	6	60.0	7	63.6	–	–
Other color	4	9.3	1	14.3	–	–	1	9.1	2	6.5
Bicolored	1	2.3	–	–	1	10.0	–	–	–	–
Multicolored (3 or more)	3	7.0	2	28.6	1	10.0	2	18.2	–	–
Suggested raw material										
Cotton	38	88.4	6	85.7	10	100.0	11	100.0	30	96.8
Hide or fur	3	6.9	1	14.3	–	–	–	–	1?	3.2?
Feathers	2	4.7	–	–	–	–	–	–	–	–
Suggested method of decoration										
Solid color	15	34.9	3	42.8	4	40.0	3	27.3	27	87.1
Negative painting/resist-dye	15	34.9	–	–	–	–	–	–	2	6.5
Tie-dye	–	–	–	–	–	–	–	–	1	3.2
Negative painting/ resist-dye + tie-dye	2	4.7	–	–	1	10.0	–	–	–	–
Painted design alone	7	16.3	2	28.6	–	–	–	–	–	–
Simple stripes alone	1	2.3	–	–	1	10.0	2	18.2	1	3.2
Feathers alone	1	2.3	–	–	–	–	–	–	–	–
Feathers + painted	1	2.3	–	–	–	–	–	–	–	–
Tapestry weave	1	2.3	–	–	1	10.0	–	–	–	–
Embroidery alone	–	–	–	–	2	20.0	5	45.4	–	–
Openwork with embroidery	–	–	1	14.3	1	10.0	–	–	–	–
Striped cloth with embroidery	–	–	1	14.3	–	–	–	–	–	–
Tie-dye with embroidery	–	–	–	–	–	–	1	9.1	–	–
Kilt visible above sash										
	8	18.6	–	–	1	10.0	–	–	22	71.0
Contrasting selvage present										
	4	9.3	2	28.6	1	10.0	3	27.3	24	77.4
Tassel placement										
Profile view, in front	2	4.7	2	28.6	1	10.0	3	27.3	–	–
Profile view, in back	–	–	1	14.3	2	20.0	6	54.5	1	3.2
Frontal view, wearer's right	3	6.9	–	–	–	–	–	–	8	25.8
Frontal view, wearer's left	–	–	–	–	–	–	–	–	9	29.1
Frontal view, one each side	2	4.7	–	–	–	–	–	–	1	3.2
None depicted	23	53.5	3	42.8	4	40.0	2	18.2	5	16.1
Section of painting missing	13	30.2	1	14.3	3	30.0	–	–	7	22.6

Pottery Mound (81.4 percent) than the Antelope Mesa sites, where fewer than half of the Kawaika'a kilts are black and a variety of colors are depicted. At pre–A.D. 1500 Awat'ovi, white kilts constitute 60 percent of the assemblage and only 20 percent are black.

In addition to a different emphasis on color, the Pottery Mound and Antelope Mesa kilt depictions also differ in their style of decoration. The Pottery Mound kilts place a much greater emphasis on what appears to be applied decoration (resist-dye and painted designs), whereas the Antelope Mesa kilts place a greater emphasis on structural patterning. Only one Pottery Mound kilt appears to be intricately woven in a tapestry or twill-tapestry weave (Hibben 1975:Figure 72; Kent 1983b:239, Figure 149k; see Figure 9.4d).

Kilts that suggest structural patterning are most common at the early Antelope Mesa sites. These include possible examples of tapestry weave (Smith 1952:Figure 51d), twill weave (Smith 1952:Figure 52a, right; Figure 9.10d), embroidery or supplementary weft (Smith 1952: Figures 52a, center, 63f; Figure 9.10d), and three that combine embroidery or supplementary weft with stripes or openwork (Smith 1952:Figures 54a, 72a, 86a; Figure 9.10f). The prevalence and diversity of these styles at the Antelope Mesa sites suggest the presence of far more sophisticated weavers in or near these communities than at Pottery Mound.

Kilts from Pottery Mound and Kawaika'a share a few similarities not found in the pre–A.D. 1500 Awat'ovi assemblage (Figure 9.11). Both feature alternating colors of trim along the lower edge of some kilts (Figure 9.11e, f), and both depict probable painted kilts with colored (not negative-painted) designs (Figure 9.11c, d) and kilts of hide or fur (Figure 9.11a, b). One hide or fur kilt from Kawaika'a is decorated with two circles (Smith 1952:Figure 66a; Figure 9.11b) and resembles the historic Hopi boy's kilt, *kokom vitkuna*, which has two circles (*sipongya*, "blossom altar") painted on a dark background (Wright 1979:13).

Post–A.D. 1500 kilt depictions. The 11 late kilts from Awat'ovi show an even greater contrast with those at Pottery Mound (see Table 9.3). Nearly two-thirds of these kilts are white, and more than half are decorated with bordered designs that are believed to represent embroidery or supplementary weft (Smith 1952:Figures 52a, 63f, 71a, b, 81a, b; see Figures 9.2d, 9.10e). When the pre- and post–A.D. 1500 samples are combined, 11 kilts with these borders are found at the Antelope Mesa sites, none at Pottery Mound. These bordered designs appear to be a relatively late style,

so it is possible that Pottery Mound was abandoned by the time this style gained popularity at Antelope Mesa.

The kilts from Kuaua are in a different class altogether. Nearly 95 percent have black backgrounds, and 87 percent are solid black (Figures 9.12, 9.13d–f). Almost 80 percent of the kilt depictions show the selvage in a contrasting color, usually red (e.g., Dutton 1963:Plate XVI). One kilt has a selvage with two alternating colors (Dutton 1963:Figure 64; Figure 9.13f), like those depicted in the Pottery Mound and Kawaika'a murals (see Figure 9.11e, f). Of the 31 kilts in the Kuaua sample, one black kilt is patterned with a single white stripe, and three are decorated in negative painting/resist- or tie-dye (Figure 9.12a–c). None of the other kilts are decorated. The negative-patterned designs appear to represent constellations of stars (e.g., Dutton 1963:Figures 56, 68) and are much simpler than the tie-dye and negative-painted designs found on the Pottery Mound and Antelope Mesa kilts. One with a large white circle and a line of smaller circles bears the closest resemblance to the Pottery Mound kilts (Dutton 1963:Figure 35a; Figure 9.12c). Another exhibits a barely visible pattern of light-ninglike elements (Dutton 1963:Figure 56; Figure 9.12a).

Most of the kilt depictions at Kuaua (71 percent) show the upper edge of the kilt extending above the sash (e.g., Dutton 1963:Plate XIV; see Figure 9.12b, d, Figure 9.13d–f). As previously noted, approximately 20 percent of the Pottery Mound kilts are also depicted in this manner, whereas none of the early or late Antelope Mesa kilts exhibit this artistic convention. This manner of depicting kilts has a uniquely Eastern Pueblo flavor.

Sashes

SASH DEPICTIONS AT POTTERY MOUND

The Pottery Mound sample contains 43 sash depictions, the vast majority of which are solid white (Table 9.4). Four others are light brown and two are a combination of white and lavender. Presumably, most if not all were intended to represent woven cotton sashes. One, with a snakeskin design, suggests a negative-painted or resist-dye technique (Hibben 1975:Figure 49, right). Based on historic Pueblo dance regalia, most of the white sashes probably represent braided sashes (e.g., Hibben 1975:Figures 2, 64, 65, 74, 75; see Figures 9.4c, 9.7c, 9.11c). The long white fringes on some depictions (e.g., Hibben 1975:Figure 100; see Figure 9.8a, fringe partially visible at right side of dress) are highly reminiscent of the pendant fringes on historic Hopi rain or wedding sashes (Kent 1983a:Figure 67).

a.   b.   c.

d.

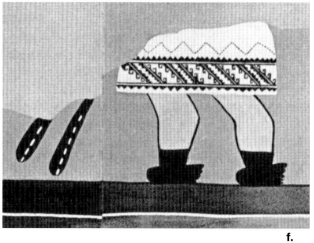

e.   f.

FIGURE 9.10

Different emphases in clothing decoration in the Pottery Mound and Antelope Mesa murals: **a–c**) garments with black backgrounds, some decorated with negative-painted or resist-dye designs, Pottery Mound, Kivas 6, 7, and 16, respectively, A.D. 1400–1500; **d**) kilts probably worked in embroidery or supplemental weft (left) and twill weave (right), Awat'ovi, Test 14, Room 3, ca. A.D. 1400–1550; **e**) kilt with probable embroidery or supplemental weft, Awat'ovi, Room 788, ca. A.D. 1500–1630; **f**) kilt with probable embroidery or supplemental weft and openwork weave, Kawaika'a, Test 4, Room 7, ca. A.D. 1375–1500. (**a–c** from Hibben [1975:Figures 47, 86, and 100, respectively], courtesy of KC Publications; **d–f** from Smith [1952:Figures 52a, 71a, and 86a, respectively], courtesy of the Peabody Museum of Archaeology and Ethnology, Harvard University.)

a.   b.

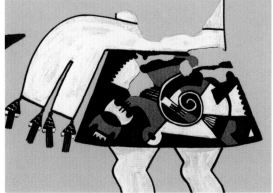

c.   d.

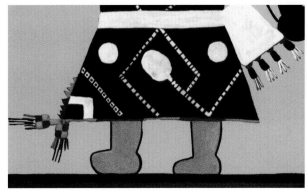
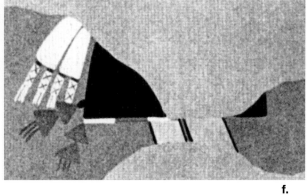

e.   f.

FIGURE 9.11

Conventions shared between Pottery Mound and Kawaika'a, but not early Awat'ovi: **a–b** show fur or hide kilts,
a) Pottery Mound, Kiva 8, ca. A.D. 1400–1500, **b**) Kawaika'a, Test 5, Room 4, ca. A.D. 1375–1500; **c–d** show probable
painted kilts with multicolored designs, **c**) Pottery Mound, Kiva 9, ca. A.D. 1400–1500, **d**) Kawaika'a, Test 5, Room 1,
ca. A.D. 1375–1500; **e–f** show two-color edging on lower edge of garment, **e**) Pottery Mound, Kiva 8, ca. A.D. 1400–1500,
f) Kawaika'a, Test 5, Room 4, ca. A.D. 1375–1500. (**a, c,** and **e** from Hibben [1975:Figures 23, 65, and 74, respectively],
courtesy of KC Publications; **b, d,** and **f** from Smith [1952:Figures 66a, 67b, and 69e, respectively], courtesy of the
Peabody Museum of Archaeology and Ethnology, Harvard University.)

a.

b.

c.

d.

FIGURE 9.12

Kuaua ritual costuming, Kiva III: **a–b**) black kilts with resist-dye or negative-painted designs suggestive of constellations, background of **a** has barely perceptible dark zigzag lines, and ends of white sash are worked in contrasting color; **c**) black kilt with resist-dye or negative-painted design resembling examples in the Pottery Mound murals, sash ends suggest embroidery or supplemental weft; **d**) black kilts with white sashes with ends worked in contrasting color. (**a–d** from Dutton [1963:Figures 56, 68, 35a, 30, and 31, respectively], courtesy of the University of New Mexico Press.)

Two other sashes have a horizontal pendant fringe decorated with shells or other tinklers (Hibben 1975: Frontispiece). Other sashes suggest warp-faced belting (Hibben 1975:Figure 71, right).

More than 20 percent of the sash depictions lack tassels. This includes front-facing figures whose tassels, if hanging behind them, would not be visible. The tassels on nearly half of the sashes are rendered in two or more colors (see Figure 9.13a), and approximately 20 percent have compound tassels decorated with geometric designs (e.g., Hibben 1975:Figures 64, 65, 92; see Figure 9.3c). Modern analogues of these geometric tassels are found on Hopi wedding mantas (Kent 1983a:Figures 35, 36). Their Hopi name, *sipolata*, translates as "blossom buds" (Wright 1979:21). The most common method of depicting sash-wearing males in the Pottery Mound murals is to show the figures in profile with their fringes hanging toward the back (27.9 percent; e.g., Hibben 1975:Figures 14, 86, 91; see Figures 9.8b, 9.10b). Among the front-facing figures with sashes, about half have the fringes hanging to

the wearer's right, the other half to the left (Hibben 1975: Figures 64, 65, 72, 74, 75).

A COMPARISON OF THE POTTERY MOUND, ANTELOPE MESA, AND KUAUA SASH DEPICTIONS

Compared to Pottery Mound and Kuaua, the Antelope Mesa mural painters made much greater use of decorated sashes, including striped sashes and sashes with striped fringes (Smith 1952:Figures 52b, 80, right; see Figures 9.5e, 9.10d, Table 9.4). At least one striped sash from Awat'ovi suggests warp-faced belting (Smith 1952:Figure 50e). The Kuaua sashes, in contrast, are almost entirely white. Sashes with long self-fringes, resembling historic Hopi rain sashes, are also much more common at the Antelope Mesa sites (e.g., Smith 1952:Figures 63f, 67d, 81a, b, 82a; see Figures 9.7b, d, 9.9d, 9.10e) than at Pottery Mound and are completely absent at Kuaua. The Kuaua sashes, on the other hand, show the greatest use (24 percent) of pendant fringes decorated with shells or other attachments (Dutton 1963: Plate XVI, Figures 6, 10, 64, 88; see Figure 9.13f).

FIGURE 9.13

Shared convention in the Pottery Mound and Kuaua murals of depicting the upper edge of the kilt above the sash:
a–c) Pottery Mound, Kivas 6, 2, and 2, respectively; **d–f**) Kuaua, Kiva III. (**a–d** from Hibben [1975:Figures 47, 39, and 19, respectively], courtesy of KC Publications; **d–f** from Dutton [1963:Figures 31, 32, and 64, respectively], courtesy of the University of New Mexico Press.)

Table 9.4. Sash Depictions

	Early Period						Late Period			
	Pottery Mound N = 43		Kawaika'a N = 10		Awat'ovi N = 10		Awat'ovi N = 16		Kuaua N = 33	
	N	%	N	%	N	%	N	%	N	%
Background color										
White	34	79.1	6	60.0	7	70.0	11	68.7	29	87.9
Black	–	–	2	20.0	–	–	2	12.5	1	3.0
Other color	5	11.6	1	10.0	–	–	2	12.5	2	6.1
Bicolored	4	9.3	–	–	2	20.0	1	6.3	–	–
Multicolored	–	–	1	10.00	1	10.0	–	–	1	3.0
Suggested raw material										
Cotton	43	100.0	1	100.0	10	100.0	16	100.0	33	100.0
Suggested method of decoration										
Solid color	41	95.4	8	80.0	7	70.0	13	81.2	30	90.9
Embroidered borders	–	–	–	–	–	–	2	12.5	2	6.1
Striped body or borders	1	2.3	1	10.0	3	30.0	1	6.3	1	3.0
Negative painted/ resist-dye	1	2.3	–	–	–	–	–	–	–	–
Unknown, section missing	–	–	1	10.0	–	–	–	–	–	–
How worn?										
Around waist	43	100.0	8	80.0	7	70.0	11	68.7	30	90.9
Low on hips	–	–	–	–	1	10.0	2	12.5	–	–
Around chest	–	–	2	20.0	2	20.0	3	18.8	–	–
Around head	–	–	–	–	–	–	–	–	3	9.1

Simple two-colored tassels appear at all sites but are especially common at Kuaua (e.g., Dutton 1963:Figures 6, 30, 96; see Figure 9.13d). Compound tassels with geometric designs, resembling those used on historic Hopi wedding mantas, appear on approximately 20 percent of the sashes from Pottery Mound, Kuaua, Kawaika'a, and late Awat'ovi (e.g., Dutton 1963:Cover, Figures 32, 54, 66, 110, 113; Hibben 1975:Figure 92; Smith 1952:Figures 72a, 72b; see Figures 9.3c, 9.11f, 9.13e) but are absent in the early Awat'ovi depictions.

The major difference between Pottery Mound and Kuaua, on the one hand, and the Kawaika'a and Awat'ovi assemblages, on the other, is the manner of displaying the sash. Approximately 20 percent of the Antelope Mesa

sashes are wrapped around the upper torsos of female or dual-gendered figures dressed in a wraparound blanket or kilt (e.g., Smith 1952:Figures 67d, 81a, b; see Figures 9.7d, 9.9c, d). None of the Pottery Mound or Kuaua sashes are displayed in this manner. A few shirt- or tunic-clad Awat'ovi male figures wear sashes low on the hips (Smith 1952:Figures 50c, f, 53b; see Figures 9.5e, 9.8f), another style not found at the eastern sites. Most importantly, more than half of the sash-wearing figures at Kawaika'a and Awat'ovi are depicted in profile with the fringes extending down the back (e.g., Smith 1952:Plates A, F, I, Figures 50e, 52a, 53b; see Figures 9.2d, 9.5e, 9.10d–f, 9.11d), compared to 28 percent at Pottery Mound and only 12.5 percent at Kuaua (e.g., Dutton 1963:Figures 8, 10). At Kuaua, nearly

Table 9.4. Sash Depictions

| | Early Period | | | | | Late Period | | | |
| | Pottery Mound N = 43 | | Kawaika'a N = 10 | | Awat'ovi N = 10 | | Awat'ovi N = 16 | | Kuaua N = 33 | |
	N	%	N	%	N	%	N	%	N	%
Fringe/tassel treatment										
Long self fringe	3	6.9	2	20.0	6	60.0	6	37.5	–	–
Striped fringe	–	–	2	20.0	2	20.0	3	18.8	–	–
Simple tassel, 1 color	–	–	–	–	–	–	–	–	6	18.2
Simple tassel, 2+ colors	18	41.9	4	40.0	–	–	4	25.0	18	54.5
Compound tassel with geometric designs	8	18.6	2	20.0	–	–	3	18.7	7	21.2
Fringe and/or tassels not depicted	12	27.9	–	–	1	10.0	–	–	2	6.1
Section of painting missing	2	4.7	–	–	1	10.0	–	–	–	–
Pendant fringe with attachments present										
	2	4.6	–	–	–	–	1	6.3	8	24.2
Fringe placement										
Profile view, in front	3	7.0	–	–	–	–	–	–	–	–
Profile view, in back	10	23.3	6	60.0	4	40.0	13	81.2	4	12.1
Frontal view, wearer's right	9	20.9	1	10.0	1	10.0	–	–	17	51.5
Frontal view, wearer's left	8	18.6	3	30.0	4	40.0	3	18.8	12	36.4
None depicted	11	25.5	–	–	–	–	–	–	–	–
Section of painting missing	2	4.7	–	–	1	10.0	–	–	–	–

all sashes occur on static front-facing figures (see Figures 9.12a, b, d, 9.13d, f). Among the front-facing figures from all sites, it is more common for the Pottery Mound and Kuaua sashes to be tied on the wearer's right and for the Antelope Mesa sashes to be tied on the wearer's left. At Pottery Mound and Antelope Mesa, nearly all of the sashes associated with female front-facing figures are tied on the wearer's left. Approximately 10 percent of the sashes at Kuaua are wrapped around the head, a feature not recorded at the other sites (see Figure 9.5d).

Differences are also seen in the pre– and post– A.D. 1500 samples. A few late sashes at Awat'ovi and Kuaua have their ends decorated with what appears to be embroidery or supplementary weft (e.g., Dutton 1963:

Figures 35a, 49; Smith 1952:Plate I, Figure 81a, b, right; see Figures 9.2d, 9.12c). This feature is not found at Pottery Mound, Kawaika'a, or pre–A.D. 1500 Awat'ovi. Like the embroidered or supplementary-weft kilt borders, this sash style appears to be a relatively late development in the late prehispanic Southwest.

Shirts and Tunics
SHIRTS AND TUNICS FROM POTTERY MOUND
The Pottery Mound sample contains at least nine possible shirts or tunics (Table 9.5). This is the most difficult category to assess because some of the depictions I have classified as shirts might have been intended to represent body painting or hide garments instead. Based on the

presence of tassels at the corner of one garment (Hibben 1975:Figure 60; see Figure 9.6d) and the suggestion of weave structures in several examples (e.g., Hibben 1975: Figure 30; see Figure 9.7a), at least four appear to be depictions of woven textiles. Two suggest openwork weaves: one a simple netting technique (Hibben 1975:Frontispiece, right) and the other weft-wrap openwork (Hibben 1975: Figure 60; see Figure 9.6d). The latter is decorated with clusters of small circles identified by Hibben's Acoma informants as constellations of stars. Another shirt with a two-dimensional checkered design suggests tapestry weave (Hibben 1975:Figure 30; see Figure 9.7a). The fourth is a striped fabric suggestive of plain weave or twill (Hibben 1975:Figure 71, left). Three of the four garments have sleeves. Despite the popularity of tie-dye and negative painting or resist-dye designs for decorating kilts and mantas at Pottery Mound, shirts decorated in this manner are lacking in the Pottery Mound sample.

The other five items in the sample could represent woven shirts, hide shirts, or simply body painting (Hibben 1975:Frontispiece, center and left, Figures 25, 26, 75). I have tentatively classified them as long-sleeved shirts because the color of the body differs from that of the hands. But if every figure with differently colored hands and bodies was intended to be wearing a shirt, then there are more shirts in the Pottery Mound murals than I have included in my sample. I suspect most of these depictions were meant to represent body painting. Two of these depictions, decorated with a star or Venus motif, could represent painted cotton or hide shirts (Hibben 1975:Figures 25, 26). Both figures appear on the same wall and wear kilts decorated with feathers.

A COMPARISON OF THE POTTERY MOUND, ANTELOPE MESA, AND KUAUA SHIRTS AND TUNICS

Some of the most significant differences between the Antelope Mesa and Pottery Mound assemblages concern the use of shirts and tunics. In the Antelope Mesa region, shirt and tunic depictions attributed to the pre–A.D. 1500 period are either white openwork shirts (Smith 1952:Figure 24a, d, k; see Figure 9.6e) or black shirts or tunics decorated in negative painting/resist-dye or tie-dye (Smith 1952:Figures 17m, 24c, 80b, 81b; see Figure 9.8f). At Pottery Mound, openwork shirts are uncommon and negative-patterned black shirts nonexistent. After A.D. 1500, depictions of tunics with embroidered borders appear in the Awat'ovi murals (Smith 1952:Figures 50f, 53b; see Figure 9.5d). None of these shirt styles are found at Kuaua.

The most interesting garment from Kuaua is a long, flared tunic with three-quarter sleeves and an undulating lower edge worn by a dual-gendered figure that Dutton's Zuni informant identified as Corn (Earth) Mother and Sky (Sun) Father, and which Dutton referred to as the Universal Deity (Dutton 1953:Frontispiece, 116–19, Figure 54; see Figure 9.5d). The undulating lower edge of the garment suggests a hide tunic, and its small rectangular motifs suggest painted decoration. The figure is surrounded by a variety of elements relating to corn, fertility, and warfare, the latter including a star or Venus symbol and a quiver with a snakelike design.

I have already noted a connection between shirts, tunics, and warfare in the Mesoamerican codices. A similar association is seen between these garments and warfare or hunting imagery in the Pueblo IV murals. The Kuaua example cited above is one excellent example, but examples are found at all mural sites, where shirt-wearing figures are frequently depicted with bows, arrows, quivers, or a star or Venus symbol, the latter identified by Schaafsma (2000:150) as an image related to warfare and hunting in both Mesoamerica and the Pueblo Southwest. At Pottery Mound, two figures that appear to be wearing shirts display a star or Venus symbol prominently on the chest, and one of these has a similar symbol on the kilt (Hibben 1975:Figures 25, 26). Other Pottery Mound figures that might be wearing shirts are depicted with bows and quivers (e.g., Hibben 1975:Frontispiece), as are several tunic-wearing figures from Awat'ovi (Smith 1952: Plate A, Figures 53b, 61b; see Figure 9.5e).

Manta Dresses and Short Shoulder Blankets

MANTA DRESSES AND SHORT SHOULDER BLANKETS AT POTTERY MOUND

The Pottery Mound mural sample includes seven women's manta dresses and one short shoulder blanket or cape, all with a black background (Table 9.6). Three manta dresses and the shoulder blanket are undecorated (Hibben 1975: Figures 17, center, 60, 99, right, 100, left; see Figures 9.6d over shoulders, 9.10c). The other four mantas are patterned with asymmetrical arrangements of diagonal lines, hooklike elements, and white circles that resemble the kilt designs. One suggests negative painting or resist-dye (Hibben 1975:Figure 45; see Figure 9.9a), and three combine tie-dye and negative painting/resist-dye motifs (Hibben 1975:Figures 74, 99 left, 100 right; see Figures 9.7c, 9.8a).

Table 9.5. Shirt and Tunic Depictions

	Early Period						Late Period			
	Pottery Mound N = 9		Kawaika'a N = 2		Awat'ovi N = 4		Awat'ovi N = 4		Kuaua N = 6	
	N	%	N	%	N	%	N	%	N	%
Garment form										
Sleeveless vests	–	–	–	–	–	–	–	–	1	16.7
Sleeveless shirts or tunics	1	11.1	1	50.0	2	50.0	–	–	–	–
Shirts or tunics with long sleeves extending to wrists	6	66.7	1	50.0	1	25.0	3	75.0	3	50.0
Shirts or tunics with short sleeves ending near elbow	2	22.2	–	–	–	–	1	25.0	2	33.3
Unknown, incomplete depiction	–	–	–	–	1	25.0	–	–	–	–
Background color										
Black	–	–	1	50.0	2	50.0	1	25.0	1	16.7
White	1	11.1	1	50.0	2	50.0	1	25.0	1	16.7
Other color	5	55.6	–	–	–	–	2	75.0	4	66.6
Bicolored	2	22.2	–	–	–	–	–	–	–	–
Multicolored (3 or more)	1	11.1	–	–	–	–	–	–	–	–
Suggested raw material										
Cotton	4	44.4	1	100.0	4	100.0	4	100.0	1	16.7
Cotton, hide, or body paint	5	55.6	–	–	–	–	–	–	5	83.3
Suggested method of decoration										
Solid color	3	33.4	–	–	–	–	1	25.0	5	83.3
Negative painting/ resist-dye	–	–	–	–	–	–	1	25.0	–	–
Tie-dye	–	–	1	50.0	1	25.0	–	–	–	–
Negative painting/ resist- + tie-dye	–	–	–	–	1	25.0				
Painted design	2	22.2	–	–	–	–	–	–	1	16.7
Simple stripes	1	11.1	–	–	–	–	–	–	–	–
Openwork	2	22.2	1	50.0	2	50.0	–	–	–	–
Tapestry weave	1	11.1	–	–	–	–	–	–	–	–
Embroidery	–	–	–	–	–	–	2	50.0	–	–
Tassel placement										
Profile view, in front	–	–	–	–	1	25.0	–	–	–	–
Profile view, in back	–	–	–	–	–	–	–	–	–	–
Frontal view, wearer's right	1	11.1	–	–	1	25.0	–	–	–	–
Frontal view, wearer's left	–	–	–	–	–	–	–	–	–	–
Frontal view, one each side	–	–	–	–	–	–	–	–	–	–
None depicted	8	88.9	2	100.0	1	25.0	4	100.0	6	100.0
Section of painting missing	–	–	–	–	1	25.0	–	–	–	–

Table 9.6. Manta Dresses, Wraparound Garments, and Shoulder Blanket Depictions

| | Early Period | | | | | | Late Period | | | |
| | Pottery Mound N = 10 | | Kawaika'a N = 8 | | Awat'ovi N = 6 | | Awat'ovi N = 11 | | Kuaua N = 0 | |
	N	%	N	%	N	%	N	%	N	%
How worn?										
Over one shoulder and under one arm (manta dress)	7	70.0	–	–	–	–	–	–	–	–
Around upper torso, under both arms (wraparound garment)	2	20.0	7	87.5	1	16.7	8	72.7	–	–
Over the shoulders or around the neck (shoulder blanket)	1	10.0	1	12.5	2	33.3	3	27.3	–	–
Unknown, shoulders missing	–	–	–	–	3	50.0	–	–	–	–
Background color										
Black	10	100.0	4	50.0	6	100.0	8	72.7	–	–
White	–	–	2	25.0	–	–	–	–	–	–
Gray	–	–	–	–	–	–	3	27.3	–	–
Multicolored (3 or more)	–	–	2	25.0	–	–	–	–	–	–
Suggested raw material										
Cotton	10	100.0	8	100.0	6	100.0	–	100.0	–	–
Suggested method of decoration										
Solid color	4	40.0	4	50.0	2	33.3	4	36.3	–	–
Negative painting/resist-dye	1	10.0	–	–	1	16.7	3	27.3	–	–
Tie-dye	–	–	1	12.5	2	33.3	1	9.1	–	–
Negative painting/ resist-dye + tie-dye	3	30.0	–	–	1	16.7	–	–	–	–
Painted	2?	20.0	–	–	–	–	–	–	–	–
Simple stripes	–	–	2	25.0	–	–	–	–	–	–
Openwork	–	–	1	12.5	–	–	–	–	–	–
Embroidery alone	–	–	–	–	–	–	2	18.2	–	–
Tie-dye with embroidery	–	–	–	–	–	–	1	9.1	–	–
Tassel placement										–
Profile view, in front	–	–	–	–	–	–	–	–	–	–
Profile view, in back	–	–	–	–	–	–	–	–	–	–
Frontal view, wearer's right	2	20.0	–	–	–	–	3	27.3	–	–
Frontal view, wearer's left	–	–	–	–	–	–	–	–	–	–
Frontal view, one each side	–	–	–	–	2	33.3	–	–	–	–
None depicted	8	80.0	8	100.0	1	16.7	8	72.7	–	–
Section of painting missing	–	–	–	–	3	50.0	–	–	–	–

All of the Pottery Mound figures that wear these manta dresses have hair whorls, except for one that appears to have the hair tied up in back (Hibben 1975: Figure 17, center). The figures with the hair whorls appear to be female dancers. In all cases, the manta dresses are tied over one shoulder and under the other, the same way in which Pueblo women wear their manta dresses today (Kent 1983a). All but one have the manta tied over the wearer's right shoulder (viewer's left) in the historic Pueblo manner (see Figures 9.7c, 9.8a, 9.9a, 9.10c). The exception has the manta tied over the wearer's left shoulder (viewer's right; Hibben 1975:Figure 99, left). Upper and lower tassels are depicted on only two of the seven mantas. In both cases, they are depicted on the wearer's right (viewer's left), the same side as the shoulder over which the manta is tied (Hibben 1975:Figure 45, 74; see Figures 9.7c, 9.9a). Four of these figures are legless, with the lower edge of the garment not shown. In all five cases in which manta dresses and fringed sashes are shown together, the sash is tied on the wearer's left (viewer's right), opposite the side where the manta is tied (see Figures 9.7c, 9.9a). This is the same convention practiced by Hopi women today (Webster and Loma'omvaya 2004:74).

The Pottery Mound sample also includes two garments (?) wrapped around the upper torsos of two nearly identical figures (Hibben 1975:Figures 38, 62; see Figure 9.9b) that appear to be "corn maidens" (Crotty 1995:264, Figure 49). Their bodies and faces are decorated with corn motifs and rows of dots that may represent corn kernels, while their hairstyles resemble the uneven bob worn by some male figures in the Kawaika'a murals. This suggests that these Pottery Mound figures may be dual gendered, like the White Corn Maiden of the Tewa (Ortiz 1969:165). Whether these figures are actually meant to be wearing garments is questionable. They are included in the sample because of their resemblance to figures with similar hairdos wearing wraparound garments in the Antelope Mesa murals (e.g., Smith 1952: Figure 67d).

The only short black shoulder blanket at Pottery Mound is worn by what appears to be a front-facing female, based on the graduated shape of the hips (Hibben 1975:Figure 60; see Figure 9.6d). This figure also wears the openwork shirt with constellation-like designs. The combination of a short black shoulder blanket with an openwork garment lends an Antelope Mesa "feel" to the costume. The constellations, on the other hand, seem more like an Eastern Pueblo feature.

A COMPARISON OF THE POTTERY MOUND, ANTELOPE MESA, AND KUAUA MANTA DRESSES AND SHORT SHOULDER BLANKETS

Small, capelike shoulder blankets occur at Pottery Mound, Kawaika'a, and Awat'ovi, but not Kuaua (see Table 9.6). They are especially common at Awat'ovi. The shoulder blanket from Pottery Mound (see Figure 9.6d) and the sole example from Kawaika'a (Smith 1952:Figure 67a), are solid black, whereas most Awat'ovi examples are decorated with tie-dye or negative painting (e.g., Smith 1952:Figures 17n, p, 81a, b; see Figure 9.2d).

The greatest difference between the Pottery Mound, Antelope Mesa, and Kuaua murals involves the depiction of female dress. Except for the two possible dual-gendered "corn maiden" figures, all of the female figures at Pottery Mound wear manta dresses in typical historic Pueblo fashion, over one shoulder and under the other. Surprisingly, there are no surviving depictions of this style at the other sites, even though manta dresses have been worn in this manner at all of the pueblos, including Hopi, for at least 250 years.[2] The fact that three of the Awat'ovi female (?) depictions are cut off at the shoulders makes it impossible to confirm or deny the presence of this style at Antelope Mesa. Smith's Figure 51c is one possible example (see Figure 9.7b).

No figures at Kuaua exhibit this style of dress, even though many were identified as female by Dutton's (1963) informants. The sole Kuaua figure with hair whorls, identified as Yellow Corn Woman or Kochininako, wears a kilt and a sash, just like the other Kuaua figures (Dutton 1963:Figure 113).

At Antelope Mesa, the most common manner of depicting female dress was with a blanket or kilt wrapped around the upper torso and under both arms (e.g., Smith 1952:Figures 67d, 78b, 81a, b; see Figure 9.7d, 9.8c, d, 9.9c, d). Based on their asymmetrical hairdos, some of these figures may be dual gendered (see Figure 9.9d). As noted, two figures from Pottery Mound, possibly also dual gendered, are portrayed in a similar manner (see Figure 9.9b). Given that all of these figures are depicted without legs, it is impossible to know the original length of these garments. The Antelope Mesa examples worn in this manner exhibit a wide range of decorative techniques, including openwork (see Figure 9.9d), stripes, negative painting/resist-dye/tie-dye (see Figures 9.8c, d, 9.9c), and embroidery or supplementary weft, some combined with tie-dye (Smith 1952:Figure 82a). Others are solid black (see Figure 9.9d). Once again, the diversity of weave structures in this assemblage points to Antelope Mesa as an important textile-production center.

One convention practiced by mural painters from all sites was the depiction of female and dual-gendered figures in the frontal position. Only one probable female from Pottery Mound is shown in profile, and that individual appears to be dead (Hibben 1975:Figure 49, second from left). At both Pottery Mound and Antelope Mesa, when tassels are shown on women's manta dresses and other wraparound garments, they are shown on the wearer's right. When sashes are depicted in association with these garments, they are tied with their fringes to the wearer's left (cf. Hibben 1975:Figures 45, 74; Smith 1952:Figures 67d, 81a, b; see Figures 9.7c, d, 9.9d). Thus, Pottery Mound and the Antelope Mesa sites share the same convention of tassel/fringe placement for their female figures, even though these figures wear garments with different kinds of decoration and wear them in different ways. Once again, Kuaua is out on its own. Only one figure in the Kuaua murals has hair whorls, and both the kilt and the sash worn by that figure have their tassels hanging to the right (Dutton 1963:Figure 113).

Blankets or Other Textiles Displayed on Walls

WALL BLANKETS AT POTTERY MOUND

In addition to mantas and shoulder blankets worn by human figures, the Pottery Mound sample includes several panels of decorated blankets or other textiles displayed on walls (Hibben 1975:Figures 17, upper, 94–96). One incomplete depiction of a probable painted blanket shows a two-dimensional design of interlocking motifs (Hibben 1975:Figure 95; see Figure 9.7e). The most complete example has a multicolored design with the bands arranged in offset quartering (Hibben 1975:Figure 96; Figure 9.14b). The layout of this blanket is strikingly similar to that found on two Pueblo III blankets from Painted Cave near Canyon de Chelly (Haury 1945:Plates 11, 12; Kent 1983b:Plate 17; Figure 9.14a). Significantly, the motifs used to decorate the bands are similar to those found on Pueblo IV Rio Grande pottery (Suzanne Eckert, personal communication 2004).

Another panel depicts as many as nine blankets or other textiles arranged as if displayed on a rack (Hibben 1975:Figure 94; Figure 9.14d). Some of these appear to be folded. The five blankets with multicolored designs appear to represent painted blankets and suggest an offset quartered layout similar to that shown in Figure 9.14b.

These alternate with four black blankets or other textiles decorated with combined tie-dye and negative-painted/resist designs (Hibben 1975:Figure 94; Figure 9.14d). Like the negative-patterned designs on the Pottery Mound kilts and mantas, most exhibit hooklike, dot-in-a-square motifs and prominent white circles. Another panel from Pottery Mound that appears to illustrate blankets on a rack features two black negative-painted blankets and two others painted with colorful Sikyatki designs (Hibben 1975:Figure 17, upper).

A COMPARISON OF THE POTTERY MOUND AND ANTELOPE MESA WALL BLANKETS

Large decorated blankets are depicted on walls at Pottery Mound and the Antelope Mesa sites, but not Kuaua. Fragmentary depictions of blankets with allover two-dimensional designs like the one from Pottery Mound are relatively common at Kawaika'a and early Awat'ovi (e.g., Hibben 1975:Figure 95; Smith 1952:44, 45a, 74c; see Figure 9.7f). One blanket from pre-A.D. 1500 Awat'ovi appears to combine painted and openwork designs (Smith 1952:Figure 45c). Other depictions of possible blankets exhibit Sikyatki designs (e.g., Smith 1952:Figures 44b, 45b). Brody (1964:123–125) has suggested that all of the large framed Sikyatki designs of the third-order layout represent textiles on walls.

Given the proximity of Antelope Mesa to the Chinle drainage where the Painted Cave blankets were found, it is surprising that the Antelope Mesa sample contains no obvious examples of blankets with offset-quartered designs. Most blanket depictions at Awat'ovi and Kawaika'a are extremely fragmentary, however, so it is possible that depictions of such blankets simply did not survive.

Systems of Design Patterning

Table 9.7 provides a basic summary of the design systems used to decorate textiles in the kiva murals. Finite or unit designs are found at all sites but are most characteristic of the early period. Although stars, birds, a variety of Sikyatki designs, and other finite designs appear on a range of garments, the most common use of a finite design system was to produce the asymmetrical, negative-patterned, black-and-white designs arranged obliquely to the warp and weft that I have characterized as tie-dye and negative painting. These designs, which may represent celestial bodies, lightning, plants, or other natural elements, are often arranged in fourfold rotation (e.g., Hibben 1975:Figures 86, 99, left; see Figures 9.4c, 9.10a, b).

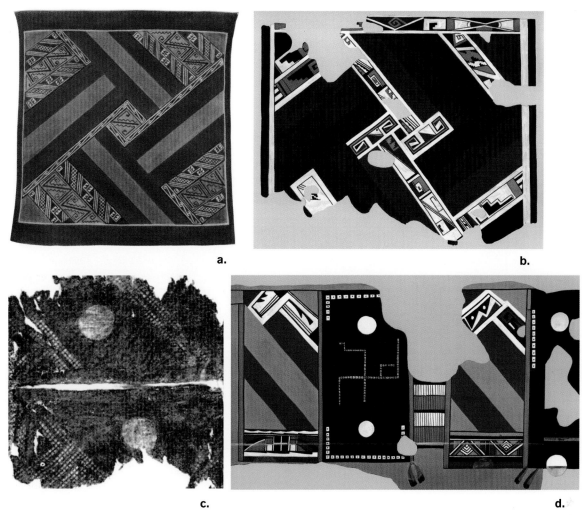

FIGURE 9.14

Evidence of Kayenta painting and dyeing traditions at Pottery Mound: **a**) artist's reconstruction of a painted cotton blanket with bands arranged in fourfold rotation, Painted Cave, ca. A.D. 1250; **b**) depiction of probable painted blanket with bands arranged in fourfold rotation, Pottery Mound, Kiva 12, ca. A.D. 1400–1500; **c**) detail of cotton shirt with negative-painted or resist-dye designs, Poncho House, ca. A.D. 1250; **d**) depiction of blankets hanging on wall, some with bands arranged in fourfold rotation, others with negative-painted or resist-dye designs, Pottery Mound, Kiva 16, ca. A.D. 1400–1500. (**a** from Haury [1945:Plate 11], courtesy of the Amerind Foundation; **b** and **d** from Hibben [1975:Figures 96 and 94, respectively], courtesy of KC Publications; **c** adapted from Guernsey [1931:Plate 63], courtesy of the Peabody Museum of Archaeology and Ethnology, Harvard University.)

Although this dynamic, asymmetrical, negative-patterned design system was shared across the entire Pueblo landscape, there are important regional differences in the types of garments to which these designs were applied. At Kuaua, they occur only on kilts (Dutton 1963: Figures 35*a*, 56). At Pottery Mound, they occur on kilts, manta dresses, and textiles (blankets?) displayed on walls (Hibben 1975:Figures 2, 45, 47, 60, 74, 75, 86, 91–94, 99, 100). At Antelope Mesa, these negative-patterned designs were applied to an even wider range of styles, including kilts, tunics, women's wraparound garments, a sash, and short shoulder blankets (Smith 1952:Plate E, Figures 17*m*, *n*, *p*, 50*c*, 51*c*, 52*a*, left, 52*b*, 65*a*, 78*b*, 88*c*). At early Awat'ovi, a similar design, but rendered in openwork, was used to

Table 9.7. Systems of Decoration

	Early Period			Late Period	
	Pottery Mound	**Kawaika'a**	**Awat'ovi**	**Awat'ovi**	**Kuaua**
Finite or unit designs					
Negative-patterned designs with motifs oblique to the warp and weft, often in fourfold rotation	17 kilts, 4 mantas worked in resist-dye or negative painting	1 tunic and 1 wraparound garment worked in tie-dye	1 kilt, 2 tunics, 2 shoulder blankets, 2 wraparound garments worked in resist-dye or negative painting; 1 openwork tunic	1 kilt, 1 wraparound garment, 3 shoulder blankets worked in resist-dye or negative painting. (Tie-dye kilt has embroidered border.)	1 kilt worked in resist-dye or negative painting
Other finite designs	1 feathered kilt with star or Venus motif; 2 shirts with a star or Venus motif; 5 kilts with bird, geometric, and abstract Sikyatki designs; 1 openwork shirt with clusters of dots (stars?); 1 kilt with small curvilinear motifs; 2 painted blankets with abstract Sikyatki designs	1 hide (?) kilt with 2 circles	Painted blankets with abstract Sikyatki designs	1 negative-painted or resist-dye shirt with circles and dashes	1 tie-dye kilt with clusters of dots (stars?)
One-dimensional band designs					
Translation, single color	–	Openwork design on 1 kilt with an embroidered border; embroidered border on 1 striped kilt	Embroidered borders on 3 kilts	Embroidered border on 1 sash; visible band of 1 tie-dye wraparound garment	Embroidered border on 1 sash
Translation with color counterchange	–	–	–	Embroidered borders on 6 kilts (1 kilt tie-dyed), 1 sash, 2 tunics	Embroidered border on 1 sash
Mirror reflection with color counterchange	–	–	–	Embroidered borders on 3 kilt borders	–
Bifold rotation	–	Embroidered border on the openwork kilt cited above	–	–	–
Simple stripes	1 kilt, 1 tunic, 1 sash	Striped kilt with embroidered border cited above; 2 sashes	1 kilt, 3 sashes (1 warp faced?)	1 sash	1 sash border, 1 sash (warp faced?)
Two-dimensional designs					
Offset quartering	Painted blankets	1 painted kilt	–	–	–
Grid design	1 openwork shirt, 1 tapestry shirt, 1 sash with a snakeskin design	1 openwork shirt, 1 openwork kilt	1 openwork shirt	–	–
Bifold rotation	1 tapestry kilt	–	1 tapestry kilt	–	–
Other two-dimensional designs	Painted blankets	Painted blankets	Painted blankets	Painted blankets	–

decorate a white tunic (Smith 1952:Figure 24k). Based on the use of a shared design system incorporating many of the same elements, it appears that the people of Pottery Mound, Antelope Mesa, and Kuaua shared much the same symbolic code, one focused on lightning, moisture, plants, and fertility (Webster et al. 2006). On the other hand, the finite constellation-like motifs found on a few Pottery Mound and Kuaua costumes (e.g., Dutton 1963: Figures 56, 68; Hibben 1975:Figure 60) are not apparent in the Antelope Mesa assemblage.

Except for simple stripes, which occur at all four sites, one-dimensional band designs occur only at Antelope Mesa and Kuaua. Most of these designs are thought to represent borders worked in embroidery or supplementary weft. At Kuaua, they are found only at the ends of sashes (Dutton 1963:Figures 35a, 49, around head; see Figure 9.12c). At Kawaika'a, these borders appear only on kilts, where they consistently co-occur with other decorative techniques, such as openwork (Smith 1952:Figure 86a; see Figure 9.10f) or striped fabrics (Smith 1952:Figure 72a). At Awat'ovi, these borders appear on a wide range of textiles—kilts, tunics, wraparound garments, and sashes—and are usually the sole decorative technique (e.g., Smith 1952:Figures 50f, 63f, 71b, 81a, b; see Figures 9.2d, 9.5e, 9.7d, 9.10d, e). An exception is a late Awat'ovi tie-dyed kilt with an embroidered border (Smith 1952:Figure 82a). These embroidered or supplementary-weft borders exhibit a more sophisticated use of color counterchange through time.

Two-dimensional designs are found during the early period at Pottery Mound and Antelope Mesa. These include painted (?) blankets decorated in offset quartering (Hibben 1975:Figures 94, 96; see Figure 9.14b, d), openwork shirts and an openwork wraparound garment with gridded designs (Hibben 1975:Frontispiece, right; Smith 1952:Figure 24a, d, g; see Figures 9.6e, 9.9d), a shirt with a checkered design suggestive of tapestry weave (Hibben 1975:Figure 30; see Figure 9.7a), and kilts with possible tapestry or twill-tapestry designs arranged in bifold rotation (Hibben 1975:Figure 72; Smith 1952:Figure 24i; see Figure 9.4d). Other probable painted blankets also exhibit two-dimensional designs (e.g., Hibben 1975: Figure 95; Smith 1952:Figure 45a; see Figure 9.7e, f).

Summary and Conclusions

Most styles of ritual clothing found in the Pueblo IV kiva murals appear to have entered the Southwest as part of an integrated costume repertoire influenced by distant ritual complexes in Mexico. These garment styles probably were not adopted piecemeal, but as components of coherent ritual assemblages, the same way they are used today. Many of the same conventions associated with these garment styles in central and western Mexico—kilts and breechcloths worn by deity impersonators and deities; kilts, sashes, and loincloths worn by warriors or deities associated with rain and death; sleeved shirts associated with warriors and weaponry; the depiction of warriors in profile with their sash ends toward the back—are found in the Pueblo IV murals. Not only did southwestern societies evidently adopt certain ritual clothing styles from the south, they also appear to have appropriated aspects of their ritual meanings. That said, no Pueblo costume assemblage is exactly like any Mexican assemblage. Rather, Pueblo people incorporated these widespread ideas and conventions into their own local frameworks, adapting them to local design styles, weaving traditions, and tastes.

Of all Mesoamerican ritual costume styles, those from central Mexico seem to show the closest connection to the Pueblo IV murals. I have already noted the paucity of available costume information for the region between central Mexico and the U.S. Southwest. Textile remains are scarce in northern Mexico, the U.S.-Mexico borderlands, and the southern Southwest, so most information must be gleaned from more durable artifact classes—ceramic designs and figurines, stone sculptures, and murals, or early historic records. Other than King's (1974) discussion of clothing depicted on Ramos Polychrome vessels, no one to my knowledge has undertaken a study of late precontact clothing styles from the northern third of Mexico. Until this occurs, the spread of southern garment styles to the northern Southwest will remain poorly understood. Likely, the Classic period Hohokam and the political center of Paquimé played a critical role in the transfer of southern ideas, garment styles, and iconography and symbolism to Pueblo societies in the northern Southwest.

While the people of Pottery Mound, Kuaua, Awat'ovi, and Kawaika'a seem to have participated in a broadly shared ritual system, they expressed their rituals through slightly different, regionally based, styles of ceremonial dress. Before discussing the differences, let us review what conventions were shared. Considering first just the pre–A.D. 1500 assemblage from Pottery Mound and Antelope Mesa, we find the same basic garment categories depicted: kilts, sashes, shirts, mantas, leggings, and so on. Pottery Mound, Kawaika'a, and Awat'ovi all have black garments

FIGURE 9.15

Types of garments with negative-painted or resist-dye design, at different sites.

☐ **Kilts**   ☐ **Wraparound garments**
☐ **Shirts/tunics**   ☐ **Shoulder blankets**
☐ **Manta dresses**

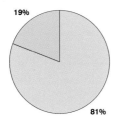

a. Types of Pottery Mound garments with negative-painted or resist-dye designs (n = 21).

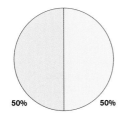

b Types of Kawaika'a garments with negative-painted or resist-dye designs (n = 2).

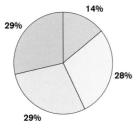

c Types of early Awat'ovi garments with negative-painted or resist-dye designs (n = 7).

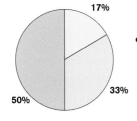

d Types of late Awat'ovi garments with negative-painted or resist-dye designs (n = 6).

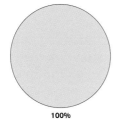

e Types of Kuaua garments with negative-painted or resist-dye designs (n = 3).

decorated in negative painting or tie-dye, and all depict painted blankets hanging on walls. Except for one female at Pottery Mound that appears to be deceased, all identifiable female figures from these three sites are depicted in the frontal position. When tassels are depicted on female wraparound garments, they are shown on the wearer's right (viewer's left), and when sashes are depicted with them, they are tied on the wearer's left (viewer's right). In other words, many of the same basic posturing and clothing conventions found in the Pottery Mound murals also occur at the pre–A.D. 1500 Antelope Mesa sites.

Despite these basic similarities between the Pottery Mound and early Antelope Mesa murals, there are also some important, more subtle, regional differences. The first, and in my mind the most significant, relates to the categories of garments to which these resist-dye or negative-painted designs were applied. At Pottery Mound, most of these designs were applied to women's manta dresses and men's kilts (Figure 9.15a). In contrast, men's kilts decorated in this manner were rare at Awat'ovi and nonexistent at Kawaika'a (Figure 9.15b, c). At the latter site, these designs were applied to what appear to be a man's tunic and a woman's wraparound garment (Figure 9.15b). Although the early and late Awat'ovi murals depict a large number of black tie-dyed garments, only one is a man's kilt. Rather, it is shoulder blankets, tunics, and women's wraparound garments that show most of this iconography at Awat'ovi (Figure 9.15c–d). Furthermore, although the Pottery Mound garments exhibit negative-painted/resist-dye designs, and designs that combine negative painting/resist- and tie-dye, none are decorated exclusively with tie-dye (that is, dot-in-a-square) motifs. In contrast, tie-dye designs are common at the Antelope Mesa sites, where examples of all three conventions are found.

Another striking difference concerns the manner of depicting female clothing. At Pottery Mound, most females wear their manta dresses over one shoulder and under the other with a sash belt tied around the waist, in the historic Pueblo style. All of these dresses are black and some are negatively patterned. At pre–A.D. 1500 Kawaika'a and Awat'ovi, female and dual-gendered figures wear their dresses wrapped around their upper torsos and under their arms, often with a highly placed sash. Not only is this a different convention from Pottery Mound, it is also completely different from the way in which Hopi women have worn their manta dresses for the past several hundred years. The only figures dressed in this manner at

Pottery Mound are two "corn maidens" who appear to be dual gendered and show strong Sikyatki influence.

Another major contrast is the far greater use of negative-painted or resist-dye decoration in Pottery Mound costuming (Figure 9.16a) compared to a greater emphasis on structural patterning, woven-in, or needlework designs at the Antelope Mesa sites (Figure 9.16b–d). Especially prior to A.D. 1500, when embroidery or supplementary weft began to eclipse many of the more complex weaves, there appears to be a wider array of fabric structures depicted in the Antelope Mesa murals than at Pottery Mound. Some of these techniques have antecedents in the Kayenta region, others in the southern deserts, suggesting a melding of northern and southern textile traditions at the Hopi region in early Pueblo IV (Webster and Loma'omvaya 2004). The early Antelope Mesa and Pottery Mound costumes also differ in their choice of background color—the Pottery Mound assemblage being predominantly black, Awat'ovi showing a greater use of white, and the Kawaika'a assemblage exhibiting the widest variability in color overall (Figure 9.17a–d). At Hopi and many of the other pueblos, this black/white dichotomy in textiles persisted into historic times, with white (cotton) and blue-black indigo-dyed (wool) versions of most garment styles produced (Whiting 1977:415–16).

Kawaika'a really is the "in-between" site as far as Pottery Mound and the Antelope Mesa sites are concerned. Pottery Mound and Kawaika'a share a number of conventions not found in the Awat'ovi murals, including fur and painted kilts and a distinctive style of two-color edging (see Figure 9.11). These commonalities suggest a closer relationship between Pottery Mound and Kawaika'a than between Pottery Mound and Awat'ovi. Still, there is no question that Kawaika'a is an Antelope Mesa site. This is especially true in regard to the depiction of male figures at Kawaika'a and Awat'ovi, where more than half of the male figures wearing sashes, many of whom appear to be warriors, are shown in profile with their sashes hanging toward the back. Only 28 percent of the Pottery Mound figures with sashes are depicted in this manner. The general pattern at Antelope Mesa was to show male figures in profile, female figures frontally. Although Pottery Mound and Antelope Mesa share the same pattern of positioning females, the males at Pottery Mound are positioned in more diverse ways.

The late site of Kuaua is a world apart from these other artistic traditions. Nearly all of the Kuaua figures appear in frontal view. Kuaua also has the most limited costume repertoire of any site, with most garments solid

FIGURE 9.16

Types of garments with various methods of costume decoration, excluding sashes, at different sites.

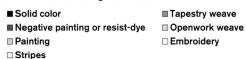

■ Solid color ▨ Tapestry weave
▨ Negative painting or resist-dye ▢ Openwork weave
▢ Painting ▢ Embroidery
▢ Stripes

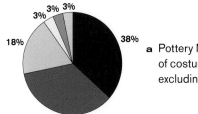

a Pottery Mound methods of costume decoration, excluding sashes (n = 60).

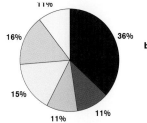

b Kawaika'a methods of costume decoration, excluding sashes (n = 19).

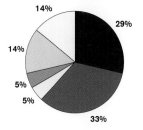

c Early Awat'ovi methods of costume decoration, excluding sashes (n = 21).

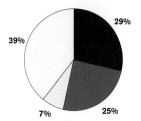

d Late Awat'ovi methods of costume decoration, excluding sashes (n = 28).

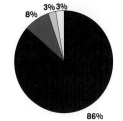

e Kuaua methods of costume decoration, excluding sashes (n = 37).

FIGURE 9.17
Predominant garment colors by types of garments, excluding sashes, at different sites.

■ Black   □ Bicolored
□ White   ■ Multicolored
■ Other

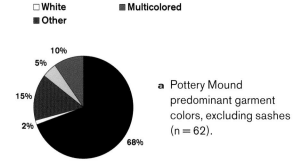

a Pottery Mound predominant garment colors, excluding sashes (n = 62).

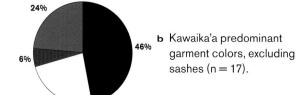

b Kawaika'a predominant garment colors, excluding sashes (n = 17).

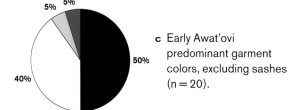

c Early Awat'ovi predominant garment colors, excluding sashes (n = 20).

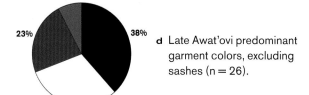

d Late Awat'ovi predominant garment colors, excluding sashes (n = 26).

e Kuaua predominant garment colors, excluding sashes (n = 37).

black, and decoration typically limited to a contrasting selvage or tassels (see Figures 9.15e, 9.16e, 9.17e). Only 13 percent of the kilts have surface designs, and only two display lightninglike motifs or prominent white circles. Most of the resist-dye designs appear to depict static constellations. There are no fancy shirts, kilts, or mantas at Kuaua, and no Hopi-style rain sashes.

Not surprisingly, it is with Pottery Mound that Kuaua finds its closest connection. Although the Kuaua murals appear to postdate the major occupation of Pottery Mound, and the two sites exhibit vastly different costume assemblages, there is evidence of cultural continuity between them. Both emphasize the use of black cloth and negatively patterned resist-dye designs over other colors and techniques. Both also frequently depict the upper edge of the kilt above the sash (see Figure 9.13), a stylistic convention rarely seen in the Antelope Mesa murals.

What do these differences in ritual clothing styles suggest about the production and exchange of ritual textiles at Pottery Mound, Antelope Mesa, and Kuaua during the late prehispanic period? In my view, the evidence suggests that most of these textiles were locally produced within their respective communities. Pottery Mound, Kawaika'a, Awat'ovi, and Kuaua all had evidence of loom holes (Crotty 1995; Dutton 1963:27; Smith 1972; Webster 1997), which indicates that the weaving of textiles on upright looms was practiced at all of these sites. Moreover, early Spanish accounts describe both the Hopi Mesas and the Middle Rio Grande as important centers of cotton production and weaving at the time of European contact (Webster 1997; 2000). Sixteenth-century chroniclers described the wearing of elaborately "painted" and "embroidered" shirts, kilts, skirts, and blankets by the Piros and Southern Tiwas of the Middle Rio Grande (Hammond and Rey 1966:85), indicating that Pottery Mound was not unique among the Eastern Pueblos in its use of highly decorated textiles.

If the painted and tie-dyed textiles depicted in the kiva murals were anything like the archaeological examples from the Kayenta region, then all would have started their lives as plain-weave cloth. Plain weaves are the easiest fabrics to make and require the least amount of specialized weaving knowledge. Given the likelihood that cotton was locally available in both regions and the fact that all of these sites contained evidence of loom holes, I see no reason why all of the plain-weave fabrics for these painted and tie-dye textiles could not have been made within each respective community.

An even more convincing case for local production is suggested by the fact that different categories of garments tend to be decorated with negative-painted or resist-dye designs at Pottery Mound, Antelope Mesa, and Kuaua. This suggests that different social conventions governed decisions about the proper types of garments that should bear these designs. A casual examination of these negative-painted/resist-dye designs also reveals the presence of different design elements and compositions at these sites. Given that garments decorated with these designs varied across regions, and the designs themselves were different, this suggests that these negative-painted/resist-dye designs were applied within each community according to local taste.

A similar argument can be made for the painted blankets at Pottery Mound. Although several exhibit the same offset-quartering layout as found in archaeological examples from the Kayenta region (Haury 1945), the design bands incorporate local designs found on Rio Grande pottery. This suggests that these designs were applied by painters familiar with local design aesthetics.

Thus, the most intriguing question may not be who was weaving these painted and tie-dyed textiles, but who was decorating them and how this skill was transmitted (see also Hays-Gilpin and LeBlanc, this volume). Nearly all known archaeological examples of painted and tie-dyed textiles come from Sinagua and Kayenta sites (e.g., Dixon 1956; Guernsey 1931; Haury 1945). This suggests that the painting of blankets and production of tie-dyed textiles during Pueblo III was largely a Western Pueblo specialty. Our perception may be skewed because so few decorated textiles have been recovered from Eastern Pueblo sites, but there is no question that these decorative techniques were important in the west. If I am correct that the cloth for these painted and tie-dyed garments was locally woven and decorated at Pottery Mound and, by extension, other sites in the Rio Grande, then who was decorating these garments? Did Western Pueblo—perhaps Keresan—ritual specialists proficient in these techniques introduce this painting and dyeing technology to Pottery Mound and other villages in the Rio Grande? Did Eastern Pueblo ritual specialists learn these techniques from practitioners in the west and bring them back to the Rio Grande? Or did

this technology spread northward along the Rio Grande from the Paquimé region, where no examples of painted or resist-dyed textiles have been found, but their presence is inferred from ceramic designs? I can offer no answers to these questions but provide some insights from the post-contact period that might help explain the presence of the fancier textiles at Pottery Mound.

Early Spanish accounts suggest that an extensive cotton weaving industry existed in the Rio Grande during Pueblo IV (Webster 1997; 2000). However, the relative lack of structurally complex textile depictions in the Pottery Mound and Kuaua murals suggests that this production was largely focused on the manufacture of plain-weave cloth. Plain-weave textiles have been recovered archaeologically from a number of Pueblo IV sites in the Rio Grande, but no intricate structural weaves have been found (Webster 1997; 2000). Archaeological textiles from the Kayenta region, together with the textile evidence from the Antelope Mesa murals, point to the Western Pueblo region, including the Hopi area, as a major locus of complex weaving technology and specialized textile production in Pueblo III and Pueblo IV. While it is likely that the painted and tie-dyed textiles in the Pottery Mound and Kuaua murals were locally woven and decorated, it is also likely that the more complex weaves—textiles like the tapestry or twill-tapestry kilt depicted in Figure 9.4d and perhaps the openwork shirt depicted in Figure 9.6d—were acquired in trade from the west. Alternately, they could have been made by Western Pueblo weavers residing at these sites.

If Western Pueblo weavers were supplying intricately woven ritual textiles to Pottery Mound and other communities in the east, what was going back in return? Historic accounts identify the Middle Rio Grande as an important source of turquoise, feathers, pigments, and other esoteric objects to the Hopi villages. Frequently, these goods were exchanged for woven textiles (Beaglehole 1937:84; Parsons 1936:1015). The mural depictions suggest that this exchange pattern may be of considerable antiquity, dating back at least as far as the fifteenth century. By combining the textile and mural evidence with data from other media, we may yet arrive at a fuller picture of the social and economic interactions of these Eastern and Western Pueblo communities. ⁙

NOTES

1. The American Museum of Natural History has five painted cotton cloth fragments that were recovered from an unidentified site in the Pinaleño Mountains, ca. 1940. The fragments, catalog number 29.1/9271 from accession 1940–1984, are decorated with brick red, blue-green, and brown-black paint, the same general color palette used to decorate the polychrome blanket from Painted Cave shown in Figure 9.14a. The fragments are small, and a design cannot be discerned. Based on other evidence (e.g., perforated plates and Pueblo-style architecture) for Kayenta migrants in this area in the mid- to late A.D. 1200s, it is possible that this textile was made by migrants from the Kayenta area.

2. Editor's note: See Chapter 8 for mention of manta dresses pictured in Tompiro rock art.

REFERENCES CITED

Anawalt, Patricia R.

1981 *Indian Clothing before Cortés: Mesoamerican Costumes from the Codices.* University of Oklahoma Press, Norman.

1990 The Emperor's Cloak: Aztec Pomp, Toltec Circumstances. *American Antiquity* 55(2):291–307.

2000 Textile Research from the Mesoamerican Perspective. In *Beyond Cloth and Cordage: Archaeological Textile Research in the Americas,* edited by Penelope Ballard Drooker and Laurie D. Webster, pp. 205–28. University of Utah Press, Salt Lake City.

Beaglehole, Ernest

1937 *Notes on Hopi Economic Life.* Yale University Publications in Anthropology 15. Yale University, New Haven, Connecticut.

Brody, J. J.

1964 Design Analysis of the Rio Grande Pottery of Pottery Mound, New Mexico. Unpublished Master's thesis, Department of Art History, University of New Mexico, Albuquerque.

2004 *Mimbres Painted Pottery.* Revised edition. School of American Research Press, Santa Fe, New Mexico.

Crotty, Helen K.

1995 Anasazi Mural Art of the Pueblo IV Period, A.D. 1300–1600: Influences, Selective Adaptation, and Cultural Diversity in the Prehistoric Southwest. Unpublished Ph.D. dissertation, Department of Art History, University of California, Los Angeles.

Dixon, Keith A.

1956 *Hidden House: A Cliff Ruin in Sycamore Canyon, Central Arizona.* Museum of Northern Arizona Bulletin 29. Northern Arizona Society of Science and Art, Flagstaff.

Dutton, Bertha P.

1963 *Sun Father's Way: The Kiva Murals of Kuaua, A Pueblo Ruin, Coronado State Monument, New Mexico.* University of New Mexico Press, Albuquerque.

Fenn, Forrest

2004 *The Secrets of San Lazaro Pueblo.* One Horse Land and Cattle Company, Santa Fe, New Mexico.

Fontana, Bernard L.

1999 *A Guide to Contemporary Southwest Indians.* Southwest Parks and Monuments Association, Tucson, Arizona.

Fox, Nancy L.

1978 *Pueblo Weaving and Textile Arts.* Museum of New Mexico Press, Santa Fe.

Guernsey, Samuel J.

1931 *Explorations in Northeastern Arizona.* Papers of the Peabody Museum of American Archaeology and Ethnology Vol. 12, No. 1. Harvard University, Cambridge, Massachusetts.

Hammond, George P., and Agapito Rey

1966 *The Rediscovery of New Mexico, 1580–1594.* University of New Mexico Press, Albuquerque.

Haury, Emil
1945 *Painted Cave, Northeastern Arizona.* Amerind Foundation No. 3. Amerind Foundation, Dragoon, Arizona.

Hibben, Frank C.
1975 *Kiva Art of the Anasazi at Pottery Mound.* KC Publications, Las Vegas, Nevada.

Hough, Walter
1914 *Culture of the Ancient Pueblos of the Upper Gila River Region, New Mexico and Arizona.* United States National Museum Bulletin 87. U.S. Government Printing Office, Washington, D.C.

Keegan, Marcia
1999 *Pueblo People: Ancient Tradition, Modern Lives.* Clear Light Publishers, Santa Fe, New Mexico.

Kent, Kate Peck
1957 *The Cultivation and Weaving of Cotton in the Prehistoric Southwestern United States.* Transactions of the American Philosophical Society Vol. 47, No. 3. American Philosophical Society, Philadelphia.
1983a *Pueblo Indian Textiles.* School of American Research Press, Santa Fe, New Mexico.
1983b *Prehistoric Textiles of the Southwest.* School of American Research Press, Santa Fe, New Mexico.

King, Mary Elizabeth
1974 Medio Period Perishable Artifacts. In *Casas Grandes: A Fallen Trading Center of the Gran Chichimeca*, Vol. 8, by Charles C. Di Peso, John B. Rinaldo, and Gloria J. Fenner, pp. 76–119. Amerind Foundation No. 9. Amerind Foundation, Dragoon, Arizona.
1979 The Prehistoric Textile Industry of Mesoamerica. In *The Junius B. Bird Pre-Columbian Textile Conference*, edited by Ann P. Rowe, Elizabeth P. Benson, and Anne-Louise Schaffer, pp. 265–78. Textile Museum and Dumbarton Oaks, Washington, D.C.

Mastache, Alba Guadalupe
2005 El Tejido en el México Antiguo. In Textiles del México de Ayer y Hoy. *Arqueología* 19:20–31.

Moulard, Barbara L.
1984 *Within the Underworld Sky: Mimbres Ceramic Art in Context.* Twelvetrees Press, Pasadena, California.

Ortiz, Alfonso
1969 *The Tewa World: Space, Time, Being, and Becoming in an Pueblo Society.* University of Chicago Press, Chicago.

Parsons, Elsie Clews
1936 *Hopi Journal of Alexander M. Stephen.* 2 vols. Columbia University Press, New York.

Pond, Gordon G.
1966 A Painted Kiva near Winslow, Arizona. *American Antiquity* 31(4):555–58.

Roediger, Virginia M.
1941 *Ceremonial Costumes of the Pueblo Indians: Their Evolution, Fabrication, and Significance in the Prayer Drama.* University of California Press, Berkeley.

Schaafsma, Polly
2000 *Warrior, Shield, and Star: Imagery and Ideology of Pueblo Warfare.* Western Edge Press, Santa Fe, New Mexico.

Smith, Watson
1952 *Kiva Mural Decorations at Awatovi and Kawaika-a.* Reports of the Awatovi Expedition No. 5. Papers of the Peabody Museum of American Archaeology and Ethnology Vol. 37. Harvard University, Cambridge, Massachusetts.
1972 *Prehistoric Kivas of Antelope Mesa, Northeastern Arizona.* Reports of the Awatovi Expedition No. 9. Papers of the Peabody Museum of American Archaeology and Ethnology Vol. 39, No. 1. Harvard University, Cambridge, Massachusetts.

Teague, Lynn S.
1998 *Textiles in Southwestern Prehistory.* University of New Mexico Press, Albuquerque.

Townsend, Richard F. (editor)
2005 *Casas Grandes and the Ceramic Art of the Ancient Southwest.* Art Institute of Chicago, Chicago, and Yale University Press, New Haven, Connecticut.

Webster, Laurie D.

1997 *Effects of European Contact on Textile Production and Exchange in the North American Southwest: A Pueblo Case Study.* Ph.D. dissertation, Department of Anthropology, University of Arizona, Tucson. University Microfilms, Ann Arbor.

2000 The Economics of Pueblo Textile Production and Exchange in Colonial New Mexico. In *Beyond Cloth and Cordage: Current Approaches to Archaeological Textile Research in the Americas*, edited by Penelope Ballard Drooker and Laurie D. Webster, pp. 179–204. University of Utah Press, Salt Lake City.

Webster, Laurie D., Kelley Hays-Gilpin, and Polly Schaafsma

2006 A New Look at Tie-dye and the Dot-in-a-Square Motif in the Prehispanic Southwest. *Kiva* 71(3):317–48.

Webster, Laurie D., and Micah Loma'omvaya

2004 Textiles, Baskets, and Hopi Cultural Identity. In *Identity, Feasting, and the Archaeology of the Greater Southwest: Proceedings of the 2002 Southwest Symposium*, edited by Barbara J. Mills, pp. 74–92. University Press of Colorado, Boulder.

Whiting, Alfred F.

1977 Hopi Textiles. In *Ethnographic Textiles of the Western Hemisphere*, edited by Irene Emery and Patricia Fiske, pp. 413–19. Irene Emery Roundtable on Museum Textiles, 1976 Proceedings. Textile Museum, Washington, D.C.

Wright, Barton

1979 *Hopi Material Culture.* Heard Museum, Phoenix, and Northland Press, Flagstaff, Arizona.

CHAPTER TEN

An Assessment of the Archaeofaunal Remains from Pottery Mound

Tiffany C. Clark

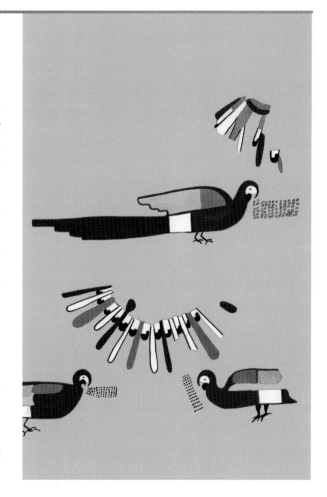

Introduction

It has long been argued that Pottery Mound was a major procurement and trading center for birds and bird products in the Lower Rio Puerco district during the Pueblo IV period (Emslie 1981; Emslie and Hargrave 1978). Much of the evidence for this argument derives from the reportedly large and diverse avifaunal assemblage that was collected by Frank Hibben during his excavations at the site in the 1950s and 1960s. Results of a more recent analysis of archaeofaunal remains recovered from stratified midden deposits by the University of New Mexico's field school in 1979 call into question the initial characterization of Pottery Mound as a specialized bird processing and distribution site. Examination of the unmodified animal bone assemblage from these latter excavations reveals that faunal procurement practices at Pottery Mound were primarily focused on the exploitation of subsistence taxa and in particular on small-sized mammalian species. Although bird remains increase slightly over time, avifauna comprises a relatively small proportion of the identified assemblage throughout the occupational span of the pueblo. Comparison with other contemporaneous sites suggests that the procurement of animal resources at Pottery Mound fits a fairly generalized faunal utilization pattern that typifies much of the Rio Grande region during the Pueblo IV period.

The chapter begins with a description of the recovery procedures, analytical techniques, and quantification methods used in the archaeofaunal study. An overview of the taxonomic composition of the Pottery Mound assemblage is then presented and the diversity and abundance of various fauna are described. Temporal variability in the distribution of the major taxonomic groups is then evaluated in order to examine changes over time in the relative importance of different animal resources. Broader patterns of faunal procurement are investigated and used to assess regional disparities in the subsistence strategies that were pursued by the residents of Pottery Mound and other contemporaneous Rio Grande villages.

Analytical Methods

Collection and Analysis

The faunal remains analyzed in this study derive from excavations that were undertaken by the University of New Mexico in 1979 (Cordell 1980). The materials were recovered from a 5 x 5 m test unit that had been placed in a midden area along the northern edge of the site (see Figure 1.3 and Appendix A). Deposits in this area were characterized by a relatively dense accumulation of stratified trash that had depths up to 3.4 m (Eckert 2003). Due to the large volume of animal bone that was obtained from these excavations, the present analysis focused only on those materials from the northwest quadrant of the test unit.

Excavation notes on file at the University of New Mexico indicate that all fill removed from the test unit was screened through 1/4 in mesh. Faunal material recovered from these screened contexts was bagged by provenience and later cleaned and sorted by taxon in the field laboratory. During this initial sort, bone tools were removed from the rest of the assemblage and bagged separately.[1]

Taxonomic identifications of the unmodified animal bone were determined through comparison with modern specimens from the reference collection that is housed in the Department of Anthropology at Arizona State University. Published reference manuals were also relied on in some cases to identify taxon not represented in the comparative collection (Gilbert 1980; Gilbert et al. 1985; Olsen 1964; 1968; Schmid 1972). During the analysis, each specimen was identified to its lowest taxonomic level. If identification to genus or species was not possible, more generalized taxonomic categories, such as family or order,

were employed. Mammal, bird, and reptilian specimens were considered "identifiable" if they could at least be assigned to the order level; fish remains were determined to be identifiable at the class level. Unidentifiable remains, largely consisting of long bone shaft fragments or small pieces of poorly preserved bone, lacked distinguishing anatomical characteristics that allowed identification to a taxonomic order. Specimens determined to be unidentifiable were separated by class (for example, Mammalia or Aves) and then sorted into rough size categories based on the shape and thickness of the bone.

Once identified to taxon, a variety of information was recorded for each specimen including anatomical element, side, completeness, portion, and degree of fusion. In addition, different types of natural and cultural modifications were also coded. All of the archaeofaunal data was then entered into a computer database.

Quantification

The faunal data were quantified using two different methods, the Number of Identifiable Specimens (NISP) and the Minimum Number of Individuals (MNI). In this analysis, NISP was used as the primary method of quantification. The NISP was determined by totaling the number of identified bone fragments at or below various taxonomic levels (i.e., class, order, family, and species) within an assemblage.

The NISP quantification method has been criticized on a number of grounds (Grayson 1984:20–24; Klein and Cruz-Uribe 1984:24–26). Researchers have argued that disparities in NISP counts among species may not always reflect differential exploitation patterns because the number of identifiable bone elements can vary substantially by taxon. In addition, taphonomic factors may also significantly impact the number of identifiable specimens per taxon. Bones that are susceptible to postdepositional breakage may have inflated NISP counts since a single fragmented bone may produce two or more countable pieces. Similarly, the bones of large mammals may be partitioned into a greater number of pieces than the elements from small game animals either by deliberate breakage during processing activities or by chance (Grayson 1984:21). In both of these cases, the interdependence of the units being counted may skew the NISP values so that they do not directly reflect the relative number of animals that contributed to the faunal assemblage. Lastly, the NISP can overemphasize the importance of species whose whole carcass was brought back to

Table 10.1. NISP and MNI Counts for the Major Taxonomic Groups by Rank Order

Rank	NISP (n)	MNI (n)
1	Lagomorph (4,475)	Lagomorph (136)
2	Bird (530)	Bird (37)
3	Rodent (361)	Rodent (36)
4	Carnivore (263)	Carnivore (3)
5	Artiodactyl (201)	Artiodactyl (2)
6	*Fish* (39)	Reptile (2)
7	Reptile (5)	*Fish* (1)

Note: Italicized taxonomic groups denote discrepancies between counting methods.

the site compared with animals that were dismembered at the kill site and only had selective portions retrieved.

Due to the potential problems associated with NISP, MNI was also calculated for the Pottery Mound assemblage. As discussed in depth by Grayson (1984:28–34), MNI is not without its own shortcomings. In this study, I primarily used MNI as a comparative tool with which to assess the accuracy of the NISP in quantifying relative taxonomic abundance. I assume that if the ordinal scale measure of taxonomic abundance was roughly similar between these two quantification methods, then it can be concluded that the NISP counts approximately reflect the contribution of the different taxa that are present in the faunal assemblage (Grayson 1984:96–110). The MNI for each genus and species was calculated using the most frequently occurring paired (i.e., left or right) element within the computerized database. Once individual MNI values were obtained, the data were combined into larger taxonomic groups (artiodactyls, lagomorphs, rodents, carnivores, birds, reptiles, and fish) and ordinally ranked. Fragments that could not be identified to genus were generally excluded from this analysis.

Comparisons of NISP and MNI counts indicate that the major taxonomic groups maintain approximately the same rank order with both methods of quantification (Table 10.1). A single discrepancy can be observed, however, in the rank of fish. This taxonomic group exhibits a small MNI value in comparison to its NISP count. The disparity reflects a basic problem with how the MNI values are determined. Specifically, MNI counts may underestimate taxa that contain relatively few paired limb elements. In the case of fish bone, the bulk of the preserved remains from Pottery Mound are composed

of rib and vertebrae fragments, neither of which can be used to calculate MNI values. A visual inspection of the identified fish remains, however, reveals discernible size differences among the specimens that suggest more than one individual was present in the assemblage. It may thus be concluded that the single NISP and MNI rank order discrepancy is likely the result of methodological shortcomings in the MNI quantification technique. Given this, the exclusive use of NISP counts in the present analysis can be considered both appropriate and valid.

Taxonomic Composition

A relatively large and well-preserved faunal assemblage was recovered from the northwest quadrant of the test unit at Pottery Mound. Of the 9,020 specimens that are examined in this study (Table 10.2), approximately 65 percent of remains can be considered identifiable. The majority of specimens are mammalian species (90 percent), with birds (9 percent), fish (1 percent), and reptiles (<1 percent) constituting relatively small proportions of the assemblage. At least 34 taxa are represented in the assemblage including 19 mammals, 12 birds, 2 reptiles, and a single fish species.

The Pottery Mound assemblage consists of fauna that are commonly associated with the grassland vegetative communities that have been documented historically in the Lower Puerco River valley (Brown 1994; Dortignac 1963). Terrestrial species make up the bulk of the zooarchaeological remains. The presence of fish, turtle, and waterbird suggests that Pottery Mound residents also occasionally exploited the aquatic and riparian habitats that would have been found prehistorically along the Rio Puerco.

Table 10.2. Distribution of Identified Archaeofaunal Remains from Pottery Mound

Scientific Name	Common Name	NISP	% NISP	MNI
Class Mammalia	**Mammals**	**5,300**	**90.2**	**177**
Order Artiodactyla	Artiodactyls			
Indeterminate Artiodactyla	Indeterminate Artiodactyls	172	2.9	n/a
Odocoileus sp.	Deer	4	<0.1	1
Antilocapra americana	Pronghorn Antelope	25	0.4	1
Order Lagomorpha	Rabbits and Hares			
Indeterminate Lagomorpha	Indeterminate Rabbits and Hares	64	1.1	n/a
Sylvilagus sp.	Cottontail	1,397	23.8	48
Lepus californicus	Black-tailed Jackrabbit	3,014	51.3	88
Order Rodentia	Rodents			
Indeterminate Rodentia	Indeterminate Rodents	107	1.8	n/a
Spermophilus variegates	Rock Squirrel	3	0.5	1
Ammospermophilus sp.	Ground Squirrel	19	0.3	1
Geomys bursarius	Plains Pocket Gopher	33	0.6	5
Onychomys leucogaster	Northern Grasshopper Mouse	2	<0.1	1
Dipodomys sp.	Kangaroo Rat	21	0.4	5
Reithrodontomys megalotis	Western Harvest Mouse	2	<0.1	1
Peromyscus sp.	White-Footed Mouse	2	<0.1	1
Eutamius sp.	Chipmunk	2	<0.1	1
Neotoma sp.	Wood Rat	133	2.3	14
Peromyscus zibethicus	Deer Mouse	3	0.1	3
Cynomys sp.	Prairie Dog	34	0.6	3
Order Carnivora	Carnivores			
Indeterminate Small Carnivora	Small-Sized Carnivores	1	<0.1	n/a
Indeterminate Large Carnivora	Large-Sized Carnivores	48	0.8	n/a
Canis sp.	Coyote/Dog	203	3.5	n/a
Canis lupus	Wolf	1	<0.1	n/a
Canis familiaris	Domestic Dog	8	<0.1	1
Urocyon cinereoargenteus	Gray Fox	1	<0.1	1
Lynx rufus	Bobcat	1	<0.1	1
Class Aves	**Birds**	**529**	**9.0**	**36**
Order Anseriformes	Ducks, Geese, and Swans			
Anas sp.	Duck	4	<0.1	1
Order Falconiformes	Hawks and Falcons			

Table 10.2. Distribution of Identified Archaeofaunal Remains from Pottery Mound

Scientific Name	Common Name	NISP	% NISP	MNI
Indeterminate Falconiformes	Indeterminate Hawks and Falcons	1	<0.1	n/a
Family Accipitridae	Eagles and Hawks			
Indeterminate Accipitridae	Indeterminate Eagles and Hawks	2	<0.1	n/a
Accipiter sp.	Hawk	1	<0.1	1
Aquila chrysaetos	Golden Eagle	1	<0.1	3
Buteo sp.	Hawk	17	0.3	1
Family Falconidae	Falcons			
Indeterminate Falconidae	Indeterminate Falcons	1	<0.1	n/a
Falco sparverius	American Kestrel	4	<0.1	1
Order Galliformes	Gallinaceous Birds			
Callipepla sp.	Quail	31	0.5	4
Meleagris gallopavo	Turkey	421	7.2	17
Order Columbiformes	Pigeons and Doves			
Zenaida macroura	Mourning Dove	8	0.1	4
Order Gruiformes	Cranes, Rails, and Allies			
Grus sp.	Crane	1	<0.1	1
Order Strigiformes	Owls			
Bubo virginianus	Great Horned Owl	2	<0.1	1
Order Piciformes	Flickers and Woodpeckers			
Indeterminate Piciformes	Indeterminate Flickers	1	<0.1	1
Order Passeriformes	Perching Birds			
Indeterminate Passeriformes	Indeterminate Perching Birds	26	0.4	n/a
Indeterminate Corvidae	Indeterminate Jays and Crows	6	0.1	n/a
Corvus corax	Common Raven	2	<0.1	1
Class Osteichthyes	**Fish**	**39**	**0.7**	**1**
Indeterminate Osteichthyes	Indeterminate Fish	37	0.6	n/a
Catostomus sp.	Sucker	2	<0.1	1
Class Reptilia	**Reptiles**	**5**	**0.1**	**2**
Order Testudines	Turtles			
Indeterminate Testudines	Indeterminate Turtles	4	<0.1	1
Order Squamata	Lizards and Snakes			
Pituophis melanoleucus	Gopher Snake	1	<0.1	1
TOTAL		**5,873**	**100.0**	**216**

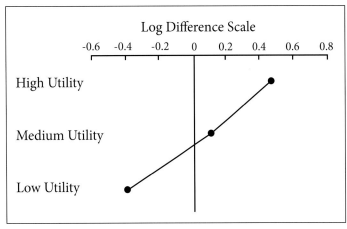

FIGURE 10.1

Ratio diagram of artiodactyl element utility groups based on NISP.

Mammalian Fauna

ARTIODACTYLS

Large game taxa account for 3.4 percent (201 specimens) of the identified bone at Pottery Mound. Although artiodactyl remains comprise a relatively small proportion of the overall assemblage, the large amount of usable meat that is associated with these animals inevitably made them an important resource. Two artiodactyl genera have historically been found in the Puerco River valley—pronghorn antelope (Antilocapra americana) and deer (Odocoileus sp.) (Henderson and Harrington 1914). Of these, antelope constitute the overwhelming majority of artiodactyl specimens from Pottery Mound. Because of the high degree of anatomical similarity between mule deer (Odocoileus hemionus) and white-tailed deer (Odocoileus virginianus), the few deer elements that are present in the assemblage were assigned to the genus level.

The high frequency of antelope in the archaeofaunal assemblage indicates that hunters at Pottery Mound procured most of their large game from grassland areas that would have surrounded the village prehistorically. Unlike deer, which tend to inhabit piñon-juniper woodlands and more montane environments, pronghorn antelope are adapted to open grassland and savannah-like habitats (Lubinski and Herren 2000:4). The general scarcity of deer in the assemblage suggests that rather than acquiring artiodactyls from upland locales, such as those found in the nearby Cebolleta Mountains, hunters preferred to procure large game from the extensive grasslands of the Lower Rio Puerco valley (Brown 1994).

A review of the ethnographic literature indicates that in the Puebloan Southwest, antelope was communally hunted either using game drives or surrounds with bows and arrows (Gnabasik 1981:100). In contrast, deer tend to be more successfully procured by individual hunters (Lange 1959:130–31). Given these different procurement strategies, the abundance of antelope bone at Pottery Mound suggests that communal types of hunting behavior were the predominant technique used to obtain large game resources.

Element representation data suggest that while the inhabitants of Pottery Mound may have hunted pronghorns in the grassland areas around the pueblo, they also traveled farther afield to procure large game. Researchers have argued that increased transport costs associated with long-distance hunting are expected to result in a disproportionate amount of high-meat-yielding elements being brought back to the village from the kill site (Bayham 1982; Binford 1978; Metcalf and Jones 1988; Speth 1983). This pattern, which is referred to as the "schlep" effect, is based on the assumption that long-distance hunters will be more selective in the body parts that they transport to their primary settlement and will discard portions of the carcass that contain little meat, fat, or other unusable parts (Binford 1978; 1981; Perkins and Daly 1968). Metcalf and Jones (1988) have developed the Food Utility Index (FUI) to study this procedure. The index serves to rank bone elements in relation to one another based on the weight of utilizable meat, fat, and marrow.

To evaluate the evidence for long-distance hunting at Pottery Mound, FUI values are first used to group artiodactyl bone elements in the assemblage into high, medium, and low utility categories.[2] Bone frequencies in these archaeologically derived utility groups are then standardized against data from a complete undisturbed

Table 10.3. Distribution of Artiodactyl Elements with Cut Marks at Pottery Mound

No.	Element	Function	NISP (percent)
1	Metapodial	Disarticulate toes, remove hide from leg	1 (6.7)
2	Pelvis	Disarticulate lower hind leg at hock joints	1 (6.7)
3	Rib shaft	Defleshing of rib slab	8 (53.3)
4	Sacrum	Defleshing the back	1 (6.7)
5	Lumbar vertebrae	Defleshing the back	2 (13.3)
6	Cervical vertebrae	Defleshing of neck and/or decapitation	1 (6.7)
7	Cranium	Decapitation	1 (6.7)

Source: Adapted from Lang and Harris 1984:Table 11.

antelope skeleton using a logged ratio technique developed by Reitz and Wing (1999:208–13). In this method, ratios of observed to expected specimens are obtained by subtracting the logged percentage of each utility group in the archaeological collection from the logged percentage of this same category in a complete skeleton.[3] The logged ratio values of the three utility groups are plotted in Figure 10.1. Positive values indicate elements that are more abundant than expected for a complete skeleton; negative values denote body parts that are underrepresented in the archaeological assemblage.

The artiodactyl elements in the Pottery Mound assemblage display a pattern that is suggestive of long-distance hunting. High-meat-yielding parts of the artiodactyl carcass are overrepresented in the assemblage, whereas those elements that contain little meat or marrow exhibit far lower frequencies than expected. These findings suggest hunters from Pottery Mound were consistently bringing back the most highly valued portions of the carcass to the village and leaving behind lower quality elements at the kill site.

Most of the cut marks that are found on artiodactyl bones are the result of butchering activities (Figure 10.2; Table 10.3). The ways in which large game carcasses were processed at Pottery Mound are quite similar to those observed at other Rio Grande pueblos, including Arroyo Hondo (Lang and Harris 1984:78–85) and Gran Quivira (Eshbaugh 1992: 28–35). The presence of cut marks on the distal portions of the metapodial (No. 1) likely represent the disarticulation of the toes and lower limbs incurred during the removal of the hide. Dismemberment of the lower hind shanks from the torso would have produced

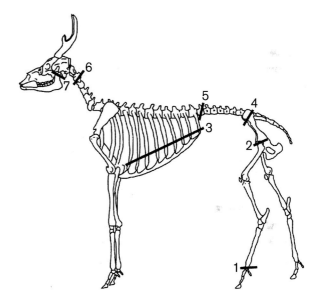

FIGURE 10.2

Location of butchering marks on artiodactyl bone at Pottery Mound. (Adapted from Lang and Harris 1984: Figure 11.)

cut marks similar to those seen on the acetabulum of the pelvis (No. 2). Lang and Harris (1984:80) attribute butchering marks on rib shafts, lumbar vertebrae, and the sacrum (Nos. 3–5) to the defleshing of the back and rib slab. Finally, the cut marks observed on the cranium (No. 6) and cervical vertebrae (No. 7) were likely sustained when the head was removed from the rest of the carcass.

Approximately 9 percent of the artiodactyl remains (18 specimens) at Pottery Mound show evidence of burning. Most of these bones are charred black (67 percent), with lower frequencies of bone displaying either white calcination (28 percent) or partial charring (6 percent). The burning of large game bone may relate to preparation for extraction of marrow and grease, as Bonnichsen (1973:9–24) notes that the practice of heating of bones to facilitate splitting results in occasional accidental burning. The occurrence of burned artiodactyl bones in the Pottery Mound assemblage could also be explained by the use of these remains as a source of fuel or by disposal practices that involved the burning of trash deposits.

LAGOMORPHS

The most abundant taxa present in the Pottery Mound assemblage are lagomorphs. In total, 76.2 percent (4,475 specimens) of the identified fauna is assigned to this order. Lagomorphs consist of two genera—black-tailed jackrabbits (Lepus californicus) and cottontails (Sylvilagus sp.). Two species of cottontails presently inhabit this portion of central New Mexico, desert cottontail (S. audubonii) and Nuttall's cottontail (S. nuttallii) (Findley et al. 1975). Given that Nuttall's cottontail is generally found in montane environments, it may be assumed that the majority of cottontails in the Pottery Mound assemblage are desert cottontail.

As can be observed in Table 10.2, jackrabbits are twice as abundant as cottontails in the Pottery Mound assemblage. The lower frequency of cottontail bone probably reflects the lack of suitable environs for this type of lagomorph. It is generally agreed that cottontails prefer areas of dense, low-growing vegetation where they can easily hide from predators (Madsen 1974; Szuter and Bayham 1989). In contrast, jackrabbits favor open environments with sparse vegetation that allows them to flee (Szuter 1991:18–20). Given that the grassland environments of the Lower Rio Puerco region would have provided an ideal habitat for black-tailed jackrabbits, the abundance of this species in the Pottery Mound faunal assemblage is not unexpected and suggests that residents procured most of their small game in the immediate vicinity of the pueblo.

The importance of lagomorphs as a food source is well documented in the prehistoric Southwest. Ethnographic accounts indicate that historic Rio Grande Pueblo groups hunted hares and rabbits using a variety of techniques (Lange 1959; Ortiz 1969; White 1942). These include a surround technique in which lagomorphs are driven into nets by groups of hunters and then killed with throwing sticks and bows and arrows (Gnabasik 1981:107). In addition to communal hunting, lagomorphs were also procured individually by setting traps and snares in agricultural fields.

Little evidence for the butchering of lagomorphs is found in the Pottery Mound assemblage. In total, cut marks were recorded on only three jackrabbit bones. The lack of butchering marks on lagomorph remains is consistent with the ethnographic data, which suggest that the whole rabbit carcass was generally roasted over a fire or boiled (Stevenson 1894; White 1932; 1962). Once cooked, the carcass would have been dismembered by hand (Olsen 1990:92).

Only 2 percent (91 specimens) of the rabbit bone sustained some degree of burn damage. Most of the burned specimens are charred black (53 percent), with lower proportions of bone exhibiting partial charring (26 percent) or white calcination (21 percent). The burning of lagomorph bone may partially be the result of cooking practices. It is expected that when rabbits were roasted over a fire, those peripheral elements that are close to the surface of the skin (for example, crania, distal limbs, and phalanges) would have been scorched or partially burned. As approximately 55 percent of the burned rabbit bone in the Pottery Mound assemblage is composed of peripheral elements, this type of cooking technique appears to have been fairly widely practiced. Other possible explanations for the burning of lagomorph remains include the use of bones as a fuel source or disposal activities in which bone was tossed into a fire after a meal.

RODENTS

A total of 361 specimens, or 6.1 percent of the identified Pottery Mound fauna, is assigned to this taxonomic order. Eleven different genera are represented among the identified taxa. The most common rodent genera, in decreasing order of abundance, are wood rats (Neotoma), prairie dogs (Cynomys), pocket gophers (Geomys), kangaroo rats (Dipodomys), and ground squirrels (Ammospermophilus) (see Table 10.2).

Large-sized rodents (for example, wood rats, prairie

dogs, and squirrels) were often considered to be important game animals among historic Puebloan groups (Henderson and Harrington 1914:19–23; Parsons 1920:59; 1977:95). While rodents were occasionally acquired through communal hunting techniques, similar to those described above for rabbits (Gnabasik 1981:107), generally small game was procured by solitary individuals. The hunting of rodents may have been undertaken during other subsistence activities, such as the gathering of wild plants or the tending of agricultural fields (Rea 1998; Underhill 1936). This practice of "garden hunting" not only served to supplement animal protein in the diet but also helped to rid cultivated fields of pests (Linares 1976).

Although some rodents were undoubtedly used as a food source, some of the small mammal bones recovered from Pottery Mound appear to have been intrusive in origin. This conclusion is based on the fact that many of the smaller-sized rodent taxa (for example, kangaroo rats, pocket gophers, and mice) lack the weathering that tends to be associated with prehistorically derived faunal material. The extremely low occurrence of burning (one specimen), along with the presence of several partially articulated skeletons, also suggests that a portion of the recovered rodent bones derive from animals that died naturally in their burrows.

No butchering marks are found on rodent remains in the Pottery Mound assemblage. The paucity of cut marks is not unexpected as rodents are assumed to be processed in similar ways as lagomorphs, with the entire carcass being roasted or boiled and then dismembered by hand. Szuter (1984:150) has reported that among certain southwestern groups, small rodents may be eaten whole or mashed into a pulp after they are cooked. If these types of processing techniques were used at Pottery Mound, it is expected that little to no trace of rodent consumption would be present in the archaeological record (with the exception of coprolites).

CARNIVORES

Specimens assigned to the order Carnivora comprise approximately 4 percent of the identified fauna (263 specimens) from Pottery Mound. The majority of these remains are from small-sized canids, most of which appear to derive from domestic dogs (Canis familiaris), or possibly coyotes (Canis latrans). Other identified carnivores in the assemblage include a single bone specimen from a wolf (Canis lupus), gray fox (Urocyon cinereoargenteus), and bobcat (Lynx rufus). A number of carnivore

bones could not be assigned to a specific genus or species; these specimens were grouped into small- and large-size categories (see Table 10.2).[4]

According to Tyler (1964), carnivores play an integral role in Puebloan cosmology and mythology. Pueblo groups hunted carnivores for their pelts, which are used in dance costumes, masks, and other ritual paraphernalia (Gnabasik 1981). At Santo Domingo and Jemez Pueblo, for example, fox skins are often part of ceremonial costumes with the pelts hung from a dancer's waist (Lange 1959:139; Parsons 1977:89). Bobcat pelts were used as collars on katsina masks at several Rio Grande pueblos, including San Felipe (White 1932:33), Santo Domingo (White 1974a:113), and Zia (White 1974b:240).

Dogs were one of the few domesticated animals in the prehistoric Puebloan Southwest and ethnographic accounts suggest they were used in a variety of different ways. One of the most common uses of dogs was as pets. For example, Fewkes (1904:27) notes that the Hopi considered dogs to be a "pet rather than a beast of burden. The good qualities of this pet were recognized and recounted in their legends." At the pueblos of Jemez and Hopi, dogs were also sometimes taken along to hunt rabbits and deer (Anell 1969:60–61; Parsons 1977:94–95). Finally, domestic canids were occasionally used as a source of meat (Lang and Harris 1984:89). It is said that the Hopi raised particular types of dogs to be eaten (Bourke 1962:253; Stephen 1936:266, 939). This practice does not appear to have been widespread, however, as Parsons (1970:23) notes that dogs were not considered to be a food source at Taos Pueblo. The presence of several cut marks on domestic dog bones from Pottery Mound suggests that the prehistoric residents of the pueblo may have butchered and eaten these animals during times of subsistence stress.

Approximately 6 percent of the carnivore bone exhibits evidence of burning. Over half of the burned bone is charred black (8 specimens), with substantially lower frequencies of white calcination (4 specimens) or partial charring (3 specimens). The burning of carnivore bone is likely a result of a number of different activities that include cooking, trash disposal, and the use of bones as fuel.

Avian Fauna

Bird remains are the second most abundant taxonomic class in the Pottery Mound assemblage. A total of 529 identified avian bones representing at least 12 different bird species were recorded during analysis.[5] Over half of these remains, 460 specimens or 87 percent of the identified bird assemblage, consists of avifauna that are generally considered to be food sources (Henderson and Harrington 1914:33–46). Identified food taxa include gallinaceous birds, specifically turkey (Meleagris gallopavo) and quail (Callipepla sp.), as well as mourning doves (Zenaida macroura).

Turkeys are the most common avian species at Pottery Mound. Although wild turkeys may have been hunted by village residents, the archaeological evidence suggests that the raising of domestic turkeys was well established in many parts of the Rio Grande region by the Pueblo IV period (Clark 2003a:17; Lang and Harris 1984:101–5; McKusick 1986:10–11; Stubbs and Stallings 1953:46–47). The extent to which domestic turkeys were used as a food source has been a point of debate, however, as some researchers contend that these birds were exclusively raised for their feathers (McKusick 1986:15). Historic Spanish accounts indicate that at the time of contact, a number of the Rio Grande pueblos used turkeys both as a source of raw materials and for food (Hammond 1966:82–83, 98, 102, 129, 135, 142; Hammond and Rey 1929:72, 79; Schroeder 1968:97–101; Schroeder and Matson 1965:100, 112, 115, 145).

Kiva murals at Pottery Mound illustrate the widespread use of turkey feathers in Pueblo IV period ceremonial contexts. Emslie and Hargrave (1978) found that wing, tail, and body feathers of this species were commonly depicted on walls of the ceremonial structures (Hibben 1975:Figures 75, 101). Similar illustrations of turkey feathers have also been identified in the kiva murals at Awat'ovi by Smith (1952:179). The diversity of ways in which the feathers are depicted in the Pottery Mound murals led Emslie and Hargrave (1978) to conclude that they were not associated with one particular use or ceremony. Rather, it appears that turkey feathers may have served a variety of ritually oriented functions during the Pueblo IV period.

Though depictions on kiva murals strongly suggest that turkeys were used for their feathers, the presence of butchered turkey bone in the Pottery Mound assemblage indicates that these large birds were also considered to be a food source. According to Lang and Harris (1984:107), the use of domesticated turkeys would have provided a relatively abundant and dependable source of high-quality meat for aggregated populations faced with limited wild meat resources. Such may have been the case at Pottery Mound, where the low proportion of artiodactyl bone in the assemblage indicates that access to large game was relatively restricted. The distribution of cut marks on turkey remains from the site suggests that these birds

were partially dismembered prior to cooking. The presence of butchering marks on both cervical vertebrae and the distal ends of several tibiotarsi indicates that portions of the carcass that contained little meat (for example, the neck and the lower scaled portion of the leg with the foot) were removed during the initial stages of processing. Cut marks on the humerus and scapula suggest that as the carcass was butchered into smaller parts, the wings were separated from the rest of the body. This type of dismemberment pattern would be expected if turkeys were cooked in pots (Lang and Harris 1984:74). The occurrence of burning on the ends of several long bones, as well as on the outer wing and foot bones, suggests that these large birds may also have been roasted whole over the fire.

Nonfood avian species in the Pottery Mound assemblage fall into three basic categories: songbirds, birds of prey, and waterfowl. Ethnographic data indicate that most of the nonfood birds were procured for their feathers, which would have been used in the manufacture of ceremonial costumes, ritual paraphernalia, and offerings (Gnabasik 1981; Tyler 1979). The lack of butchering marks and relatively low frequency of burning associated with these remains substantiates the conclusion that these species were generally not consumed by the residents of Pottery Mound.

Songbirds are found to be the most abundant nonfood bird with 7 percent (35 specimens) of the identified avian specimens. The majority of these remains were classified to the Corvidae (crows and jays) family in the order Passeriformes (perching birds). A single specimen from a woodpecker (order Piciformes) is also represented in the bird assemblage. Habitat preference information presented by Emslie (1981:856) suggests that most of these songbird species could have been procured in the grassland areas around the village.

The bird of prey species that were identified in the assemblage are also expected to have been locally available. These birds comprise approximately 5 percent (29 specimens) of the identified avian specimens. The majority of these bones consist of hawks, eagles, and falcons (order Falconiformes), along with a small number of owls (order Strigiformes). The most ritually important bird of prey found in the Pottery Mound assemblage is the golden eagle (Aquila chrysaetos). Emslie and Hargrave (1978) note that golden eagle feathers are depicted in a number of the kiva murals at Pottery Mound and suggest that their plumage had a variety of functions. Ethnographic accounts also attest to the ritual importance of golden eagles, with historic Pueblo groups using eagle feathers in rituals related to leadership succession, agricultural productivity, hunting, curing, and war (Gnabasik 1981). While other birds of prey were not considered to be as ritually significant as eagles, hawk and owl plumage may have also been routinely collected by Pueblo groups for use in katsina masks and prayersticks (Lange 1959:476–77, 481–83, 509–10; Stevenson 1894:Plate 32e; White 1974a:117).

Waterfowl species found in the Pottery Mound assemblage include four duck (*Anas* sp.) bones and a cranial fragment from an unidentified crane (*Grus* sp.). A review of the ornithological literature suggests that most of the ducks and cranes that are found in the region today are migratory birds that would have only been in the area during the winter months (Sibley 2000:82–88, 156–57).[6] It is expected that the waterfowl would have been attracted to the marsh areas that existed along the prehistoric banks of the Rio Puerco. The low occurrence of these migratory birds in the Pottery Mound assemblages suggests that waterfowl species were not intensively targeted by hunters but rather were acquired as a result of opportunistic procurement practices. The depiction of waterfowl on the Pottery Mound kiva murals is fairly limited, with a single illustration of a whooping crane (*Grus americana*) reported by Hibben (1975:33). Taken together, these data suggest that waterbirds may not have been as ritually important as some of the other avian taxa at Pottery Mound. Feathers from waterfowl were used, however, to make prayersticks at Santo Domingo (White 1974a:163), Jemez (Parsons 1977:104), and Zuni (Ladd 1963), as well as fetishes at Zia (White 1974b:307).

Fish Remains

The 39 fish bones that were recovered from the midden deposits at Pottery Mound primarily consist of cranial, rib, and vertebral elements from unidentified fish species. The only bones that are identifiable to genera are two operculum fragments, both of which appear to derive from an unidentified sucker (Catostomus sp.). Comparisons with modern specimens indicate that at least some of these fish were quite large in size with one individual having an estimated body length between 40 and 50 cm.

Ethnographic data suggest that fish were a minor food source for many of the Rio Grande Pueblo groups (Gnabasik 1981:243–44). Snow's (2002) summary of the bony fish remains recovered from prehistoric archaeological sites in New Mexico, however, suggests that this pattern may be a historic phenomenon. Her review of the extant literature found that it was not uncommon for prehispanic groups with access to riverine environments to catch and consume fish. The importance of these taxa as a source of food is also supported by early Spanish accounts, which describe communal fishing expeditions by Pueblo groups along the Rio Grande in the spring and summer months (Adams and Chavez 1975:7; Hammond 1966:210; Hodge et al. 1945:43).

Although the specific fish species that were available prehistorically in the Rio Puerco are not known, a number of native taxa have been reported in the nearby Rio Grande. These include the shovelnose sturgeon (*Scaphirhynchus platorynchus*), longnose gar (*Lepisosteus osseus*), smallmouth buffalo fish (*Ictiobus bubalus*), flannelmouth sucker (*Catostomus latipinnis*), Rio Grande mountain sucker (*Pantosteus plebeius*), Rio Grande chub (*Gila nigrescens*), Rio Grande shiner (*Notropis jemezanus*), and American eel (*Anguilla rostrata*) (Koster 1957). The recovery of *Catostomus* remains from Pottery Mound suggests that at least some of these species may have been locally procured in the Lower Rio Puerco. Longnose gar may also have been present in some of the nearby waterways, as McKusick (1981:43) notes that Hibben's excavations at Pottery Mound recovered a palatine from a longnose gar in Room West 2. In addition, the longnose gar is pictured on Layer 11, Kiva 10 at Pottery Mound (student drawing, Hibben Center Archives, University of New Mexico, Albuquerque). While the small number of fish bones in the assemblage suggests that aquatic taxa were never heavily relied on as a food source, the residents of Pottery Mound appear to have occasionally procured fish to meet their basic subsistence needs.

Reptilian Remains

Reptiles are extremely rare at Pottery Mound and comprise less than 1 percent of the faunal assemblage. Four of the five reptile specimens that were identified derive from turtle carapaces. Ethnographic data indicate that while not considered a major food source, turtles were procured by a number of Rio Grande Pueblo groups, who made rattles from the shells of the animals (Lange 1959; Parsons 1970; 1977; White 1962; Whitman 1947).

The fragmentary nature of the turtle remains did not allow identification to genus. Two species of turtles are found historically in this area of central New Mexico—the ornate box turtle (*Terrapene ornata*) and the painted turtle (*Chrysemys picta*) (Olsen 1968:96–97). Though the former species is expected to have been locally available

Table 10.4. Summary of Unidentified Fauna from Pottery Mound

Size Category	NISP	% NISP
Class Mammalia	**2,227**	**70.8**
Large Mammal	282	9.0
Medium Mammal	338	10.7
Small Mammal	1,607	51.1
Class Aves	**862**	**27.4**
Large Bird	766	24.4
Medium Bird	48	1.5
Small Bird	32	1.0
Unidentified Bird	**16**	**0.5**
Unidentified Animal	58	1.8
TOTAL	**3,147**	**100.0**

in the grassland habitats of the Lower Rio Puerco valley, painted turtle colonies are geographically restricted to major waterways in the region (Lang and Harris 1984:113). The nearest known colony of painted turtles to Pottery Mound is located along a stretch of the Rio Grande that runs from Corrales, New Mexico, on the north to El Paso, Texas, on the south (Degenhardt and Christiansen 1974). Assuming that the distribution of this aquatic species has not changed substantially since prehistoric times, the residents of Pottery Mound would have acquired these animals either through trade or by traveling some distances (at least 20 km) to procure the turtles directly.

A single vertebrate from a gopher snake (*Pituophis melanoleucus*) was also recovered during the Pottery Mound excavations. The complete vertebral element shows no signs of weathering or burning. The condition of the bone suggests that it may be intrusive. While snakes were used in certain Pueblo rituals, generally they were not considered a food source (Henderson and Harrington 1914; Stevenson 1894; White 1962).

Unidentified Remains

In total, 3,147 specimens in the Pottery Mound assemblage are considered unidentifiable (Table 10.4). The distribution of bone in the unidentified faunal assemblage closely parallels that for identified remains. The majority of unidentified specimens (1,607 specimens or 51 percent of the unidentified remains) are composed of indeterminate small mammals, the bulk of which likely represent nondiagnostic fragments of lagomorph bone. Medium- or carnivore-sized mammalian specimens are found in substantially lower abundances with 338 specimens, or 11 percent of unidentified bone, assigned to this category. Finally, large mammal bones comprise a relatively low proportion of the unidentified faunal assemblage. Most of this bone is assumed to be highly fragmented artiodactyl elements.

Unidentified bird remains are also found to display similar distributional patterns as those seen among the identified avian bone. Specimens assigned to the "unidentified large bird" category are far more abundant than either medium- or small-sized bird specimens. The majority of unidentified large bird remains are probably domesticated turkeys. Five eggshell fragments from unidentified large birds are also recorded in the assemblage. The eggshells either represent the remains of domestic turkeys that had been raised at Pottery Mound or possibly wild bird eggs that were collected and eaten by the residents of the pueblo.

Table 10.5. Percent of Taxa by Time Period at Hummingbird Pueblo and Pottery Mound

Taxonomic Group	Hummingbird Pueblo		Pottery Mound	
	Phase 1	Phase 2	Phase 2	Phase 3
Artiodactyls	3.8	2.8	9.2	3.4
Lagomorphs	84.7	79.2	80.0	76.1
Rodents	9.8	10.3	1.5	6.2
Carnivores	0.7	0.5	3.1	4.5
Fish	–	–	–	0.7
Reptiles	–	0.1	–	0.1
Birds	0.9	7.1	6.2	9.1
TOTAL NISP	**950**	**1652**	**65**	**5809**

Note: Hummingbird Pueblo fauna data were taken from Eckert 2003: Appendix C.

Temporal Patterns in Faunal Procurement Practices

Temporal patterning in the exploitation of animal resources at Pottery Mound is assessed in this study through a comparative analysis of the faunal distribution data from early and late phase occupational assemblages. To evaluate changes in faunal procurement through time, the identified bone specimens from Pottery Mound were first grouped by provenience into one of two temporal phases, Phase 2 (A.D. 1350–1400) and Phase 3 (1400–1450/1490), previously defined by Eckert (2003).[7] The relative frequencies of the major taxonomic groups within each assemblage were then calculated based on total NISP counts (Table 10.5). Due to the small sample size associated with the Phase 2 Pottery Mound assemblage (NISP = 65), faunal data from the Lower Rio Puerco site of Hummingbird Pueblo (LA 578) were also included in the analysis for comparative purposes (see Figure 10.4). According to Eckert (2003:40), Hummingbird Pueblo was established in the late thirteenth century (Phase 1), with occupation at the village continuing until the early 1400s (Phase 2). The large collection of faunal remains that was recovered from Phase 1 and 2 deposits at Hummingbird Pueblo provides the opportunity to assess long-term temporal trends in faunal utilization patterns for the Lower Rio Puerco district as a whole. Taxonomic distributions of identified zooarchaeological remains in the Hummingbird Pueblo assemblages are presented in Table 10.5.

Examination of the frequencies of the major taxonomic groups in the phase assemblages from Hummingbird Pueblo and Pottery Mound demonstrate that there are relatively few changes in the use and exploitation of mammalian fauna in the Lower Rio Puerco district during the late Pueblo III and Pueblo IV periods. All of the phase assemblages contain extremely large proportions of lagomorph remains, indicating that these smaller game animals were a consistent and abundant meat source for the inhabitants of the Lower Rio Puerco district. The relatively high frequencies of rodents that are observed in both the early and late phase assemblages at Hummingbird Pueblo suggest that residents of this village also procured other types of small game animals, in particular prairie dogs (*Cynomys* sp.), to meet their dietary needs (Clark 1998). Although rodents do not appear to have been extensively used as a food source at Pottery Mound, the slight increase that is seen in these remains through time (1.5 percent to 6.2 percent) suggests the possible intensification of small mammal usage in the latter phase of occupation.

The most notable temporal change that is observed in the distribution of the mammalian taxa is a slight decrease in the frequency of artiodactyl remains in the Phase 3 assemblage at Pottery Mound. This pattern suggests that while large game may have been somewhat plentiful during the initial phase of the village's occupation, the intensive hunting of these animals eventually resulted in the reduction of local artiodactyl populations in the areas

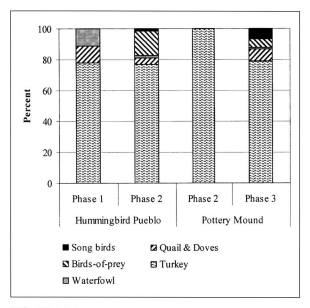

FIGURE 10.3

Percent of bird taxa by time period from Hummingbird Pueblo and Pottery Mound.

surrounding the pueblo. The overhunting of large game has been documented at several other nucleated Pueblo IV period villages in the Rio Grande region, including Arroyo Hondo (Lang and Harris 1984) and Gran Quivira (Spielmann 1988). Interestingly, no evidence of large game depletion is observed at the nearby site of Hummingbird Pueblo, where artiodactyls are found to comprise a small proportion of both the Phase 2 and Phase 3 samples. The consistently low frequencies of artiodactyl remains that characterize Hummingbird Pueblo, in combination with the small sample size of the Phase 2 assemblage at Pottery Mound, suggest that the elevated frequency of large game bone may be the result of sampling error. As such, this patterning should be viewed with some caution.

Though the acquisition of mammalian taxa in the Lower Rio Puerco remains largely unchanged throughout the late Pueblo III and Pueblo IV periods, such does not appear to have been the case for avifauna. Specifically, a marked increase can be observed over time in the exploitation of birds at Hummingbird Pueblo (Clark and Eckert 2004; Eckert 2003). Whereas avian bone accounts for less than 1 percent of the total identified fauna in the Phase 1 assemblage, over 7 percent of the Phase 2 sample is composed of bird specimens (see Table 10.5). The increased procurement of avifauna in the Pueblo IV period does not

appear to have been a site-specific phenomenon, as both the Phase 2 and 3 assemblages at Pottery Mound are also found to contain relatively high frequencies of avian bone.

Examination of the various bird species that are represented in the assemblages from Hummingbird Pueblo and Pottery Mound provides additional insight into the changing use of avifauna in the Lower Rio Puerco district during the Pueblo IV period (Figure 10.3). Although turkeys comprise the overwhelming majority of identified bird remains in all the phase assemblages, subtle temporal shifts can be observed in the frequencies of the wild bird taxa.[8] For example, at Hummingbird Pueblo very few nonfood wild birds are found in the Phase 1 assemblage. This can be contrasted with the relatively high frequency of birds of prey, along with small quantities of waterfowl and songbird species, which characterize the Phase 2 assemblage. While the interpretation of the Phase 2 assemblage at Pottery Mound is limited by small sample size (NISP = 4), most of the wild bird species in the Phase 3 avian assemblage are composed of birds of prey and songbirds.

Taken together, these data indicate a regional pattern for the increased procurement of both turkey and nonfood wild birds during the Pueblo IV period. Eckert (2003:130) posits that the intensified use of avian species reflects the incorporation of feathers into a new ritual regime that developed in the area during the fourteenth century. She argues that the adoption of this new religious ideology served to integrate the diverse populations that had aggregated in the Lower Rio Puerco district in the late 1200s (see also Adams 1991; Schaafsma 1980:244–45; Schaafsma and Schaafsma 1974).

Regional Comparisons of Faunal Utilization Patterns

Initial studies of the archaeofaunal remains from Pottery Mound suggested that the site was a major procurement and distribution center for birds and bird products during the Pueblo IV period (Emslie 1981; Emslie and Hargrave 1978). The data examined in the present analysis indicate that while avian usage in the Lower Rio Puerco district increased in the fourteenth century, birds comprise a relatively small percent of the faunal assemblage in both the early and late phases of occupation. These initial findings suggest an economy that was oriented toward the acquisition of subsistence taxa, rather than the procurement of ritually important bird species for redistribution or trade.

Table 10.6. Taxonomic Frequencies of Fauna from Pueblo IV Rio Grande Sites

Taxonomic Group	Pottery Mound (LA 416)	Hummingbird Pueblo (LA 578)	Qualacu (LA 757)	Pueblo del Encierro (LA 70)	Gran Quivira (LA 120)	Tijeras Pueblo (LA 581)	Arroyo Hondo (LA 12)
Artiodactyls	3	3	5	4	25	28	8
Lagomorphs	76	81	60	30	60	38	43
Rodents	6	10	6	27	2	18	30
Carnivores	4	1	0	3	1	2	2
Fish	1	0	17	2	0	0	<1
Reptiles	<1	<1	7	1	<1	<1	<1
Turkey	2	4	1	21	1	14	10
Wild Birds	7	1	4	12	11	0	7
TOTAL NISP	**5,874**	**2,602**	**574**	**5,835**	**13,669**	**4,759**	**11,431**

How does the use of birds at Pottery Mound compare to other Pueblo IV period villages in the Rio Grande region? Were birds more intensively procured at Pottery Mound or are patterns of avifauna exploitation similar to other contemporaneous settlements in the region? If Pottery Mound specialized in the procurement and processing of birds, then the site should exhibit substantially higher frequencies of avian remains compared to other Pueblo IV sites in the Rio Grande region. To investigate possible regional differences in avifaunal use, I compare the Pottery Mound assemblage to published and unpublished data from a number of Pueblo IV village sites in the northern and central portions of the Rio Grande region (Figure 10.4). Site assemblages examined in this study include: Hummingbird Pueblo (Eckert 2003), Qualacu (James 1987), Pueblo del Encierro (Harris 1978), Gran Quivira (Clark 2003b), Tijeras Pueblo (Young 1980), and Arroyo Hondo (Lang and Harris 1984). Though the sampled sites are characterized by slightly different environmental settings and occupational histories, broad regional trends in faunal procurement practices may be discerned through interassemblage comparisons. The distributions of the major taxonomic groups in each site assemblage are shown in Table 10.6.

An examination of bird bone frequencies indicates that the extent to which avian taxa were exploited by Pueblo IV period populations varies substantially among the sampled assemblages. The large quantity of turkey and

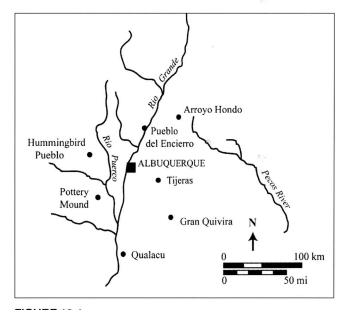

FIGURE 10.4
Location of sites examined in comparative faunal analysis.

Table 10.7. Brainerd-Robinson Similarity Coefficients Comparing Percentages of Faunal Samples from Different Sites

	Pottery Mound	Hummingbird Pueblo	Qualacu	Gran Quivira	Pueblo del Encierro	Tijeras Pueblo	Arroyo Hondo
Pottery Mound	—	183	152	151	105	110	119
Hummingbird Pueblo	183	—	149	142	100	105	114
Qualacu	152	149	—	144	96	118	111
Gran Quivira	151	142	144	—	98	156	132
Pueblo del Encierro	105	100	96	98	—	146	161
Tijeras Pueblo	110	105	118	156	146	—	143
Arroyo Hondo	119	114	111	132	161	143	—

wild birds at Pueblo del Encierro suggests that the residents of this Rio Grande village considered avifauna to be an important animal resource. In contrast, the procurement of avian taxa was much more limited at the sites of Hummingbird Pueblo and Qualacu, where low frequencies of bird bone characterize the identified assemblages. Although Pottery Mound exhibits a greater abundance of wild birds than either of these villages, the moderately low frequencies of avifauna that were recovered from midden deposits support my initial conclusions and suggest that the site was not a major bird procurement or distribution center during the Pueblo IV period.

To assess broader faunal utilization patterns among the sampled Pueblo IV period sites, Brainerd-Robinson (BR) similarity coefficients are also used to statistically evaluate intersite differences in the distribution of the major taxonomic groups. The BR coefficient is a city-block metric that was originally designed to measure similarities among pottery assemblages in terms of proportions of different ceramic types (Shennan 1997:233). In this study, different taxonomic groups substitute for pottery types. To calculate the coefficient, one simply totals the percentage differences between taxonomic groups (using percentages in Table 10.6) for each pair of archaeological assemblages and then subtracts this value from 200, the maximum possible percentage similarity between two assemblages. BR coefficients for each pair of site assemblages are presented in Table 10.7.

The BR coefficients indicate that of all the sampled sites, the faunal assemblage from Pottery Mound is most similar to Hummingbird Pueblo. The high BR coefficient (183) that was obtained from this pair of assemblages suggests that during the Pueblo IV period, the residents of the Lower Rio Puerco valley followed similar faunal procurement strategies that focused on the acquisition of small mammalian taxa (see Table 10.6). The moderately high coefficients that are found between Pottery Mound and the sites of Qualacu (152) and Gran Quivira (151) suggest that these subsistence practices may have been fairly widespread, though some noticeable differences exist among the faunal assemblages from these sites. A comparison of the taxonomic distributions in Table 10.6 demonstrates that while all three assemblages contain large quantities of lagomorph bone, Qualacu has substantially more fish and Gran Quivira exhibits a higher frequency of artiodactyl remains. The abundance of fish at Qualacu is not surprising given that the site is situated on the banks of the Rio Grande (Marshall 1987). Similarly, Gran Quivira is located in close proximity to the Medanos Plains, an extensive grassland area that is expected to have supported large herds of pronghorn antelope that would have been readily exploited by Jumanos hunters (Clark 2003b).

The Pottery Mound faunal assemblage displays marked differences when compared to the collections of animal bone from Pueblo del Encierro, Tijeras Pueblo, and Arroyo Hondo. However, BR coefficients indicate that the latter three sites are generally quite similar to one another. Assemblages from these sites exhibit lower proportions of lagomorphs with higher frequencies of turkeys and rodents (see Table 10.6). These results indicate that while small animals were an important component of the diet throughout the Rio Grande region, variation exists in the specific types of subsistence fauna that were exploited by different populations.

Intersite disparities in faunal utilization among the sampled Pueblo IV sites appear to largely correspond to regional topographic and environmental differences. The villages of Pottery Mound, Hummingbird Pueblo, and Qualacu are all found in grassland environments at relatively low elevations (below 1,800 m or 5,904 ft; Brown and Lowe 1980). Similar biotic communities are found in the area around Gran Quivira, though this village is located at a much higher elevation (1,982 m or 6,500 ft). The exploitation of a shared set of taxa that are associated with these grassland habitats would explain the high level of correspondence that is seen in the faunal assemblages from these sites. In contrast, the similarities in fauna procurement practices at Arroyo Hondo, Tijeras Pueblo, and Pueblo del Encierro may be explained by the location of these sites in, or adjacent to, juniper-piñon woodlands and montane conifer forests that characterize higher elevation areas of the Rio Grande region.

Although geographic factors play a role in structuring faunal subsistence strategies, it appears that populations throughout the Rio Grande region emphasized the same basic principles in their acquisition of animal resources. At most pueblos, residents concentrated on procuring smaller-sized animals rather than expending the effort to travel further afield to hunt large game. The local abundance of these small game animals would have provided a reliable source of meat that could have been obtained with relatively little effort. While somewhat speculative, it can be suggested that this type of "least cost" faunal procurement strategy may have been preferred given the labor and time constraints that would have been associated with other subsistence pursuits, including agricultural and wild plant gathering activities.

Conclusion

To summarize, the analysis of the archaeofaunal remains from the Pueblo IV site of Pottery Mound suggests a pattern of animal usage that was oriented toward the exploitation of subsistence taxa. The predominance of lagomorphs in the assemblage documents the economic importance of these small mammals in the Pueblo diet. Although artiodactyls were only occasionally procured by hunters from Pottery Mound, the large amount of meat that was associated with these large game animals inevitably made them an important food source. The relatively low frequencies of nonintrusive rodents, carnivores, reptiles, birds, and fish indicate that these animals were not extensively procured as subsistence items and likely contributed only minor amounts of meat to the diet.

While few temporal changes in the acquisition of subsistence taxa are observed between the early and late phase occupations at Pottery Mound, a marked increase in the exploitation of avian fauna is observed during the Pueblo IV period in the Lower Rio Puerco area. Intersite analyses indicate that despite the intensification of bird use, no definitive evidence was found to support Emslie's (1981) early depiction of Pottery Mound as a site of major importance for birds and bird products. Rather, examination of the frequencies of terrestrial and riverine economic taxa among the sampled assemblages reveals that Pottery Mound adheres to a fairly generalized pattern of faunal procurement that typifies a number of sites in the central Rio Grande region. ⁘

NOTES

1. As worked bone artifacts were not available to the author at the time of analysis, these materials are not considered in the present study.

2. High utility elements include the scapula, sternum, rib, thoracic vertebrae, pelvis, sacrum, femur, and tibia; medium utility elements include the humerus, cervical and lumbar vertebrae, radius, ulna, tarsals, astragalus, and calcaneus; low utility elements include the skull, teeth, atlas, axis, metacarpal, metatarsal, carpals, and phalange.

3. Element utility group values presented in the ratio diagram are based on the formula: $d = \log_{10}X - \log_{10}Y$; d is the logged ratio; X is the percentage of each utility group (percent NISP of high, medium, or low utility groups) in the total artiodactyl assemblage; and Y is the percentage of this same utility group in a complete skeleton.

4. Small-sized carnivores include animals that are smaller than a coyote or dog; large carnivores are those animals that are dog sized or larger.

5. It should be noted that Emslie (1981:853) identified 50 bird species in the Pottery Mound faunal assemblage that was collected by Hibben. The marked disparity in taxonomic richness between the two avifaunal assemblages is likely the result of sample size differences. Grayson (1984:132–51) and others have shown that the number of species represented in an assemblage (i.e., species richness) is highly correlated to the overall number of identified specimens (i.e., the assemblage size). Given that the identified avifaunal assemblage from Hibben's excavations was over six times larger than the assemblage examined in this study (3,472 specimens versus 529 specimens, respectively), it is not unexpected that Emslie's analysis identified a greater number of bird taxa.

6. Exceptions to this include mallards (*Anas platyrhynchos*) and northern pintails (*Anas acuta*), both of which can be found in the area year-round. In addition, cinnamon (*Anas cyanoptera*) and blue-winged (*Anas discors*) teals are more commonly found in the area during the summer months (Sibley 2000:87).

7. Using ceramic seriation data from Pottery Mound and Hummingbird Pueblo, Eckert (2003) has defined three phases of Pueblo IV occupation in the Lower Rio Puerco district: Phase 1 (A.D. 1275–1350), Phase 2 (A.D. 1350–1400), and Phase 3 (A.D. 1400–1450/1490).

8. In this analysis, it is assumed that most of the turkey at Pottery Mound represents the remains of domesticated individuals.

REFERENCES CITED

Adams, E. Charles
    1991   *The Origin and Development of the Pueblo Katsina Cult.* University of Arizona Press, Tucson.

Adams, Eleanor B., and Fray Angélico Chávez
    1975   *The Missions of New Mexico 1776: A Description by Fray Francisco Atanasio Dominquez.* University of New Mexico Press, Albuquerque.

Anell, Bengt
    1969   *Running Down and Driving of Game in North America.* Studia Ethnographica Upsaliencia XXX. Berlingska Boktrijckeriel, Sweden.

Bayham, Frank E.
    1982   Diachronic Analysis of Prehistoric Animal Exploitation at Ventana Cave. Unpublished Ph.D. dissertation, Department of Anthropology, Arizona State University, Tempe.

Binford, Lewis R.
    1978   *Nunamiut Ethnoarchaeology.* Academic Press, New York.
    1981   *Bones: Ancient Men and Modern Myths.* Academic Press, New York.

Bonnichsen, Robson
    1973   Some Operational Aspects of Human and Animal Bone Alteration. In *Mammalian Osteo-Archaeology: North America*, edited by B. Miles Gilbert. Missouri Archaeological Special Publications. University of Missouri, Columbia.

Bourke, John G.
    1962   *The Snake Dance of the Moquis of Arizona.* First published 1884. Charles Scribner's Sons, New York.

Brown, David E.
    1994   Part 4—Grasslands. In *Biotic Communities, Southwestern United States and Northwestern Mexico*, edited by David E. Brown, pp. 107–42. University of Utah Press, Salt Lake City.

Brown, David E., and Charles H. Lowe
    1980   *Biotic Communities of the Southwest.* USDA Forest Service General Technical Report RM-78. Rocky Mountain Forest and Range Experiment Station, Fort Collins, Colorado.

Clark, Tiffany C.
    1998   Report on the Vertebrate Faunal Remains from Hummingbird Pueblo (LA 578). Report on file, Department of Anthropology, University of Colorado, Boulder.

2003a   Archaeofaunal Remains from Pueblo Blanco (LA 51). In *Politics and Economy at Pueblo Blanco, New Mexico: Final Report of the 1999 and 2000 Field Seasons*, edited William M. Graves and Katherine A. Spielmann. Report submitted to the USDA Forest Service, Cibola Office, Albuquerque, New Mexico.

2003b   Final Report of the Archaeofaunal Remains from Gran Quivira Pueblo (LA 120), Torrance County, New Mexico. Report on file, Department of Anthropology, Arizona State University, Tempe.

Clark, Tiffany C., and Suzanne Eckert

2004   The Importance of Avifauna in Pueblo IV Ritual Systems: A Case Study from the Lower Rio Puerco, New Mexico. Poster presented at the 69th Annual Meeting of the Society for American Archaeology, Montreal.

Cordell, Linda

1980   University of New Mexico Field School Excavations at Pottery Mound, New Mexico, 1979, Preliminary Report. Manuscript on file, Maxwell Museum of Anthropology, University of New Mexico, Albuquerque.

Degenhardt, William G., and J. L. Christiansen

1974   Distribution and Habitats of Turtles in New Mexico. *Southwestern Naturalist* 19:21–46.

Dortignac, Edward J.

1963   Rio Puerco: Abused Basin. In *Aridity and Man*, edited by C. Hodge, pp. 507–15. American Association for the Advancement of Science, Publication 74. Washington, D.C.

Eckert, Suzanne L.

2003   Social Boundaries, Immigration, and Ritual Systems: A Case Study from the American Southwest. Unpublished Ph.D. dissertation, Department of Anthropology, Arizona State University, Tempe.

Emslie, Steven D.

1981   Prehistoric Agricultural Ecosystems: Avifauna from Pottery Mound, New Mexico. *American Antiquity* 46(4):853–61.

Emslie, Steven D., and Lyndon L. Hargrave

1978   An Ethnobiological Study of the Avifauna from Pottery Mound, New Mexico. Paper presented at the 43rd Annual Meeting of the Society for American Archaeology, Tucson.

Eshbaugh, David C.

1992   Aboriginal Butchering Practices at Gran Quivira Pueblo: An Examination of Cut Marks. In *Subsistence and Exchange at Gran Quivira Pueblo, New Mexico*, edited by K. Spielmann, pp. 21–37. Submitted to the National Park Service, Southwestern Regional Office, Santa Fe, New Mexico.

Fewkes, J. Walter

1904   *Two Summers' Work in Pueblo Ruins*. In Bureau of American Ethnology Twenty-Second Annual Report, 1900–1901, pp. 3–195. U.S. Government Printing Office, Washington, D.C.

Findley, James S., Arthur H. Harris, Don E. Wilson, and Clyde Jones

1975   *Mammals of New Mexico*. University of New Mexico Press, Albuquerque.

Gilbert, B. Miles

1980   *Mammalian Osteology*. B. Miles Gilbert, Laramie, Wyoming.

Gilbert, B. Miles, Larry D. Martin, and Howard G. Savage

1985   *Avian Osteology*. B. Miles Gilbert, Flagstaff, Arizona.

Gnabasik, V.

1981   Faunal Utilization by the Pueblo Indian. Unpublished Master's thesis, Department of Anthropology, Eastern New Mexico University, Portales.

Grayson, D. K.

1984   *Quantitative Zooarchaeology*. Academic Press, San Diego, California.

Hammond, George P.

1966   *The Rediscovery of New Mexico, 1580–1594: The Explorations of Chamuscado, Espejo, Castaño de Sosa, Morlete, and Leyva de Bonilla and Humaña*. University of New Mexico Press, Albuquerque.

Hammond, George P., and Agapito Rey

1929   *Pérez de Luxán, Diego. Expedition into New Mexico Made by Antonio de Espejo, 1582–1583, as Revealed in the Journal of Diego Pérez de Luxán, a Member of the Party*. Quivira Society, Los Angeles.

Harris, Arthur H.
 1978 Section H, Faunal Remains from LA 70. In *Archaeological Excavations at Pueblo del Encierro, LA 70, Cochiti Dame Savage Project, Cochiti, New Mexico. Final Report 1964–1965*. Laboratory of Anthropology Note No. 78. Santa Fe, New Mexico.

Henderson, Junius, and John P. Harrington
 1914 *Ethnozoology of the Tewa Indians*. Bureau of American Ethnology Bulletin 56. U.S. Government Printing Office, Washington, D.C.

Hibben, Frank C.
 1975 *Kiva Art of the Anasazi at Pottery Mound*. KC Publications, Las Vegas, Nevada.

Hodge, Frederick Webb, George P. Hammond, and Agapito Rey (translators and editors)
 1945 *Fray Alonso de Benavides Revised Memorial of 1634*. University of New Mexico Press, Albuquerque.

James, Steven R.
 1987 Faunal Analysis. In *Qualacu, Archaeological Investigation of a Piro Pueblo*, edited by Michael P. Marshall, pp. 93–108. U.S. Fish and Wildlife Service, Office of Contract Archaeology, University of New Mexico, Albuquerque.

Klein, Richard G., and Kathryn Cruz-Uribe
 1984 *The Analysis of Animal Bones from Archaeological Sites*. University of Chicago Press, Chicago.

Koster, William J.
 1957 *Guide to the Fishes of New Mexico*. University of New Mexico Press, Albuquerque.

Ladd, Edmund J.
 1963 Zuni Ethno-Ornithology. Unpublished Master's thesis, University of New Mexico, Albuquerque.

Lang, Richard W., and Arthur H. Harris
 1984 *The Faunal Remains from Arroyo Hondo Pueblo: A Study in Short-Term Subsistence Change*. School of American Research Press, Santa Fe, New Mexico.

Lange, Charles H.
 1959 *Cochiti: A New Mexico Pueblo, Past and Present*. University of Texas Press, Austin.

Linares, Olga F.
 1976 Garden Hunting in the American Tropics. *Human Ecology* 4(4):331–49.

Lubinski, Patrick M., and Vicki Herren
 2000 An Introduction to Pronghorn Biology, Ethnography, and Archaeology. *Plains Anthropologist* 32:3–12.

McKusick, Charmion R.
 1986 *Southwest Indian Turkeys: Prehistory and Comparative Osteology*. Southwest Bird Laboratory, Globe, Arizona.

Madsen, Rees Low
 1974 The Influence of Rainfall on the Reproduction of Sonoran Desert Lagomorphs. Unpublished Master's thesis, Department of Biological Sciences, University of Arizona, Tucson.

Marshall, Michael P.
 1987 *Qualacu, Archaeological Investigation of a Piro Pueblo*. U.S. Fish and Wildlife Service, Office of Contract Archaeology, University of New Mexico, Albuquerque.

Metcalf, J., and K. Jones
 1988 A Reconstruction of Animal Body-Part Utility Indices. *American Antiquity* 53:486–504.

Olsen, John W.
 1990 *Vertebrate Faunal Remains from Grasshopper Pueblo, Arizona*. Anthropological Papers, Museum of Anthropology 83. Museum of Anthropology, University of Michigan, Ann Arbor.

Olsen, Stanley J.
 1964 *Mammal Remains from Archaeological Sites*. Papers of the Peabody Museum of American Archaeology and Ethnology Vol. 56, No. 1. Harvard University, Cambridge, Massachusetts.
 1968 *Fish, Amphibian and Reptile Remains from Archaeological Sites: Part I. Southeastern and Southwestern United States*. Papers of the Peabody Museum of American Archaeology and Ethnology Vol. 56, No. 2. Harvard University, Cambridge, Massachusetts.

Ortiz, Alfonso
 1969 *The Tewa World: Space, Time, Being, and Becoming in a Pueblo Society*. University of Chicago Press, Chicago.

Parsons, Elsie C.

1920 Notes on Isleta, Santa Ana, and Acoma. *American Anthropologist* 20:162–86.

1970 *Taos Pueblo.* Originally published 1936, General Series in Anthropology No. 2. George Banta, Menasha, Wisconsin. Johnson Reprint, New York.

1977 *The Pueblo of Jemez.* Originally published 1925, Department of Anthropology, Phillips Academy, Andover, Massachusetts, Yale University Press, New Haven, Connecticut. University Microfilms, Ann Arbor.

Perkins, D., Jr., and P. Daly

1968 A Hunter's Village in Neolithic Turkey. *Scientific American* 219(5):96–106.

Rea, Amadeo M.

1998 *Folk Mammalogy of the Northern Pimans.* University of Arizona Press, Tucson.

Reitz, Elizabeth J., and Elizabeth S. Wing

1999 *Zooarchaeology.* Cambridge Manuals in Archaeology. Cambridge University Press, Cambridge.

Schaafsma, Polly

1980 *Indian Rock Art of the Southwest.* School of American Research, Santa Fe, and University of New Mexico Press, Albuquerque.

Schaafsma, Polly, and Curtis F. Schaafsma

1974 Evidence for the Origins of the Pueblo Kachina Cult as Suggested by Southwestern Rock Art. *American Antiquity* (4):535–45.

Schmid, E.

1972 *Atlas of Animal Bone for Prehistorians, Archaeologists, and Quaternary Geologists.* Elsevier Publishing Company, New York.

Schroeder, Albert H.

1968 Birds and Feathers in Documents Relating to Indians of the Southwest. In *Collected Papers in Honor of Lyndon Lane Hargrave,* edited by Albert H. Schroeder, pp. 95–114. Papers of the Archaeological Society of New Mexico 1. Museum of New Mexico, Albuquerque.

Schroeder, Albert H., and Dan S. Matson

1965 *A Colony on the Move: Gaspar Castaño de Sosa's Journal, 1590–1591.* School of American Research, Santa Fe, New Mexico.

Shennan, Stephan

1997 *Quantifying Archaeology.* 2nd edition. Edinburgh University Press, Edinburgh.

Sibley, David Allen

2000 *National Audubon Society: The Sibley Guide to Birds.* Alfred A. Knopf, New York.

Smith, Watson

1952 *Kiva Murals Decorations at Awatovi and Kawaika-a.* Papers of the Peabody Museum of American Archaeology and Ethnology Vol. 37, pp. 173–83. Harvard University, Cambridge, Massachusetts.

Snow, Cordelia Thomas

2002 Fish Tales: The Use of Freshwater Fish in New Mexico from A.D. 1000 to 1900. In *Forward into the Past: Papers in Honor of Teddy Lou and Francis Stickney,* edited by Regge Wiseman, Thomas O'Laughlin, and Cordelia Snow. Papers of the Archaeological Society of New Mexico 28. Archaeological Society of New Mexico, Albuquerque.

Speth, John D.

1983 *Bison Kills and Bone Counts: Decision Making by Ancient Hunters.* University of Chicago Press, Chicago.

Spielmann, K. A.

1988 Changing Faunal Resource Procurement at Gran Quivira Pueblo, New Mexico. Paper presented at the 53rd Annual Meeting of the Society for American Archaeology, Phoenix.

Stephen, Alexander M.

1936 *Hopi Journal of Alexander M. Stephen.* Columbia University Contributions to Anthropology Vol. XXIII. Columbia University Press, New York.

Stevenson, Matilda Coxe

1894   *The Sia.* Bureau of American Ethnology Eleventh Annual Report, 1889–1890, pp. 3–157. Smithsonian Institution, Washington, D.C.

Stubbs, Stanley A., and W. S. Stallings Jr.

1953   *The Excavation of Pindi Pueblo, New Mexico.* Monographs of the School of American Research and the Laboratory of Anthropology No. 18. School of American Research, Santa Fe, New Mexico.

Szuter, C. R.

1984   Faunal Exploitation and the Reliance on Small Animals among the Hohokam. In *Hohokam Archaeology along the Salt-Gila Aqueduct Project, Volume VII: Environment and Subsistence*, edited by L. Teague and P. Crown, pp. 139–70. Cultural Resource Management Division, Arizona State Museum, University of Arizona, Tucson.

1991   *Hunting by Prehistoric Horticulturalists in the American Southwest.* Garland Publishing, New York.

Szuter, C. R., and F. Bayham

1989   Sedentism and Animal Procurement among Desert Horticulturalists of the North American Southwest. In *Farmers as Hunters: The Implications of Sedentism*, edited by Susan Kent, pp. 80–95. Cambridge University Press, Cambridge.

Tyler, Hamilton A.

1964   *Pueblo Animals and Myths.* University of Oklahoma Press, Norman.

1979   *Pueblo Birds and Myths.* University of Oklahoma Press, Norman.

Underhill, Ruth Murray

1936   *The Autobiography of a Papago Woman.* Memoirs of the American Anthropological Association No. 46. American Anthropological Association, Menasha, Wisconsin.

White, Leslie A.

1932   *The Pueblo of San Felipe.* Memoirs of the American Anthropological Association No. 38. American Anthropological Association, Menasha, Wisconsin.

1942   *The Pueblo of Santa Ana, New Mexico.* Memoirs of the American Anthropological Association No. 60. American Anthropological Association, Menasha, Wisconsin.

1962   *The Pueblo of Sia, New Mexico.* Bureau of American Ethnology Bulletin 184. U.S. Government Printing Office, Washington, D.C.

1974a   *The Pueblo of Santa Domingo, New Mexico.* Originally published 1935, Memoirs of the American Anthropological Association No. 43, American Anthropological Association, Menasha, Wisconsin. Kraus Reprint, Millwood, New York.

1974b   *Zia—The Sun Symbol Pueblo.* Originally published 1962, The Pueblo of Sia, New Mexico, Bureau of American Ethnology Bulletin 184, U.S. Government Printing Office, Washington, D.C. University of New Mexico and Calvin Horn, Albuquerque.

Whitman, William

1947   *The Pueblo Indians of San Ildefonso: A Changing Culture.* Columbia University Contributions to Anthropology No. 34. Columbia University Press, New York.

Young, Gwen

1980   Analysis of Faunal Remains. In *Tijeras Canyon, Analyses of the Past*, edited by L. Cordell, pp. 88–120. Maxwell Museum of Anthropology and University of New Mexico Press, Albuquerque.

CHAPTER ELEVEN

Discussion of the Pottery Mound Essays and Some Alternative Proposals

David R. Wilcox

When Polly Schaafsma asked me to be the outside discussant for a two-day advanced seminar at the School of American Research (SAR) and later at a Society for American Archaeology (SAA) symposium on new research concerning the site of Pottery Mound in Valencia County, New Mexico, along the Lower Rio Puerco of the East, I leaped at the chance. Unlike Polly, or Gwinn and Patricia Vivian, I had not worked at the site. And I never knew Frank Hibben, who directed excavations there intermittently from 1954 to 1987. Unlike Kelley Hays-Gilpin, Steven LeBlanc, or Suzanne Eckert, I am not a ceramic specialist, and unlike Helen Crotty, Kelley, Steve, or Polly, I am not a specialist in the study of southwestern iconography (or rock art); nor like Laurie Webster am I a textile expert, or, like Tiffany Clark, a zooarchaeologist. I am, however, like Michael Adler, an architectural analyst.

I do bring certain other strengths to the table. Unlike any of the others, I am deeply knowledgeable about Hohokam archaeology and what Hohokam platform mounds are (Wilcox 1987; 1991a; 1999a; Wilcox and Shenk 1977), an issue relevant to the interpretation of the architecture and stratigraphy of Pottery Mound (Hibben 1966; 1975).[1] Twenty years ago I (Wilcox 1986a) also looked closely at the history of debate about the

cultural connections between the American Southwest and Mesoamerica, proposing my own model (Wilcox 1986b), and reassessing it periodically ever since (Wilcox 1995; 1999b; 2000a). In 1964 I was trained as an archaeological stratigrapher by Alice Kehoe, and I brought these skills to bear in Saskatchewan and New York and New England before applying them at Grasshopper Pueblo near Cibecue, Arizona, and then in what proved to be my dissertation research on the Casa Grande Ruin near Coolidge, Arizona (Wilcox and Shenk 1977; see also Wilcox 1999b). The basis of that study was what architects call "elevation drawings," but to me they were profiles, and in an appendix to that report I (Wilcox 1977) set forth my principles in "On Drawing Profiles," which were initially written down for the benefit of field school students at Grasshopper Pueblo.

Perhaps Polly knew that I have long been fascinated by scientific debate and its historical analysis, as someone who first read T. C. Chamberlin's (1965) classic paper on "The Method of Multiple Working Hypotheses" when I was an undergraduate. Chamberlin (1965) warned against the seduction of "ruling theories," pointing out that all scientists must face the psychological danger of letting what begins as a "working hypothesis," after it is repeated several times with no seeming contradiction, become accepted as fact. His way of overcoming this problem was to embrace as many different working hypotheses as one could imagine, playing them against one another. The larger implication of this perspective is that science is structured by debates on many levels, what the American philosopher Nicholas Rescher (1985) calls a "strife of systems"; science is not simply about "paradigms" (cf. Kuhn 1962). I long have sought to understand how scientists operating from very different perspectives or assumptions can find middle ground (Scheffler 1967; Wilcox 2004; Wilcox and Shenk 1977:172) and build a new, if temporary, consensus, as A. V. Kidder (1927) succeeded so dramatically in doing at the first Pecos Conference (Wilcox 2005a; Wilcox and Fowler 2002).

Let there be no mistake: this volume presents a debate on many levels and along numerous dimensions about the meaning of what has been found at the Pottery Mound site. At the 2005 Society for American Archaeology (SAA) symposium I characterized my role as that of an umpire whose job was to articulate the "rules of play" and to point out when players stepped out of bounds. But surely Polly knows that I also am a protagonist in these debates, as passionately interested as anyone

about the explanation for the patterning now revealed in the archaeological record of Pottery Mound.

Together with Laurie Webster, Polly participated in a week-long advanced seminar I co-organized in October 2001 on the anthropological question of Zuni origins (Gregory and Wilcox 2007). As a part of that exercise, I assembled what we call the Coalescent Communities Database of all known sites with 13 rooms or more found throughout the entire North American Southwest for the period A.D. 1200–1700 (Gregory and Wilcox 2007; Wilcox 2005a; Wilcox et al. 2006; see also Hill et al. 2004). Polly and Curtis Schaafsma helped enormously in that research. Not only can we now see the population of Zuni in its multiscalar contexts of neighbor-to-neighbor relationships, from local to macroregional scales, the same can be done for the Pottery Mound site. Along with my colleagues David Gregory and J. Brett Hill (Wilcox et al. 2006; 2007), I have used the data in the Coalescent Communities Database to construct a series of settlement pattern maps for each 50-year period from A.D. 1200 to 1600. Their analysis reveals many previously unknown or poorly appreciated patterns that suggest a plethora of new hypotheses for future research. It thus has become possible to infer the social, economic, and political contexts of the Pottery Mound site in a way that is much more comprehensive and less ad hoc, laying the foundations for a fresh evaluation of current debates (presented in this volume) about its place in southwestern archaeology.

In what follows, I first discuss briefly the essays found in this volume, playing the role of umpire and evaluating the strengths and weaknesses of the arguments made in them. I then weigh in with my own perspective on the site and its interpretation and end with some suggestions for future work. The genesis of this volume has been a "movable feast" of intellectual discussions and give and take that has taught all of us much, both at the two formal gatherings, and through e-mail exchanges. At the SAR one memorable day, David Phillips, the director of the new Hibben Center at the University of New Mexico (UNM), which now has charge of most of the publicly available archival records on the Pottery Mound site, brought to Santa Fe the profile drawing of the north face of the 10-foot-wide, 551-foot-long east-west bulldozer trench Professor Hibben precociously had cut through the south part of the mound. How excited we felt to see how detailed it was; at my suggestion Phillips agreed to collaborate with Michael Adler and his students to scan it. Thanks also to Phillips and Adler, in July 2004 a field trip was arranged to visit both the Hummingbird site (LA 578) and Pottery Mound (LA 416), which I was able to do in the company of the geomorphologist Fred Nials. Seeing both of these sites firsthand has helped enormously to understand what's what at them.

This volume for the first time publishes the bulldozer trench profile without any elaboration in Appendix C. Phillips has also produced a new composite map of the site that is more comprehensive than any earlier effort (see Figure 1.3). Curtis Schaafsma has helpfully compiled in Appendix D summary data on the ceramic type frequencies recorded in various of the excavations at Pottery Mound, including those from a 5 x 5 m test pit excavated immediately north of the extant mound by Linda Cordell (1980) in 1979 for UNM. Intensive studies of data from this test pit are presented in this volume by Suzanne Eckert (Chapter 4) and Tiffany Clark (Chapter 10). Cordell (2004) was an important contributor to the SAR seminar.

At the SAA symposium, Jean Ballagh and David Phillips (2005) presented a useful paper, a preliminary account of their project to assemble and write up the results of each year of excavation at Pottery Mound during the Hibben era. Rather wistfully, they wondered aloud why this volume was being prepared before they finished their project (Ballagh and Phillips 2005). The answer is clear: with the passing of Frank Hibben there was much pent-up interest in the site and a widely shared desire to bring together current perspectives about its interpretation so that the debate can be more explicitly joined, thus sharpening the questions that should be asked about the data as its analysis proceeds. This volume, then, is a preliminary effort. No consensus has been achieved and, indeed, would probably be premature. But I think it succeeds admirably in presenting much of what is currently known about this important site, putting the data into the theoretical contexts of modern southwestern archaeology and stimulating a much larger interest in the site's relevance to the interests of many other archaeologists and the general public.

A Brief Critique of the Essays

The Platform Mound Issue

Gwinn Vivian (Chapter 2) reviews the history of Frank Hibben's thinking about the Pottery Mound site, showing how his interpretation shifted from a conception of internal southwestern explanation to an external one involving Mesoamerican influences. Like Cordell (2004), his wife Patricia (Chapter 5), and Adler (Chapter 3), he is skeptical about Hibben's (1966; 1975) claim of a so-called pyramidal substructure to the mound. Apparently it was the red clay soil, probably a terrace deposit along the Rio Puerco, that misled him. Is there any other reason to suppose a platform mound was present?

Looking at the profile (Appendix C), one might also point to a pattern in the adobe walls recorded there. Making a photocopy of the profile, I used the meter scale to mark off tick marks along the horizontal datum line, arbitrarily starting from the east end and numbering westward. From 23 m west (of the east end of the trench) to 78 m west is an adobe roomblock at least four strata deep. At the bottom, in what I will call Stratum 1, is Kiva 13 (from 44 to 48 m west), although it is likely it intruded downward from Stratum 2, above. Farther west, in that same stratum, we see a series of vertical wall stubs with adobe floors near their base that appear to be capped by a layer coded "R": this keys out as "Red clay chunks/ additional extraneous material." Might this be the top of what, in the Hohokam region of southern Arizona, could be interpreted as a "platform mound" on whose surface other adobe structures were then successively built?

The best archaeological stratigraphers to study Hohokam platform mounds have been Julian Hayden (1940) and David Gregory (1987; 1991; Gregory et al. 1988). There are two ways such mounds were created: (1) by building a succession of walls that formed cells that were deliberately filled in; and (2) by deliberately filling in extant rooms (which had floors) and capping them so other structures could be erected on the raised platform. It may be the latter scenario that Hibben thought he saw in the profile of his terrible trench, especially from 48 to 63 m west. If so, closer inspection should have led to the rejection of such a hypothesis. The rooms in this section of the profile were clearly dug *down* into the red clay stratum, not raised up above it. The surface on which the rooms of Stratum 2 (as I will call it) were built is close to being at what was then ground level. Thus, it seems that Pottery Mound is more analogous to a Middle Eastern tell, raised up by a succession of razed rooms, rather than a Hohokam platform mound.

The Moral Issue

Patricia Vivian (Chapter 5) recounts the tragic story of how the marvelous murals exposed in the Pottery Mound kivas were destroyed forever by Frank Hibben's decision to successively scrape them away as each layer was recorded as best they could be at that time. Was this, then, the wanton destruction of what we should recognize today as a world-class art form, from motives of expediency or hubris?[2] Clearly, the methods used were inadequate, there was a technique whereby the murals could have been peeled, as was done at Awat'ovi and Kawaika'a (Smith 1952), and the memory today of having been a party to such destruction is deeply painful. What we should join in saying today, I think, is that the approach taken was wrong and that when the day arrives, as I believe it will, when new southwestern murals are discovered, modern methods should be used to preserve them in perpetuity.

What remains of the Pottery Mound murals are what historians call "secondary sources": the color (now fading) and black and white photographs, the drawings, and the artists' renderings. As P. Vivian discusses, this adds another layer of uncertainty about the exact colors once proclaimed in the originals, perhaps subtly distorting the intended meanings. All artists' reproductions, just like all profiles (Wilcox 1977), are interpretations, and it is not now possible to ask a host of questions about, for example, the differences of technological style in the original brushstrokes that modern scholars would like to know. Were these murals painted by individuals acting alone, by groups of artists acting as coordinated teams, or are they collages assembled by different artists interacting from different perspectives in the same context? We may not now be able to answer such questions with any assurance. Nevertheless, even admitting these moral and scientific shortcomings, an impressive and highly evocative corpus of data about the mural art of Pottery Mound has been preserved and does provide an adequate basis for proposing many insights about the beliefs of the people who produced this imagery, as many of the papers in this volume show.

The Mera Diagram and the Size and Chronology of Pottery Mound

In connection with my work assembling the Coalescent Communities Database (Wilcox et al. 2007), I learned about the hundreds of site diagrams made by H. P. Mera that are curated at ARMS (Archaeological Research Management System), Laboratory of Anthropology, Museum of New Mexico in Santa Fe. One of them is of LA 416, Pottery Mound (Figure 11.1). It shows a high southern mound and a lower northern roomblock, with a third roomblock emerging from under the high mound

along the north side, east end. In Figure 11.1 this diagram is shown in relationship to the recent map constructed by David Phillips (see Figure 1.3).[3]

Already in the 1920s, arroyo cutting along the Rio Puerco of the East was digging into the north edge of the rooms (Warner 1928) and this process was accelerating during the 1950s (Brody 1964) and later (Hibben 1987). In the decade from 1954 to 1964, Brody (1964) estimates that several thousand square feet of site (i.e., about 40–50 rooms) were lost. Today little remains of the northern roomblock shown in Mera's diagram. It appears that the UNM test pit (see Figure 11.1) was dug in between the high southern mound and the northern roomblock.

In Warner's (1928) day, he said the edge of the arroyo was 1,000 ft (305 m) north of the middle of the mound; he also estimated the total number of rooms then extant at 500, with an average room size of 6 x 10 ft (5.574 m²). This indicates a total room area of about 2,787 m², and with the open spaces his maps show in the midst of the rooms (probably plaza space), the total extent of the architecture was perhaps the size of an acre, or 4,047 m². Judging by Mera's diagram (see Figure 11.1), half of this area is now eroded away. Warner's (1928) statement that the site extended over 15 acres might refer to the extent of the sherd scatter, not to the architecture.

Perhaps we should question Warner's assertion that the middle of the high mound was 1,000 ft (305 m) from the arroyo, where walls were eroding out. Mera's northern roomblock is about 100 paces north of the northern edge of the high mound; Phillips's map (see Figure 11.1) places the edge of the 1953 arroyo edge, at most, about 105 m north of the north edge of the southern high mound. In Figure 11.1, we see that the north edge of the northern roomblock seen by Mera is parallel to the edge of the 1953 arroyo edge, but a little farther north. These data suggest that the major erosion since Warner's day did not begin until the early 1950s.

Ceramic analyses of the samples recovered in Hibben's early field school work (Voll 1961) showed that the high mound was basically a Glaze A site, with only a trace of Glaze B and a bit more Glaze C pottery (see Appendix D). Perhaps as many as 200 sherds of Glaze C were reportedly found during the 1954 work, mainly in the high mound and Kiva 1 (Ballagh and Phillips 2005). Looking more closely at Voll's (1961) data, we find that the six surface rooms that were probably located in the southern edge of Mera's northern roomblock contained a relatively greater amount of Glaze C than he reports elsewhere. This may mean that

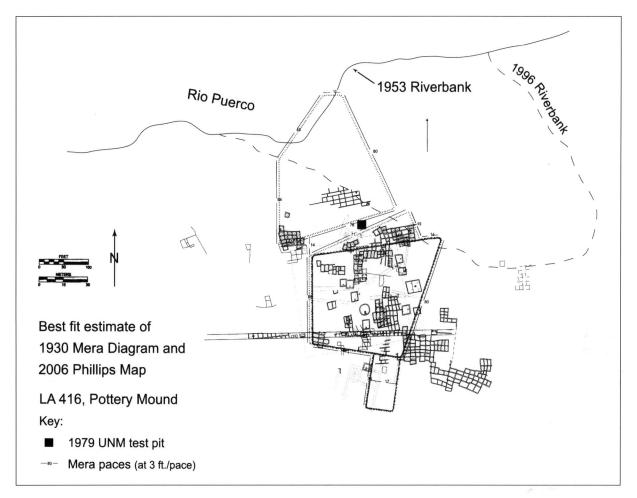

FIGURE 11.1

H. P. Mera diagram of LA 416, Pottery Mound, superimposed on David Phillips's recent composite map of this site (see Figure 1.3, this volume). (Courtesy of the Laboratory of Anthropology, Museum of New Mexico, Santa Fe.)

there was both vertical (in the high mound) and horizontal (in the northern roomblock) stratigraphy at the site. Mera also recorded later glazes at the site (R. G. Vivian, Chapter 2); did they come from a later part of the northern roomblock? Alternatively, the site may have begun as a small village in the range of 100–250 rooms and expanded in early Glaze C times to a medium village of about 500 rooms.

Brody (1964) argued that Pottery Mound Polychrome, most of whose designs he thought were similar to the style on Sikyatki Polychrome (a Jeddito Yellow Ware type manufactured at Hopi) but with an entirely different technology, was temporally equivalent (on design-style grounds) to Glaze C pottery, which Schaafsma (2002) dates to A.D. 1450–1490. One of the typical motifs

on the outside of Pottery Mound Polychrome bowls is a narrow red stripe edged on both sides by a black glaze line (Brody 1964:79). The same motif is also common on Espinoso Glaze Polychrome (Glaze C) in the Rio Grande, and Harlow (1965) reports it on his Alphabeta Polychrome, Glaze-on-white, at Acoma, which, however, he dates to A.D. 1375–1440; this motif is not found farther west (Harlow 1965). Interestingly, Voll (1961:43) reports a few sherds from Pottery Mound with "a white paste, sherd tempered, black glaze-on-red interior slip and white exterior slip; rim sherds showed a diagonal red stripe outlined in black glaze on the exterior." This description matches Harlow's (1965) Beta-Two Polychrome type, which he dates to A.D. 1395–1465. The currently accepted chronological model for

Sikyatki Polychrome (Hays-Gilpin and van Hartesveldt 1998; Smith 1971) has it beginning ca. A.D. 1375, a generation earlier than Brody (1964), following Colton (1955), thought. These data partly support Brody's (1964) inference, but with Pottery Mound Polychrome probably beginning contemporaneously with Sikyatki Polychrome, ca. A.D. 1375, and continuing to be made into early Glaze C times, or ca. A.D. 1450–1475, right about where Voll (1961) thought (cf. Appendix D, this volume).

Although analogous to Sikyatki Polychrome, Pottery Mound Polychrome, Brody (1964:114) found, had designs that "tend to be far more rigid and formal, [and] use less motifs and textural variations than those found on true Sikyatki."[4] Compared to "true Sikyatki," Pottery Mound Polychrome "seems pale and listless" (Brody 1964:95). This could be due to the early date of Pottery Mound Polychrome and Brody's comparison of it to what Smith (1971) later called "flamboyant" Sikyatki Polychrome. Hays-Gilpin and LeBlanc (Chapter 7) recognize that early Sikyatki Polychrome is not painted in what they regard as "Sikyatki style"; however, Hays-Gilpin (personal communication 2006), who has directly examined many Pottery Mound Polychrome pots, regards their style as being a version of the "flamboyant" Sikyatki style. In Sikyatki Polychrome that style does not appear until after the depopulation of Homol'ovi II (which might be as late as A.D. 1425, given the large quantities of Sikyatki Polychrome found there; cf. Adams [2004]). This still leaves several generations when the flamboyant style may have coexisted at both Hopi sites and Pottery Mound. However, in Appendix D, Curtis Schaafsma finds that Pottery Mound Polychrome was already present early in the site's use history. This might mean that the flamboyant style moved from east to west rather than the other way (cf. Crotty, Chapter 6; Hays-Gilpin and LeBlanc, Chapter 7).

The earliest, Glaze A, kivas excavated at Pottery Mound lacked mural art (Crotty, Chapter 6), which probably means that the earliest kivas to be painted were built ca. 1375, as Bramlett's (1963) analysis (cited in Crotty's chapter) implies. The bottom line is that it is most likely that Sikyatki Polychrome and Pottery Mound Polychrome, as well as the earliest murals at Hopi and the Homol'ovis, are part of a horizon style (Willey and Phillips 1958) that found contemporaneous expression at these distant sites (cf. Eckert, Chapter 4; Crotty, Chapter 6; and Hays-Gilpin and LeBlanc, Chapter 7). Whether either influenced the other, or whether both were inspired by a third, outside, source, is discussed further in the following sections.

Adler (Chapter 3) finds that the Hummingbird site (LA 578) began ca. A.D. 1250, while Pottery Mound (LA 416), farther down the Rio Puerco of the East near its mouth, may have been founded as much as a century later. Unexplained by this view is the fairly high frequency of Socorro Black-on-white found at the site (Appendix D). Perhaps there was an earlier pithouse component; the profile (Appendix C) between 128 and 133 m west shows what appears to be a pithouse cut into the red clay subsoil.[5] The absence at Pottery Mound of Los Padillas Glaze Polychrome (made close by in the Middle Rio Grande area [Franklin 1996]) or Arenal Glaze Polychrome, which date to A.D. 1315–1350 (Schaafsma 2002), supports the view that the pueblo was not founded until ca. A.D. 1350.[6] The significance of this finding of a chronological difference between the founding of Hummingbird and Pottery Mound is explored further in what follows.

What is Style?

The revival, on new methodological grounds, of arguments for aboriginal migrations (Anthony 1990; Clark 2001; Lyons 2003) has produced many fascinating arguments for the coresidence of ethnically distinct people at Pueblo IV villages during the 1300s and 1400s. Concepts of style often play a key role in such arguments (Clark 2007). At the SAR seminar and the SAA symposium there was much animated discussion about this, and the essays by Adler (Chapter 3), Eckert (Chapter 4), Crotty (Chapter 6), Hays-Gilpin and LeBlanc (Chapter 7), and P. Schaafsma (Chapter 8) marshal the data on style in many different ways to reach quite divergent positions. The basic difference is the debate between P. Schaafsma, who argues that the Pottery Mound murals are primarily an expression of Rio Grande style, and the others, who variously argue for Western Pueblo influence, or even Western Pueblo presence, to explain many aspects of the mural and ceramic art.

As an opening gambit at the SAA symposium, I suggested the rule that "labels are not explanations." What is "Sikyatki style," for example? Is it just a label for features (motifs) that look like forms found at Hopi on Sikyatki Polychrome pottery? Taking up this challenge, Hays-Gilpin and LeBlanc (Chapter 7) present a nuanced and carefully reasoned analysis of the stylistic relationships of Hopi and Pottery Mound. They find that the portrayals of textiles (analyzed in greater detail by Webster, Chapter 9) are some of the strongest evidence for linkage. They propose alternative scenarios whereby Hopi, or Keresans from Hopi, or perhaps Keresans from elsewhere with the requisite religious knowledge, could have painted many of the Pottery Mound murals. Crotty (Chapter 6) objects, however, because most of the murals with Hopi- (Sikyatki-) like elements also contain others expressive of a different style. I think she makes a good point.[7]

Interestingly, Brody (1964), some 40 years ago, saw the basic fact, something that only recently became clear to me. He says that the "larger Sikyatki designs of the third layout order in the Jeddito [at Hopi] are framed top and bottom, as noted by Smith [1952]; they also have side frames near the wall corners, and are thus completely within a prescribed area and *may also represent textiles*" (1964:125, emphasis added). So far as I am aware, Webster (Chapter 9) does not analyze these panels. Brody (1964:125) goes on to say the following: "If this assumption is correct, the abstract Sikyatki style of design was never used on the murals except in a representational way; *the style had nothing to do with mural art*; but on the murals, it had to do with textile art" (emphasis added). In the next paragraph he says further that "though the decorative character of the design style is inescapable, it is used only because it is an integral part of an object or thing depicted; and the design style belongs to the object or thing, *not to the painting*" (1964:125, emphasis added).

This point goes a long way to clarify the current debate: like the famous story about the elephant, each party has hold of a part, but none have yet formulated effective methodologies for analyzing the whole. P. Schaafsma's (Chapter 8) mention of the concept of a "cosmovision" seems to me to be a glance in the right direction, as is the recognition by most of these authors that many of the murals have a narrative structure. No adequate analysis of them *as narratives*, however, has yet been achieved.[8]

Shortcomings of Arbitrary Units of Analysis

Fifty years ago, the English archaeologist Sir Mortimer Wheeler (1956) severely chastised American archaeologists for using arbitrary metric levels to excavate sites. This approach destroys the depositional structure of artifact proveniences in the name of expediency. Regretfully, the 1979 UNM test pit (Cordell 1980) was dug using arbitrary 20 cm levels. The samples recovered were thus "destratified," mixing together sets of sherds or animal bone that were deposited in discrete events. Listen to the late Kit Sargeant, who dutifully excavated these samples using arbitrary levels, but who also observed the profiles

thus exposed and thought hard about what their depositional structure meant:

> There are several possible explanations which occur to my mind [to explain] the *sharply angled deposits* of the midden in which we are excavating:
>
> 1. This was a sloping bank to the river during prehistoric times.
> 2. A wash or small arroyo draining toward the river which was used as a trash dump and burial area.
> 3. Drainage channel which might have been dammed for domestic water purposes.
> 4. A purposely excavated trench to obtain clay for pottery or for building purposes.
> 5. The excavated catchment basin for water or perhaps a walk-in-well [cited in Cordell 2004, emphasis added].[9]

Looking at the Mera diagram (see Figure 11.1) in light of the scenarios suggested by Sargeant, we might suggest that the narrow passageway between the northern and southern roomblocks was a gully (rather than a narrow plaza).[10] In any case, Sargeant's observation report of "sharply angled deposits" that must have been crosscut by 2.5 x 2.5 m wide arbitrary metric levels (an issue I brought up at the SAR seminar) suggests that the temporal assumptions made by Eckert (2003; Chapter 4) or Clark (Chapter 10) must be regarded with extreme caution.[11] The UNM test pit needs to be reopened and profiled by people with in-depth knowledge of archaeological stratigraphy and the advice of a geomorphologist.

Nor is the assumption warranted that the sample taken from this test pit is in any way representative of the site as a whole, either in its chronological data or its faunal data. Looking at the profile of the bulldozer trench (Appendix C), we see in the interval 20 to 23 m west a steeply sloping stratified series of charcoal and other lenses—probably a trash midden that dips away from the eastern edge of the roomblock. The 1979 UNM test pit was in a similar relationship to the north edge of the high mound and the south edge of the northern roomblock (see Figure 11.1). But when were these roomblocks erected in this section of the site? We have no a priori reason to think they were there throughout the sequence of occupation at the site, nor that trash was deposited in that section in any continuous and long-lasting way; it may have accumulated very rapidly. Clark (Chapter 10) found that most of the animal bone in her sample came from the upper levels. We have no a priori way of knowing whether this sample represents the remains of only a couple of feasting events or a continuous, episodic rain of debris deposited over many decades (as she assumes). Her comparisons with other site assemblages is thus suspect, as is her critique of Emslie's (1981) hypothesis about the relatively greater importance of bird procurement at Pottery Mound than other sites he knew about. Emslie's sample was six times as large as that from the northwest quadrant of the 1979 UNM test pit and came from many different proveniences across the site—and thus should be much more representative, as a whole, than that analyzed by Clark.

I also remain deeply skeptical about Eckert's assignment of ethnic labels to the technological temper-classes her analysis documented. There are alternative possibilities that have yet to be ruled out. For example, people from Pottery Mound might have been resident among the Western Pueblos (Acoma, Zuni, Hopi) for a time and returned with new knowledge about how to make pottery (see Helms [1979] and Ware and Blinman [2000] for more paradigmatic discussions of this scenario; see also P. Schaafsma, Chapter 8, on the importance of visiting back and forth among the Pueblos). Alternatively, possibly the small number of pots that have long been regarded as (badly made) copies of Zuni or Acoma pottery (Brody 1964:31; Voll 1961) had different forms that required different strength characteristics, etc.

What About Trade?

A possibility most of the essays in this volume tend to shy away from, neglect, or reject is that some of the ceramic variability present at Pottery Mound is due to trade with other groups. In contrast, Brody (1964:25, 27, 66, 74, 76) proposes an interesting model of trade based on the presence of design motifs or styles that vary widely from the norm found at the site; such material accounts for about 3 percent of the decorated pottery.

> The trade route from Pottery Mound to Pecos would follow the Rio Grande to Tijeras Canyon, cross the eastern slope of the Sandias, going north, by Paa-ko, to the Galisteo Basin and its towns, and finally to Pecos. . . . It is likely that some if not all of the narrow banded vessels found at Pottery Mound were not manufactured there, rather that they were imported from the eastern slope of the Sandias where pottery making methods and

materials were sometimes identical to those of Pottery Mound [Brody 1964:25].

Going the other way, a small amount of Pottery Mound Polychrome, classified as San Clemente Polychrome by Mera (1933:4) and Lambert (1954:77; see also Toulouse and Stephenson 1960:23), may have been traded eastward. Indeed, what is classified as San Clemente Polychrome may have been made at Pottery Mound and traded out (Brody 1964:137).

More recently, Franklin (1996) in his analysis of Valencia Pueblo ceramics from the Los Lunas area (about 12 mi east of Pottery Mound) says that Pottery Mound Polychrome "is found, in small quantities, along the Rio Grande at Valencia Pueblo, and also at Gran Quivira [Hayes et al. 1981:91]. Whether or not it was manufactured outside Pottery Mound site itself has not been determined." Of San Clemente Polychrome, Franklin (1996:76) says its high frequency at Pottery Mound is seen nowhere else, pointing to its center of production being Pottery Mound; furthermore, "this type is present, but not dominant, at Valencia and the Middle Rio Grande basin; it is almost absent everywhere else." Building on earlier studies by Shepard (1942), Warren (1980; 1981), and Hayes and others (1981), Franklin (1996:71) argues that "trade with the Rio Grande [eastward] was intense during Glaze A," which pottery type he argues persisted into Glaze C times (1996:30, 74). Pottery Mound was connected to this east-west exchange sphere, but a realignment in the fifteenth century may be what led to a region-wide demographic decline (Franklin 1996:91; see below for a further discussion of this hypothesis). Modern sourcing studies on a macroregional scale to test these trade models would be most welcome.

Rio Grande–Style Rock Art and the Murals

Schaafsma (2000; Chapter 8) carefully compares the rock art of the Rio Grande macroregion and northwestern Chihuahua with the imagery portrayed in the Pottery Mound murals. The structure of the mural images facilitates such comparison, as Brody (1964:115–16) recognized: "The only pictorial space considered [in the Pottery Mound murals] is that occupied by the figures; and with that characteristic, these wall paintings closely resemble rock art, especially pictographs, of that and later periods." Schaafsma makes a strong case for the representational content of the murals fitting in closely with that seen in what she has called the "Rio Grande Style" of Pueblo IV rock art. In contrast, she shows that in the Hopi region there is no broad "landscape context" in the rock art for either the kiva murals there or the Sikyatki pottery designs. Her suggestion that textiles with "Sikyatki-style" designs moved westward is possible, but so too is the possibility that they moved from Hopi eastward. The Middle Rio Grande (and possibly the Pottery Mound area) did become a production zone for cotton (Hill 1998), but when that occurred remains unknown.

Mesoamerican Connections

Provocatively, Hibben (1966; 1975) changed his mind about his interpretation of Pottery Mound, perhaps because he was influenced by his friend Charles Di Peso's (1974) excavations at Paquimé (aka Casas Grandes) in northwestern Chihuahua, or William Wasley's (1960) excavations of the Gatlin platform mound near Gila Bend, Arizona, which he attributed to Mesoamerican influence (see R. G. Vivian, Chapter 2). We have seen that his inference of a platform mound (or pyramid) does not hold up to critical scrutiny (see preceding). But there are other bases for postulating some form of external Mexican influence. Webster (Chapter 9) elegantly shows that the textiles pictured in southwestern murals may reflect Mesoamerican meanings. Hays-Gilpin and LeBlanc (Chapter 7) show that the ceramics from northwestern Chihuahua, especially Ramos Polychrome, have a bearing on the development of what they define as "Sikyatki style." P. Schaafsma (1998; 2000; Chapter 8) also sees important connections in both rock art and the murals with the "cosmovision" centered in the Casas Grandes world (see also Schaafsma and Riley 1999). However, to her mind, the populations responsible for the rock art found in the Jornada area of southeastern New Mexico are critically important in understanding the structure of connectivity between Paquimé and the Rio Grande pueblos, a point I discuss further in what follows.

Once again, it is a point made by J. J. Brody (1964:116; 1970) that is of key importance to this discussion. What are the antecedents of southwestern Pueblo IV murals? "Iconographically and stylistically they seem to be without precedent in the area, and yet they occur in contexts that are certainly indigenous" (Brody 1970:102). After a thoughtful consideration of this problem, based on what was then known, he concludes as follows:

It seems clear that all of the visual elements which characterize Pueblo IV mural art were present in the Southwest in earlier periods, and it is probable that the later form was the result of a synthesis of several of the earlier local prototypes, especially including ceramic design. The impulse to synthesize may have been based on a conceptual system ["cosmovision"?] which came into the Southwest from Mexico along with many iconographic elements adopted by some of the Anasazi during Pueblo IV times [Brody 1970:109].

Since then, P. Schaafsma (1980; 1992; 1998; 2000), as to the first point, has presented a wealth of new imagery to consider in evaluating relevant local precedents for the Pueblo IV designs, most of which are outside of the Ancestral Pueblo cultural tradition. She agrees with the second point, that "the impulse to synthesize" may have come from Mexico (personal communication 2006). Webster's analysis (Chapter 9), the only discussion here that fully considers a spatial scale comparable to Brody's (1970) analysis, appears to reach much the same conclusion. There the matter must rest until future studies can bring new knowledge to bear.

Putting Pottery Mound into a Macroregional Cultural Context

"It is time, once again, to begin thinking about Southwestern archaeology as a whole" (Wilcox 2005a:9). Some time ago, I (1991b; see also Wilcox 1995) began such an attempt, noticing that there was a macroregional system centered on Paquimé where thousands of sherds of both Gila and El Paso polychromes were found (see Di Peso et al. 1974)—more than at any other excavated site. Gila Polychrome, a type of Roosevelt Red Ware, is distributed widely northwestwardly from Paquimé through the Safford Valley and Point of Pines and on to the Mogollon Rim country (the center of the development of Fourmile Polychrome, a type of western White Mountain Red Ware), and as far north as Bidahochi Pueblo (personal observation). El Paso Polychrome is distributed northeastwardly from Paquimé through the Jornada area of southeastern New Mexico as far east as the bison-hunting villages in the Roswell area on the edge of the High Plains (Speth 2003). As part of our recent Zuni Origins study (Gregory and Wilcox 2007), we asked Arthur Vokes to assemble a macroregional database of all known marine shell, copper bells, macaws, and turquoise found in the North American Southwest. Post–A.D. 1250, these data show a similar bilobed spatial pattern to that apparent in the distribution of Gila and El Paso polychromes (Vokes and Gregory 2007: Figure 17.12). These data together strengthen the case for Paquimé having had a profound intellectual influence on the southern Southwest and on southern Pueblo groups. With its single copper bell (Cordell 2004; Vargas 1995) and the numerous scarlet macaw images in its murals (Hibben 1975), Pottery Mound was clearly on the northern edge of this interaction sphere.

At Zuni, Kwakina Polychrome in its color scheme is an analogous type to Gila Polychrome, as is the white-slipped variety of San Clemente Polychrome at Pottery Mound. At Hopi, the addition of a matte red to Jeddito Black-on-yellow created Sikyatki Polychrome, just as its addition to yellow-slipped San Clemente created Pottery Mound Polychrome.[12] On the same time horizon, ca. A.D. 1375, a red matte paint was also added to some Roosevelt Red Ware, creating what Patrick Lyons (personal communication 2005) proposes to call "Los Muertos Polychrome" (see Haury 1945); it has also been called "Perry Mesa Polychrome" (Wilcox 1987). These color schemes, as Hays-Gilpin and LeBlanc (Chapter 7) note, harken back to Chihuahuan polychromes and especially to Ramos Polychrome—which is temporally antecedent to the northern types—but lasts into the middle 1400s. If, as seems likely, the colors had ideological or metaphoric meanings, we must begin to look much more intently at the "cosmovision" centered at Paquimé to understand what was going on here. Crown's (1994) excellent study of Gila Polychrome probably should be rethought from this perspective. Rather than Hopi influencing Pottery Mound, or vice versa, Paquimé may have influenced both, causing a parallel development to occur.

Along the northeastern axis, in the Jornada region of southeastern New Mexico, the influence of Paquimé was expressed differently. P. Schaafsma (personal communication 2006) informs me that "anything that smacks of Sikyatki is absent from these Jornada contexts." The villages there are also much smaller than those along the northwestern axis, and so the ceremonial organizations may similarly have been very different. Yet it is from this Jornada region that P. Schaafsma infers that the ideologies expressed in her Rio Grande style of rock art swept northward along the Rio Grande and beyond. One way to shed more light on this, that so far as I know has not yet been seriously examined, is to compare the iconography of El Paso/Villa Ahumada polychromes to that of Roosevelt Red Ware.

There is, however, an east-west dimension to all of this, capping the triangle for which the distributions of Gila and El Paso polychromes define the other two sides. Rio Grande Glaze Ware is known to suddenly emerge in the Middle Rio Grande valley (Albuquerque to Los Lunas) ca. A.D. 1315, after a century of experience with intrusive eastern White Mountain Red Ware (Franklin 1996:83). The emergence of the katsina ideology (Schaafsma 1994) soon spread along the same east-west *oikoumene*, even as the depopulation of the Pueblo, Colorado, drainage (at Wide Ruin, ca. A.D. 1300) and the Cebolleta Mesa (ca. A.D. 1350) began to break apart its settlement contiguity, neighbor-to-neighbor, from Hopi to Gran Quivira and beyond. The discovery at Speth's (2003) Roswell sites of an increase in pottery coming from long-distance sources *both* to the southwest and the west suggests that an east-west exchange structure extended all the way to this northeastern vertex of the Paquimé Pueblo IV macro-regional system (see also Franklin 1996). If the katsina ideology is expressed in the so-called Sikyatki style, then its evolution from a rather rigid and formal artistic expression (Brody 1964; see previous) to a more flamboyant one (at Hopi) may be an "internal" Puebloan development. However, there are masked figures in the Paquimé rock art style, and "kachina-like masks are more frequent among the designs on Ramos and Villa Ahumada Polychrome (Di Peso et al. 1974:Vol. 6)" (Schaafsma 1998:40). A wider comparative examination of the religious meanings of masks in the Americas would be helpful (see Brundage 1985; Lévi-Strauss 1979).

How significant the Pueblo IV economic relationships were in terms of autonomy versus interdependency on multiple spatial scales has yet to be adequately measured (Wilcox 2005a). The Coalescent Communities Database (CCD), and the resulting maps of successive 50-year periods (Figures 11.2–11.5), should help us to formulate better research questions to address this fundamental issue (see also Wilcox et al. 2006; 2007).[13] Table 11.1 summarizes the demographic data from the CCD for many of the neighbors of Pottery Mound. These results should be regarded as preliminary, as the kind of intensive consultation with local specialists to fine-tune the life-history models of the sites (number of rooms per time period) and their chronologies has yet to occur; only once it does can what we hope will become a widespread consensus be achieved. I continue to believe, however, that the *trends* apparent in these maps and in Table 11.1 will hold up to critical scrutiny (Wilcox et al. 2007).

Table 11.1. Rise and Decline of Pottery Mound's Puebloan Neighbors, A.D. 1350–1500, Compiled from the Coalescent Communities Database

Pueblo Site Cluster or Site	Demographic Comments
Jemez	takeoff in the west, mid-1400s
Zia	takeoff in the mid-1400s?
Cochiti	some decline or reorganization, mid-1400s
Kuapa	reorganized 1350–1400 and mid-1400s
LA 85	ends by 1400
Tyuoni	expansion, mid-1400s
Perage/San Ildefonso	reorganized late 1400s, also mid-1300s (Guaje Mesa goes out by 1350)
Puye	takeoff mid-1400s or reorganization; Old Santa Clara (Pueblo Estrella) gone by 1400; Santa Clara takes off 1500
Espanola Basin	takeoff mid-1300s
Picuris	takeoff early 1400s
Taos	takeoff mid-1400s
Santa Cruz Valley	ends by 1450 (squeezed out between Picuris and Nambe)
Nambe	takeoff mid-1300s
Santa Fe	takeoff 1300 (Arroyo Hondo first 1,000-room pueblo); decline in late 1300s; ends by 1450
Tonque	takeoff mid-1300s; shrinks early 1400s
Galisteo Basin	takeoff mid-1300s, again mid-1400s; shrinks early 1500s
Pecos	takeoff 1500
Sambrillo	ends by 1350
Chilili	persists, 1250–1670
San Miguel	ends by 1350
Rio Hondo/Roswell	ends by 1425
Corona/Gallo	ends by 1400
SE New Mexico	ends by 1375
Alamogordo	ends by 1350
Three Rivers	ends by 1400
Mesilla	ends by 1400
East of Black Range	ends by 1400
Mimbres/Black Range	ends by 1400
Alamosa Creek	ends by 1400
La Magdalena	persists, 1350–1700
Gran Quivira region	takeoff and reorganization mid-1400s
Chupadera Arroyo	reorganized 1450
Tompiro	takeoff early 1400s

Table 11.1 continued on page 239

Table 11.1 continued from page 238

Table 11.1. Rise and Decline of Pottery Mound's Puebloan Neighbors, A.D. 1350–1500, Compiled from the Coalescent Communities Database

Pueblo Site Cluster or Site	Demographic Comments
Quarai	ends by 1450; takeoff 1525
Piro	takeoff early 1300s; reorganized 1525
Isleta	takeoff early 1300s; decline in south mid-1400s
Albuquerque	takeoff early 1300s; second takeoff mid-1400s
Bootheel	reorganized 1350; ends 1400–1450
Gallinas Springs	ends by 1325
Lower Puerco of the E	ends by 1475
Middle Puerco of the E	ends by 1400 except Pueblo del Ojito and Hummingbird
Upper Puerco of the E	ends by 1400
Cebolleta Mesa	ends by 1350
Acoma	takeoff mid-1300s
Jaralosa	ends by 1385
El Morro area	ends by 1375
Pescado area	ends by 1375
Cliff	ends by 1425–1450
Casas Grandes	ends by 1450

Source: After Wilcox et al. 2007.

The network positions of Pottery Mound and its upstream neighbor, Hummingbird Pueblo, are clarified by these maps.[14] Hummingbird lies at the south end of the Middle Rio Puerco of the East settlement system that took off ca. A.D. 1225 as Keresan-speaking populations in the southern part of the old Chacoan world moved westward, southward, and eastward (see Ford et al. 1972; Wilcox 2005b; Wilcox et al. 2007). Its founding ca. A.D. 1250 may indicate that some of these populations moved a bit south to establish a trade linkage between the Western Keresans at Acoma and the Eastern Keresans at Zia, something that should be investigated in future research (cf. Adler, Chapter 3). Pottery Mound, in contrast, lies closest to the Southern Tiwa–speaking groups in the Los Lunas area and the Piro farther south; the mouth of the Rio Puerco of the East is situated on the cultural boundary between these two groups (see Marshall and Walt 1984; Wilcox 1991b). P. Schaafsma (Chapter 8) documents close ties to

this section of the Rio Grande, with ties as well to the Galisteo Basin and the Salinas Pueblos east of Abó Pass (which is east of the mouth of the Rio Puerco). However, Franklin's (1996) comparisons show that Pottery Mound was closer ceramically to the Southern Tiwa province. On the basis of the predominance of the evidence, Pottery Mound would appear to have its closest cultural affiliation to the Southern Tiwa.

A pattern that can be tracked through time in the maps (see Figures 11.2–11.5) and in Table 11.1 is the dissection of the east-west axis of the Pueblo IV macroregional system. The marked demographic decline along the eastern fringe of the Puebloan world and then in the lower Middle Rio Grande (including Pottery Mound) supports Franklin's (1996:91) finding of a profound realignment of exchange relationships. We thus have identified a *regional economic context* for the depopulation of the Pottery Mound site.

Please note in regard to Figures 11.2 through 11.5: The nested lines around the sites are the results of a cost-surface analysis by Brett Hill using three measures of interaction to cluster sites: 7 km catchment areas, the distance one can walk and come back in a day (18 km), and the distance one can walk in a day with a pack (36 km). This analysis takes into account the energy costs of crossing slopes of different magnitude.

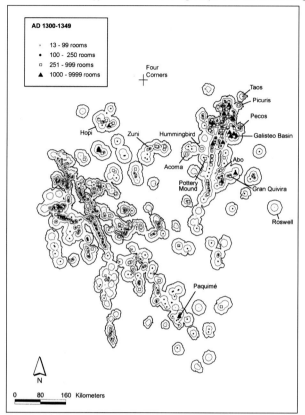

FIGURE 11.2
Coalescent Communities Map of the North American Southwest, A.D. 1300–1349 (after Wilcox et al. 2007).

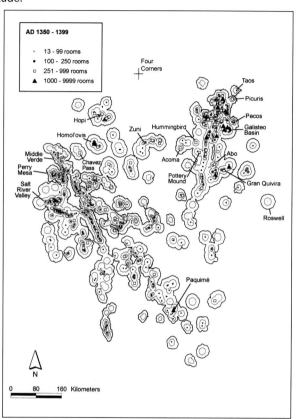

FIGURE 11.3
Coalescent Communities Map of the North American Southwest, A.D. 1350–1399. (After Wilcox et al. 2007.)

A second pattern is probably also of fundamental importance in explaining this outcome. By ca. A.D. 1400, the whole Mogollon Rim country cleared out, sharply delineating the northern Pueblo Southwest from the remnants of the southern Southwest (see Figure 11.4). Only a generation or so after the beginning of the style horizon expressed in black-and-red on yellow pottery (Sikyatki, Matsaki,[15] Pottery Mound, and Cieneguilla polychromes[16]), ties with the probable ideological source for some of these concepts was apparently severed, reducing the economic sphere of Paquimé and probably contributing to its decline. Much the same story was happening along the northeastern axis, though perhaps for different reasons. Meanwhile, the Hopi macroeconomy (Wilcox 2005c; 2006) indicated

by the distribution of Hopi Yellow Ware also shrank, no doubt requiring a fundamental retrenchment and reorganization. It succeeded, if the flamboyant style of Sikyatki Polychrome and the Hopi kiva murals are any indication—though why this happened remains a mystery. One economic factor may have been the emergence of the early protohistoric period's Puebloan macroeconomy based on the beginnings of the so-called dog-nomad trade between Plains bison hunters and the large Plains-edge pueblos from Taos to Gran Quivira—but that is another story beyond the scope of this discussion (but see Wilcox 1981; 1984; 2005a; Wilcox et al. 2006; 2007). Within a generation or so, as this world was just emerging, Pottery Mound was no longer a place of occupation (see Figure 11.5).

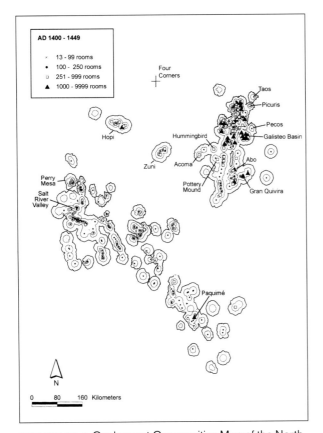

FIGURE 11.4 Coalescent Communities Map of the North American Southwest, A.D. 1400–1449. (After Wilcox et al. 2007.)

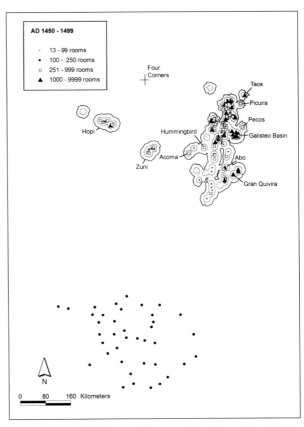

FIGURE 11.5 Coalescent Communities Map of the North American Southwest, A.D. 1450–1499. (After Wilcox et al. 2007.)

Future Directions of Pottery Mound Research

Many new directions for future research on Pottery Mound are alluded to in the above discussion and in the other essays in this volume. Here I just want to repeat one of the "rules of the game" I enunciated at the 2005 SAA symposium: no guts, no glory. Pottery Mound continues to erode away. Let us join together in urging those now responsible for the site to formulate a serious management plan for its preservation and further study. Aerial photographs need to be taken from which a comprehensive planimetric map can be made. Then all the earlier maps and profiles need to be reconciled with the overall map, so we can better understand the relationships of the parts to the whole—a process well begun by David Phillips (see Figure 1.3). As Linda Cordell (2004) has said, a geomorphological model needs to be created for the site and the depositional context of its locality along the Lower Rio Puerco of the East. I recommend that plans be

put in place and funding found to reopen Hibben's bulldozer trench and to fully record the profiles in microstratigraphic detail for both the north and the south sides. The same should be done with the 1979 UNM 5 x 5 m test pit. Both efforts should incorporate the expertise of a geomorphologist. Pollen and other soil samples could be taken at the same time and studied. An archival study broader even than is currently under way should be initiated in which all available aerial photographs and other geomorphological data about the site and its locality are assembled and analyzed. In this way it may be possible to chart the progressive destruction of the site, resolving important questions about its original size and extent. New ways to intervene to stop the continuing erosion of the site should be designed and implemented. Let our credo be that long since proposed by the Chicago architect Daniel Hudson Burnham: "Make no little plans," he said, "they have no magic to stir men's blood" (Hines 1979:xvii). ▪▪

ACKNOWLEDGMENTS

First thanks go to Polly Schaafsma for inviting me to be an outside discussant in this series of discussions of the Pottery Mound. Special thanks also go to Curtis Schaafsma, David Phillips, and Michael Adler for providing firsthand access to New Mexico sites and their insights about them. The participants in this volume have been unfailingly kind and timely. Thanks also go to David Gregory and J. Brett Hill of the Center for Desert Archaeology (CDA) for their collaboration on interpreting the Coalescent Communities Database and to William Doelle, the president of CDA, and Jim Holmlund, Western Mapping Company, for their support while I was assembling it. David Gregory, Polly Schaafsma, and Kelley Hays-Gilpin read the draft of this essay and provided important corrections and insights. At the Museum of Northern Arizona I want to thank Director Robert Breunig for his support and Jodi Griffith for drafting a copy of the Mera diagram of LA 416 and preparing versions of the other figures for use here. I also thank the Laboratory of Anthropology, Museum of New Mexico, Santa Fe, for permission to publish this version of the Mera diagram. For any errors of fact or interpretation I alone am responsible.

NOTES

1. Not only did I observe Gregory's excavations of Mound 8 at Las Colinas and at Pueblo Grande, David Doyel's at Escalante, Jerry Howard's at Mesa Grande, and those of Douglas Craig, Owen Lindauer, and David Jacobs in Tonto Basin mounds, I have read Christian Downum's superb but as yet unpublished monograph on the excavations of the Pueblo Grande mound.

2. From Hibben's point of view, he knew that the site was eroding rapidly into the Rio Puerco of the East. This probably was his justification for using a bulldozer to cut a huge trench through the site. To peel a mural apparently would have required first cleaning it all off, but they saw that it faded badly when that was done, as P. Vivian discusses. Brody (1970:102, 104) explains Hibben's solution: "The procedure was then established of uncovering each wall in sections and recording each section both by hand and photographically. A reconstruction of the entire wall was then made from these copies." While I do not think this was the best approach, it probably should not be concluded that it was a wanton act of hubris.

3. Mera's diagram has measurements in paces. From Curtis Schaafsma (personal communication 2006) I learned that studies by Jonathan Haas and Winifred Creamer had established that Mera's "pace" was a yard long, or 3 ft. I assume in Figure 11.1 that his north arrow points to true north, as does that on the Phillips map (personal communication 2005). Taking the two known points seen in the profile

of the Hibben bulldozer trench, the adobe walls were exposed on the surface as points of reference and the north edge of the escarpment of the extant mound as another. Jodi Griffith, the Museum of Northern Arizona draftsperson, used a computer to reconcile the two maps as shown in Figure 11.1. The edge of the 1953 and 1996 riverbanks are taken from an earlier version of the Phillips map. Note the location of the 1979 UNM test pit in this "best fit" composite map.

4. "When the same style of design is found on pottery types of the same age but belonging to different wares, those types are then said to be analogous" (Colton 1953:71).

5. In working out the percentages in the various "strat tests" excavated by Hibben, C. Schaafsma (Appendix D; personal communication 2006) discovered that in the west test at the base there is a dominant assemblage of types that go with Socorro Black-on-white, which supports the hypothesis that there was an earlier component.

6. Curtis Schaafsma first pointed this out to me and to others. He also points out that in all the tests for which we have data (see Appendix D), Cieneguilla Glaze-on-yellow is reported in the deepest levels; he dates this type as beginning ca. A.D. 1370 (1995; 2002). Maybe so; but I think, in the first place, we should be cautious because Hibben's tests were conducted using gross 50 cm arbitrary levels, causing artificial mixture of deposits. Bramlett's (1963) analysis (cited in Crotty, Chapter 6) may

still prove to be the most correct; Voll (1961) also believed that the occupation started earlier than A.D. 1370 (see following). Is Cieneguilla Glaze-on-yellow analogous to Jeddito Black-on-yellow, which was first made at Hopi ca. A.D. 1325? If so, given that the former was apparently made in large quantities at Pottery Mound (Eckert 2003; Appendix D), then perhaps it dates earlier at Pottery Mound than it does in the Galisteo Basin where C. Schaafsma's (1995; 2002) dating was derived from a depositionally meaningful stratigraphic study at Las Madres (LA 25). More detailed comparative ceramic studies across the whole east-west distribution of the early Pueblo IV northern Southwest are needed.

7. A comparison of the tables in Chapters 6 and 7 reveals discrepancies about what different scholars recognize as "Sikyatki style." In general, it is not clear to me that all scholars from Brody (1964) on have had the same referent in mind for this concept. Hays-Gilpin and LeBlanc (Chapter 7) have helped to clarify what should be the referent, appealing to what Smith (1971) called "flamboyant" Sikyatki style, but pointing out that the style of early Sikyatki Polychrome is different.

8. A new approach to interpreting mural and ceramic art has recently been proposed by Sekaquaptewa and Washburn (2004). Arguing that what are portrayed are not simply representational symbols but metaphors, they turn to the Hopi language found in publicly sung songs to demonstrate the metaphorical nature of these concepts and apply this perspective in interesting ways to the interpretation of certain mural panels and ceramic images. While I (1981; 2004) believe there are grounds for doubting the complete continuity of Hopi religious beliefs from the Pueblo IV period into the present, something these authors seem unwilling to doubt or test, nevertheless their proposals are stimulating and insightful.

9. Sargeant did draw profiles of at least some of the exposures in this test pit, but they could not be found recently (Cordell 2004). The two excavated quadrants of this test pit need to be reopened and detailed, depositionally meaningful profiles need to be made of all eight faces, just as is now being done in the mound in front of Pueblo Bonito

by Wirt Wills (personal communication 2005). Until then, it is not possible to be sure exactly how "sharply angled" the deposits were. Measuring off the bulldozer trench profile, I get 24 degrees for the slope of the probable trash deposits on the east side of the high mound. A photograph taken by Curtis Schaafsma in the 1980s of the strata exposed in the arroyo bank not far from the UNM test pit suggests 20 degrees (P. Schaafsma, personal communication 2006). Some of Sargeant's scenarios might imply even steeper slopes.

10. When we visited Pottery Mound, I noticed a sediment-filled channel in the arroyo face across from the site but did not then know enough to look for the relationship to a possible channel between Mera's north and south roomblocks. Nor did we walk around to the east and then north so we could look back at the face of the arroyo cut through the site to see if a sediment-and-trash-filled channel was present in the appropriate place. Might it be, we may wonder, that during the time Pottery Mound was occupied the Puerco was a braided stream and the site was located on its outermost (southern) channel? A geomorphologist should be able to help us better conceptualize such questions and to answer them.

11. In particular, Eckert's suggestion that "it can be assumed that each level represents approximately six years of accumulation" is entirely speculative and without foundation. We should also note that her data (see Chapter 4) do not seriate, which is another reason for thinking that the deposits sampled may have accumulated much faster than she assumes. I am not even persuaded that the two-part chronological grouping suggested by Eckert (2003) and Clark (Chapter 10) is sound.

12. This important comparison was driven home to me when we were at the Pottery Mound site in July 2004 and Curtis Schaafsma held an impromptu ceramic seminar, explaining what Pottery Mound Polychrome was compared to San Clemente Polychrome; I immediately saw the similarity, technologically, to Sikyatki.

13. The sites are classified into four size classes: hamlets and small, medium, and large villages. A cost-surface analysis by J. Brett Hill is shown in the nested enclosures of the sites, taking the energetics

of crossing different slopes into account for three measures of interaction: 7 km catchments, 18 km to go and come back in a day, and 36 km to go in a day on foot with a pack (see Wilcox et al. 2007).

14. I show Pottery Mound on Figure 11.2 for the A.D. 1300–1349 period because when it was made I was following Voll's (1961) assessment of its beginning. In light of the above discussion, I now doubt that it should be shown on this map. If it was founded a bit before A.D. 1350, it probably was only a small village or hamlet initially. Similarly, I now would add it to the post-1450 map.

15. The current chronological model for Matsaki Polychrome at Zuni (Kintigh 1985) has its beginning about A.D. 1400. It would be worth critically reexamining this calibration to see if it might be better moved back to A.D. 1375. The eminent ceramicist Emil W. Haury (1931:44, Plate 13) reported a bowl of Matsaki Polychrome from the Show Low Ruin, which is thought to have been depopulated by A.D. 1400.

16. Franklin (1996:87) describes Cieneguilla Polychrome as being Cieneguilla Glaze-on-yellow with red matte paint added; both were types made in the Galisteo Basin.

REFERENCES CITED

Adams, E. Charles

2004 Homol'ovi: A 13th–14th Century Settlement Cluster in Northeastern Arizona. In *The Protohistoric Pueblo World, A.D. 1275–1600*, edited by E. Charles Adams and Andrew I. Duff, pp. 119–27. University of Arizona Press, Tucson.

Anthony, David W.

1990 Migration in Archeology: The Baby and the Bathwater. *American Anthropologist* 92(4):895–914.

Ballagh, Jean, and David Phillips

2005 Rediscovering Pottery Mound. Paper presented at the 70th Annual Society for American Archaeology Meeting, Salt Lake City.

Bramlett, William O., Jr.

1963 Manuscript and notes from 1963. Manuscript on file, Maxwell Museum of Anthropology, University of New Mexico, Albuquerque.

Brody, J. J.

1964 Design Analysis of the Rio Grande Glaze Pottery of Pottery Mound, New Mexico. Unpublished Master's thesis, University of New Mexico, Albuquerque.

1970 The Kiva Murals of Pottery Mound. *Verhandlungen des XXXVIII Internationales Amerikanistenkongresses*, Stuttgart-München, 12. bis 18. August 1968, Band II, pp. 101–10.

Brundage, Burr Cartwright

1985 *The Jade Steps: A Ritual Life of the Aztecs.* University of Utah Press, Salt Lake City.

Chamberlin, T. C.

1965 The Method of Multiple Working Hypotheses. *Science* 148(3671):754–59.

Clark, Jeffrey J.

2001 *Tracking Prehistoric Migrations: Pueblo Settlers among the Tonto Basin Hohokam.* Anthropological Papers of the University of Arizona No. 65. University of Arizona Press, Tucson.

2007 Archaeological Concepts for Assessing Mogollon-Zuni Connections. In *Zuni Origins, Toward a New Synthesis of Southwestern Archaeology*, edited by David A. Gregory and David R. Wilcox. University of Arizona Press, Tucson, in press.

Colton, Harold S.

1953 *Potsherds, An Introduction to the Study of Prehistoric Southwestern Ceramics and Their Use in Historic Reconstruction.* Museum of Northern Arizona Bulletin No. 25. Northern Arizona Society of Science and Art, Flagstaff.

1955 *Pottery Types of the Southwest.* Museum of Northern Arizona Ceramic Series No. 3. Northern Arizona Society of Science and Art, Flagstaff.

Cordell, Linda S.

1980 University of New Mexico Field School Excavations at Pottery Mound, New Mexico, 1979, Preliminary Report. Manuscript on file, Maxwell Museum of Anthropology, University of New Mexico, Albuquerque.

2004 Advanced Seminar on Pottery Mound, School of American Research, May 11–12. Manuscript on file, School of American Research, Santa Fe, New Mexico.

Crotty, Helen K.

1995 Anasazi Mural Art of the Pueblo IV Period, A.D. 1300–1600: Influences, Selective Adaptation, and Cultural Diversity in the Prehistoric Southwest. Unpublished Ph.D. dissertation, University of California, Los Angeles.

Crown, Patricia

1994 *Ceramics and Ideology, Salado Polychrome Pottery.* University of New Mexico Press, Albuquerque.

Di Peso, Charles C.

1974 *Casas Grandes, A Fallen Trading Center of the Gran Chichimeca.* Vols. 1–3. Amerind Foundation, Dragoon, Arizona.

Di Peso, Charles C., John B. Rinaldo, and Gloria J. Fenner

1974 *Casas Grandes, A Fallen Trading Center of the Gran Chichimeca.* Vols. 4 and 6. Northland Press, Flagstaff, Arizona.

Eckert, Suzanne L.

2003 Social Boundaries, Immigration, and Ritual Systems: A Case Study from the American Southwest. Unpublished Ph.D. dissertation, Arizona State University, Tempe.

Emslie, Steven D.

1981 Prehistoric Agricultural Ecosystems: Avifauna from Pottery Mound, New Mexico. *American Antiquity* 46(4):853–61.

Ford, Richard I., Albert H. Schroeder, and Stewart L. Peckham

1972 Three Perspectives on Puebloan Prehistory. In *New Perspectives on the Pueblos*, edited by Alfonso Ortiz, pp. 19–39. University of New Mexico Press, Albuquerque.

Franklin, Hayward H.

1996 *Valencia Pueblo Ceramics.* Manuscript on file, Separate No. P2785, ARMS, Laboratory of Anthropology, Museum of New Mexico, Santa Fe.

Gregory, David A.

1987 The Morphology of Platform Mounds and the Structure of Classic Period Hohokam Sites. In *The Hohokam Village: Site Structure and Organization*, edited by David E. Doyel, pp. 183–210. American Association for the Advancement of Science, Glenwood Springs, Colorado.

1991 Form and Variation in Hohokam Settlement Patterns. In *Chaco & Hohokam: Prehistoric Regional Systems in the American Southwest*, edited by Patricia L. Crown and W. James Judge, pp. 159–94. School of American Research, Santa Fe, New Mexico.

Gregory, David A., David R. Abbott, Deni J. Seymour, and Nancy M. Bannister

1988 *The 1982–1984 Excavations at Las Colinas, The Mound 8 Precinct.* Arizona State Museum Archaeological Series Vol. 162, No. 3. University of Arizona, Tucson.

Gregory, David A., and David R. Wilcox (editors)

2007 *Zuni Origins: Toward a New Synthesis of Southwestern Archaeology*, edited by David A. Gregory and David R. Wilcox. University of Arizona Press, Tucson, in press.

Harlow, Francis H.

1965 Acoma Glazed Pottery. Manuscript on file, No. P1598, Laboratory of Anthropology, Santa Fe, New Mexico.

Haury, Emil W.

1931 Showlow and Pinedale Ruins. In *Recently Dated Pueblo Ruins in Arizona*, pp. 4–79. Smithsonian Miscellaneous Collections Vol. 82, No. 11. Smithsonian Institution, Washington D.C.

1945 *The Excavation of Los Muertos and Neighboring Ruins in the Salt River Valley, Southern Arizona.* Papers of the Peabody Museum of American Archaeology and Ethnology Vol. 24, No. 1. Harvard University, Cambridge, Massachusetts.

Hayden, Julian D.

1940   *Excavations, 1940, at University Indian Ruin.*
       Southwestern Monuments Association
       Technical Series Vol. 5. Southwestern
       Monuments Association, Globe, Arizona.

Hayes, Alden C., Jon N. Young, and A. H. Warren

1981   *Excavations of Mound 7, Gran Quivira National
       Monument, New Mexico.* Publications in
       Archaeology No. 16. U.S. National Park
       Service, Washington D.C.

Hays-Gilpin, Kelley, and Eric van Hartesveldt (editors)

1998   *Prehistoric Ceramics of the Puerco Valley, The
       1995 Chambers-Sanders Trust Lands Ceramic
       Conference.* Museum of Northern Arizona
       Ceramic Series No. 7. Museum of Northern
       Arizona, Flagstaff.

Helms, Mary W.

1979   *Ancient Panama, Chiefs in Search of Power.*
       University of Texas Press, Austin.

Hibben, Frank C.

1966   A Possible Pyramidal Structure and Other
       Mexican Influences at Pottery Mound, New
       Mexico. *American Antiquity* 31(4):522–29.

1975   *Kiva Art of the Anasazi at Pottery Mound.* KC
       Publications, Las Vegas, Nevada.

1987   Report on the Salvage Operations at the site
       of Pottery Mound, New Mexico, during the
       Excavation Seasons of 1977–1986. Manuscript
       on file, ARMS, Laboratory of Anthropology,
       Museum of New Mexico, Santa Fe.

Hill, J. Brett

1998   Agricultural Production and Specialization
       among the Eastern Anasazi during the Pueblo
       IV Period. In *Migration and Reorganization:
       The Pueblo IV Period in the American
       Southwest*, edited by Katherine A. Spielmann,
       pp. 209–32. Arizona State University
       Anthropological Research Papers No. 51.
       Arizona State University, Tempe.

Hill, J. Brett, Jeffery J. Clark, William H. Doelle, and
       Patrick D. Lyons

2004   Prehistoric Demography in the Southwest:
       Migration, Coalescence, and Hohokam
       Population Decline. *American Antiquity*
       69:689–716.

Hines, Thomas S.

1979   *Burnham of Chicago, Architect and Planner.*
       University of Chicago Press, Chicago.

Kidder, Alfred V.

1927   Southwestern Archeological Conference.
       Science 66(1716):489–91.

Kintigh, Keith W.

1985   *Settlement, Subsistence, and Society in Late
       Zuni Prehistory.* Anthropological Papers of the
       University of Arizona No. 44. University of
       Arizona Press, Tucson.

Kuhn, Thomas

1962   *The Structure of Scientific Revolutions.*
       University of Chicago Press, Chicago.

Lambert, Marjorie F.

1954   *Paa-ko, Archaeological Chronicle of an
       Indian Village in North Central New Mexico.*
       School of American Research Monograph
       No. 19. School of American Research,
       Santa Fe, New Mexico.

LeBlanc, Stephen A.

1980   The Dating of Casas Grandes. *American
       Antiquity* 45:799–806.

Lévi-Strauss, Claude

1979   *The Way of the Masks.* Translated by Sylvia
       Modelski. University of Washington
       Press, Seattle.

Lyons, Patrick D.

2003   *Ancestral Hopi Migrations.* Anthropological
       Papers of the University of Arizona No. 68.
       University of Arizona Press, Tucson.

Marshall, Michael P., and Henry J. Walt

1984   *Rio Abajo: Prehistory and History of a
       Rio Grande Province.* Historic Preservation
       Division, New Mexico Historic Preservation
       Program, Santa Fe.

Mera, Harry P.

1933   *A Proposed Revision of the Rio Grande
       Glaze Paint Sequence.* Laboratory of
       Anthropology Technical Series Bulletin
       No. 5. Archaeological Survey, Laboratory of
       Anthropology, Santa Fe, New Mexico.

Rescher, Nicholas

1985   *The Strife of Systems: An Essay on the Grounds and Implications of Philosophical Diversity.* University of Pittsburgh Press, Pittsburgh, Pennsylvania.

Schaafsma, Curtis F.

1995   The Chronology of Las Madres Pueblo (LA 25). In *Of Pots and Rocks; Papers in Honor of A. Helene Warren*, edited by Meliha S. Duran and David T. Kirkpatrick, pp. 155–66. Papers of the Archaeological Society of New Mexico Vol. 21. Archaeological Society of New Mexico, Albuquerque.

2002   *Apaches de Navajo, Seventeenth-Century Navajos in the Chama Valley of New Mexico.* University of Utah Press, Salt Lake City.

Schaafsma, Curtis F., and Carroll L. Riley (editors)

1999   *The Casas Grandes World.* University of Utah Press, Salt Lake City.

Schaafsma, Polly

1980   *Indian Rock Art of the Southwest.* School of American Research, Santa Fe, New Mexico.

1992   *Rock Art in New Mexico.* Revised Edition. Museum of New Mexico Press, Santa Fe.

1998   Paquime Rock Art Style, Chihuahua, Mexico. In *Rock Art of the Chihuahuan Desert Borderlands*, edited by Sheron Smith-Savage and Robert J. Mallouf, pp. 33–44. Center for Big Bend Studies Occasional Papers No. 3. Sul Ross State University, Alpine, Texas.

2000   *Warrior, Shield, and Star.* Western Edge Press, Santa Fe, New Mexico.

Schaafsma, Polly (editor)

1994   *Kachinas in the Pueblo World.* University of New Mexico Press, Albuquerque.

Scheffler, Israel

1967   *Science and Subjectivity.* Bobbs-Merrill, New York.

Sekaquaptewa, Emory, and Dorothy Washburn

2004   They Go Along Singing: Reconstructing the Hopi Past from Ritual Metaphors in Song and Image. *American Antiquity* 69(3):457–86.

Shepard, Anna O.

1942   *Rio Grande Glaze Paint Ware: A Study Illustrating the Place of Ceramic Technological Analysis in Archaeological Research.* Contributions to American Anthropology and History No. 39. Carnegie Institute of Washington Publication No. 528. Carnegie Institution of Washington, Washington, D.C.

Smith, Watson

1952   *Kiva Mural Decorations at Awatovi and Kawaika'a, with a Survey of Other Wall Paintings in the Pueblo Southwest.* Papers of the Peabody Museum of American Archaeology and Ethnology Vol. 37. Harvard University, Cambridge, Massachusetts.

1971   *Painted Ceramics of the Western Mound at Awatovi.* Papers of the Peabody Museum of American Archaeology and Ethnology No. 38. Harvard University, Cambridge, Massachusetts.

Speth, John D. (editor)

2003   *Life on the Periphery, Economic Change in late Prehistoric Southeastern New Mexico.* Memoirs of the Museum of Anthropology, University of Michigan, No 37. Museum of Anthropology, University of Michigan, Ann Arbor.

Toulouse, Joseph, Jr., and Robert L. Stephenson

1960   *Excavations at Pueblo Pardo.* Museum of New Mexico Papers in Anthropology No. 2. Museum of New Mexico, Santa Fe.

Vargas, Victoria D.

1995   *Copper Bell Trade Patterns in the Prehispanic U.S. Southwest and Northwest Mexico.* Arizona State Museum Archaeological Series No. 187. University of Arizona, Tucson.

Vokes, Arthur H., and David A. Gregory

2007   Trade and Exchange Networks for Exotic Goods in the American Southwest and Northwest Mexico. In *Zuni Origins: Toward a New Synthesis in Southwestern Archaeology*, edited by David A. Gregory and David R. Wilcox. University of Arizona Press, Tucson, in press.

Voll, Charles

1961 The Glaze Paint Ceramics of Pottery Mound. Unpublished Master's thesis, University of New Mexico, Albuquerque.

Ware, John A., and Eric Blinman

2000 Cultural Collapse and Reorganization: The Origin and Spread of Pueblo Ritual Organizations. In *The Archaeology of Regional Interaction: Religion, Warfare, and Exchange across the American Southwest and Beyond*, edited by Michelle Hegmon, pp. 381–409. University Press of Colorado, Boulder.

Warner, Thor

1928 Rio Puerco Ruins. *American Anthropologist*, n.s., 30:85–93.

Warren, Helene

1980 A Petrographic Study of the Pottery. In *Contributions to Gran Quivira Archeology*, edited by Alden C. Hayes. National Park Service, Washington, D.C.

1981 Description of Pottery Tempering Materials of Gran Quivira. In *Excavation of Mound 7, Gran Quivira National Monument, New Mexico*, by Alden C. Hayes, Jon N. Young, and A. H. Warren, Appendix. Publications in Archeology No. 16. U.S. National Park Service, Washington, D.C.

Wasley, William W.

1960 A Hohokam Platform at the Gatlin Site, Gila Bend, Arizona. *American Antiquity* 26(2):244–62.

Wheeler, Mortimer

1956 *Archaeology from the Earth*. Penguin, Baltimore, Maryland.

Wilcox, David R.

1977 On Drawing Profiles. In *The Architecture of the Casa Grande and Its Interpretation*, by David R. Wilcox and Lynette O. Shenk, pp. 213–17. Arizona State Museum Archaeological Series No. 115. University of Arizona, Tucson.

1981 Changing Perspectives on the Protohistoric Pueblos, A.D. 1450–1700. In *The Protohistoric Period in the North American Southwest, A.D. 1450–1700*, edited by David R. Wilcox and W. Bruce Masse, pp. 378–409. Arizona State University Anthropological Research Papers No. 24. Arizona State University, Tempe.

1984 Multi-Ethnic Division of Labor in the Protohistoric Southwest. In *Collected Papers in Honor of Harry L. Hadlock*, edited by Nancy L. Fox, pp. 141–56. Papers of the Archaeological Society of New Mexico No. 9. Archaeological Society of New Mexico, Albuquerque.

1986a A Historical Analysis of the Problem of Southwestern-Mesoamerican Connections. In *Ripples in the Chichimec Sea*, edited by F. Joan Mathien and Randall H. McGuire, pp. 9–44. Southern Illinois University Press, Carbondale.

1986b The Tepiman Connection: A Model of Southwestern-Mesoamerican Interactions. In *Ripples in the Chichimec Sea*, edited by F. Joan Mathien and Randall H. McGuire, pp. 135–53. Southern Illinois University Press, Carbondale.

1987 *Frank Midvale's Investigation of the Site of La Ciudad*. Arizona State University Anthropological Field Studies No. 19. Arizona State University, Tempe.

1991a Hohokam Social Complexity. In *Chaco & Hohokam: Prehistoric Regional Systems in the American Southwest*, edited by Patricia L. Crown and W. James Judge, pp. 253–76. School of American Research, Santa Fe, New Mexico.

1991b Changing Context of Pueblo Adaptations, A.D. 1250–1600. In *Farmers, Hunters and Colonists: Interaction between the Southwest and the Southern Plains*, edited by Katherine A. Spielmann, pp. 128–54. University of Arizona Press, Tucson.

1995 A Processual Model of Charles C. Di Peso's Babocomari Site and Related Systems. In *The Gran Chichimeca: Essays on the Archaeology and Ethnohistory of Northern Mesoamerica*, edited by Jonathan E. Reyman, pp. 281–319. Avebury, London.

1999a A Peregrine View of Macroregional Systems in the North American Southwest, A.D. 750–1250. In *Great Towns and Regional Polities*, edited by Jill E. Neitzel, pp. 115–42. University of New Mexico Press, Albuquerque.

1999b A Preliminary Graph-Theoretic Analysis of Access Relationships at Casas Grandes, Chihuahua. In *The Casas Grandes World*, edited by Curtis Schaafsma and Carroll Riley, pp. 93–104. University of Utah Press, Salt Lake City.

2000a El Nexo Tepiman: Un Modelo de Interacción entre Mesoamérica y Suroeste Norteamericano. In *Relaciones, Estudios de Historia y Sociedad* No. 82:59–84. El Colegio de Michoacán, Zamora, Michoacán, Mexico.

2000b A Peregrine View of Hohokam Archaeology. *Bulletin of Old Pueblo Archaeology Center* pp. 1–6.

2002 The Wupatki Nexus: Chaco-Hohokam-Chumash Connectivity, A.D. 1150–1225. In *The Archaeology of Contact: Processes and Consequences. Proceedings of the Twenty-Fifth Annual Conference of the Archaeological Association of the University of Calgary*, edited by Kurtis Lesick, Barbara Kulle, Christine Cluney, and Meaghan Peuramaki-Brown, pp. 218–34. Archaeological Association of the University of Calgary, Alberta.

2004 Looking for Middle Ground: Archaeology on the Colorado Plateau Today. In *The Colorado Plateau: Cultural, Biological, and Physical Research*, edited by Charles van Riper III and Kenneth Cole, pp. 11–18. University of Arizona Press, Tucson.

2005a Big Issues, New Syntheses. Big Picture Archaeology. *Plateau* 2(1):8–21.

2005b Things Chaco, A Peregrine Perspective. Big Picture Archaeology. *Plateau* 2(1):36–55.

2005c Perry Mesa and Its World. Big Picture Archaeology. *Plateau* 2(1):22–35.

2006 Final Report, La Plata Mapping Project: Mapping and Artifact Collections at NA11648, Comparisons with Other Verde Confederacy Sites, and Its Context within the Hopi Macroeconomy. To be submitted to the Agua Fria National Monument, Phoenix. Manuscript on file, Museum of Northern Arizona, Flagstaff.

Wilcox, David R., and Don D. Fowler
2002 The Beginnings of Anthropological Archaeology in the North American Southwest: From Thomas Jefferson to the Pecos Conference. *Journal of the Southwest* (Summer): whole issue.

Wilcox, David R., David A. Gregory, and J. Brett Hill
2007 Zuni in the Puebloan and Southwestern Worlds. In *Zuni Origins, Toward a New Synthesis of Southwestern Archaeology*, edited by David A. Gregory and David R. Wilcox. University of Arizona Press, Tucson, in press.

Wilcox, David R., David A. Gregory, J. Brett Hill, and Gary Funkhouser
2006 The Changing Contexts for Warfare in the North American Southwest, A.D. 1200–1700. In *Southwestern Interludes: Papers in Honor of Charlotte J. and Theodore R. Frisbie*, edited by Regge Wiseman, Thomas O'Laughlin, and Cordelia Snow, pp. 203–32. Archaeological Society of New Mexico No. 32. Archaeological Society of New Mexico, Albuquerque.

Wilcox, David R., and Lynette O. Shenk
1977 *The Architecture of the Casa Grande and Its Interpretation.* Arizona State Museum Archaeological Series No. 115. University of Arizona, Tucson.

Willey, Gordon R., and Philip Phillips
1958 *Method and Theory in American Archaeology.* University of Chicago Press, Chicago.

Appendix A

Site Maps of Pottery Mound (LA 416)
A Detail Mosaic

Compiled by David A. Phillips Jr.

South Bulldozer Trench, 1961

No structural features
west of this point
in trench

LA 416, Pottery Mound
Detail Mosaic

This map tile

ALL TILES: known excavated rooms are shown with
diagonal lines to opposite corners (except kivas, rooms
in South Bulldozer Trench, and "salvage era" rooms).
Probable 1960-1961 excavated rooms shown with
dashed diagonal lines.

Known field mappers: F. Hibben, R. Schorsch,
R. G. Vivian, Charles Voll, James Faris.
Other details from rendering and kiva plans
by W. Bramlett and 1975 published map.
Rendered in 2006 by D. Phillips with assistance
of M. Adler, P. Kay, C. Schaafsma, and P. Schaafsma.
Map is as accurate as available data allow, but
spatial relationships are approximate.

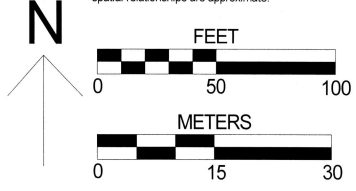

N

FEET

0   50   100

METERS

0   15   30

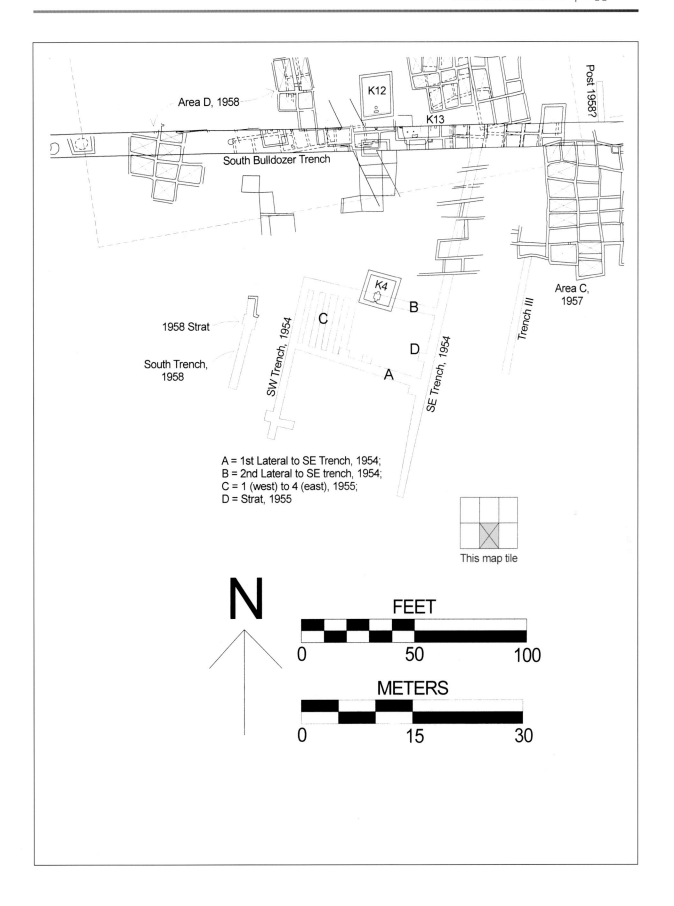

Area D, 1958

K12

K13

Post 1958?

South Bulldozer Trench

1958 Strat

South Trench,
1958

SW Trench, 1954

C

K4

B

D

A

SE Trench, 1954

Trench III

Area C,
1957

A = 1st Lateral to SE Trench, 1954;
B = 2nd Lateral to SE trench, 1954;
C = 1 (west) to 4 (east), 1955;
D = Strat, 1955

This map tile

N

FEET

0   50   100

METERS

0   15   30

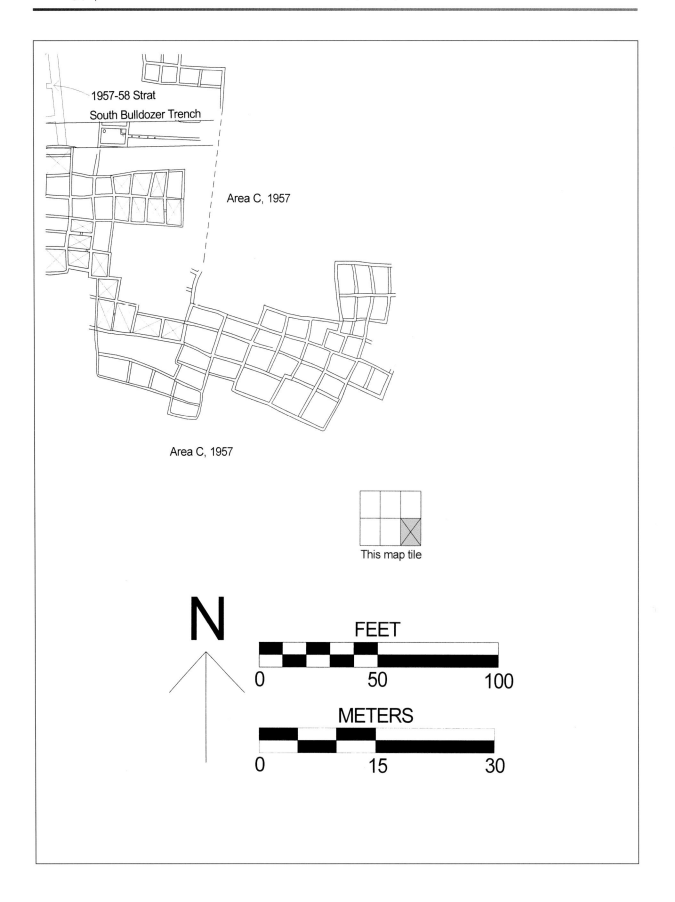

1957-58 Strat
South Bulldozer Trench

Area C, 1957

Area C, 1957

This map tile

N

FEET

0   50   100

METERS

0   15   30

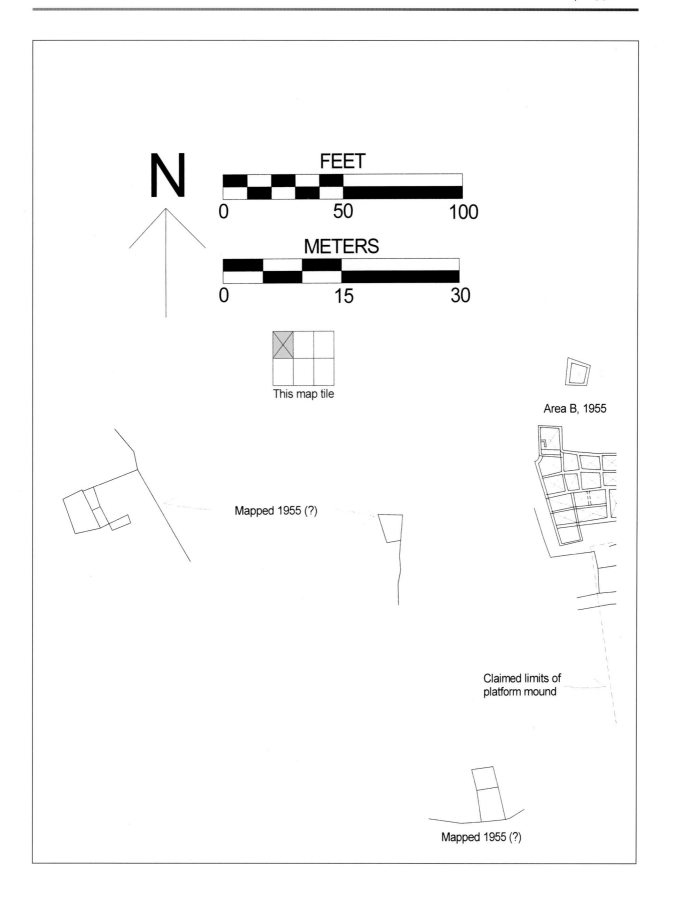

N

FEET

0   50   100

METERS

0   15   30

This map tile

Mapped 1955 (?)

Area B, 1955

Claimed limits of
platform mound

Mapped 1955 (?)

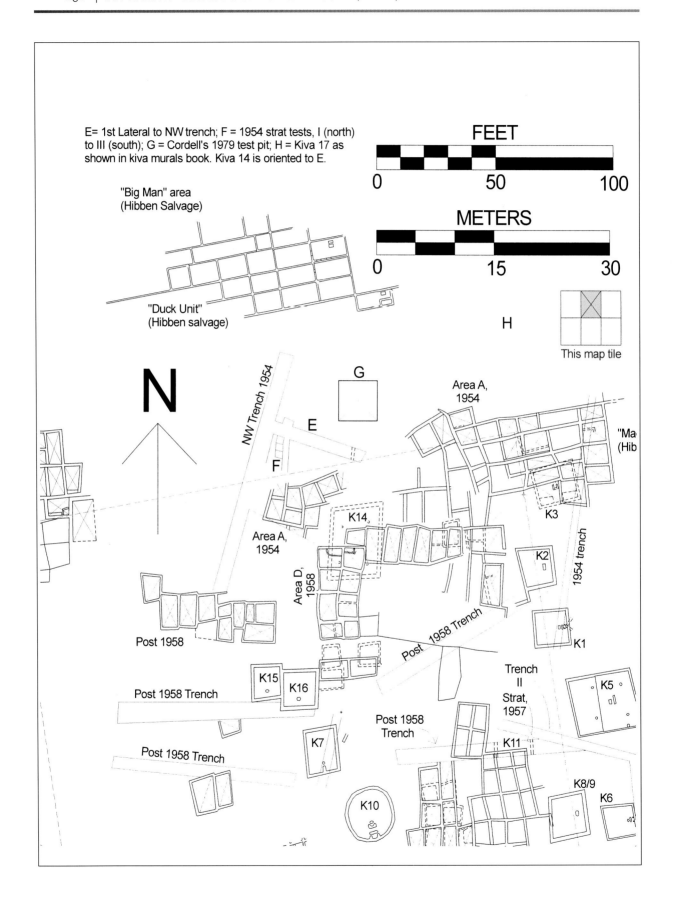

E= 1st Lateral to NW trench; F = 1954 strat tests, I (north)
to III (south); G = Cordell's 1979 test pit; H = Kiva 17 as
shown in kiva murals book. Kiva 14 is oriented to E.

"Big Man" area
(Hibben Salvage)

"Duck Unit"
(Hibben salvage)

FEET

0   50   100

METERS

0   15   30

H

This map tile

N

NW Trench 1954

E

F

G

Area A,
1954

"Ma
(Hib

K3

K14

Area A,
1954

K2

1954 trench

Area D,
1958

Post 1958 Trench

Post 1958

K1

K15

K16

Trench
II

Strat,
1957

K5

Post 1958 Trench

K7

Post 1958
Trench

K11

Post 1958 Trench

K8/9

K10

K6

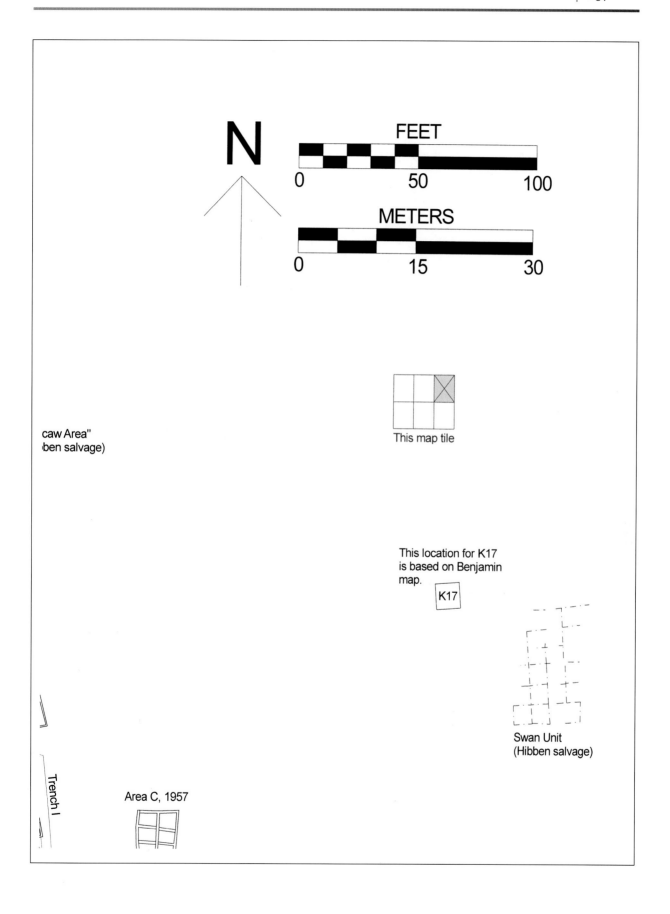

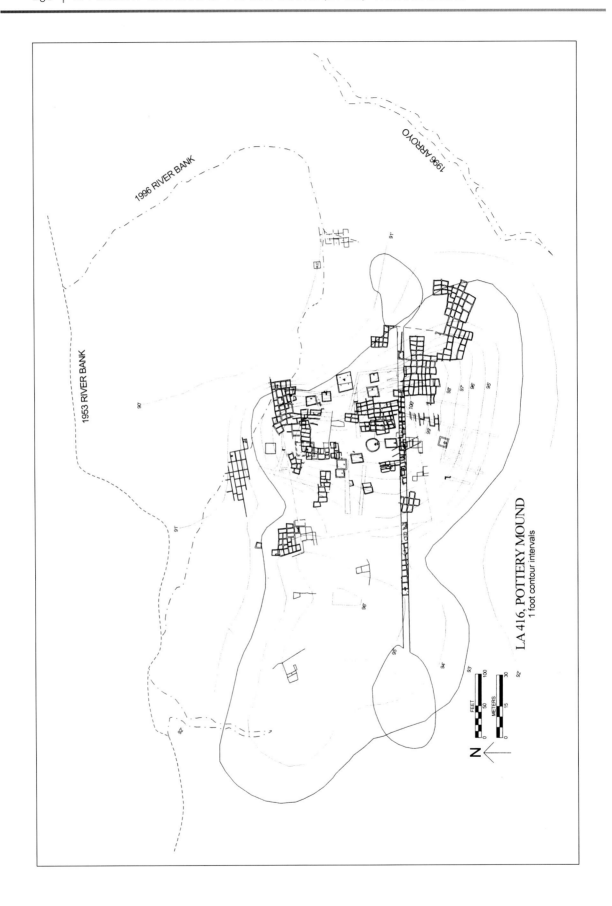

LA 416, POTTERY MOUND
1 foot contour intervals

Appendix B

Room Data, Pottery Mound Pueblo

Michael A. Adler

Appendix B: Room Data, Pottery Mound Pueblo

Unit	Room Number	N Wall length	S Wall length	E Wall length	W Wall length	Avg NS length (m)	Avg EW length	Room floor area	room long axis orient	hearth location and size	storage features	date excavated	comments
B	2	1.37	1.28		3.35	1.326	3.35	4.445	NS	1W (13x22)		1955	Banquette along S Wall. Walls are 11.5 inches thick.
B	3	2.9	2.9	2	2.06	2.896	2.02	5.847	EW	1 N wall (13x22)	2 bins	1955	Banquette along E wall
B	4	2.08		3		2.082	3	6.237	NS	1N (13x22)	1, NE corner	1955	3 separate floor levels encountered in excavations of room and subfloor contexts
B	5	2.08	2.08	3.9	3.86	2.082	3.86	8.039	NS				Door goes between rms 5 and 7. Either large room or 2 smaller rooms with missing cross-wall. Rooms to W all small, with cross-wall.
B	6	1.6	1.58	3.3	3.35	1.588	3.3	5.244	NS	hearth with vent shaft on E wall		1955	Hearth with vent shaft – room block kiva?
B	7												"concealed door" in S wall
B	9		2.01	1.8		2.012	1.83	3.679	EW			1955	measurements estimated off of map, looks to be same size as rm 14
B	10				6.33		6.33		NS				Banquette (40x13)
B	11	2.13	2.13	1.9	1.65	2.134	1.79	3.821	EW			1955	Door between 5 and 7
B	12	2.13	2.13	1.8	1.83	2.134	1.83	3.902	EW				estimated off of map, same size as rm B11
B	13	1.6	1.6	1.9	1.98	1.6	1.96	3.129	NS	1S Wall		1955	

Appendix B: Room Data, Pottery Mound Pueblo (continued)

Unit	Room Number	N Wall length	S Wall length	E Wall length	W Wall length	Avg NS length (m)	Avg EW length	Room floor area	room long axis orient	hearth location and size	storage features	date excavated	comments
B	14		2.03	1.8		2.033	1.83	3.718	EW	1N, 1S, 1E walls		1955	Carpenter notes say rms 14 and 9 are ONE room, but map has possible dividing wall. Should be treated as 1 or 2 rooms? ALSO, labeled as B10 on Benjamin map, but this is not correct label
B	15	3.35	3.28	1.9	1.93	3.315	1.91	6.315	EW				Room 15 is labeled as Room 16 in T.B. Hughes field notes 1955, probably a labeling mistake
B	16		2.29	2	2.2	2.286	2.08	4.749	EW	1		1955	Room 15 is labeled as Room 16 in T.B. Hughes field notes 1955, probably a labeling mistake
B	17	3.48	3.12	1.7	1.83	3.303	1.76	5.828	EW				
B	18		2.44	2		2.438	1.98	4.831	NS				Subfloor wall found under E wall
B	19	2.06	2.46	1.8	2.16	2.26	1.98	4.478	EW	1 S	1 NW part of room	1955	possible center post pit, irregular room shape
B	20		2.08	1.7	2.03	2.082	1.84	3.836	EW	1 (23x12)			earlier walls under N, S, and E walls
B	22	2.29	2.08	1.7	1.83	2.184	1.75	3.827	NS			1955	door 13" wide in N wall painted designs on W Wall. Looks like Rm 13. Sterile soil at 7.25 ft under surface.
C	3	3.35	3.3	1.9	2.13	3.327	2.03	6.759		1 (sealed)		1957	Banquette under uppermost floor.
C	3.1	3.3	3.3	1.8	1.8	3.301	1.8	5.956				1957	room under 3
C	5			3.4	3.43		3.43						
C	6	2.41	2.31	3.5	3.43	2.362	3.45	8.161					

Appendix B: Room Data, Pottery Mound Pueblo (continued)

Unit	Room Number	N Wall length	S Wall length	E Wall length	W Wall length	Avg NS length (m)	Avg E/W length	Room floor area	room long axis orient	hearth location and size	storage features	date excavated	comments
C	7	3.4	3.35	1.9	1.96	3.377	1.93	6.526				1957	
C	8	2.84	2.77	1.9	1.85	2.806	1.85	5.199				1957	
C	9												
C	10	2.59		2.5	2.34	2.591	2.4	6.219	N/S		1 SE corner	1957	4 floor levels excavated
C	11	2.16		3.3		2.159	3.28	7.074	N/S				
C	12	3.28	3.38	1.9	2.08	3.327	1.98	6.585	E/W				
C	23	3.81	3.81	1.7	1.73	3.81	1.73	6.573	E/W	1N		1957	flute found in room fill
C	24											1957	
D	1	2.71	2.44	2	2.04	2.576	2.04	5.26	E/W		1 NE corner	1958	Bin in NE corner
D	2	2.26	2.14	2.3	2.26	2.199	2.3	5.061				1958	
D	3	2.51	2.44	2.5	2.44	2.477	2.46	6.086				1958	Walls under floor
D	4	2.14	2.1	2.5	2.5	2.123	2.5	5.306		4	square pit in middle of room, possible post hole	1958	pit in middle of room. West wall oriented 22 degrees N of E, rooms filled in prior to construction of later rooms. Rooms D3,4,6,27 are abutted to room 5
D	5	2.21	2.21	3.2	3.33	2.21	3.28	7.241	N/S			1958	
D	6	2.21	2.23	3.2	3.23	2.217	3.23	7.164	N/S				

Appendix B: Room Data, Pottery Mound Pueblo (continued)

Unit	Room Number	N Wall length	S Wall length	E Wall length	W Wall length	Avg NS length (m)	Avg E/W length	Room floor area	room long axis orient	hearth location and size	storage features	date excavated	comments
D	7	2.03	2.23	4.3	4.06	2.134	4.2	8.968				1958	
D	8				4.34		4.34		N/S			1958	
D	9	2.23				2.234							
D	10								E/W				
D	12											1958	possibly subdivided room, very small
D	13	3.28	3.28	2.2	2.23	3.277	2.23	7.321		1 near SW corner	1SE corner	1958	hearth in W 1/2 of room, 1 storage bin
D	18	3.48		2.3		3.48	2.33	8.108	E/W			1958	
D	19	3.79	3.66	2.2	2.33	3.722	2.28	8.493	E/W			1958	inverted T-shaped doorway in N wall, with slab in front of it (possible ventilator?)
D	20	3.33	3.48	2.3	2.06	3.403	2.19	7.465	E/W			1958	
D	24	3.73	3.25	2.1	2.11	3.493	2.11	7.368	E/W			1958	
D	25		3.25			3.249			E/W				
D	26	1.58	1.58	1.7	1.72	1.576	1.72	2.704				1958	2 floor levels
D	26.1&27.1	2.69	2.69	2.2	2.16	2.691	2.16	5.808				1958	possibly erroneous measurements, noted by Weeks
D	7	2.06	2.23	4.3	4.06	2.146	4.17	8.937	N/S			1958	

Appendix B: Room Data, Pottery Mound Pueblo (continued)

Unit	Room Number	N Wall length	S Wall length	E Wall length	W Wall length	Avg NS length (m)	Avg EW length	Room floor area	room long axis orient	hearth location and size	storage features	date excavated	comments
Duck	2	4.5	4.5	2.4	2.44	4.5	2.44	10.98	EW	3			sealed with adobe, called the "shaman burial room", arch mag date of 1400+33 from U of Ok. Notes by Benjamin describe rooms 2 and 3 as identical in size, but other notes indicate rm 2 as smaller than described by Benjamin
Duck	3	4.5	4.5	2.4	2.44	4.5	2.44	10.98	EW				evidence of underlying room, 3 feet below surface. Room measurements based on estimated south wall location/length.
Duck	4	4.2	4.2	2.1	2.1	4.2	2.1	8.82	EW	0	0	1979	loom holes in floor, two earlier floors located at 2.5 and 3.0 m below ground surface
Duck	5	4.2	4.2	1	1	4.2	1	4.2	EW			1979	room destroyed by looters
Duck	6	1.6	1.6	1.6	1.6	1.6	1.6	2.56	EW			1979	room filled with sterile sand, above two burial pits, passageway from Rm 6 to Rm 11
Duck	7		3			3							room destroyed by looters, falling into Puerco
Duck	8												nearly all of room falling into Puerco
Duck	9	5	5	2.7	2.7	5	2.7	13.5	EW	2			cache pit in room, lots of ritual items
Duck	10	3.5	3.5	1.5	1.5	3.5	1.5	5.25	EW	2			ritual cache (the "treasure room) in room
													evidence of 2 more levels of underlying rooms, earlier structures. Hearths on every lower floor
Duck	11	3	3	2.5	2.5	3	2.5	7.5	EW	1	1	1980	
Duck	12	3.2	3.2	2.5	2.5	3.2	2.5	8	EW	1		1980	evidence of underlying room

Appendix B: Room Data, Pottery Mound Pueblo (continued)

Unit	Room Number	N Wall length	S Wall length	E Wall length	W Wall length	Avg NS length (m)	Avg EW length	Room floor area	room long axis orient	hearth location and size	storage features	date excavated	comments
Duck	13		5.48			5.48							burial pit under floor has skull (male,40) and two femora with cut marks
Duck	14	3.56	3.56	2.6	2.56	3.56	2.56	9.114	EW			1980	estimated off of map of Duck labeled October 1979
Duck	15	3.35	3.35	2.5	2.47	3.35	2.47	8.275	EW	2	1	1980	estimated off of map of Duck labeled October 1979. Three levels of construction noted in Cordell, extensive pot hunting
Duck	16	3.2	3.2	2.5	2.5	3.2	2.5	8	EW			1980	possible pass-through to room 15 indicated on map
Duck	17	3.5	3.5	2.5	2.5	3.5	2.5	8.75	EW			1980	
Duck	18		0						EW				not excavated
Duck													hearth in NW corner, slab-lined, lots of artifacts deposited in fill and on floor, deer scapula decorated with black spots
Duck	19	4.2	4.2	2	2	4.2	2	8.4	EW	1	0	1980	
Duck	20	3	3	2	2	3	2	6	EW				
Duck	20.1	3	3	2.2	2.2	3	2.2	6.6	EW				room directly under room 20, walls slightly offset
Duck	20.2	3	3	2.3	2.3	3	2.3	6.9	EW				room directly under room 20.1, walls slightly offset, earliest room
Duck	21												not excavated
Duck	22												only partially excavated
Duck	23	4.2	4.2	1.6	1.6	4.2	1.6	6.72	EW				three levels of room floors, most of fill was wind blown sand, dug by pothunters earlier

Appendix B: Room Data, Pottery Mound Pueblo (continued)

Unit	Room Number	N Wall length	S Wall length	E Wall length	W Wall length	Avg NS length (m)	Avg EW length	Room floor area	room long axis orient	hearth location and size	storage features	date excavated	comments
Duck	24	4.2	4.2	1.8	1.82	4.2	1.82	7.644	EW	1	1		ventilator in north wall, fir pit, altar? In center of room
Duck	25	4.2	4.2			4.2			EW				majority of room caved into Puerco, north wall leaning toward river, lots of materials in fill and on floor
Duck	26												not excavated
													lost of sand on floor, looks to have been abandoned prior to roof burning/collapse. Also white ash in fill between floor and roof fall.
Duck	27	4.36	4.24	1.7	1.6	4.3	1.66	7.138	EW	2	0	1980-81	
F	2	3.55	3.4	2.5	2.18	3.478	2.34	8.123	NW				

Appendix C

Profile of the 1961 Bulldozer Trench

Compiled by Michael A. Adler

MAP KEY

[A] Adobe chunk
[B] Burned adobe (bright red)
[Cl] Charcoal flecks (light)
[F] Undifferentiated fill
[G] Gray fine ash
[O] Brown and Light Clay

[Fb] Burned fill
[S] Sand - water deposited
[Su] Backdirt / disturbed soil
[Xg] Green clay chunks
[W] Sand - wind deposited
[R] Red clay chunks / additional extraneous material

[X] Red clay - water deposited mud
[ ] Architectural adobe - walls and floors
[ ] Heavy charcoal/ash deposit
[CH] Heavy charcoal

MAP SCALE

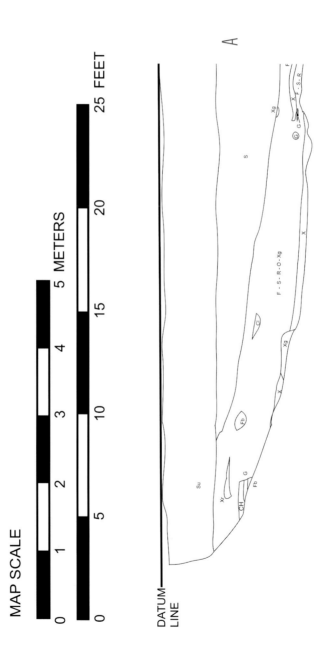

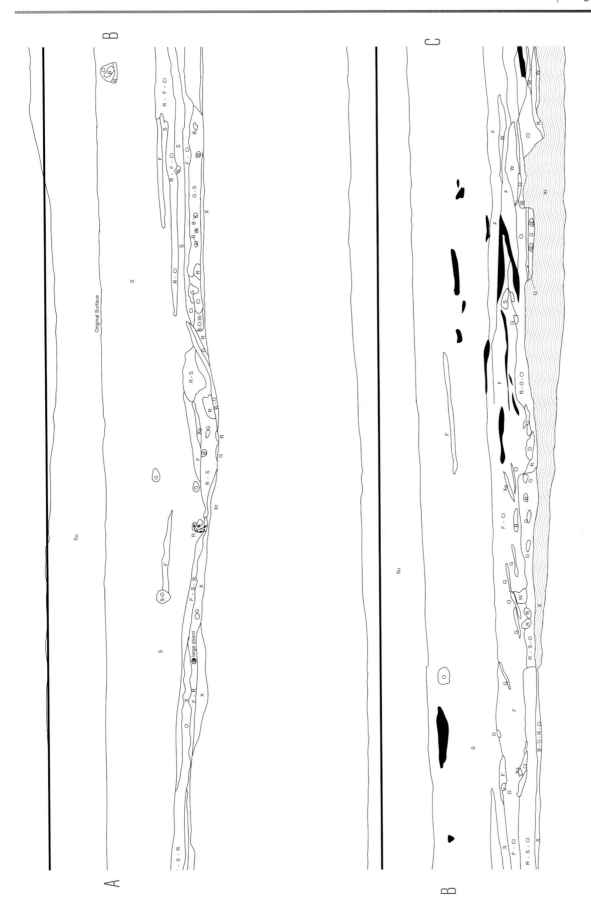

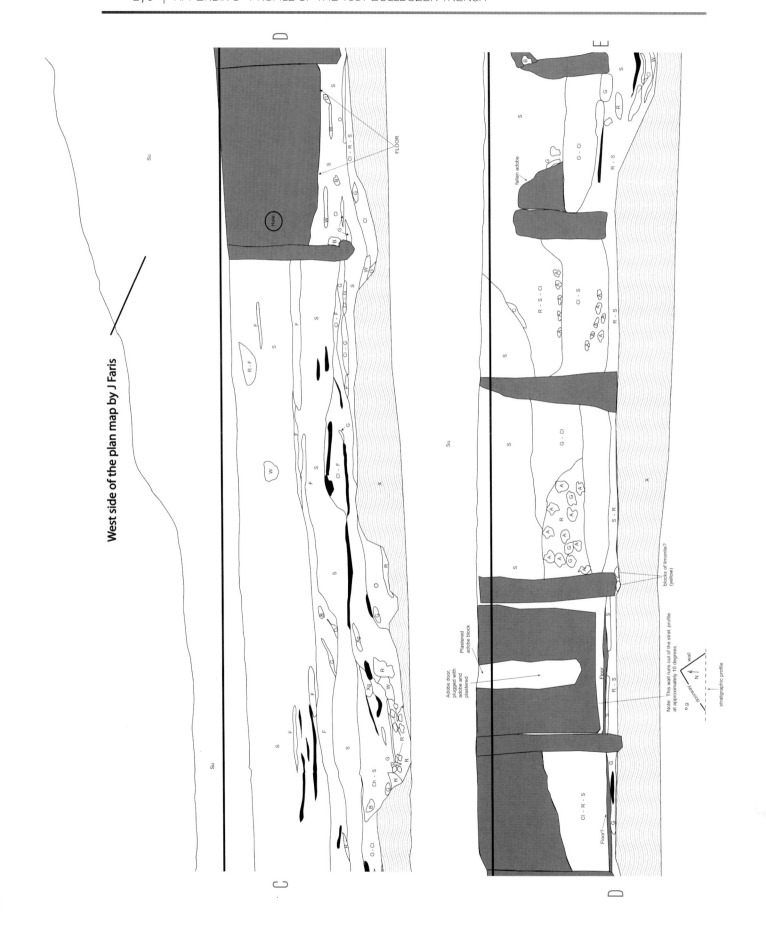

West side of the plan map by J Faris

Note: This wall runs out of the strat. profile at approximately 10 degrees

stratigraphic profile

Adobe door plugged with adobe and plastered

Plastered adobe block

blocks of limonite? (yellow)

fallen adobe

FLOOR

Floor

Floor?

Hole

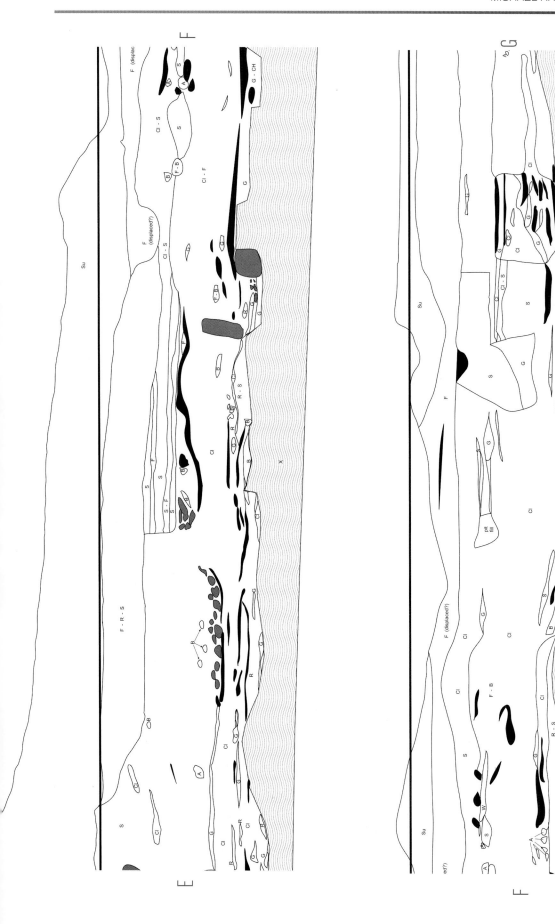

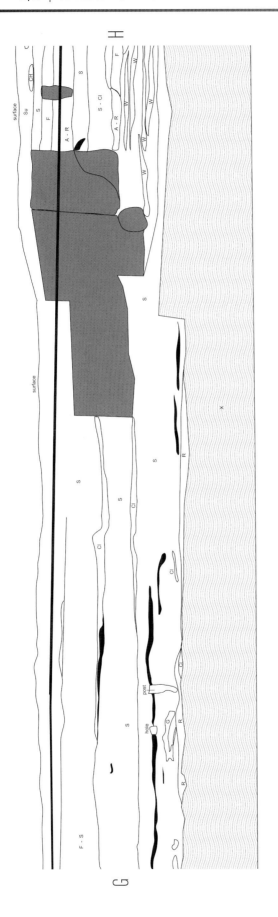

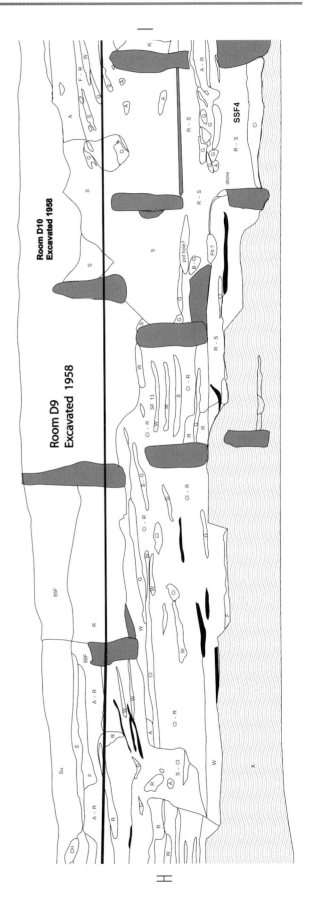

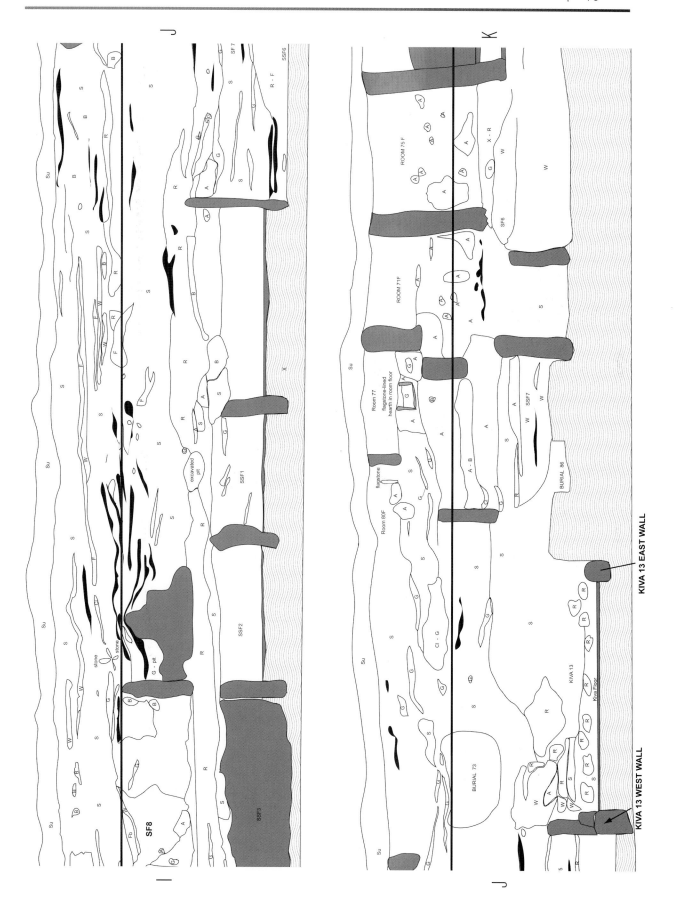

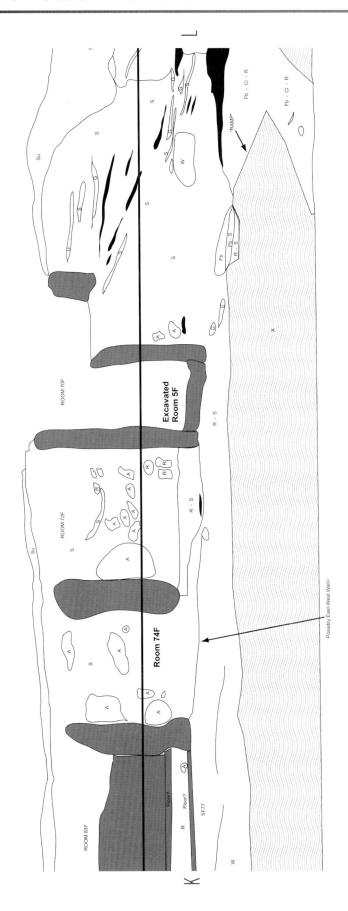

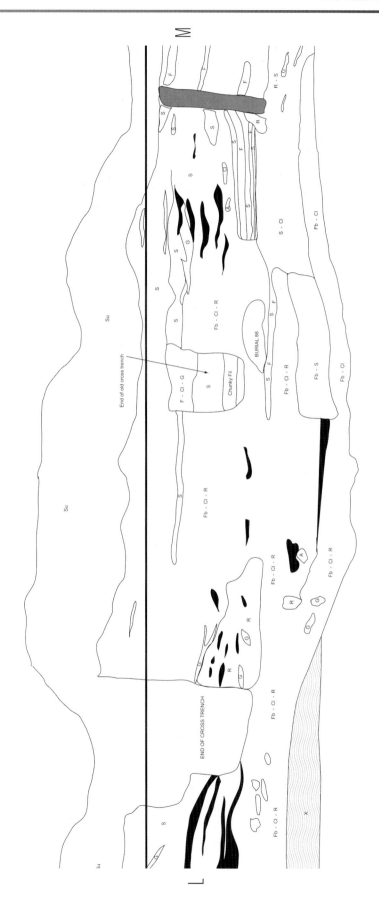

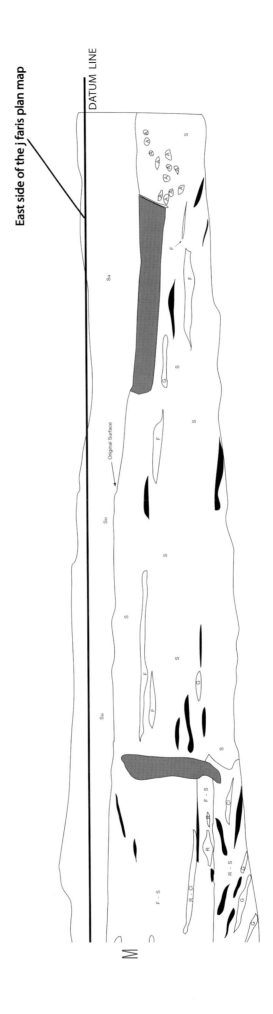

East side of the j faris plan map

Appendix D

Compilation of Excavated and Previously Reported Ceramics from Pottery Mound

Curtis F. Schaafsma

This compilation of excavated and previously reported ceramics is motivated by two primary considerations. One is to obtain a reliable ceramic assemblage for the site as a whole and the second is to determine as adequately as possible the chronology of the site. The compilation is derived from Charles Voll's (1961) master of arts thesis, Linda Cordell's (1980) preliminary report of her 1979 field school, and Frank C. Hibben's (1987) report of his salvage excavations between 1977 and 1986. Combined, these sources report more than 44,000 sherds that provide a good understanding of the ceramics present at the site and their relative proportions. Only Hibben presents stratigraphic tallies and some of his stratigraphic tallies are presented in order to obtain some idea of the chronology of the site overall.

The present effort was prompted by an inconsistency between the excavated data in these reports and the surface ceramic assemblage reported by H. P. Mera. For example, Voll (1961:40) stated that "no Group D, E or F sherds or European glaze wares occurred at Pottery Mound." In contrast Mera (1940:18) said of Pottery Mound (LA 416): "But as this paper deals principally with the duration of occupation it will suffice to say that this covered a span

from A to E." As the compiled data presented here will show, Voll was correct in regard to excavated ceramics. It would appear that Mera collected surface ceramics that somehow differ from what is present beneath the surface. All of this has a major bearing on the time frame of the site since Mera's Glaze E would not have existed until after 1515 (1940:5), meaning that Pottery Mound would have been occupied almost until the arrival of the Coronado party in 1540. As is discussed in what follows, the excavated ceramics indicate that Pottery Mound was primarily abandoned between 1425 and 1450, with a minor component persisting until shortly after 1450.

The ceramics summarized here came from a variety of places within the site and were excavated in a number of different contexts. Cordell excavated a stratified test pit in the northern section of the site (see Appendix A and Figure 1.3), which she divided into four portions or quadrants. All of the ceramics from these quadrants and from all levels were tallied together for her 1980 report and it is these data that are presented here. Eckert (2003) tallied the ceramics from the northwest quadrant by level and presented these data in her dissertation as Appendix A, Table A.1. She addresses these ceramics in her chapter for this volume as well (Eckert, Chapter 4). However, since her ceramic categories or types are not comparable with the ceramic categories used by the others, there will be no effort made here to integrate her material.

Voll did his work as a graduate student working directly for Frank Hibben. He had access to a wide variety of sherd collections obtained by Hibben's field schools as well as tests he made. Voll stated:

> The ceramic samples used in this thesis were (1) sherds from a one meter square stratitest located in the first lateral to the northwest trench, (2) sherds from a one meter square stratitest, Block 157, located ten feet west of the southwest corner of Kiva 5, (3) sherds excavated from six shallow rooms located on the edge of the Rio Puerco arroyo and which have eroded into the arroyo, (4) sherds from the fill of Kiva 8, and (5) approximately 500 large sherds saved from all sections of the site [1961:12].

These proveniences are indicated on the composite site map prepared by David Phillips (see Appendix A and Figure 1.3) with the exception of the six rooms that were somewhere north of the main site. Voll presents ceramic summaries for the first lateral to the northwest trench (1961:Table 4), Block 157 (1961:Table 3), the six shallow rooms (1961:Table 6), and the fill of Kiva 8 (1961:Table 5). The compilation presented here is derived from these tables. Voll does not present summary data on the approximately 500 large sherds, but clearly some of his generalities are based on them. For example, he mentions eight sherds of Glaze B (1961:31), but there are no Glaze B sherds in his summary tables. He presented no stratigraphic data and each provenience is presented as a simple summary regardless of what levels he might have had in his excavations.

Voll's (1961) thesis is especially important since he makes an extensive review of the literature and details what ceramic categories he is recognizing and cites the relevant studies. One can be fairly sure what he was doing and what he meant by a discrete type or other category. For a recent and comprehensive review of the types involved, refer to Hayward Franklin's (1996) report on Valencia Pueblo, some 12 mi to the east of Pottery Mound. Franklin knows that the Rio Grande Glaze ceramic typology is grounded in Mera (1933) and Kidder and Shepard (1936) and has gradually been refined over the years. It is this typological structure that I am discussing and will

be endeavoring to present in this compilation. I will also utilize the type names assigned by Mera in 1933 and in particular will adhere to his precise spellings in all cases. For example, Espinoso Glaze-polychrome was named by Mera (1933:5) and that is how one spells "Espinoso." I (2002:Table 8.1) have recently offered dates for these types and utilized Mera's type names in all cases.

Cordell (personal communication 2005) presented ceramic information derived by Kit Sargeant. Kit was working within the same typological structure as Voll and Franklin and I can assume that her categories and/or types are comparable to theirs. It has been impossible to establish who did the ceramic tables presented in Hibben's 1987 report, but Joan Mathien has suggested that it was Kit Sargeant. Unfortunately, Kit has since passed away. At any rate, the tables in Hibben's report are quite good and it is essential that they be given wider distribution.

Hibben's 1987 report covers his salvage operations along the edge of the cut bank of the Puerco between 1977 and 1986. He was working under state permit in this period and the 1987 preliminary report was presented as part of his 1987 request for a continuation of the state permit. It represents a great deal of work and the collections from this salvage operation at the Maxwell Museum should be studied and a full report prepared. The report is a public document and has been in the Laboratory of Anthropology library in Santa Fe since 1987.

Overall, the combined ceramic data from these sources give us a much better understanding of the overall ceramic assemblage and the site chronology than has previously been available.

Ceramic Assemblage

The goal here is to compile the ceramic data from the previously mentioned sources and derive an overall ceramic assemblage for Pottery Mound that provides a useable understanding of the relative proportions of the various types and kinds of ceramics that are present. In essence, this would be equivalent to the "expected" proportions if one were to be doing a Chi Square statistical evaluation of the probable meaning of variations from the expected values. In other words, do the "observed' proportions in any provenience mean anything in their deviation from the "expected' values? While none of this compilation is subjected to statistical procedures, this comparison indicates the larger goal of deriving a ceramic assemblage.

Table D.1. Percentages of Decorated Ceramics per Provenience Derived from Voll's (1961) Tables 3, 4, 5 and 6

Ceramic Types and Categories	Table 3 Block 157	Table 4 Lateral	Table 5 Kiva 8	Table 6 6 Rooms	Combined Count	Combined Percentage
Agua Fria Glaze-on-red	34.736	21.726	13.904	10.748	1,379	19.137
Cieneguilla Glaze-on-yellow	5.858	5.238	9.606	5.503	509	7.064
San Clemente Glaze-polychrome	12.129	15.082	28.386	18.917	1,464	20.316
Pottery Mound Glaze-polychrome	.083	.048	3.070	4.213	136	1.887
Pinnawa Glaze-on-white, local	.248	.145	.542	1.462	38	.527
Red Glaze, local temper	37.954	29.777	36.403	39.639	2,543	35.290
Yellow Glaze, local temper	3.135	24.394	6.103	11.866	848	11.768
Kwakina Glaze-polychrome	1.320	.388	.289	.258	35	.486
Pinnawa Glaze-on-white	.908	.630	.072	.430	31	.430
Acoma/Zuni red sherds	.495	.824	.181	2.494	57	.791
Acoma/Zuni white sherds	.660	.436	.072	—	19	.264
Espinoso Glaze-polychrome	—	.097	.108	1.978	28	.389
Red Rio Grande Glaze	.165	.048	.614	1.634	39	.541
Yellow Rio Grande Glaze	—	.048	.181	.860	16	.222
Jeddito Black-on-yellow	—	—	.072	—	2	.028
Sikyatki Polychrome	.248	.048	—	—	4	.056
Hopi yellow sherds	.660	.291	.325	—	23	.319
Abiquiu Black-on-gray	.330	.097	—	—	6	.083
Socorro Black-on-white	.908	.679	.072	—	27	.375
gray sherds	.083	—	—	—	1	.014
white on red sherds	.083	—	—	—	1	.014
Total Decorated Sherds	N = 1,212	N = 2,062	N = 2,769	N = 1,163	7,206	100.001

Source: Charles Voll, "The Glaze Paint Ceramics from Pottery Mound" (Master's Thesis, University of New Mexico, Albuquerque, 1961).

The most comprehensive data set is derived from Voll's (1961) thesis. Voll derived ceramics from a number of proveniences and his work approximates a sample of the whole site. He presented counts of the ceramics from these various places in a series of tables that tally the ceramics per provenience. I converted all of his counts to percentages and prepared a summary table of the decorated ceramics (Table D.1). The combined percentage column gives a good start on deriving an assemblage for the site as a whole. Voll separated the culinary sherds from each provenience and tallied them separately. I have

followed his lead on this and separated them, too (Table D.2). For the most part, these sherds constitute statistical "noise" and are best removed if possible. Later, in dealing with Hibben's stratigraphic data, I will present tables that leave the culinary in the sample, which is unfortunate, but time does not allow me to recalculate these large data sets. Also, in all of these tables I have calculated the percentages to three decimal places, not to provide spurious accuracy, but to allow small samples to be manifest.

Voll's data are extremely useful for a starting point. He divided the ceramics into discrete categories and tallied

Table D.2. Percentages of Culinary Sherds per Provenience Derived from Voll's (1961) Tables 3, 4, 5 and 6.

Culinary Ceramic Categories	Table 3 Block 157	Table 4 Lateral	Table 5 Kiva 8	Table 6 6 Rooms	Combined Count	Combined Percentage
local culinary (combined)	99.916	99.540	99.669	100.000	6,418	99.767
white paste (Acoma/Zuni?)	.084	.460	.248		13	.202
yellow paste (Jeddito Corr.)			.008		2	.031
Total Culinary	N = 1,190	N = 1,304	N = 2,419	N = 1,520	6,433	100.000

Source: Charles Voll, "The Glaze Paint Ceramics from Pottery Mound" (Master's Thesis, University of New Mexico, Albuquerque, 1961).

them consistently in the various proveniences. However, it immediately becomes apparent that there are problems integrating his data with the other sources. Voll, for example, separated "Agua Fria Glaze-on-red" from "red Glaze, local temper." Are these one and the same thing? Should one lump these into a single sample? As seen in the following, Hibben in his 1987 report gives counts for "Glaze A/Red" and mentions nothing about "red Glaze, local temper." In my overall assemblage development I have taken the liberty of assuming that most of the "red Glaze, local temper" must be "Agua Fria Glaze-on-red" and that without question this would be "Glaze A." There are statistically minor problems as well, such as Hibben consistently reporting Los Lunas Smudged and related types while Voll reports none of that sort of pottery.

Hibben provided ceramic data counts in tabular form from two primary locations along the edge of the Puerco escarpment on the north edge of the site (see Appendix A and Figure 1.3). These are a stratified trash deposit he termed the Big Man area (Figure D.1; Hibben 1987:31) and a series of superimposed rooms termed the Duck Unit (Figure D.2). The Duck Unit rooms abut the Big Man Unit, as can be seen in the southeast corner of Figure D.1. The 1985 escarpment of the Puerco was actively eroding this area and portions of it were lost shortly after excavation. However a great deal of it remained in 1987 when I visited the site and took many photographs of this area and the nature of the stratigraphic layers (Schaafsma 1987). Overall, this is an extraordinarily valuable sample and should be studied completely. As can be seen from Figure D.1, many sections were excavated with many sherds recovered, and only the sections with diagonal lines were tallied for the 1987 report. All of the other sections

still need to be analyzed. As mentioned, the ceramic analysis was apparently done by Kit Sargeant under Hibben's overall supervision.

The compilation of Hibben's Big Man Unit is presented in Table D.3. Hibben's ceramic categories are presented exactly as presented in the 1987 report, except for minor spelling changes, such as "Sikyatki" instead of "Sitkyatki." Table D.3 gives the summary counts for each provenience. Since my addition differed from Hibben's, I have given both sums at the bottom of the table. My sums were used to calculate the summary percentages in the right-hand column. It is this data that should be compared with Voll's data to derive an overall assemblage. It will not take long to realize that the 45.748 percent Plain Utility in this assemblage will have to be removed in order to make a realistic comparison with Voll's decorated ceramics.

To render Hibben's data from the Big Man Unit into a form that was approximately compatible with Voll's ceramic data, Table D.4 was prepared. This table has all of the culinary ceramics removed and a number of categories combined, such as the two kinds of "San Clemente" that are tallied separately on Table D.3.

The nearby Duck Unit was detailed on a 1982 map prepared by Hibben (see Figure D.2). A couple of minor errors and omissions are noted on Figure D.2. The position of the Rio Puerco escarpment in 1980 and 1982 is indicated, showing the need for this salvage excavation. In his 1987 report Hibben presented tabular counts of the ceramics from Rooms 9, 10, 14, 15, and 19. Presumably the ceramics from the other rooms indicated on the map as having been excavated are at the Maxwell Museum and are yet to be studied.

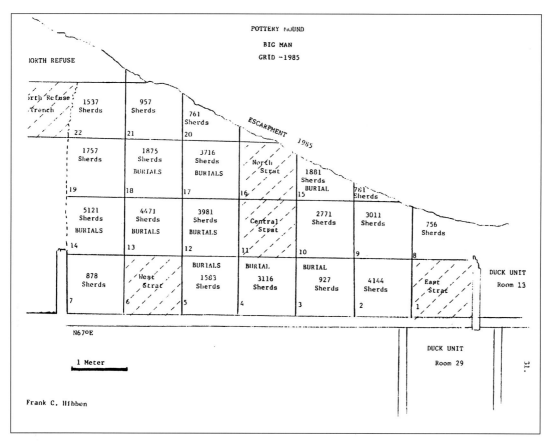

FIGURE D.1.

Frank C. Hibben's (1987) report, from plan of Big Man Unit on page 31 of the report.

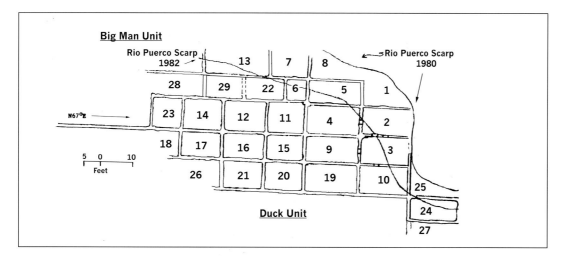

FIGURE D.2.

Frank C. Hibben's (1982) map of the Duck Unit. Corrections and additions by C. Schaafsma, are based on a 1985 site map prepared by B. C. Benjamin. Copy on file at the Maxwell Museum of Anthropology, University of New Mexico, Albuquerque.

Table D.3. Frank C. Hibben's (1987) Report, Summary of Ceramics in the Big Man Unit

Ceramic Type or Kind	East Strat	West Strat	Central	North Strat	Total Type	Percent
Glaze A/Red	1,279	753	1,357	1,039	4,428	19.915
Glaze A/Yellow	513	673	1,100	1,192	3,478	15.642
Pottery Mound Poly	161	299	354	107	921	4.142
San Clemente	105	240	48	119	512	2.303
San Clemente Poly	41	88	95	75	299	1.345
Zuni (Acoma) Glaze	44	345	33	100	522	2.348
Jeddito	87	115	135	113	450	2.024
Sikyatki	42	47	33	60	182	.819
Jeddito Corrugated	25	25	5	54	109	.490
Plain Utility	2,366	486	3,577	3,743	10,172	45.748
Micaceous Utility	21	57	17	29	124	.558
Glaze A St. Johns	7	49	0	25	81	.364
Socorro B/W	106	89	65	125	385	1.732
Socorro Corrugated	38	124	128	56	346	1.556
Los Lunas Smudged	20	51	18	51	140	.630
Galisteo B/W	7	0	25	4	36	.162
Fingernail Incised	4	14	0	0	18	.081
Matte Red/Brown (?)	3	0	0	0	3	.013
Los Lunas Smudged Decorated Corrugated	0	21	0	0	21	.094
Unknown	0	4	0	0	4	.018
Santa Fe B/W (?)	0	0	0	4	4	.018
Total By Schaafsma	**4,869**	**3,480**	**6,990**	**6,896**	**22,235**	**100.002**
Total By Hibben	**4,869**	**3,480**	**6,990**	**6,902**	**22,241**	

Source: Frank C. Hibben, "Report on the Salvage Operations at the Site of Pottery Mound, New Mexico, during the Excavating Seasons of 1977–1986" (manuscript on file, Laboratory of Anthropology No. P2662 and P2663, Santa Fe, New Mexico, 1987).

Of the superimposed rooms in the Duck Unit, Hibben said:

Throughout the Duck Unit excavations through the floors of the various rooms revealed another set of rooms with walls at variance with those above and further digging revealed yet a third architectural level beneath. In several instances different colored adobe used in the walls accentuated this tri-partheid addition. The fact that the room tiers of Pottery Mound, in many areas, reveal three, or in some instance four,

architectural levels, is a feature of the entire site. In most instances the underlying rooms show a plan different from the level or levels below and above [1987:7].

The summary of ceramics from the tallied rooms in the 1987 report are presented here as Table D.5. As with Table D.3 my addition differs from Hibben's and the percentages calculated in the right-hand column were done with my sums. Hibben's are presented for consistency with his report. The assemblage has less "noise" from the presence of the Plain Utility (only 4.344 percent), but a separate

Table D.4. Frank C. Hibben's (1987) Report, Decorated Ceramics from the Big Man Unit, Merged to Conform to Voll's (1961) Categories in Order to Develop the Overall Site Summary in Table 8

Ceramic Type or Kind	Total	Percent	Notes
Glaze A/Red	4,428	39.182	
Glaze A/Yellow	3,478	30.776	
Pottery Mound Polychrome	921	8.150	
San Clemente	811	7.176	Hibben's two kinds of San Clemente are merged here.
Zuni (Acoma) Glaze	522	4.620	Glaze A St John's is merged with these on Table 8.
Jeddito	450	3.982	It is assumed that this is Jeddito Black-on-yellow.
Sikyatki	182	1.610	
Glaze A St. Johns	81	.717	These 81 sherds are merged with Zuni/Acoma pottery on Table 8.
Socorro B/W	385	3.407	
Galisteo B/W	36	.319	
Matt(e) Red/Brown	3	.027	
Santa Fe B/W	4	.035	
Total Decorated	**11,301**	**100.001**	

Sources: Frank C. Hibben, "Report on the Salvage Operations at the Site of Pottery Mound, New Mexico, during the Excavating Seasons of 1977–1986" (manuscript on file, Laboratory of Anthropology No. P2662 and P2663, Santa Fe, New Mexico, 1987).

Charles Voll, "The Glaze Paint Ceramics from Pottery Mound" (Master's Thesis, University of New Mexico, Albuquerque, 1961).

table was nonetheless prepared that has the utility pottery removed (Table D.6).

Cordell's (1980) preliminary report of her 1979 excavation has summary ceramic counts and percentages of the overall excavation on pages 7 and 8. With the exception of Pottery Mound Polychrome, all of the Glaze A types and varieties were grouped as "Glaze A." Of this grouping, Cordell (1980:7) said Glaze A includes "Agua Fria B/r, Cieneguilla, San Clemente and Los Padillas." More recently she has reiterated this set of types as being in the "Glaze A" reported in 1980 (Cordell 2004:4), including the reference to Los Padillas Glaze Polychrome. She specifically excludes Glaze C: "We did not find Glaze C in context in the excavation unit" (2004:4).

Cordell's ceramic data are presented here as Table D.7 with a final column calculated by me that has the two kinds of culinary removed to give percentages on the decorated ceramics only. Recognizing that Pottery Mound Polychrome is a version of Glaze A (to be discussed more fully in what follows), it is valid to combine the 1.676 percent of this type with the 94.366 percent "Glaze A"

to obtain an overall percentage of "Glaze A" of 96.042 percent of all decorated pottery from the test pit.

The ceramic tallies from Voll, Hibben, and Cordell are combined into Table D.8. All the versions of Glaze A that are discriminated by Hibben and Voll, with the exception of Pottery Mound Polychrome, are lumped on this table as "Glaze A" in order to make use of Cordell's data. As with Cordell's ceramics, if the percentage of Glaze A overall (85.436 percent) is combined with the percentage of Pottery Mound Polychrome (5.858 percent) then "Glaze A" constitutes 91.294 percent of the overall assemblage based on a combined sherd count of 44,535. Obviously, Pottery Mound was primarily a Rio Grande Glaze A site.

I have included eight sherds of two types of Glaze B on Table D.8 that were reported by Voll (1961:31) to emphasize the fact that the site was in existence in the time period of these types of Glaze B (1420–1450; Schaafsma 2002:Table 8.1). As has been well known since Mera's time, Glaze B was mainly made north of Albuquerque and was very little traded to the south. Speaking of Glaze B, Mera (1940:3) said, "Farther south, where this form occurs only

Table D.5. Frank C. Hibben's (1987) Report, Summary of Ceramics in the Duck Unit

Ceramic Type or Kind	Room 9	Room 10	Room 14	Room 15	Room 19	Total	Percent
Glaze A/Red	870	745	944	1,610	1,375	5,544	38.348
Glaze A/Yellow	664	499	600	866	579	3,208	22.190
Pottery Mound Poly	278	78	515	245	226	1,342	9.283
San Clemente	373	67	128	463	235	1,266	8.757
San Clemente Poly	129	53	39	400	70	691	4.780
Zuni (Acoma) Glaze	193	231	69	123	78	694	4.800
Jeddito	72	24	31	117	118	362	2.504
Sikyatki	27	46	8	35	131	247	1.709
Jeddito Corrugated	20	0	7	33	43	103	.712
Plain Utility	179	55	145	128	121	628	4.344
Micaceous Utility	19	9	38	11	32	109	.754
Glaze A St. Johns	0	11	19	40	18	88	.609
Socorro B/W	13	6	10	6	50	85	.588
Socorro Corrugated	8	4	4	7	22	45	.311
Los Lunas Smudged	6	4	8	2	14	34	.235
Galisteo B/W	6	5	0	0	0	11	.076
Total By Schaafsma	**2,857**	**1,837**	**2,565**	**4,086**	**3,112**	**14,457**	**100.000**
Total By Hibben	**2,876**	**1,817**	**2,558**	**4,025**	**3,102**	**14,378**	

Source: Frank C. Hibben, "Report on the Salvage Operations at the Site of Pottery Mound, New Mexico, during the Excavating Seasons of 1977–1986" (manuscript on file, Laboratory of Anthropology No. P2662 and P2663, Santa Fe, New Mexico, 1987).

Table D.6. Frank C. Hibben's (1987) Report, Decorated Ceramics from the Duck Unit, Merged to Conform to Voll's (1961) Categories in Order to Develop the Overall Site Summary in Table 8

Ceramic Type or Kind	Total	Percent	Notes
Glaze A/Red	5,544	40.951	
Glaze A/Yellow	3,208	23.696	
Pottery Mound Poly	1,342	9.913	
San Clemente	1,957	14.456	Hibben's two kinds of San Clemente are merged here.
Zuni (Acoma) Glaze	694	5.126	Glaze A St John's is merged with these on Table 8.
Jeddito	362	2.674	It is assumed that this is Jeddito Black-on-yellow.
Sikyatki	247	1.824	
Glaze A St. Johns	88	.650	These 88 sherds are merged with Zuni/Acoma pottery on Table 8.
Socorro B/W	85	.628	
Galisteo B/W	11	.081	
Total Decorated	**13,538**	**99.999**	

Sources: Frank C. Hibben, "Report on the Salvage Operations at the Site of Pottery Mound, New Mexico, during the Excavating Seasons of 1977–1986" (manuscript on file, Laboratory of Anthropology No. P2662 and P2663, Santa Fe, New Mexico, 1987).

Charles Voll, "The Glaze Paint Ceramics from Pottery Mound" (Master's Thesis, University of New Mexico, Albuquerque, 1961).

Table D.7. Linda Cordell's (1980) Excavation Ceramics as Presented on Pages 7–8 of the Report

Ceramic Types	Counts	Cordell's Percentages	CFS Percentages of Decorated Types Only[a]
Glaze A[b]	11,825	49.000	94.366
Pottery Mound Polychrome	210	.005	1.676
Jeddito B/Y	306	1.000	2.442
Acoma Glaze[c]	111	.500	.886
Sityatki	15	.005	.120
Galisteo B/W	5	.002	.040
Socorro B/W	57	.020	.455
Clapboard Utility	16	.008	—
Other Utility	11,774	48.000	—
Cordell Total	**24,321**	**100**	—
CFS Total	**24,319**	—	**99.985**

Source: Linda Cordell, "University of New Mexico Field School Excavations at Pottery Mound, New Mexico, 1979, Preliminary Report" (manuscript on file, Maxwell Museum of Anthropology, University of New Mexico, Albuquerque, 1980).
Notes: [a]Decorated types total 12,529. CFS recalculated the percentages of decorated types to provide comparison with Voll's data. The two kinds of utility were excluded.
[b]"Glaze A" includes "Agua Fria G/r, Cieneguilla, San Clemente and Los Padillas" (1980:7).
[c]"Acoma Glaze" combines all the Zuni/Acoma types.

Table D.8. Summary of Excavated, Decorated Ceramics from Pottery Mound

Ceramic Types or Categories	Cordell 1980	Voll 1961	Hibben 1987 Duck Unit	Hibben 1987 Big Man Unit	Combined Count	Combined Percentage
Glaze A	11,825	6,798	10,709	8,717	38,049	85.436
Pottery Mound Glaze-polychrome	210	136	1,342	921	2,609	5.858
Largo Glaze-on-yellow	0	4	0	0	4	.009
Largo Glaze-polychrome	0	4	0	0	4	.009
Espinoso Glaze-polychrome	0	28	0	0	28	.063
Acoma/Zuni Glazes	111	142	782	603	1,638	3.678
Jeddito Black-on-yellow	306	2	362	450	1,120	2.515
Sikyatki Polychrome	15	4	247	182	448	1.006
Hopi yellow sherds	0	23	0	0	23	.052
Socorro Black-on-white	57	27	85	385	554	1.244
Galisteo Black-on-white	5	0	11	36	52	.117
Abiquiu Black-on-gray	0	6	0	0	6	.013
Total Decorated Sherds	**12,529**	**7,174**	**13,538**	**11,294**	**44,535**	**100.000**

Sources: Linda S. Cordell, "University of New Mexico Field School Excavations at Pottery Mound, New Mexico, 1979, Preliminary Report" (manuscript on file, Maxwell Museum of Anthropology, University of New Mexico, Albuquerque, 1980).
Frank C. Hibben, "Report on the Salvage Operations at the Site of Pottery Mound, New Mexico, during the Excavating Seasons of 1977–1986" (manuscript on file, Laboratory of Anthropology No. P2662 and P2663, Santa Fe, New Mexico, 1987).
Charles Voll, "The Glaze Paint Ceramics from Pottery Mound" (Master's Thesis, University of New Mexico, Albuquerque, 1961).

sporadically, Group A is believed to have merged directly into C with no intermediate forms." Simply put, regardless of how long "Glaze A" was made at Pottery Mound, there is no need to expect a Glaze B component, and there is not one.

Addressing Table D.8, it is apparent that of the three investigators whose work is summarized here, the only Glaze C or Espinoso Glaze Polychrome that is reported are Voll's (1961) 28 sherds. Referring back to his original counts, 2 of these are from the "First Lateral to Northwest Trench" (1961:Table 4), 3 are from the fill of Kiva 8 (1961:12, Table 5), and 23 are from the six shallow rooms to the north of the site that had eroded into the Puerco by 1961 (1961:12, Table 6). The primary consideration at this point is the fact that out of 44,535 sherds, most of the actual Glaze C (23) came from six shallow rooms that were separated from the main village. The chronological implication of this is discussed in what follows.

All of the Acoma/Zuni Glazes are grouped together and they make up 3.678 percent of all the decorated ceramics. These are extremely interesting but will not be elaborated here. The persistent presence of a kind of pottery called "Glaze A St. Johns" on Hibben's tables has been combined by me into the Acoma/Zuni Glaze group. I do not know what is meant by this kind of pottery and it is possible that it is essentially what Cordell refers to as "Los Padillas." Basically all of this sort of pottery needs to be reanalyzed with a consistent terminology.

For years people have been excited about the clearly large proportion of Hopi pottery at Pottery Mound. Now, at least, we can work with some realistic percentages. There is 2.515 percent of Jeddito Black-on-yellow (as nearly as I can make out, and assuming that Hibben's "Jeddito" is Jeddito Black-on-yellow), 1.006 percent Sikyatki Polychrome, and .052 percent (23) Hopi yellow sherds. Together they amount to 3.573 percent of the decorated pottery. At this point I have presumed that Voll's Hopi yellow sherds have some sort of decoration. I have also set aside the Jeddito Corrugated on Hibben's tables. Perhaps they are the same as Voll's yellow sherds. Nonetheless about 3.5 percent of the decorated sherds are trade from the Hopi area.

Overall there is 1.244 percent Socorro Black-on-white, which is discussed in what follows. Everybody except Voll reported some Galisteo Black-on-white, which totals .117 percent. Finally, the six sherds of Abiquiu Black-on-gray constitute .013 percent.

Clearly all of these ceramic collections should be restudied with a consistent terminology. Nevertheless, the summary assemblage on Table D.8 provides a good assessment of the ceramics present at the site and their relative proportions. Returning to Voll's (1961:40) generalization that "no Group D, E or F sherds or European glaze wares occurred at Pottery Mound," we can now refer to quite sound data to endorse that statement. I would now say that Mera (1940:20–21) was wrong to include LA 416 (Pottery Mound) on his Period 3 (1490–1515) and Period 4 (1515–1650) maps. We can also add that there is very little Glaze C (Espinoso Glaze Polychrome) to justify including LA 416 on the Period 2 (1490–1490) map (Mera 1940:20–21). This is not to say that Mera did not pick up off the surface these later types of pottery. Somehow, there was later pottery on the surface than is found beneath the surface. It is also important to note that in the entire assemblage there is no St. Johns Polychrome. This will become an important point when discussing the chronology. The assemblage on Table D.8 also confirms the validity of Voll's (1961:50) statement that "no Gila Polychrome was found at Pottery Mound." When perusing a large ceramic assemblage such as that on Table D.8, one has to begin looking for what is missing that could be there.

Chronology

Only Hibben provides tabulated ceramic data that can be used for chronological purposes within the typological structure that the three sources used here have worked in. His data come from the Big Man Unit and the Duck Unit discussed previously.

To my knowledge, the tabulated ceramics from the superimposed rooms in the Duck Unit presented in Hibben's 1987 report constitute the most reliable stratigraphic data available from Pottery Mound. The room walls provided horizontal spatial control; the upper levels appear to have been excavated in 20 cm layers; and most importantly, the floors determined closed vertical control. Accordingly, most of this discussion addresses my tables compiled from Hibben's Duck Unit.

Hibben provided tabulated ceramic counts per level from Rooms 9, 10, 14, 15, and 19. My tables prepared from these sources include Table D.9 (Room 9), Table D.10 (Room 10), Table D.11 (Room 14), Table D.12 (Room 15), and Table D.13 (Room 19). All of these tables present counts per level, except for Table D.12 in which I have converted Hibben's counts to percentages. It is the percentages in Table D.12 that I will primarily discuss here.

Table D.9. Frank C. Hibben's (1987) Report, Ceramic Counts per Level in Room 9 of the Duck Unit

Ceramic Type or Kind	20 cm	40 cm	60 cm	80 cm	Floor 1 1.8 m	1st Sub-Floor	2nd Sub-Floor	Floor 2 2 m	Floor 3 2.8 m	Type Total
Glaze A/Red	133	96	142	31	186	28	21	132	101	870
Glaze A/Yellow	141	117	83	70	117	16	9	28	83	664
Pottery Mound Poly	26	31	29	43	99	17	3	6	24	278
San Clemente	33	18	25	14	51	63	14	21	134	373
San Clemente Poly	14	7	22	4	35	11	3	8	25	129
Zuni (Acoma) Glaze	16	8	14	5	2	19	22	11	96	193
Jeddito	12	11	26	4	19	0	0	0	0	72
Sikyatki	3	7	0	4	4	3	1	2	3	27
Jeddito Corrugated	1	3	6	0	2	6	1	0	1	20
Plain Utility	22	16	11	10	34	21	7	25	33	179
Micaceous Utility	3	2	6	0	1	3	1	3	0	19
Socorro B/W	6	0	1	1	0	4	1	0	0	13
Socorro Corrugated	1	2	1	1	0	1	2	0	0	8
Los Lunas Smudged	1	0	2	0	0	3	0	0	0	6
Galisteo B/W	3	0	0	0	0	1	1	1	0	6
Level Total Count	**415**	**318**	**368**	**187**	**550**	**196**	**86**	**237**	**500**	**2,857**

Table D.10. Frank C. Hibben's (1987) Report, Ceramic Counts per Level in Room 10 of the Duck Unit

Ceramic Type or Kind	20 cm	40 cm	60 cm	80 cm	Floor 1 1.8 m	Floor 2 2.3 m	Floor 3 2.8 m	Type Total
Glaze A/Red	119	111	143	14	172	114	72	745
Glaze A/Yellow	115	114	122	17	83	31	17	499
Pottery Mound Poly	21	16	13	0	14	7	7	78
San Clemente	7	4	3	11	18	13	11	67
San Clemente Poly	3	3	1	0	12	3	31	53
Zuni (Acoma) Glaze	93	91	6	18	3	3	17	231
Jeddito	2	0	0	0	22	0	0	24
Sikyatki	2	3	0	0	9	6	26	46
Plain Utility	14	3	2	1	14	7	14	55
Micaceous Utility	0	3	0	0	3	0	3	9
Glaze A St. Johns	0	0	0	0	2	6	3	11
Socorro B/W	3	0	0	0	0	1	2	6
Socorro Corrugated	0	2	0	0	1	1	0	4
Los Lunas Smudged	4	0	0	0	0	0	0	4
Galisteo B/W	2	0	0	0	0	3	0	5
Level Total Count	**385**	**350**	**290**	**61**	**353**	**195**	**203**	**1,837**

Source for Tables D.9–D.13:

Frank C. Hibben, "Report on the Salvage Operations at the Site of Pottery Mound, New Mexico, during the Excavating Seasons of 1977–1986" (manuscript on file, Laboratory of Anthropology No. P2662 and P2663, Santa Fe, New Mexico, 1987).

Table D.11. Frank C. Hibben's (1987) Report, Ceramic Counts per Level in Room 14 of the Duck Unit

Ceramic Type or Kind	Level				Floor 1 1.8 m	Floor 2 2.3 m	Type Total
	20 cm	40 cm	60 cm	80 cm			
Glaze A/Red	166	172	160	216	193	37	944
Glaze A/Yellow	101	93	113	71	181	41	600
Pottery Mound Poly	78	87	94	101	142	13	515
San Clemente	32	27	18	11	19	21	128
San Clemente Poly	14	3	7	8	4	3	39
Zuni (Acoma) Glaze	6	5	8	22	27	1	69
Jeddito	3	0	2	4	8	14	31
Sikyatki	1	3	2	1	0	1	8
Jeddito Corrugated	2	1	4	0	0	0	7
Plain Utility	29	31	42	23	17	3	145
Micaceous Utility	13	4	2	11	7	1	38
Glaze A St. Johns	12	3	1	2	1	0	19
Socorro B/W	7	0	0	0	0	3	10
Socorro Corrugated	3	1	0	0	0	0	4
Los Lunas Smudged	4	2	1	1	0	0	8
Level Total Count	471	432	454	471	599	138	2,565

Table D.12. Frank C. Hibben's (1987) Report, Ceramic Percentages per Level in Room 15 of the Duck Unit

Ceramic Type or Kind	Level				Floor 1 1.3 m	Floor 2 1.8 m	Floor 3 2.6 m	Type Total
	20 cm	40 cm	60 cm	80 cm				
Glaze A/Red	39.091	29.889	34.227	44.316	56.364	39.713	36.239	1,610
Glaze A/Yellow	22.857	14.785	17.508	37.123	21.273	19.856	19.266	866
Pottery Mound Poly	4.286	2.226	9.621	3.016	4.727	19.139	2.752	245
San Clemente	14.545	27.186	14.669	1.392	3.455	6.459	5.352	463
San Clemente Poly	14.156	20.668	15.931	1.160	2.182	3.349	4.434	400
Zuni (Acoma) Glaze	.649	—	1.104	.928	3.273	2.632	11.927	123
Jeddito	.390	.159	.946	1.160	2.727	3.349	11.162	117
Sikyatki	.390	.477	1.893	1.624	1.818	—	—	35
Jeddito Corrugated	—	.318	—	.696	.364	2.153	2.599	33
Plain Utility	1.429	3.657	3.312	7.425	3.636	1.675	2.141	128
Micaceous Utility	.390	—	—	.464	.182	.957	.153	11
Glaze A St. Johns	1.039	.477	—	—	—	.718	3.976	40
Socorro B/W	.390	.159	.315	—	—	—	—	6
Socorro Corrugated	.390	—	.158	.696	—	—	—	7
Los Lunas Smudged	—	—	.315	—	—	—	—	2
Level Total Count	N = 770	N = 629	N = 634	N = 431	N = 550	N = 418	N = 654	N = 4,086

Source for Tables D.9–d.13:
Frank C. Hibben, "Report on the Salvage Operations at the Site of Pottery Mound, New Mexico, during the Excavating Seasons of 1977–1986" (manuscript on file, Laboratory of Anthropology No. P2662 and P2663, Santa Fe, New Mexico, 1987).

Table D.13. Frank C. Hibben's (1987) Report, Ceramic Counts per Level in Room 19 of the Duck Unit

| Ceramic Type or Kind | Level | | | | | | | | |
	20 cm	40 cm	60 cm	80 cm	Floor 1 1.2 m	1st Sub-Floor 1.4 m	Floor 2 2.0 m	Floor 3 2.8 m	Type Total
Glaze A/Red	401	316	218	271	90	17	29	33	1,375
Glaze A/Yellow	141	122	94	103	73	11	14	21	579
Pottery Mound Poly	41	13	10	24	34	83	17	4	226
San Clemente	121	26	3	39	15	18	13	0	235
San Clemente Poly	16	13	2	1	12	23	3	0	70
Zuni (Acoma) Glaze	3	11	7	3	19	4	14	17	78
Jeddito	26	0	13	4	14	19	3	39	118
Sikyatki	3	4	39	3	61	3	1	17	131
Jeddito Corrugated	4	0	0	0	6	5	2	26	43
Plain Utility	27	14	21	6	11	16	21	5	121
Micaceous Utility	17	3	2	6	0	3	0	1	32
Glaze A St. Johns	1	3	6	0	0	4	0	4	18
Socorro B/W	10	7	7	13	3	6	2	2	50
Socorro Corrugated	7	5	0	1	1	7	1	0	22
Los Lunas Smudged	3	0	0	0	3	4	3	1	14
Level Total Count	**821**	**537**	**422**	**474**	**342**	**223**	**123**	**170**	**3,112**

Source for Tables D.9–D.13:

Frank C. Hibben, "Report on the Salvage Operations at the Site of Pottery Mound, New Mexico, during the Excavating Seasons of 1977–1986" (manuscript on file, Laboratory of Anthropology No. P2662 and P2663, Santa Fe, New Mexico, 1987).

The first thing I would like to address is the stratigraphic occurrence of Pottery Mound Polychrome. In the fill over Floor 3 of Room 15 at a depth of 2.6 m Pottery Mound Polychrome constitutes 2.752 percent (18 sherds) of the total assemblage for that level. A perusal of the other rooms will show that at the lowest levels (usually Floor 3), Pottery Mound Polychrome is always present in substantial numbers. Since the fill over Floor 3 (in Rooms 9, 10, 15, and 19) is a closed find, Pottery Mound Polychrome has to have been in existence at the time of this deposit, which appears to have been during the early years of the site.

The stratigraphic evidence presented here pulls Pottery Mound Polychrome back into being basically a color variation of San Clemente Polychrome, as originally noted by Mera (1933:4), who stated in his definition of San Clemente Polychrome that "in this variety a white or tan slip is substituted for the usual red for bowl interiors and a few examples are known which have in addition an extra matte color incorporated in the design." It is the version of San Clemente Polychrome with matte color in the design that Russell Schorsch named "Pottery Mound Polychrome" in 1954, according to Voll (1961:Table 2). Speaking of "Pottery Mound Glaze-Polychrome," Voll (1961:22) said, "It was identical to San Clemente Glaze-Polychrome in all characteristics except in the use of matte red paint." To me that means that when doing his ceramic counts, Voll simply treated the San Clemente sherds with some matte red paint as Pottery Mound Polychrome. He rarely had any sherds large enough to identify the style of painting. He did not use style as a primary sherd identification criterion. As he said:

Pottery Mound Glaze-Polychrome was the only Pottery Mound ceramic type which showed the influence of a western design style, and this design style appears to have been borrowed from the Hopi Yellow Ware type Sikyatki Polychrome which occurred as a common trade ware. The lack of whole vessels and the small number of Pottery Mound Glaze-Polychrome sherds made it impossible to determine how closely this design style was copied [1961:51].

Voll correctly regarded it as derived from San Clemente Glaze Polychrome and treated it as "Group A," which he dated to 1350–1450.

I would now maintain that the stratigraphic evidence from the superimposed rooms of the Duck Unit confirms the typological placement of Pottery Mound Polychrome with the other kinds of Glaze A and that it has a temporal span that is the same as the other kinds of Glaze A. In all probability this temporal span will be essentially the 1350–1450 period presented by Voll (1961:59, Table 2). A final comment has to do with dating Sikyatki designs on Pottery Mound Polychrome. Voll (1961:60) noted that "this type appears to make heavy use of Sikyatki Polychrome style designs." However, having realized that Pottery Mound Polychrome is recognized in his analysis as being "identical to San Clemente Glaze-Polychrome, but designs contain small red-filled areas and sometimes isolated matte red elements" (1961:60), there is no way to determine when in the life span of this type the Sikyatki design elements appear. More work needs to be done with the pottery from these deep levels.

The next consideration based on the tables for the Duck Unit is "Glaze A/Yellow," which is simply a synonym for Cieneguilla Glaze-on-yellow or Polychrome (Mera 1933:3–4). The beginning date of Cieneguilla Glaze-on-yellow is 1370 (Schaafsma 2002:Table 8.1) based on stratigraphic placement at Las Madres Pueblo in the middle of the Galisteo Basin (Schaafsma 1995) and corroborated by stratigraphy and tree-ring dates at Arroyo Hondo Pueblo (Habicht-Mauche 1993:10). Hayward Franklin (1996:12), working at Valencia Pueblo some 12 mi east of Pottery Mound, offered the beginning date of 1375 for Cieneguilla Glaze-on-yellow. This is one of the few types that has such a precise chronological beginning date.

Since "Glaze A/Yellow" constitutes 19.266 percent (126 sherds) of the total assemblage over Floor 3 in Room 15 (Table D.12) and is well represented in the lowest levels of the other rooms, these proveniences would date after 1370. Since these floors apparently date from the beginning of the Pottery Mound Pueblo, I would submit this as evidence that Pottery Mound began shortly after 1370.

Having made the case that Pottery Mound Polychrome should be grouped for summary purposes with the other kinds of Glaze A, then one can look at Table D.12 to gain some idea of the overall assemblage. In the top 20 cm layer Glaze A constitutes 94.935 percent of the assemblage. Hopi ceramics make up .780 percent and Zuni (Acoma) Glazes make up .649 percent. There is no kind of pottery that dates later than the upper limit of Glaze A in this area, which reasonably could be 1450. Specifically, there is no Glaze C. In the lowest level of Room 15, Glaze A makes up 68.043 percent. This decrease in proportion compared with the topmost 20 cm layer is basically due to the increase in Zuni (Acoma) Glazes (11.927 percent) and Hopi (13.761 percent) ceramics. The patterns discussed for Room 15 are repeated in the other rooms as well. Overall, throughout the time span represented in Room 15, Pottery Mound was a Rio Grande Glaze A pueblo with an interesting amount of trade with the western pueblos of Acoma, Zuni, and Hopi, especially in the early years. The stratigraphic evidence and the ceramic dating discussed previously would indicate that Room 15 and the other rooms of the Duck Unit date from shortly after 1370 until some time between 1425 and 1450.

As a brief aside, having established that the deepest levels date sometime soon after 1370, it should be recalled that there is Pottery Mound Polychrome in all of these levels and that it, too, would date to around 1370. Then we can return to the earlier point that we cannot yet determine, when in the life span of that type of pottery the Sikyatki designs appear, but if they were present on Pottery Mound Polychrome at the beginning of that type, then Sikyatki designs at Pottery Mound would date to around 1370 also.

Adjacent to the Duck Unit is the Big Man Unit, an area of stratified deposits (see Figures D.1 and D.2). Hibben (1987:31) defined this area with a series of 1 m "Strats," as they are described on his map in the 1987 report (see Figure D.1). Four of these strats were presented as tabular counts in the 1987 report. I prepared four tables from these sources (Tables D.14, D.15, D.16, and D.17). In Table D.14 of the West Strat, Hibben's counts have been converted into percentages. In Table D.15 of the Central Strat test percentages were calculated with the original counts provided in parentheses. In Tables D.16 (North Strat test) and D.17 (East Strat test) only the original counts are provided.

These stratigraphic tests were done with arbitrary levels in a complex area where there were some gentle slopes to the actual layers of about 20 degrees (Schaafsma

Table D.14. Frank C. Hibben's (1987) Report, Ceramic Percentages per Level in the West Strat Test of the Big Man Unit

Ceramic Type or Kind	Level						TOTAL
	0 to 0.5 m	1 m	1.5 m	2.0 m	2.5 m	3.0 m	
Glaze A/Red	22.030	21.503	22.353	22.162	25.294	7.097	753
Glaze A/Yellow	16.244	18.844	22.745	24.595	23.824	2.581	673
Pottery Mound Poly	8.832	12.832	8.235	5.676	3.235	3.871	299
San Clemente	8.934	7.168	6.536	4.324	6.176	1.935	240
San Clemente Poly	1.929	2.428	3.529	2.973	2.353	1.290	88
Zuni (Acoma) Glaze	11.675	9.249	12.941	3.784	9.118	3.871	345
Jeddito	2.234	6.936	2.092	3.514	.882	.645	115
Sikyatki	.711	1.965	1.438	2.432	.882	—	47
Jeddito Corrugated	.305	.231	1.830	.811	.588	.645	25
Plain Utility	21.421	12.254	12.026	14.054	4.118	7.097	486
Micaceous Utility	.406	1.618	2.484	.811	2.941	4.516	57
Glaze A St. Johns	2.132	1.618	.784	1.351	.588	.645	49
Socorro B/W	.609	.578	.654	4.865	6.471	21.290	89
Socorro Corrugated	1.421	1.618	1.307	4.595	8.235	26.452	124
Los Lunas Smudged	.609	1.040	.915	2.973	.882	9.677	51
Fingernail Incised	.203	—	.131	.270	1.176	3.871	14
Los Lunas Smudged Decorated Corrugated	—	—	—	.811	3.235	4.516	21
Unknown	.305	.116	—	—	—	—	4
Column/level Total	**985**	**865**	**765**	**370**	**340**	**155**	**3,480**

Table D.15. Frank C. Hibben's (1987) Report, Ceramic Percentages per Level in the Central Strat Test of the Big Man Unit

Ceramic Type or Kind	Level				Row Percent And (Total)
	0 to 0.5 m	1.0 m	2.0 m	3.0 m	
Glaze A/Red	25.270 (613)	22.519 (479)	10.052 (136)	11.900 (129)	19.413 (1,357)
Glaze A/Yellow	17.390 (422)	18.947 (403)	13.378 (181)	8.671 (94)	15.737 (1,100)
Pottery Mound Poly	4.580 (111)	4.372 (93)	9.090 (123)	2.490 (27)	5.064 (354)
San Clemente	.701 (17)	.893 (19)	.517 (7)	.461 (5)	.687 (48)
San Clemente Poly	1.150 (28)	.846 (18)	2.291 (31)	1.661 (18)	1.359 (95)
Zuni (Acoma) Glaze	.080 (2)	.141 (3)	1.552 (21)	.646 (7)	.472 (33)
Jeddito	1.690 (41)	1.551 (33)	1.035 (14)	4.336 (47)	1.931 (135)
Sikyatki	.490 (12)	.188 (4)	.443 (6)	1.015 (11)	.472 (33)
Jeddito Corrugated	.120 (3)	—	.148 (2)	—	.072 (5)
Plain Utility	46.040 (1,117)	48.472 (1,031)	60.459 (818)	56.365 (611)	51.173 (3,577)
Micaceous Utility	.450 (11)	.141 (3)	.222 (3)	—	.243 (17)
Socorro B/W	.580 (14)	.517 (11)	.148 (2)	3.506 (38)	.930 (65)
Socorro Corrugated	.950 (23)	1.269 (27)	.443 (6)	6.642 (72)	1.831 (128)
Los Lunas Smudged	.120 (3)	—	.0739 (1)	1.292 (14)	.258 (18)
Galisteo B/W	.370 (9)	.141 (3)	.148 (2)	1.015 (11)	.358 (25)
Column Percent (Total)	**99.981 (2,426)**	**99.997 (2,127)**	**100.001 (1,353)**	**100.000 (1,084)**	**100.000 (6,990)**

Source for Tables D.14–D.17: Frank C. Hibben, "Report on the Salvage Operations at the Site of Pottery Mound, New Mexico, during the Excavating Seasons of 1977–1986" (manuscript on file, Laboratory of Anthropology No. P2662 and P2663, Santa Fe, New Mexico, 1987).

Table D.16. Frank C. Hibben's (1987) Report, Ceramic Counts per Level in the North Strat Test of the Big Man Unit

Ceramic Type or Kind	Level				Total
	0 to 0.5 m	1.0 m	2.0 m	3.0 m	
Glaze A/Red	177	337	302	223	1,039
Glaze A/Yellow	143	562	315	172	1,192
Pottery Mound Poly	31	26	39	11	107
San Clemente	43	16	45	15	119
San Clemente Poly	17	21	31	6	75
Zuni (Acoma) Glaze	29	27	20	24	100
Jeddito	41	32	30	10	113
Sikyatki	14	6	19	21	60
Jeddito Corrugated	11	14	26	3	54
Plain Utility	1,201	1,082	976	484	3,743
Micaceous Utility	11	6	5	7	29
Glaze A St. Johns	14	3	2	6	25
Socorro B/W	7	11	1	106	125
Socorro Corrugated	3	7	21	25	56
Los Lunas Smudged	1	0	19	31	51
Galisteo B/W	1	2	1	0	4
Santa Fe B/W (?)	0	3	1	0	4
Level Total Count	**1,744**	**2,155**	**1,853**	**1,144**	**6,896**

Table D.17. Frank C. Hibben's (1987) Report, Ceramic Counts per Level in the East Strat Test of the Big Man Unit

Ceramic Type or Kind	Level				Total
	0 to 0.5 m	1.0 m	2.0 m	3.0 m	
Glaze A/Red	113	489	571	106	1,279
Glaze A/Yellow	71	150	176	116	513
Pottery Mound Poly	19	22	102	18	161
San Clemente	17	39	36	13	105
San Clemente Poly	11	2	17	11	41
Zuni (Acoma) Glaze	15	19	8	2	44
Jeddito	36	3	34	14	87
Sikyatki	16	12	13	1	42
Jeddito Corrugated	3	15	3	4	25
Plain Utility	77	1,052	711	526	2,366
Micaceous Utility	3	9	6	3	21
Glaze A St. Johns	2	3	1	1	7
Socorro B/W	1	2	29	74	106
Socorro Corrugated	1	2	12	23	38
Los Lunas Smudged	0	0	3	17	20
Galisteo B/W	3	3	1	0	7
Fingernail Incised	2	0	1	1	4
Matte Red/Brown (?)	3	0	0	0	3
Level Total Count					**4,869**

Source for Tables D.14–D.17: Frank C. Hibben, "Report on the Salvage Operations at the Site of Pottery Mound, New Mexico, during the Excavating Seasons of 1977–1986" (manuscript on file, Laboratory of Anthropology No. P2662 and P2663, Santa Fe, New Mexico, 1987).

1987:Photo No. 11), so there has to be some mixing. Accordingly, the stratigraphic evidence is not as reliable as that from the superimposed rooms of the Duck Unit. Given the fact that the horizontal extent of these strat tests was 1 m x 1 m (see Figure D.1), each arbitrary level could not have mixed too many natural levels, such as those apparent in the previously mentioned photograph. On the other hand, large vertical levels such as the 1 m increments used in the Central Strat test (Table D.15) obviously increase the problem. Since smaller vertical levels reduce the problem of using arbitrary levels in deposits with sloping natural strata, primary reliance here will be placed on the West Strat test (Table D.14) where half-meter vertical levels were used. As an aside, it is fortunate that Cordell (1980:4) utilized 20 cm vertical control in the levels of her nearby test pit, rendering her levels far more reliable.

The main thing I would like to bring out in this discussion is the ceramic assemblage in the three lowest levels of the West Strat test (Table D.14). Here at a depth of over 2 m there is a sudden rise in Socorro Black-on-white and a set of related types that constitute an early assemblage. It is this assemblage that, especially at a depth of 3 m, brings down the relative proportion of the Glaze A series. Nonetheless, it is essential to note that Pottery Mound Polychrome and Glaze A Yellow are present in significant proportions in all of the deepest deposits, which corroborates the evidence presented for the Duck Unit. This deposit must have ceramics from an older occupation that was very likely contemporary with LA 2569 about 5 mi up the Rio Puerco (Fenenga and Cummings 1956). This settlement had coursed adobe rooms (Fenenga and Cummings 1956:Figure 167), a round, east-oriented kiva (1956:Figure 166), and a Socorro Black-on-white period ceramic assemblage (1956:Figure 175) similar to the Socorro assemblage in the lowest levels of the West Strat test (Table D.14). Significantly, both the ceramic assemblage from LA 2569 and the West Strat test lack St. Johns Polychrome, which implies that they both date before 1200. This implication would agree with the single tree-ring date for LA 2569 of A.D. 1183 reported by Robinson and Cameron (1991:23). This assemblage suggests that before 1200 there was a small settlement similar to LA 2569 at the location where over 170 years later, other people came in and built Pottery Mound Pueblo.

Summary

The ceramic data compiled here indicate that Pottery Mound began soon after 1370. The almost complete lack of Glaze C from any of the excavations indicates that the primary occupation terminated before 1450. The peculiar surface assemblage reported by Mera could relate to a small remnant component that is represented by the six shallow rooms collected by Voll. This component would have existed after 1450, but given the small actual amount, 28 sherds total, this residual occupation could not have lasted much past 1450. A reasonable termination date for Pottery Mound overall is 1460. However, the primary occupation would seem to be between 1370 and before 1450. There is no basis for contending that there is a continuity with the Socorro Black-on-white occupation that probably existed at the location before 1200.

REFERENCES CITED

Cordell, Linda S.

1980   University of New Mexico Field School Excavations at Pottery Mound, New Mexico, 1979, Preliminary Report. Manuscript on file, Maxwell Museum of Anthropology, University of New Mexico, Albuquerque.

2004   Advanced Seminar on Pottery Mound, School of American Research, May 11–12. Manuscript on file, School of American Research, Santa Fe, New Mexico.

Eckert, Suzanne L.

2003   Social Boundaries, Immigration, and Ritual Systems: A Case Study from the American Southwest. Unpublished Ph.D. dissertation, Department of Anthropology, Arizona State University, Tempe.

Fenenga, Franklin, and Thomas S. Cummings

1956 LA 2569: Cerros Mojinos, A Late Pueblo II–Early Pueblo III Village on the Rio Puerco near Los Lunas, New Mexico. In *Pipeline Archeology*, edited by Fred Wendorf, Nancy Fox, and Orian L. Lewis, pp. 242–55. Laboratory of Anthropology, Santa Fe, New Mexico, and Museum of Northern Arizona, Flagstaff.

Franklin, Hayward H.

1996 Valencia Pueblo Ceramics. Office of Contract Archaeology, University of New Mexico, Albuquerque. Manuscript on file, Laboratory of Anthropology No. P2785, Santa Fe, New Mexico.

Habicht-Mauche, Judith A.

1993 *The Pottery from Arroyo Hondo Pueblo, New Mexico: Tribalization and Trade in the Northern Rio Grande*, Part I. Arroyo Hondo Archaeological Series Vol. 8. School of American Research, Santa Fe, New Mexico.

Hibben, Frank C.

1987 Report on the Salvage Operations at the Site of Pottery Mound, New Mexico, during the Excavating Seasons of 1977–1986. Manuscript on file, Laboratory of Anthropology Nos. P2662 and 2663, Museum of New Mexico, Santa Fe. Manuscript on file, Maxwell Museum of Anthropology, University of New Mexico, Albuquerque.

Kidder, Alfred V., and Anna O. Shepard

1936 *The Pottery of Pecos, Vol. 2: The Glaze Paint, Culinary, and Other Wares*. Papers of the Phillips Academy, Southwestern Expedition, No. 7. Yale University Press, New Haven, Connecticut.

Mera, Harry P.

1933 *A Proposed Revision of the Rio Grande Glaze Paint Sequence*. Technical Series Bulletin No. 5. Laboratory of Anthropology, Santa Fe, New Mexico.

1940 *Population Changes in the Rio Grande Glaze-Paint Area*. Technical Series Bulletin No. 9. Laboratory of Anthropology, Santa Fe, New Mexico.

Robinson, William J., and Catherine M. Cameron

1991 *A Directory of Tree-Ring Dated Prehistoric Sites in the American Southwest*. Laboratory of Tree-Ring Research, University of Arizona, Tucson.

Schaafsma, Curtis F.

1987 Report on Pottery Mound (LA 416). Manuscript on file, LA-416 site folder at the Archaeological Records Management System, Laboratory of Anthropology, Santa Fe, New Mexico.

1995 The Chronology of Las Madres Pueblo (LA 25). In *Of Pots and Rocks: Papers in Honor of A. Helene Warren*, edited by M. S. Duran and D. T. Kirkpatrick, pp. 155–65. Papers of the Archaeological Society of New Mexico Vol. 21. Archaeological Society of New Mexico, Albuquerque.

2002 *Apaches de Navajo: Seventeenth-Century Navajos in the Chama Valley of New Mexico*. University of Utah Press, Salt Lake City.

Voll, Charles B.

1961 The Glaze Paint Ceramics of Pottery Mound, New Mexico. Unpublished Master's thesis, Department of Anthropology, University of New Mexico, Albuquerque.

List of Contributors

Michael A. Adler
 Associate Professor,
 Department of Anthropology
 Southern Methodist University
 Dallas, Texas

Tiffany C. Clark
 Research Archaeologist
 Desert Archaeology, Inc.
 Tucson, Arizona

Linda S. Cordell
 Professor Emeritus and Senior Scholar
 University of Colorado and
 School of American Research
 Boulder, Colorado, and Santa Fe, New Mexico

Helen K. Crotty
 Research Associate
 Museum of Indian Arts and Culture/
  Laboratory of Anthropology
 Santa Fe, New Mexico

Suzanne L. Eckert
 Assistant Professor,
 Department of Anthropology
 Texas A&M University
 College Station, Texas

Kelley Hays-Gilpin
 Professor, Department of Anthropology
 Northern Arizona University
 Flagstaff, Arizona

Steven A. LeBlanc
 Director of Collections,
 Peabody Museum of Archaeology and Ethnology
 Harvard University
 Cambridge, Massachusetts

David A. Phillips Jr.
 Curator of Archaeology,
 Maxwell Museum of Anthropology
 University of New Mexico
 Albuquerque, New Mexico

Curtis F. Schaafsma
 Curator of Anthropology Emeritus
 Museum of Indian Arts and Culture/
  Laboratory of Anthropology
 Santa Fe, New Mexico

Polly Schaafsma
 Research Associate
 Museum of Indian Arts and Culture/
  Laboratory of Anthropology
 Santa Fe, New Mexico

Patricia Vivian
 Witch Well, Arizona

R. Gwinn Vivian
 Witch Well, Arizona

Laurie D. Webster
 Independent Textile Consultant and
  Visiting Scholar,
 Department of Anthropology
 University of Arizona
 Tucson, Arizona

David R. Wilcox
 Senior Curator of Archaeology
 Museum of Northern Arizona
 Flagstaff, Arizona

Index

Note: entries followed by an *f* or *t* refer respectively to subject matter contained in figures or tables.

supplemental weft, and weaving, 182–83, 185, 186*f*, 191, 201

Szuter, C. R., 215

taxonomic composition, of avifaunal assemblage from Pottery Mound, 209–18

technological style, definition of, 57

Tedlock, Dennis, 18, 79

temper, of glaze-decorated bowls at Pottery Mound, 58–61, 63, 66, 68, 69n3

temporal patterns, in faunal procurement strategies, 219–20, 223

textiles: and iconography of kiva murals at Pottery Mound, 98, 117, 119–22, 155–56; and Pueblo IV ritual clothing, 168–203; and rock art of Rio Grande region, 155–56; and Sikyatki style, 130, 237

tie-dyed textiles, 175, 177, 180, 182, 192, 196, 200, 203

Tijueras Pueblo, 138, 221–23

Tiwa region, and wall paintings, 6

Tonto Ruins, 172, 174*f*

tools, and kiva murals, 81

Torres, Dee, 77

Tovakwa (LA 481), 144

trade, and ceramics at Pottery Mound, 236

Tsesmeli, Lia, 39

turkeys, 216, 220, 221, 222, 224n8. *See also* birds

turtles. *See* reptiles

Tusayan Polychrome, 125

Tyler, Hamilton A., 215

University of New Mexico field schools, and Pottery Mound, xii, 15–16, 18–19, 22, 32–33, 75–82, 208. *See also* Hibben Center

Valencia Pueblo (LA 953), 2, 236, 278, 290

Van Keuren, Scott, 113, 115

Van Pool, Christine, 127

Vargas, Victoria D., 24

Vaughn, John, 18, 76

Villagrá, Gaspar Pérez de, 6

Vivian, Patricia Bryan, 9, 20, 78, 79, 81, 82, 231–32, 243n2

Vivian, R. Gwinn, xii, 6, 9, 18, 32, 76, 231

Vokes, Arthur, 237

Voll, Charles, 18, 19, 20, 21, 24, 232, 233, 234, 244n6, 245n14, 277, 278, 279–80, 283, 286, 289–90, 293

Voth, H. R., 125, 127

Vytlacil, Natalie, 18, 76

warfare: and iconography of kiva murals at Pottery Mound, 96, 144–52; recent research on regional in Pueblo IV period, 31; and ritual clothing in Pueblo IV Southwest, 175, 192; and rock art in Rio Grande region, 144–52. *See also* shields

Warner, Thor, 17, 20, 232

warp-faced belts, 172, 188

Warren, Helene, 18, 236

Washburn, Dorothy, 244n8

Wasley, William, 237

waterfowl, 216, 217, 220, 224n6. *See also* birds

Webster, Laurie, 9, 10, 111, 119, 160, 230, 235, 237

Weidner, Kathy, 16, 105n5

Wendorf, D. F., 29

Wheeler, Sir Mortimer, 235

White House site, 177

Whiteley, Peter, 126, 127

White Mountain Red Ware, 113, 238

Wilcox, David R., 8, 10, 18, 229–30, 237

Wills, Wirt, 244n9

Wimberly, Mark, 17

Wing, Elizabeth S., 213

"working hypothesis," and scientific method, 230

Wright, Barton, 175

Yen, Sofia, 76

Zia Pueblo, 215, 217

Zuni: and Coalescent Communities Database, 230; and feathers from waterfowl, 217; influence of Paquimé on, 238; and influences on pottery and kiva decoration at Pottery Mound, 55, 66, 67; and integration in modern ritual organizations, 56. *See also* Pueblo(s)

Zuni Glaze Ware, 61*f*, 62, 63, 66, 67

DISCARDED